Oracle Security

Oracle Security

Marlene Theriault and William Heney

O'REILLY®

Beijing · Cambridge · Köln · Paris · Sebastopol · Taipei · Tokyo

Oracle Security

by Marlene Theriault and William Heney

Printed in the United States of America.

Published by O'Reilly & Associates, Inc., 101 Morris Street, Sebastopol, CA 95472.

Editor: Deborah Russell

Production Editor: Ellie Fountain Maden

Printing History:

October 1998: First Edition.

This book is printed on acid-free paper with 85% recycled content, 15% post-consumer waste. O'Reilly & Associates is committed to using paper with the highest recycled content available consistent with high quality.

ISBN: 1-56592-450-9 [4/99]

This book is dedicated to:

My father, Paul R. Siegel, M.D., whose love of life and dedication as a true physician have helped and inspired every person who has ever known him;

My mother, Lillian M. Siegel, who was an elementary school teacher and continues to teach us all the deeper lessons of life;

My sister, Judith R. Zieske, who sees beyond;

My son, Marc I. Goodman, a self-made man, who can accomplish anything he attempts;

and Nelson J. Cahill, who succeeds beyond measure.

—Marlene Theriault

To my wife Ellen. Thanks for your support.

—William Heney

Table of Contents

Preface

On an almost daily basis, we hear stories of yet another computer system that has been compromised by someone—a curious teenager, a disgruntled employee, or a corporate or political spy. We are baffled and bemused by the number of "hackers" who have been able to get into systems that have, up until now, been viewed as invulnerable. Government computers, corporate computers, and university systems are all fair game. It would appear that no system is completely safe.

In this book, you will find tactics, methods, and approaches to help you better protect your Oracle database and your computer systems as a whole. Our objective in writing this book is to provide you with the information and tools you need to ensure that your data remains safe. We emphasize the tools provided within the basic Oracle software that can help you build as complete a security system as your company requires. We are not here to sell you extra products. However, in the last chapter of the book, we do provide a brief overview of three extra-cost Oracle products: Trusted Oracle, the Advanced Networking Option, and the Oracle Application Server (formerly referred to as the Web Application Server).

The book will explain how to implement basic security concepts and more complex security actions from both a database and an applications perspective. We will also examine the auditing of the database and application areas. Since today more and more emphasis is being placed on World Wide Web-enabled interaction with the Oracle database, we'll also touch on methods for securing both the database and applications for Internet and Web interaction.

What This Book Is

This book is intended to help you understand and implement security within and for your Oracle database systems. Although we touch on many products and strategies, our main goal is to provide you with a clear understanding of the basic tools available with the standard Oracle product delivery.

This book is divided into three parts:

Part I, Security in an Oracle System

This part of the book introduces security in an Oracle system and outlines the main files, database objects, and Oracle security concepts you need to understand before attempting to adopt the security strategies presented in this book.

Chapter 1, *Oracle and Security*, outlines the threats to your system and database, introduces the various levels of security in an Oracle system, and briefly discusses the concepts and products that the book will explore.

Chapter 2, *Oracle System Files*, introduces the physical operating system files that are particularly important to your system's security.

Chapter 3, *Oracle Database Objects*, introduces the various database objects that help implement database security—for example, tables, triggers, roles, and profiles.

Chapter 4, *The Oracle Data Dictionary*, introduces the data dictionary and discusses its relevance to database security.

Chapter 5, *Oracle Default Roles and User Accounts*, describes the roles and user accounts Oracle creates automatically when the database is initialized, and explains why they are important to security.

Chapter 6, *Profiles, Passwords, and Synonyms*, discusses how you can use Oracle's user profile, password, and synonym features to secure your system; these features include password expiration times, account locking for passwords, and account "hiding" for synonyms.

Part II, Implementing Security

This part of the book describes the specific steps we recommend to make your Oracle system and database more secure. It includes a number of sample applications you might want to adapt for your own organization's use.

Chapter 7, *Developing a Database Security Plan*, discusses the importance of creating policies and a security plan as a first step in securing your system and database.

Chapter 8, *Installing and Starting Oracle*, describes what you need to do to install and start Oracle databases and to begin to implement security—for example, determine the appropriate system-level approach for accessing the database.

Chapter 9, *Developing a Simple Security Application*, provides a basic example of a security application you may wish to adapt for your own environment.

Chapter 10, *Developing an Audit Plan*, describes auditing in an Oracle system and discusses the choices you need to make about when and how to audit events.

Chapter 11, *Developing a Sample Audit Application*, provides a simple but effective audit trail application you may wish to build upon.

Chapter 12, *Backing Up and Recovering the Database*, discusses the available types of backup and recovery options from a security perspective.

Chapter 13, *Using the Oracle Enterprise Manager*, describes the use of the OEM, a basic GUI toolkit provided by Oracle to simplify many aspects of database administration, including security management.

Chapter 14, *Maintaining User Accounts*, provides a sample application you may wish to adapt for maintaining user accounts within your own system.

Part III, Enhanced Oracle Security

This part of the book describes some types of security that might be appropriate in certain types of environments.

Chapter 15, *Using the Oracle Security Server*, discusses the use of the OSS (supplied with the basic Oracle RDBMS), which uses encryption and certificates of authority to enable more secure access to your data.

Chapter 16, *Using the Internet and the Web*, suggests a number of strategies for protecting your site from the risks posed by Internet and Web connections.

Chapter 17, *Using Extra-Cost Options*, looks briefly at several extra-cost Oracle products that you may wish to purchase for enhanced security—Trusted Oracle, the Advanced Networking Option, and the Oracle Application Server.

Appendix A, *References*, provides a list of additional books and online resources.

What This Book Is Not

Often while writing this book we've had to stop and say, "Wait a minute. That's outside the scope of this book." We have tried to hold a clear view from the beginning of what we wanted to present. As we said earlier, our goal is to provide you with the information you need to implement security on your system using only the basic Oracle-standard code.

We did not want to write a "you have to do things this way" book. We have tried to show alternatives and options you can take—or ignore—based on your own company's needs and desires. We've tried to resist the temptation to make this book a larger work that tries to be all things to all people. This book is not a guide to additional products that Oracle or any third-party vendors sell to enhance your system and database security. And, although we include an overview of additional security measures you can use to protect your systems, we are not trying to provide a general guide to system security, nor are we trying to provide all the details you need to operate in a high-security environment. There are many wonderful books that address the specifics of operating system, Internet, web site, and firewall security; see Appendix A for a list of some of these books.

Audience for This Book

If you are a general Oracle user or someone who is exploring the possibility of using Oracle products in your company, and you are concerned about using these products securely, this book will give you an overview of how Oracle works and the steps you can take to build a safe environment for the products.

If you are an Oracle database administrator, this book will provide you with an in-depth understanding of the internal Oracle composition that is the basis of Oracle security. If you are a new DBA, you will find guidance on how to set up and manage security for your database.

If you are an Information Systems (IS) manager, you will gain insight into how to establish an effective security and audit plan. You will also gain knowledge about the tools available to your facility that can aid in securing your systems.

Conventions Used in This Book

The following conventions are used in this book:

Indicates a tip, suggestion, or general note. For example, we'll tell you if you need to use a particular Oracle version or if an operation requires certain privileges.

Indicates a warning or caution. For example, we'll tell you if Oracle does not behave as you'd expect or if a particular operation has a negative impact on performance.

Italic
Used for script names, filenames, and directory names, and Oracle usernames.

`Constant width`
: Used for code examples.

`Constant width italic`
: In some code examples, indicates an element (e.g., a filename) that you supply.

UPPERCASE
: In code examples, generally indicates Oracle keywords.

lowercase
: In code examples, generally indicates user-defined items such as variables, parameters, etc.

punctuation
: In code examples, enter exactly as shown.

/ and */*
: In code examples, these characters delimit a comment, which can extend from one line to another.

[ ]
: In syntax descriptions, square brackets enclose optional items.

This book contains many examples of SQL scripts that we hope will help improve your database security. Wherever possible in this code, we've followed the conventions listed above. Using these conventions helps make the usage clear and also ensures consistency both within this book and across the O'Reilly Oracle line. However, we don't endorse this style for everyone and recognize that in the real world, DBAs and developers write code in a far less structured and consistent style. Where we obtained working scripts from other sources, we have preserved the original formatting to avoid any possible confusion.

Platforms and Versions of Oracle

Most of the examples described in this book were developed on a Windows NT operating system; however, SQL scripts are very portable, and most of them will run as is on UNIX and other operating systems.

Most of the scripts also work with most versions of Oracle, from Oracle 7.x (and, in many cases, earlier) through Oracle 8.0.4 (and beyond).

Note that all scripts included in this book are available via Web or FTP access; see "Comments and Questions."

Comments and Questions

Please address comments and questions concerning this book to the publisher:

> O'Reilly & Associates, Inc.
> 101 Morris Street
> Sebastopol, CA 95472
> 800-998-9938 (in the U.S. or Canada)
> 707-829-0515 (international or local)
> 707-829-0104 (fax)

You can also send us messages electronically. For corrections and amplifications for the book, as well as for copies of the scripts found in this book, check out *http://www.oreilly.com/catalog/orasec*. See the ads at the end of the book for information about all of O'Reilly & Associates' online services.

Acknowledgments

Any book, no matter how seemingly small or easy, takes a great deal of thought and hard work to come to fruition. There are so many people who have been involved in making this book a reality. All of them deserve more thanks than there is room for in this brief section.

From Both of Us

The entire staff at O'Reilly & Associates has worked long and hard to process our words and chicken scratches and make a readable, educational, and, we hope, enjoyable book. Particular thanks go to Debby Russell for her hours and hours of editing and commenting, and her suggestions to help make this book better and better. Many thanks as well to Steve Abrams, who converted files, did lots of pre-production work on the text, and otherwise helped move things along efficiently so we could meet an ambitious schedule.

Both of us would like to extend a very special "thank you" to Christopher Hamilton. Chris graciously provided us with the complete audit trail application you will find in Chapter 11. His approach to audit tracking is simple, yet incredibly effective. Thanks, Chris!

Thanks also go to Gustavo Saurez for providing expert help, guidance, and endless patience while we were learning the inner workings of the Oracle Security Server Manager.

Several people worked diligently to provide technical reviews of this book to ensure its accuracy. We would like to extend a heartfelt "thank you" to: Dave Kreines for his comments on Chapter 1 and John Beresniewicz for his comments on structure; Michael Olin for both his wonderfully prolific and detailed comments on all of the chapters and his refreshing sense of humor throughout his feedback; James Viscusi and Craig Nickerson for detailed observations which helped to reform some chapters and make the whole better than the sum of the parts; and David Ambors, who provided some excellent suggestions for the backup and recovery chapter.

From Marlene Theriault

First, I would like to thank both Matthew Theodoseau for creating the original outline upon which this book has, in part, been based, and Tony Ziemba, who brought me to this project. Without the involvement of these two men, Bill and I would never have written this book.

Next, I would like to thank William Heney for his many hours of hard work to bring this book to completion. I've known and worked with Bill for several years and believe that his skills, knowledge, and abilities have made him the very best choice I could have made for a coauthor.

I have known Martin Rosman for many years, both as a top-notch database administrator and, more importantly, as a friend. Marty was willing to perform the first, and probably hardest, technical editing of the book. His keen insights and eagle eye have helped to make this book better rounded and more accurate. Thanks, Marty, I owe you...maybe even sushi for life! James Viscusi willingly (courageously?) took on the task of providing the second technical review and even agreed to act as one of our "formal" reviewers. Thanks, Jim, you're a brave man!

In the world of DBAs, some people stand out as "the best." I am grateful to Eyal Aronoff and Kevin Loney for not only being there to help and guide me through this complex and sometimes confusing Oracle world but, more importantly, for being my friends.

There are few words that can describe how my relationship with Rachel Carmichael has changed my life and helped to bring me to the completion of this book. Since meeting at the first East Coast Oracle user conference (ECO '91—A Wizard's Gathering), we have coauthored two award-winning papers; become deeply involved as "co-DBAs," "tag team" presenters, and best friends; and encouraged each other to learn and grow. Our ability to "fill in the holes" in each others' knowledge has helped us to help countless others.

I would like to thank all of my friends and associates at The Johns Hopkins University Applied Physics Laboratory for providing me with an outstanding example of how a security-conscious shop should be run. Particular thanks go to my immediate supervisor, Craig Nickerson (who generously took his vacation time to act as a reviewer), and his supervisor, David Sager, for staunchly supporting me and for demonstrating over and over again their belief in me and their faith in my talents and abilities.

Special thanks go to my family, who seem to be my greatest cheering section. For his patience and ongoing support through all of the long months of writing this book and for his ability to keep me calm and centered when my world seemed to be going in six different directions at once, a giant "thank you" goes to my "most special love," Nelson Cahill.

From William Heney

When Marlene invited me to work with her on this book, my first thought was to not do it, but her enthusiasm for the project turned out to be catching. My thanks to Marlene for making it seem like a good and fun thing to do. I still believe it was a good thing to do.

One of my former co-workers, Mike Adams, deserves special mention because he is the one who understood my request for the role-switching code and developed the first version.

My wife, Ellen Black, deserves a special note of thanks for quietly picking just the right times to ask the "how's the book going?" question.

I

Security in an Oracle System

This part of the book introduces security in an Oracle system and sets the scene for later parts of the book. It describes files and database objects of special significance to Oracle security, and it examines the use of the Oracle data dictionary from a security perspective. It also describes the most important Oracle security concepts you'll need to be aware of as you implement security in your own system—privileges, views, default roles and user accounts, profiles, passwords, and synonyms.

In this chapter:
- *What's It All About?*
- *The Oracle Security Model*
- *Procedures, Policies, and Plans*
- *If I Had a Hammer...*

1
Oracle and Security

When Marlene Theriault's 91-year-old father learned that she was writing a book, his first question was, "What's it about?"

"Security," she said.

Astounded, her father asked, "You're writing a book about social security?"

To each one of us, the word "security" may mean something different, depending on how and where the word is used. To the elderly, security may mean a government-issued check deposited to their bank account each month. To a woman traveling alone, security may mean a hotel room door locked with both a deadbolt and a heavy chain. To a movie star or politician, it may mean a bodyguard who travels everywhere with them. To your company, it may mean maintaining a guard force to ensure that your office buildings are safe.

Just as a guard force helps ensure that people do not enter buildings or areas in which they don't belong, in the computer world "security" may translate into hardware, software, and a set of technical and personnel procedures that together help ensure that unauthorized people do not gain access to areas of information they should not see—and that authorized people do not jeopardize your system and data by exceeding their authority.

What's It All About?

There are many facets to computer security. Most security practitioners identify the following different aspects of security:

Secrecy and confidentiality
: Data should not be disclosed to anyone not authorized to access it.

Accuracy, integrity, and authenticity

Accuracy and integrity mean that data can't be maliciously or accidentally corrupted or modified. Authenticity is a variant on this concept; it provides a way to verify the origin of the data.

Availability and recoverability

Systems keep working, and data can be recovered efficiently and completely (with no loss of accuracy or integrity) in case of loss.

These terms may all appear to be quite similar, but in reality they are very different. And, different systems have mechanisms that achieve these goals in different ways. For example, encryption is a way of enforcing secrecy and confidentiality. Passwords and digital signatures aid in enforcing authenticity. Backups are a way of helping to guarantee availability and recoverability. Auditing helps ensure accuracy and integrity. Depending on your specific environment and user base, some of these aspects of security may be more important than others. In a classified military environment, for example, secrecy is usually the most important goal. In a banking environment, accuracy and integrity of data may be more important. For most of us, availability and recoverability of data may be more important than anything else as we go about our daily work.

What is your environment? Where are the threats to your system's security coming from? What actions can you take to protect your Oracle databases? How much action is enough to protect your company's valuable data without compromising your systems' performance and your employees' rights?

Potential Threats

Let's begin to answer these questions by looking at the various potential threats to our systems. If you're reading this chapter at work, stop reading and take a moment to look around you. What do you see? Rooms or cubicles with personal computers on almost every desk? Computer rooms filled with expensive equipment to enable employees to perform their work from various areas throughout your facility? Networks of computers, routers, disk farms, and cabling to connect all of the equipment (and users) together? And people. Your fellow employees—all busily working away—entering or extracting information from your databases or the World Wide Web. Okay. So some of them are just sitting around talking right now. But, they'll eventually go back to their PCs and do something—even if it's just to play solitaire.

If you're reading this chapter at home, you might have a computer in your living room, den, kitchen, study, or any other room in your home. You might have Internet and electronic mail access available through your telephone company or an Internet service provider. You might even have access to the Internet from your television set through your television cable company. You might use a modem to connect remotely to your place of business and access your database accounts or various systems via your home computer and telephone line. If you log in remotely, how do you ensure that the information transmitted between your home and your office is protected from interception and viewing by someone else? Suppose that data *were* intercepted by a competitor? What would the damage to your company be?

More and more companies and individuals are computerizing, using the Internet, and hosting or at least using Web sites. More and more companies are placing their valuable information on computers and in databases. A company's greatest asset is its data—and the people who control, manage and interact with that data. As an Oracle DBA, system administrator, manager, or computer system user, you are charged, in one way or another, with protecting your company's data.

What are the main threats to your system and your Oracle databases? Your hardware probably does not pose much of a security threat to your system. Of course, the equipment might be stolen or might break down, which will keep you from performing your work. You will want to adopt physical security measures (such as fire alarms, locked doors, etc.) to protect the hardware. And of course you will want to back up your databases to ensure that you can recover data if you suffer a hardware failure. Similarly, your software poses certain threats: it may contain bugs or viruses that will keep you from being able to do your work and that may damage your data.

Although hardware and software threats are real, the most significant threat to your systems and data is presented by the people who use them and the people who would like to—people you know well and people you might never have seen or will never see. There are all kinds of potential intruders who might want to gain access to your database and data because they perceive that your data holds some value to them. Perhaps they:

- Believe that by accessing your data they will gain a competitive edge
- Believe that they have been harmed in some way by your company and want to retaliate
- Want to prove that they *can* get into a "protected" system
- Are agents from other countries trying to gain information to help their country
- Are just curious and want to browse

What's the Harm?

It's clear that there are many types of threats to your Oracle databases. But how serious a problem is this? What damage could occur if people outside your organization access your company's private data? Look at it a another way. On a personal level, what's wrong with someone who isn't honest obtaining your charge account number and the charge card's expiration date, or someone getting your name and social security number? What damage could a thief do with these pieces of information?

With your charge card number and its expiration date, anyone could charge items to the card. Worse yet, with your name and social security number, a person could actually impersonate you! A friend of ours once lost his wallet. He took all of the steps he believed were necessary to protect himself—he notified his charge card companies, replaced his automatic bank teller card, and got a new driver's license. He felt pretty safe after taking these actions and believed that would be the end of any problems caused by the loss of his wallet.

He was wrong. About a month later, charge card bills began to arrive. But they were not charge cards with numbers he recognized. In fact, they were not even charge cards for companies with which he did business. Someone had stolen his identity. They had obtained a counterfeit driver's license with their picture on it but with our friend's name and address. The thief began to open charge accounts all over town using our friend's information. And, of course, merchandise was charged on all of these accounts. Thus began a nightmare that was to last for several months. As quickly as our friend learned of accounts that had been opened in his name, notified those companies about the fraud, and closed the accounts, more accounts were opened and more merchandise was charged. Eventually, our friend did manage to stop new accounts from being opened, and he straightened out the mess caused by the theft of his identity. But his credit history remained damaged long after the initial loss of his wallet occurred.

How anxious are you to have personal information made available to someone whom you don't know?

From a corporate perspective, your company's identity might not be easily stolen and used, but company-private data obtained from your database might provide a corporate thief with enough information to underbid your company on a lucrative job. It could even give him enough information to be able to transfer assets outside your organization. Browsing your database could give an intruder information about your employees' salaries (he might then try to hire them away from you), or information about their personal or medical histories (blackmail might even be a possibility). And if an intruder can read your data, he might also be able to change it, which could throw your systems and database into disarray and damage your corporate reputation.

How can you keep such threats from turning into realities? The first thing you need to do is to understand how your systems and databases actually work, and how you can develop policies and apply tools that will protect these valuable assets.

The Oracle Security Model

The Oracle security model is a multi-layered one. It incorporates the protection of files and objects both inside and outside the database, as well as a variety of administrative policies and technical strategies. This section provides a brief overview of the range of features that comprise "Oracle security." Subsequent chapters will describe these features and explain how they work together.

Layers of Security

Have you ever wrapped a very tiny present and decided to have some fun with the person receiving the gift? You put the very small gift-wrapped package into a larger box, put some kind of filler in the box to hold the package still, wrap that package in the same or different wrapping paper, and put it into another box. You continue using larger and larger boxes until the true size of the gift is totally hidden from view. Like packing one box inside of another, there are actually several layers of security involved in setting up and maintaining the protection of your database and system. In some respects, you are hiding layers of files and data from the general user's view. You are also making some determination about how much security is enough to protect your own particular system, database, applications, and specific data.

The layers of security which you can implement consist of the following:

- Protecting the Oracle operating system files—the RDBMS and Oracle software
- Protecting the application code which interacts with your Oracle database
- Controlling connections to the database
- Controlling access to the database tables through roles, grants, triggers, and procedures
- Controlling access to a table through views, triggers, and procedures
- Ensuring recoverability of your corporate data
- Enabling more complex forms of security such as data encryption, digital signatures, and single sign-on
- Supporting Web site structures and database access

The Physical Entities

In this book, we divide the examination of the components of an Oracle system into two main areas—Oracle operating system files (the physical entities) and Oracle database objects (the logical entities).

This section summarizes the physical (external) components of an Oracle system—the Oracle system files, the database processes, and the System Global Area. We'll describe these components in greater detail in Chapter 2, *Oracle System Files.*

The Oracle system files

The following files are significant from a security point of view. It is vital that you protect these files to the full extent allowed by your system:

The physical files that make up the database tablespaces
: These include the redo log files, control files, archive log files, datafiles[*] for data, datafiles for the rollback segments, datafiles for the indexes, etc.

The initialization parameter file
: This file contains Oracle's initialization parameters. In your system, the file has the name *INIT<DATABASE SID>.ORA*, where *DATABASE SID* is the system identifier (SID) of your database. In this book, we generally refer to it as the *INIT.ORA* file.

The configuration file
: The configuration file, called *CONFIG.ORA*, contains configuration information about the database. The information includes the location of the control files, the database block size, the location of the various dump files, etc.

Network configuration files
: The network configuration files are used for client interaction with the database. These files include (but are not limited to) *LISTENER.ORA*, *SQLNET.ORA*, *TNSNAMES.ORA*, etc.

The Oracle distribution files
: The Oracle distribution files include all of the code that is delivered and that you install on your system in order to build, interact with, and maintain Oracle databases. You need to keep in mind that there are some usernames and passwords embedded in the Oracle distribution files.

---

* The term "datafiles" (all one word) is used by Oracle to designate certain components of a database tablespace; we follow that convention in this book. In a few places, you may also find references to "data files" (two words) that refer to actual data within a file.

Backup files

Backup files are copies of the database that you create either through the Oracle-supplied backup utilities or by making copies of the files using operating system utilities. Backups should include all of the files listed here plus any configuration management files.

The detached processes and the SGA

The Oracle detached processes and the System Global Area (SGA) are not files, but are included here because they are controlled from the operating system level and are part of a running Oracle database.

The Oracle detached processes

The detached processes include (but are not limited to) the process monitor (PMON), the system monitor (SMON), the database writer (DBWR), the log writer (LGWR), and other processes; the particular set depends on the way you configure your database.

The System Global Area (SGA)

The SGA is a set of memory-resident structures shared by the processes that interact with a database. Among the set of memory-resident structures in the SGA are the database buffer cache, the redo log buffer, the shared pool, and the data dictionary cache.

The Logical Entities

The following list summarizes the main internal database objects; Oracle protects and maintains these entities directly, and uses them to enforce security in your system. We'll describe these entities in greater detail in Chapter 3, *Oracle Database Objects*, and explain how they're used in practical ways in later chapters.

Users

Database accounts created by the DBA. Users are given privileges to connect to a database to perform work. Users might (but do not have to) own objects. Privileges are granted to users by the DBA, by an authorized user, or by the object's owner based on the user's required tasks.

Schema

The complete collection of objects owned by a user account.

Privileges

Mechanisms given to users to enable actions to be performed on either data or objects. There are two levels of privileges: system-level privileges and object-level privileges.

Roles

A group of privileges or objects that can be used to pass one or more privileges to one or more users. Roles can be hierarchical—that is, a role can be granted to another role.

Profiles

Two different forms of profiles exist within an Oracle database: the product profile table, used to control access to SQL, SQL*Plus, and PL/SQL; and the system resource profile, used to control various resources a user might consume. Included within the system resource profile are parameters you can set to enable the new Oracle8 password utility features.

The rest of the internal components are all objects. The word "object," as we use it in this book, refers to any item owned by a user. A more strict definition of an object would be "an entity which takes up space in a database." The objects include:

Tables

Building blocks used to store data.

Triggers

Stored programs associated with a table. A trigger is executed when the event on which it is based occurs. The events that will "fire" a trigger are commands that perform INSERT, UPDATE, or DELETE actions.

Views

Views are used within an Oracle database to enable just a subset of information to be extracted from a table or group of tables. Views provide a definition of what data is to be retrieved and how. A view essentially "rides" on top of one or more tables and acts as a filter to enable users to see only a subset of the columns within the table or tables. Views are actually "quasi-objects" because they do not store data.

Stored programs

Programs written in PL/SQL can be stored in a compiled form within the database. There are two types of stored programs: procedures and functions. A function must return a value, while a procedure does not have to return a value.

Synonyms

Other names for an object—think of synonyms as nicknames. A synonym is used in an Oracle database to provide location transparency of objects and object owners.

The Oracle Data Dictionary

Oracle provides a special set of views you can use to "see into" the database internal data dictionary. The data dictionary contains the description of all of the objects in the database—tables, views, stored programs, etc. These views, as a whole, are referred to as the *data dictionary*. Using the data dictionary, you will be able to view and track all of the objects that exist in your database. The data dictionary is described in detail in Chapter 4, *The Oracle Data Dictionary*. Within that chapter, you'll see how the data dictionary views are created, and you'll examine the views which are of particular importance to you from a security perspective. We'll also look at a special view called DICTIONARY. This view houses the name and description of each of the data dictionary views to which a user has been granted access. We'll explain the composition of the file used to create the data dictionary, and you will see how the views are associated with the underlying database tables.

Oracle from the Outside

Before you ever install the Oracle source code for the first time, you will want to consider the steps you must take to ensure that unauthorized people don't have access to that system code. How can you protect the physical files that comprise your Oracle database system from the operating system level? You can place the files in a set of directories which are owned by an operating system account that belongs to a special group. No one outside of the special group would be allowed to interact with the files on more than a "read-only" basis. Most operating systems provide a mechanism to establish permissions on files to either enable or disable various forms of access to those files, for example:

- On a Windows NT system, you can use the *cacls* command or Windows NT Explorer to set the system file protection.
- On a UNIX system, you can specify permission masks using the *chmod* and *chown* utilities.
- On an OpenVMS system, you can use a *set protection* command to enable or disable file-level interaction.

Chapter 8, *Installing and Starting Oracle*, suggests approaches you can use to begin to protect your database from the operating system level. Likewise, you will want to protect the application code that interacts with the database.

Oracle from the Inside

There are a number of facilities available within the database that you can use for security. Oracle supplies default roles and user accounts in the database that simplify the assignment of privileges to users. The Oracle-supplied roles and users are described in Chapter 5, *Oracle Default Roles and User Accounts.* If you decide to use these mechanisms, you must carefully evaluate how that decision could help or hurt your overall security policies and plan.

From within the database, there are many other mechanisms you can use to protect your company's data. You can grant to or revoke from users access to objects, like tables and views, within your database. There are different levels and forms of access to the data within the database tables, which you can control by creating views and then permitting only selected users access to those views. On a more automated basis, you can create triggers and procedures to perform actions behind the scenes. A few possible tasks a trigger or procedure might perform include:

- Populate another table with information based on the actions being taken on the primary table
- Remove information from another table based on the actions being taken on the primary table
- Capture information about the data before it is modified
- Issue an alert to let someone know a table has been modified

Connecting to the Database

Oracle provides several different mechanisms you can use to authorize connection to an Oracle database. Among the connection mechanisms are:

- Username and password
- An account that relies on operating system validation to enable database access
- Remote access, with or without a username and password

If you create an account for a user, you can either create the account with a specific password or create the account with the keywords *IDENTIFIED EXTERNALLY.* If you create the account with a password, the user will type his username and password to connect to the database. If you create the account with the keywords IDENTIFIED EXTERNALLY, the user will only have to type in a username and password to access the operating system. From there, the user will simply use the "/" command to access the database. The third form of access is through the use of a remote client via any of the following:

- SQL*Net
- Net8 (for Oracle8)
- A third-party connection such as ODBC, using a tool such as Microsoft Access, SQL*Plus, or the Oracle-supplied Oracle Enterprise Manager (OEM) utility (for DBA access only)

With Oracle8, a password utility is provided to enable you to control the complexity and composition of passwords as well as the length of time a password will remain valid (password aging). Another new feature, the user profile, lets you control how often a user may reuse various passwords over a period of time (password history). You can either pre-expire a user's password or set the password to expire after a specific length of time. You can lock an Oracle account either automatically (because there have been too many failed login attempts) or explicitly (because you want to prevent access to a specific account). Chapter 6, *Profiles, Passwords, and Synonyms*, discusses the password features.

Backup and Recovery

As we mentioned earlier, availability is a key tenet of computer security. In every computer system, backup facilities are integral to keeping your system and data available for use. You can't protect against every form of data loss. Backup and recovery facilities keep a loss from becoming a disaster.

The level of protection you need to provide for your database will depend on many different elements. If your system is a development environment, for example, you might not have to provide as rigid a security implementation as you would use on a full-scale production system unless you are migrating production data back to your development system for testing purposes. Under those circumstances, you will need to determine if the data being migrated must be filtered to block sensitive data from being compromised.

For a production system, you will need to consider the following when you begin to plan your backup strategy:

- How much and what type of information your company can afford to lose
- What specific data would cause the most severe problems to your company if it were lost
- How long your system could be offline (down) while data was being recovered
- How much money your company is willing to spend to ensure that you have redundant systems

All of these issues are relative. Your backup and recovery approach will be dictated, in part, by your responses to these considerations. Regardless of how rigid or flexible your backup strategies need to be, you must be sure that you've implemented a backup and recovery structure that will give you the best protection for your environment within your corporate budget constraints. In Chapter 12, *Backing Up and Recovering the Database*, we look at a variety of backup and recovery issues and implementations.

More Complex Approaches

Suppose that you've adopted the basic measures necessary to protect your Oracle files—you've established roles, privileges, views, triggers, and procedures to protect your Oracle database objects, and you've created and implemented your backup and recovery strategies, policies, plan, and procedures. What's left? In recent years, more and more organizations have begun to use strong forms of encryption to protect their data. As hackers have devised more clever ways to compromise your computer systems and databases, the industry has responded by devising better and more complex ways to protect your systems.

We all know the story of the hungry wolf who disguised himself as a sheep to fool the shepherd and mingle with the unsuspecting herd. He was then able to easily kill a sheep for his dinner. The "sheep's clothing" idea is alive and well, and it threatens your company's data. Intruders have various ways of intercepting your data or even assuming your online identity. Using programs known as *sniffers* and *spoofers*, intruders can monitor your Internet traffic and capture your username or password for future use. They also have found ways of disguising their messages so they appear to originate from your own Internet address. There are also many other ways, both brute force and automated, of guessing passwords and thereby gaining access to your computer and database.

There are now software tools you can use to protect your system from these intrusions. One way to protect your database is through the use of software that certifies a user really is who he says he is. Once a user has obtained an electronic credential attesting to his authenticity, the user can access any database for which he has been approved. Provided with the base Oracle8 software, a utility called the Oracle Security Server (OSS) Manager (see Chapter 15, *Using the Oracle Security Server*) enables you to generate and implement the following forms of security:

Certificate of authority
: A user credential that says that a user is really who he claims to be

Digital signature
: An encrypted section of code that authenticates that a message was sent by a specific user

Single sign-on
: The ability to connect once to a system presenting a username and password and be granted access to other systems or databases based on your ability to have gained access to the original system; once you've been authenticated, you won't need to present any further usernames or passwords

In the base product set, Oracle does not provide software for the encryption or decryption of data. However, Oracle does provide—for an additional fee—a product called the Advanced Networking Option (ANO), which can be used for that purpose. Products that are available at an additional price and can be used to further enhance your site's security are described in Chapter 17, *Using Extra-Cost Options.*

Web Sites

With the explosive way the world has embraced the use of the Internet, intranets, and the World Wide Web, we now have more ways our systems can be compromised, and there is much more to be learned about defending those systems.

There are many reasons why more and more businesses and government agencies are joining the ranks of those who host, or at least use, web sites. The major reason to host a web site is to improve communication between employees, (through an intranet) or between your company and potential, current, or past customers (through the Internet). The ease of reaching a large number of people with minimum expense is very appealing. The Internet enables small businesses, with very limited funds, to reach larger audiences of potential customers easily. Large companies can also benefit from the volume of Internet traffic.

Because of the high interest and activity in the web arena, we've included some brief information about web security in Chapter 16, *Using the Internet and the Web.* Within its base software, Oracle does not provide any security utilities specifically for use with your web site. However, Oracle does have a product called the Oracle Application Server available for an additional fee (see Chapter 17). The Oracle Application Server works very well with the security protocols built in to the Oracle database. It also has its own stand-alone security.

Procedures, Policies, and Plans

Whether you are an IS manager, a system administrator, or a database administrator, there are many different procedures, policies, and plans you may be called on to help develop as your organization plans its security. In this book, we use the following definitions:

Procedures
: These map out, in a step-by-step fashion, the actions you need to take to perform a job successfully.

Policies
: These detail your company's rules and reflect your company's standards and code of ethics.

Plans
: These are documents that outline the approaches to be used to implement and enforce your company's policies.

Within the realm of database security, you may need to construct the following:

- Security policies and an accompanying security plan
- An auditing plan and procedures
- A database backup and recovery plan and procedures

The auditing plan and the database backup and recovery plan are sometimes included in the security plan.

The following sections briefly examine these different entities and discuss why they are important to your organization.

Security Policies and Security Plan

Over lunch on several days during the International Oracle User Group conference (IOUG-A Live) in the spring of 1998, we casually discussed with several groups of DBAs the topic of Oracle security and security plans. To a person, everyone agreed that security policies (which outline the company's position on security issues) and a security plan (which describes, in detail, how the policies will be implemented and enforced) are vital to an organization. However, all of the DBAs we talked with admitted that they have been fighting an uphill battle to get their company's management to allocate the funds and lend the support needed to create such security policies and to write and enforce a workable security plan.

Why does your company need to take the time, effort, and expense to create and implement security policies and plans? This section touches on some of the issues you need to consider when creating security policies and a security plan.

What does a stated set of security policies and plan "buy" for you and your company? Suppose that your company has no written security policies and no security plan in effect. Ima Ticdoff, an Oracle user who works in the payroll department, gets angry with her boss one day and decides to "show him a thing or two." She doesn't want to do anything really damaging; she just wants to cause a bit of discomfort; and she doesn't want to get caught. She logs on to the database and modifies her boss's accrued vacation time from ten days to one day. Vacation accrual is posted on each employee's paycheck. When the next paychecks come out, Ima's boss notices the error in vacation accrual and begins to check into what happened. A thorough and time-consuming investigation shows that the boss's record is the only one that has been modified.

Since there is no security plan in effect, there is no auditing enabled to check who made the change to the boss's records. Even if he finds out that Ima is responsible for the modification, how can he prove that she intentionally changed the record? Worse yet, if he does prove that her actions were intentional, with no stated policy on what an employee can or cannot do, and what actions will be taken if a security breach occurs, there may be little the boss can do to discipline Ima. With the current climate of labor laws and court decisions, if the boss and your company take action against Ima, they may find themselves in the middle of a very unpleasant lawsuit that they might not win.

If your company has a stated policy on what actions will or will not be tolerated from employees and what steps will be taken if the policies are breached, action can more easily be taken against an employee who oversteps the stated boundaries. If policies are clear, each employee should understand what is expected of him or her and can help to implement the policies and protect the corporate data.

If your company has been resisting writing and implementing security policies and a security plan, show your management the latest newspaper articles on security breaches that have cost companies millions of dollars in lost revenues from damage to databases. Next, show your management Chapter 7, *Developing a Database Security Plan*, which identifies the issues you must consider when forming a security policy and which maps out the steps you'll need to take to create an Oracle security plan for your company.

Whether your organization decides to implement a small and informal security plan, puts resources into a more formal and in-depth security policy and plan, or chooses to do nothing at all, you will at least have taken a proactive stance in attempting to help your organization more effectively protect the databases in your care.

Auditing Plan and Procedures

One of the problems with the Ima incident was a lack of auditing on the system. An auditing plan is a natural follow-on to a corporate security plan. Any database you oversee should be examined to determine if there are objects that need special attention, or actions or privileges that should be monitored. Once you have identified areas that are appropriate to audit, you will want to write the procedures to document the steps you'll need to take to enable and enforce auditing on your database.

Oracle provides different levels of auditing that you can enable from your database as follows.

Statement-level auditing

Performed to capture information when a specific type of Data Definition Language (DDL) or Data Manipulation Language (DML) statement is either attempted or completed (either successfully or unsuccessfully). This type of auditing can be very broad or very specific. The statement-level audits are based on the type of SQL statement presented.

System privilege auditing

Performed to capture information when a specific system privilege is used.

Object auditing

Performed to capture information when a specific object or group of objects are accessed (either successfully or unsuccessfully).

In Chapter 10, *Developing an Audit Plan*, we discuss when and why you might want to create an auditing plan and how to implement one or another form of auditing within your database. We describe how auditing works, the various forms of auditing, and the ramifications of enabling auditing on your database. Let's look at some of the reasons you would implement auditing and some areas in which auditing might make sense:

- Specific tables whose data is vitally important to your company would be excellent potential candidates for auditing.
- You may want to keep track of who is creating one or more specific kinds of objects in your database to help ensure that an unauthorized person is not siphoning off information to which he or she should not have access.
- You may want to track accounts that have had failed connection attempts because you suspect that someone is attempting to guess their way into your database.

If you've enabled the Oracle-supplied auditing utilities, you'll be able to implement auditing within your database, either very broadly or very narrowly (depending on your needs), to gain an overall view of actions being taken in your database.

A Problem with Auditing—and a Solution

With the various forms of auditing provided by Oracle, you can determine that a specific table was accessed and when the table was modified, but you cannot tell what action was taken or what data was inserted, modified, or deleted.

Think back to the Ima incident once again. The boss knew that someone had modified his record. After investigation, he knew that his record was the only one that had been modified in error. After going through his payroll receipts and time cards, he was able to prove that he had 10 hours of vacation time accrued and was able eventually to get the time reinstated. The cost to her company from Ima's "prank" was very high in wasted time and effort.

Might there be an easier way of tracking Ima's data modifications? In Chapter 11, *Developing a Sample Audit Application*, we provide an application you can use (either completely or in part) to enable information to be captured at the column level of a table. If the audit trail application had been active in the database on the table which Ima modified, the following information would have been captured:

- What the data looked like before the change
- What the data looked like after the change
- Who had made the change
- What time the change was made

There would have been no time-consuming investigation or need to provide proof of the original data. The damage Ima caused could have been repaired easily at a very low cost to the company in time and effort—and Ima would have gotten caught!

Backup and Recovery Plan and Procedures

An Oracle technical support person once told a story about the time he was manning a support line and a customer called in. The conversation went something like this:

Customer: "Hi. I'm a DBA at this company and my database just crashed. What should I do?"

Oracle: "When was your last database backup taken?"

Customer: "Backup? Oh, we've never taken a backup."

Oracle: "When did you do your last export of the database?"

Customer: "Export? Oh, we've never taken an export of the database. What should I do?"

The support person's reply was, "I'd recommend that you update your resume and send it out really quickly...but *don't* send it to us!"

We've said how important backups are. But recovery is important too. You need a backup plan that outlines the various forms of backup you'll use, as well as a recovery plan that outlines the procedures you'll follow to recover your database in case of a minor data loss or a full-fledged disaster. In Chapter 12, we discuss the forms of backup available to you and the elements you should consider including in your backup and recovery plans and procedures.

No matter how thorough your data protection plans and procedures are, there is always the potential for hardware failure, acts of God, and human errors. A speaker at a conference we attended once told his audience to go home, walk in to the computer room, and "pull the plug on one of your disks on your test system." He was suggesting that the attendees verify that their backup and recovery plans were, in fact, effective and usable. We wholeheartedly agree with that speaker that you need to test your backup and recovery plans to ensure that they are valid and workable—but we hesitate to advise you to physically tamper with your disks!

If I Had a Hammer...

Oracle provides many software tools, operating system files, and database constructs that help you protect your data. Some tools, delivered with the basic Oracle system, you are likely to use every day; others you might use only in certain environments and situations to impose a higher level of security on your system. There are also "add-on" tools you can purchase from Oracle at additional cost that provide higher levels of data protection. This section takes a quick look at the various available tools and examines what each of these tools provides for you.

What's "Free"?

There are two particular products delivered with the basic Oracle8 product set that will help you implement better database security. They are the Oracle Enterprise Manager (OEM) and the Oracle Security Server (OSS) Manager.

Oracle Corporation currently delivers the OEM with the base product set. The OEM is a set of utilities which are personal computer-based and use a graphical user interface (GUI). These utilities provide a way to manage one or more of your databases from a single computer. The components of the OEM are easy to use and let you perform many of your day-to-day DBA functions either interactively or on an automatic, scheduled basis.

The OEM is delivered with Oracle8 and includes the following features:

- A set of database administration tools
- An event monitor you can configure to watch for specific situations within your databases
- A job scheduler to perform maintenance tasks on a scheduled basis
- A graphical interface to the Recovery Manager tools (not available in Oracle7)

The OEM is supported to work with Oracle version 7.1.6 databases and higher.

Chapter 13, *Using the Oracle Enterprise Manager*, describes the OEM.

Although the Recovery Manager is listed as a part of the OEM, you can use this product as a stand-alone utility.

The Oracle Security Server Manager is also delivered with Oracle's base product set, starting with the first delivery of Oracle8. The OSS can be used to implement a more complex security structure for more sensitive data. The OSS was originally supposed to be bundled inside the OEM toolkit. However, in version 8.0.4 of the Windows NT product set, the OSS is installed separately and appears as a separate set of menu options. The OSS lets you implement the following security features:

- User authentication through electronic credentials
- Digital signatures
- Single sign-on

All of these features are implemented "stand-alone." In other words, you do not have to have any third-party products (e.g., Kerberos) or any other Oracle-supplied products (e.g., the Advanced Networking Option) to use this utility. Although OSS is new with Oracle8, you can use its features with Oracle7 databases as well. Chapter 15 describes the OSS.

What Isn't Free?

Oracle markets several additional, extra-cost products you can use to enhance your security:

Trusted Oracle
: Provides multi-level security (MLS) primarily within government agencies where data access is based on security clearance levels.

Advanced Networking Option
: Used to encrypt and decrypt all data that is transferred over SQL*Net or Net8 to and from a database.

Oracle Application Server (formerly Web Application Server)
: Used to serve a broad spectrum of applications for Web-based interaction. With each new version of the Oracle Application Server, new security features are introduced or current features are enhanced.

Chapter 17 briefly describes these products.

2

In this chapter:

- *What's in the Files?*
- *The Instance and the Database: Starting an Oracle Database*
- *Types of Database Files*

Oracle System Files

When we say the word "refrigerator," what do you think of? Do you picture a large, rectangular box with one door or two? Or do you picture the objects inside—fresh vegetables, dairy products, ripe fruit? What does a refrigerator have to do with Oracle and security? Well, nothing, really, except that you can see the exterior of a refrigerator and not have any idea what the box contains. You see the structure—its shape and features—but the contents are a mystery to you until you open the door and look inside.

Just as the refrigerator has an outside structure, an Oracle database is comprised of a number of complex pieces of software that enable you to create data storage areas (databases) and to develop applications that interact with the databases. Once a database is created, you can see the "objects" inside. Unlike a refrigerator, which is a physical entity containing only physical objects, an Oracle database is comprised of both physical files and logical representations (the objects inside).

To determine what actions you need to take to protect your system, you first need to understand the composition of that system. You need to understand what part each component plays within the system and how the pieces interact. Once you have a basic grasp of the Oracle components, you'll be better able to create your security policies and implement a sound security plan for your organization.

This chapter provides an overview of the Oracle components that comprise the Oracle file system (external components) that are relevant to RDBMS security. Chapter 3, *Oracle Database Objects*, describes the logical (internal) database components or objects.

What's in the Files?

The physical components of an Oracle database system consist of the basic, delivered Oracle software and various storage files for each database. The storage files contain different forms of information. Those most relevant to security are:

Tablespace datafiles
: These datafiles can contain data, indexes, rollback segments, or temporary segments. Rollback segments and temporary segments are explained here. Data and indexes will be explained in Chapter 3.

Rollback segments
: These segments are used to keep track of the way the data looked before it was changed. During recovery, any uncommitted (saved) transactions still in the rollback segments are used to "roll back" these changes to restore the database to the last stable state.

Temporary segments
: These segments are allocated by Oracle when a user session requires an area in which a sort operation must be performed. Temporary segments are used by the RDBMS as a "scratch pad" to build temporary tables in order to do work requested by the user. These segments are created in the tablespace that has been designated the TEMPORARY tablespace.

Control file
: A form of binary storage file used to keep track of the status of the physical structure of a database. This file enables the database to start up and is used for database recovery. It records several critical maximum values and tracks the archive log numbers as well as the location and status of each tablespace datafile in the database.

Redo log files
: Another set of binary storage files that keep track of all changes made to the database. There must be at least two online redo logs associated with each database. The online redo logs are written to and reused in a circular fashion.

Archive log files
: These are companion files to the redo log files. If archivelog mode is enabled for your database, after each redo log file is filled, an archive log file is created with a copy of the filled redo log file. The archive log file is placed in an alternate storage area whose location you have designated in the *INIT.ORA* file for the database. The archive log files within this alternate storage area are sequentially numbered so that the new file will not overwrite an older file.

Initialization file
This is the startup parameter file. As we've mentioned, we refer to this file as the *INIT.ORA* file, though it will usually be named in your system as *INIT<DATABASE SID>.ORA*. It is used to modify the default initialization parameters used by Oracle when you start a database.

Configuration file
This file, *CONFIG.ORA*, contains configuration information. It can include information about the locations of control files and the database name. Other information, like the location of dump files, can be included in the configuration file. Although this file is optional, we mention it here because many sites choose to use a configuration file as well as an initialization parameter file. Some Oracle installers automatically create a configuration file as an include file for the initialization parameter file. Configuration files are recommended by Oracle Corporation for use with the parallel server option. The creation of the configuration file during the software installation is platform-specific, so not all installations have a configuration file.

System Global Area (SGA)
This is a "file in memory," a set of memory-resident structures. When the database is started, the initialization parameters are read, the detached Oracle processes are created and started, and a section of memory is reserved for the System Global Area. Although it is not actually a physical file, the SGA is included here because of its tight coupling with the control file and the tablespace datafiles.

The idea of differentiating Oracle system files (external components) and Oracle database objects (internal components) for an Oracle RDBMS might at first seem strange, since we speak of the database as an entity in and of itself. In reality, the "database" is comprised of many different parts that are generally viewed as a whole system. This chapter and Chapter 3 together describe the parts from a security perspective.

The Instance and the Database: Starting an Oracle Database

Many people use the terms *instance* and *database* interchangeably, but the instance and the database are actually separate entities. Let's look at what happens when the database is started from the Server Manager utility (*svrmgrl*, *svrmgrm*, or *svrmgr30* for Oracle8 on Windows NT). The startup process follows:

- The background processes are started.
- The System Global Area (SGA) is allocated in memory.

- The background processes open the various files.
- The database is ready for use.

During the startup, messages are displayed that notify you of what is happening. Here is a sample startup sequence:

```
SVRMGR>  startup
ORACLE instance started.
Total System Global Area       11865072 bytes
Fixed Size                        33708 bytes
Variable Size                  10672196 bytes
Database Buffers                1126400 bytes
Redo Buffers                      32768 bytes
Database mounted.
Database opened.
```

You can see that the *instance* is started before the files that constitute the database are opened. The instance consists of the background processes and the SGA. The SGA totals are listed before the database is started but after the "ORACLE instance started" message. The *database* is the collection of logical objects and physical files necessary to support the system, and the *database system* is the instance, SGA, and files. Figure 2-1 shows the components of the database system after the database has been started.

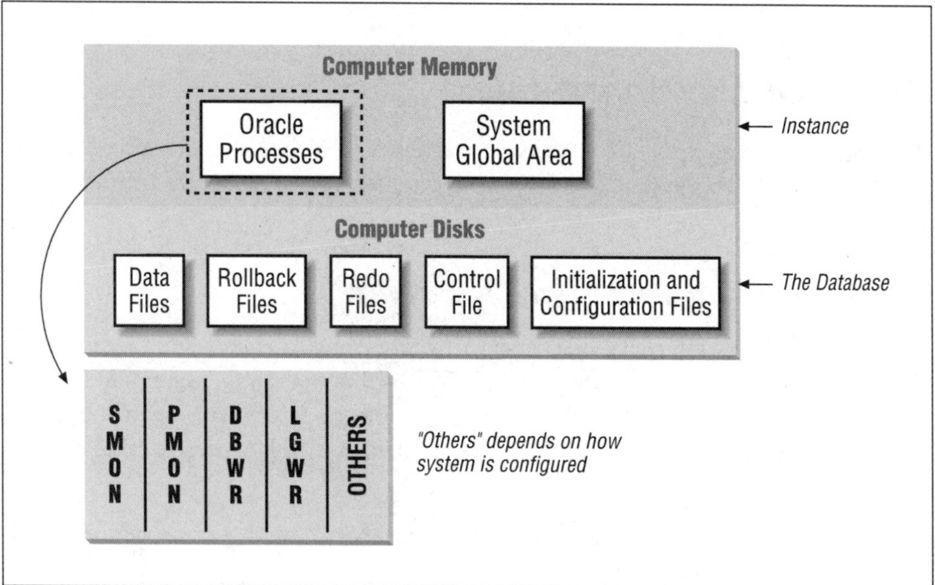

Figure 2-1. Components of the database system after startup

Now, while what we've said is technically accurate, you'll find the actual usage at Oracle sites to be quite different. Many people use the terms "instance," "database," and "database system" interchangeably. In this context, they are referring to the entire system: the background processes, the System Global Area, and the data, control, and redo log files.

What the Oracle System Files Really Are

The Oracle components we discuss in this chapter are all actually just operating system files (except for the SGA, which is a memory-resident structure). The physical database files must be protected at the operating system level from intrusive access by any user. These files are never written to directly by any user application, though they are written to on behalf of user processes. Oracle owns these files and will manage them. Users should never have any operating system privileges on these files beyond the privileges Oracle instructs you to set in the installation guide for your system.

You name the physical database files when the database is initialized and when additional datafiles are added. There are no mandatory names for any of these files. You, as the DBA, can select their names. The only restrictions are that the names cannot contain blanks or special characters, and they must conform to the operating system name requirements, and cannot exceed 30 characters in length.

Types of Database Files

The database is comprised of several different types of files that serve different functions within the system. We describe each component in the following sections.

Tablespace and Tablespace Datafiles

A tablespace is an internal object used to represent a physical storage area. It is the logical name for an entity used to access the operating system files called *datafiles*. In this book, when we speak of a tablespace we will mean the logical tablespace name as well as the files assigned to it. Oracle uses a tablespace to house the following different kinds of structures:

- Database object structures—like tables, indexes, packages, procedures, triggers, etc.
- Rollback segments
- Temporary sort segments

A tablespace must have one or more datafiles assigned to it; otherwise, it cannot be created. These files may be on one or more disks. When you create a table or index, you will specify the tablespace in which the object is to be created. If this is not done, then your default tablespace will be used. The STORAGE clause used in the CREATE statement will determine how much space is allocated from the tablespace. Several examples of STORAGE clauses appear in the following sections. When this initial allocation is filled, more space will be assigned, this time according to the NEXT parameter in the STORAGE clause. The DBA monitors space utilization and, as the tablespace becomes full, will need to add more datafiles or rebuild the tablespace to combine the current datafiles and increase the allocation of space.

Figure 2-2 shows the layout of a tablespace's datafiles on more than one disk.

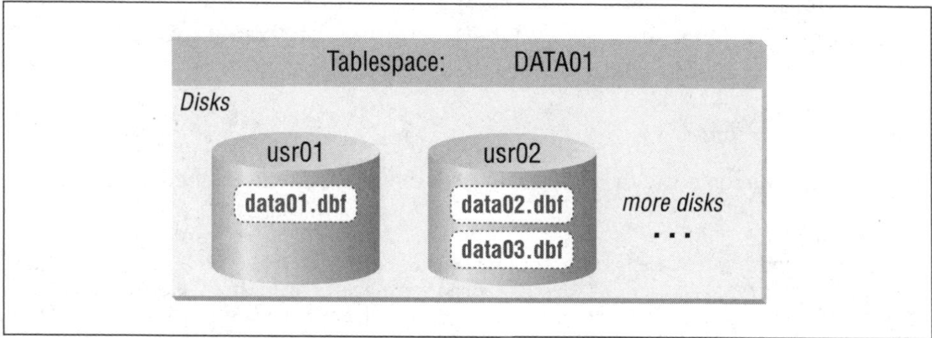

Figure 2-2. A tablespace datafiles layout

Tablespace names

Tablespace names are usually chosen to represent the type of data being stored. The name is usually generic in nature. For example, in a small system there may be a DATA_01 tablespace and an INDEX_01 tablespace. Larger systems may use somewhat more specific names such as AR_01, AR_02, PER_01, and so on. While the examples shown here follow a name and number convention, there is nothing to stop you from using names such as D, I, PERSONNEL, ACCOUNTS_RECEIVABLE, and so on. The only restrictions are that tablespace names:

- Cannot usually be more than 30 characters
- Cannot contain blanks or special characters
- Cannot use certain reserved words

Some of the obvious reserved words are CREATE, INSERT, and UPDATE. The list is quite lengthy, however, and we suggest that you look in the Oracle DBA manuals for a complete list.

You might want to use tablespace names that represent the form of data they contain. For example, in an Financials application database, you might have tablespaces named PO_DAT or GL_IDX, for Purchase Order and General Ledger applications, respectively. If you find that another form of data needs to be stored in an application, you can always create another tablespace—with an equally meaningful name—to store the new data.

Another approach is to use more general names as mentioned previously (DATA_01, etc.), particularly if you will be hosting more than one type of application in the database. This removes the arbitrary restriction that only Purchase Order data can be stored in the PO_DAT tablespace. Since each of the authors feels that one method is preferable to the other, we recommend that you let your design team make the decision about the naming convention which will be used.

We recommend that, whenever possible, you keep the files for data tablespaces on different disks from their index tablespaces and, preferably, on different controllers for better performance.

Creating a tablespace

A tablespace is created with a CREATE TABLESPACE statement such as the following:

```
SQL> CREATE TABLESPACE base_accounting
        DATAFILE '/usr06/oradata/prod/data/baseacct01.dbf' SIZE 5M REUSE,
        DATAFILE '/usr07/oradata/prod/data/baseacct02.dbf' SIZE 5M REUSE,
        DATAFILE '/usr08/oradata/prod/data/baseacct03.dbf' SIZE 5M REUSE,
        DATAFILE '/usr09/oradata/prod/data/baseacct04.dbf' SIZE 5M REUSE,
        DATAFILE '/usr06/oradata/prod/data/baseacct05.dbf' SIZE 5M REUSE,
        DATAFILE '/usr07/oradata/prod/data/baseacct06.dbf' SIZE 5M REUSE,
        DATAFILE '/usr08/oradata/prod/data/baseacct07.dbf' SIZE 5M REUSE,
        DATAFILE '/usr09/oradata/prod/data/baseacct08.dbf' SIZE 5M REUSE
     ;

tablespace created
```

In this example, the "base_accounting" tablespace has been created.

In this example, the files that constitute the tablespace are on different disks—a fact that is transparent to the user.

Creating a table within a tablespace

When you are creating a table, the tablespace can be referenced explicitly in the CREATE TABLE statements or implicitly by allowing the table to be created within the tablespace that has been defined as the user's default tablespace. For example, user *mary* has been defined with a default tablespace called tools. An appropriate space quota has been granted to *mary* on this tablespace. If *mary* creates a table and does not include a tablespace parameter in the CREATE statement, the table will be created in the tools tablespace. There is no harm in including the tablespace parameter for the default tablespace. In the following script, the tablespace is referenced explicitly:

```
SQL> CREATE TABLE general_ledger
       (entry_id           NUMBER          NOT NULL,
        transaction_id     NUMBER          NOT NULL,
        trans_amount       NUMBER(12,4)    NOT NULL,
        document_id        VARCHAR2(20),
        <and other column definitions>
       )
       TABLESPACE base_accounting
       STORAGE (INITIAL 25M  NEXT 1M PCTINCREASE 0)
       ;

table created
```

Creating an index for a table in a tablespace

In order to improve the speed with which Oracle retrieves data, you might create an index on a table. To improve performance, create the index in a separate tablespace and, preferably, on a different disk. The CREATE statement for an index for the base_accounting table created earlier might look like this:

```
SQL> CREATE UNIQUE INDEX gl_ui ON general_ledger (entry_id)
             TABLESPACE base_accounting_indx
                STORAGE (INITIAL 4M NEXT 500K PCTINCREASE 0);

index created
```

In both statements, you can see that reference is made only to the logical object (the tablespace) and not to the underlying physical objects (the datafiles). Oracle will automatically store the objects within the datafiles associated with the tablespaces mentioned in the CREATE statements.

File placement and naming

As shown in the example, the files used for the tablespaces may be placed anywhere on the computer's storage disks, although there are some general rules that you should follow to avoid performance problems. The file protection should prevent any user from ever being able to modify these files directly from the operating system level. As mentioned before, modification of these files is the sole responsibility of the Oracle processes. File names are usually chosen by the DBA in cooperation with the system administrator or in compliance with the company's security policy. As was illustrated in the CREATE TABLESPACE example, the datafile names should bear some relationship to the tablespace to which they belong.

Tablespace security

From a security standpoint, the only issue in maintaining tablespace security is operating system control of access to the datafiles. No user ever has to manipulate the database datafiles directly in any manner from the operating system level. Users should not have any privileges on these files. The underlying datafiles for the tablespaces must be owned by the account that was used to install the Oracle software. This account is usually named *oracle*.

The actual datafiles are created by Oracle with the CREATE TABLESPACE or ALTER TABLESPACE commands and they are maintained automatically by Oracle.

Redo Log Files

The redo log is used to record data that can be used to reconstruct all changes made to the database. Redo logs are created primarily to be used for recovery from a disk crash—assuming that a file-level backup has been performed and that archivelog mode has been enabled. The logs can, however, be used to recover from other forms of failure. In the event that the database has become corrupted as a result of a malicious action or a break-in, a known good backup can be restored and the archive redo logs applied to bring the database back to a good state prior to the corruption. The data in the redo logs is only intended to be read by the kernel during database recovery. Like datafiles, redo log files are binary. They are created indirectly when the database is first created, and they are maintained automatically. Each database has at least two or more redo log files. Only one redo log or redo log group is ever in use at a time, and the log files are used in a circular fashion.

Log switches

In a system with two redo log files, as one file is filled, the kernel marks it as closed and begins writing to the next one. This is referred to as a *log file switch* or *thread switch*. When the second log file is filled, the switch process is repeated and the first file is used again. When a log switch occurs, the contents of the first redo log file will be overwritten as the log file fills up again. If the database is a development system that is backed up often, recovery from a disaster may only need to be performed to the point when the backup was made. If, however, there will be a need to restore the system to a point in time after the last full backup, the DBA will need to perform full, file-level backups and enable archivelog mode on the database to allow Oracle to automatically save off each redo log file as the log switches occur.

Redo logs and archivelog mode enabled—coupled with scheduled file-level backups—are tools that could bail you out of a disaster situation. For UNIX users working with Oracle7 databases, Oracle provides a backup utility called the Oracle7 Enterprise Backup Utility, which can be used for backup and restore operations. Chapter 12, *Backing Up and Recovering the Database*, provides more information on backup considerations and implementation.

How redo log files are created

Redo log files are created when the database is created. They are specified in the CREATE DATABASE statement, as in the following example:

```
SRVRMGR>  CREATE DATABASE finprod
2>   DATAFILE /usr02/oradata/data/system01.dbf SIZE 75M REUSE
3>   CONTROLFILE REUSE
4>   LOGFILE /usr03/oradata/logfile/finlog01.dbf SIZE 1M,
5>           /usr04/oradata/logfile/finlog02.dbf SIZE 1M,
6>           /usr05/oradata/logfile/finlog03.dbf SIZE 1M,
7>           /usr03/oradata/logfile/finlog04.dbf SIZE 1M,
8>           /usr04/oradata/logfile/finlog05.dbf SIZE 1M,
9>           /usr05/oradata/logfile/finlog06.dbf SIZE 1M
10>  /
```

The redo log files, like the tablespace files, are created and owned by the Oracle system account and should never be made accessible to any other user for any purpose. In the example above, two different redo log files have been placed on each of three disks. *finlog01.dbf* will be written to first on disk usr03. When either the redo log file completely fills or a designated checkpoint size is reached, *finlog02.dbf* will be written to on disk usr04. When this log file fills or the checkpoint limit is reached, *finlog03.dbf* will be written to on disk usr05. The sequence will continue through the log files sequentially. Notice that if *finlog03.dbf* becomes damaged, there is no copy of it on the system to fall back on since there is only one unique file defined for each redo log. To avoid this, you may want to implement redo log groups as described in the next section.

Using redo log groups

Another approach to creating redo logs for your system is to create redo log groups, a form of *mirroring*. This is done by creating the log files in sets of repeated groups of files, preferably on two or more different disks, so that if one member of a set becomes damaged the others will be available to use for quick recovery. An example of a CREATE statement for redo log groups is shown here:

```
SRVRMGR> CREATE DATABASE finprod
2>   DATAFILE /usr02/oradata/data/system01.dbf SIZE 75M reuse
3>   CONTROLFILE REUSE
4>   LOGFILE GROUP 1 (/usr03/oradata/logfile/finlog01a.dbf,
5>                    /usr04/oradata/logfile/finlog01b.dbf) SIZE 1M,
```

```
6>  LOGFILE GROUP 2 (/usr03/oradata/logfile/finlog02a.dbf,
7>                   /usr04/oradata/logfile/finlog02b.dbf) SIZE 1M,
8>  LOGFILE GROUP 3 (/usr03/oradata/logfile/finlog03a.dbf,
9>                   /usr04/oradata/logfile/finlog03b.dbf) SIZE 1M
10>  MAXDATAFILES 300
11>  /
```

In this example, there are three sets or groups of redo logs with two members each on two separate disks. The files defined as *finlog01a.dbf* and *finlog01b.dbf* will be written on disks usr03 and usr04 respectively. At switch time, both *finlog02a.dbf* and *finlog02b.dbf* files will be opened for writing.

MAXDATAFILES parameter

If you think you might need to create a large number of datafiles (more than 32), you can include the MAXDATAFILES parameter in the CREATE DATABASE statement. For example, adding MAXDATAFILES = 100 will allow you to create as many as 100 total datafiles within the database. The use of a larger number for MAXDATAFILES does not impact performance and does enable a larger number of datafiles to be created in the system if needed. If you set MAXDATAFILES to a large number, the only impact you might see on your system is an increase in the size of your control file.

In earlier versions of Oracle, the only time that MAXDATAFILES could be set was at database creation time. If the maximum number of datafiles specified in this statement had to be increased later, the only way you could increase the maximum number of datafiles allowed was to recreate the database—sort of a brute force approach, not to mention a time-consuming effort. As of version 7.2, there is a way (which will be discussed shortly) to edit the control file to modify this parameter. There is no performance impact and only a slight increase in the size of the control file, so setting the MAXDATAFILES value initially to a larger size is recommended.

Control File

Each database has at least one control file. This is a small binary file (like the redo log file) that contains information on the status of the database. The information in the control file is critical to database operation and recovery. The database will not start without the control file. Like the other Oracle files, this file should never be available to any user and must be owned by the *oracle* install user. The control file is unreadable except by the instance background processes. The control file contains:

- The database's internal identification number, name, and the timestamp of when the database was created.

- Tablespace information and the name, location, size, and a checksum value for each tablespace's datafiles.
- The name, size, and location of each online redo log file.
- The log history and archived log information.
- Backup set, piece, datafile, and redo log information (very important for recovery).
- The current redo log sequence number and checkpoint information.
- Datafile copy information.
- Values for five of the MAX... parameters. (MAXLOGFILES, MAXLOGMEMBERS, MAXDATAFILES, MAXINSTANCE, MAXLOGHISTORY). These are always present, even if they are not specified in the database initialization file. In that case, the default values will be shown.

Modifying control files

In order to view or change any of the parameters in the control file, you must convert it to a readable text file. The command to dump the control file to a format in which it can be worked on is as follows:

```
SRVMGR>  ALTER DATABASE BACKUP CONTROLFILE TO TRACE;
```

In this example, the file is dumped with a default name to a default location. This default location is defined by the ORA_DUMP_DEST parameter in the database initialization file. The file produced by the command is a text file with a name similar to *ora20117.trc*.

Alternatively, the control file can be written to a specific, DBA-defined location by using a command with the following syntax:

```
SRVMGR> ALTER DATABASE BACKUP CONTROLFILE TO '$ORACLE_HOME/mdir/mfil.sql';
```

A sample control file

Whether the default directory or a directory path and file name is used, the output file from the above commands will have a SQL section that will look something like the following example:

```
# The following commands will create a new control file and use it
# to open the database.
# No data other than log history will be lost. Additional logs may
# be required for media recovery of offline datafiles. Use this
# only if the current version of all online logs are available.
STARTUP NOMOUNT
CREATE CONTROLFILE REUSE DATABASE "DOCX" NORESETLOGS ARCHIVELOG
    MAXLOGFILES 32
    MAXLOGMEMBERS 2
    MAXDATAFILES 32
```

```
    MAXINSTANCES 16
    MAXLOGHISTORY 1600
LOGFILE
  GROUP 1 'C:\orawin95\datadocx\docxlog1.dbf'  SIZE 500K,
  GROUP 2 'C:\orawin95\datadocx\docxlog2.dbf'  SIZE 500K,
  GROUP 3 'C:\orawin95\datadocx\docxlog3.dbf'  SIZE 500K
DATAFILE
  'C:\orawin95\datadocx\docxsys1.dbf',
  'C:\orawin95\datadocx\newts01.dbf',
  'C:\orawin95\datadocx\newts02.dbf'
;
```

Note that all of the MAX... values are present, even if values were not specified during database initialization.

This section of code is followed by several commands that will restart the database, recreate the control file, and perform a recovery. The file contains instructions on how it can be edited to change the MAX... parameter values as well as the LOGFILE and DATAFILE specifications. If you change either of the latter two parameters, be sure that the files you specify are made available or the database will not recreate the control file.

The primary purpose of backing up and editing the control file is to change one of the MAX... parameters—most commonly the MAXDATAFILES value.

How Oracle uses control files

In Oracle8, if the Oracle Enterprise Manger is used in conjunction with the Recovery Manager (RMAN utility) to perform backups (as described in Chapters 12 and 13), the backup history will be stored both in the Recovery Catalog and in the control files for each database. It is possible that this file will become very large; you need to take this into consideration both from a disk storage perspective and from a security perspective. Control file size is normally static, but it may begin to grow if the RMAN facility is enabled. This tool does write to the control files on a regular basis, so this increase in size does not mean there has been a security breach and that someone is tampering with your system files.

Oracle will maintain as many copies of the control file as you declare in the CONTROL_FILES parameter in the initialization file (described in the next section). This parameter is used to specify the name and location of all control files to be maintained. The control files are created indirectly when the database is first created and are maintained automatically. If you want to have additional copies of the control file, you should shut down the database and copy one of the existing control files to the new locations. Remember to maintain the same security protections on the new files as on the original ones, and be certain that *oracle* is the file owner. Modify the initialization file that will be used to start the database to include a reference to the new file and its location along with the original ones, and restart the database. The new file will be maintained automatically.

There should always be at least two, and preferably more, copies of the control file in different directories on different disks and, ideally, on different controllers. The information in all of the copies is identical. These multiple copies are for protection against disk failure. Like all of the other files, these should be available only to the *oracle* system account. If one of the control files on a system becomes damaged and the database won't start up, when the damaged control file is determined, merely replace the damaged copy with one of the other copies of the control file from a different disk and restart the database.

Initialization File

The initialization file is one of the two Oracle database files that are readable. (The other readable file is the configuration file known as *CONFIG.ORA*, which we will discuss later in this chapter.) There is no information in the initialization file that is of use to users, so it should be protected the same way as the datafiles so users cannot read it. The file must exist but does not necessarily have to contain much information since most parameters have default values. Parameters are added to change default values as part of database performance tuning.

The initialization file is a text file and will be created either by the installation process or by the DBA using any text editor. As we've mentioned, depending on the operating system you are using, this file may be named using the form *INIT<DATABASE SID>.ORA*. If the system identifier (SID) is "payroll," for example, then the file will be named *INITPAYROLL.ORA*. For simplicity, in this book we refer to this file as the *INIT.ORA* file.

Oracle's sample initialization file

Oracle provides a starting initialization file containing the most commonly modified parameters. For each of these there are three entries: one for a small, a medium, and a large database. The medium and large values are commented out with a "#" sign. The values of these parameters, however, are only suggested starting points and it is very rare that these default values are retained in a production system. There are 156 parameters that can be specified in a version 7.3.0.0.0 database. The number of parameters available will vary depending on the version of Oracle you are using. A few examples of the types of entries found in the Oracle-provided initialization file follow; in Chapter 8, *Installing and Starting Oracle*, you'll find a full set, along with an indication of which you'll need to pay particular attention to from a security perspective.

```
control_files = C:\orawin95\database\ctl1orcl.ora

compatible = 7.3.0.0.0

db_file_multiblock_read_count =  8                  # INITIAL
# db_file_multiblock_read_count = 8                                          # SMALL
# db_file_multiblock_read_count = 16                                         # MEDIUM
# db_file_multiblock_read_count = 32                                         # LARGE

db_block_buffers =  200                             # INITIAL
# db_block_buffers = 200                                                     # SMALL
# db_block_buffers = 550                                                     # MEDIUM
# db_block_buffers = 3200                                                    # LARGE

shared_pool_size =  3500000                         # INITIAL
# shared_pool_size = 3500000                                                 # SMALL
# shared_pool_size = 6000000                                                 # MEDIUM
# shared_pool_size = 9000000                                                 # LARGE
```

All lines that start with "#" are comments. The initialization file is read when the database is created and every time the database is started. Any changes to the file will not take effect until the database is stopped and restarted. This file can have references to other files, and the default file does contain one such reference to the configuration file (*CONFIG.ORA*) in the IFILE parameter.

Releases of Oracle up to version 7.2 had a bug that restricted the size of the *INIT.ORA* file. The file could be larger than the maximum size, but in many cases no error would be generated as most of the critical information usually occurs early in the file. In the earliest releases, this value was 2K and became 8K just prior to Version 7.2. As of version 7.2, this restriction no longer exists. If you are working on a version that has this restriction, you should either remove all of the comments delivered with the default initialization parameter file or move them to the bottom of the file. Make sure that all comments and remarks you want to store in this file are also placed at the bottom of the file.

Evolution of an initialization file

The production initialization file may start out as a copy of the development file but will probably change rapidly as you tune your production system. Remember that the initialization file is modified and maintained by the DBA and should be available only to and through the *oracle* system account. The wise DBA will always insert an entry in the bottom of the file reflecting each change that has been made to this file. A complete record of the value prior to the change and the new value, with a date and the initials of the person who made the change, should always be logged. In this way, there will be no question of who performed a change to the file, what change was made, and when that change occurred. A change that proves to be in error can be easily backed out if the old value is retained. An audit trail of who has been making changes will help to identify who is interacting with the parameters. A sample entry audit trail entry in the *INIT.ORA* file might look like this:

```
# Revision History:
#    04/10/98  - mlt -  increased shared_pool_size from 9000000 to 12000000
```

An alternative method is to make the comments in-line:

```
shared_pool_size = 12000000     # 4/10/98 old - 9000000 - mlt
```

If you encounter problems after increasing the SHARED_POOL_SIZE, you will know the previous value and can easily restore it or select a value between the old and new values. The revision history does not have to be complex or difficult to maintain.

Configuration File

The configuration file (*CONFIG.ORA*) is a text file that contains information that, in earlier Oracle versions, was included in the initialization parameter file. In fact, when the installation procedure creates a configuration file, the sample *INIT.ORA* file will usually contain an "IFILE=...CONFIG.ORA" statement meaning that the contents of the *CONFIG.ORA* file are to be read as a part of reading the *INIT.ORA* file. In effect, the *CONFIG.ORA* file is simply an extension of the *INIT.ORA* file. As with *INIT.ORA*, changes made in the configuration file do not take effect until the database is restarted. The question, then, is this: if these entries in the configuration file used to be in the initialization file, why are they now in a separate file? One answer is that placing the configuration information in a separate file simplifies the maintenance of initialization parameters when the parallel server option is used. Also, if you use more than one *INIT.ORA* file for different processing situations, they can all call the same *CONFIG.ORA* file for the static part of the parameter list. For example, one *INIT.ORA* file may be used for build while another may be used for batch processing and still another used for normal daily use.

In most installations where a parallel server is not being used or multiple *INIT.ORA* files are not used, the configuration file contents can be merged into the *INIT.ORA* file and the configuration file can be discarded.

Contents of the configuration file

The parameters in the typical configuration file are those that would be shared by multiple instances all accessing the same physical database files—that is, a parallel server configuration. All the instances constituting a parallel server system must use the same database name that is specified by the DB_NAME parameter. Consequently, the DB_NAME parameter is one of the lines in the configuration file. So, while each instance requires its own initialization file, the common parameters can be put into the configuration file which, as previously described, may be referenced by the *INIT.ORA* file. If a change is made in the configuration file, then all instances are affected and all instances will easily see the change.

A sample *CONFIG.ORA* file is provided for some—but not all—versions of Oracle. In a Windows NT Oracle version 8.0.4 system, no *CONFIG.ORA* file is provided but reference is made in the *INIT.ORA* file to placing multiple instance-specific parameters into another file and using the IFILE parameter to point to this other file. There is also no configuration file for Personal Oracle on Windows 95, but there is for most UNIX installations.

The production *CONFIG.ORA* file is usually a copy of the development file. The file is modified and maintained by the DBA through the *oracle* installation account and should be available only to the *oracle* system account. A sample *CONFIG.ORA* file might look like the following:

```
# Do generic setup.
db_name = "MY_DB"
ifile    = ORA_SYSTEM:INIT.ORA
db_block_size = 8192

control_files              = (my_disk01:[oracle.my_db]ora_control1.con,
                              my_disk02:[oracle.my_db]ora_control2.con,
                              my_disk03:[oracle.my_db]ora_control3.con)
background_dump_dest       = ora_dump
user_dump_dest             = ora_dump
#
# Add specific parameters for instance MY_DB below.
#
# e.g. rollback_segments = (rb1,rb2,...)
```

In this example, the parameters included are very database-specific. The database name and size, as well as the control file and dump file information, are included. However, no parameter values (like a size for DB_BLOCK_BUFFERS) are included here.

In this chapter:
- *The User Interface: User Versus Schema*
- *Objects*
- *Tables*
- *Table Triggers*
- *Views*
- *Stored Programs*
- *Synonyms*
- *Privileges*
- *Roles*
- *Profiles*

3
Oracle Database Objects

In Chapter 2, *Oracle System Files*, we described the Oracle operating system files—the physical files that are particularly important to Oracle security. This chapter looks at the internal Oracle components that are accessible only after the database is started. In contrast to the external components, which are individual data files, these components cannot be physically "touched" or identified from outside the database. They exist as components within the large operating system files created for Oracle. They contain the objects and the data dictionary. You *can* manipulate these components, but only by using the SQL language.

The User Interface: User Versus Schema

In May, 1998 at the Mid-Atlantic Association of Oracle Professionals' spring conference, one of the sessions played a game of trivia during which many questions about Oracle were asked. One of the "stumper" questions was this: "What was the forerunner of the SQL*Plus language called?" The answer, in case you ever end up in a trivia game yourself, is UFI—User Friendly Interface. UFI was an early SQL command interpreter. The DBA would use UFI to create users much as they would use SQL today. Users would log in to the database via UFI. The DBA could also give the user enough privileges to create tables and other objects. SQL has since become the standard language for manipulating data in modern relational databases.

Just as the SQL name has changed over time, so has other nomenclature. For example, let's look next at the changes in the terms "user" versus "schema."

The Schema Concept

Oracle7 introduced the schema concept. Like the "instance" vs. "database" terms we discussed in Chapter 2, "user" and "schema" are frequently used interchangeably. A *user* is equivalent to a computer account. The DBA will create a user account, assign a password, and define a default working tablespace, a temporary sort area, and quota—if the user is to be allowed to create any database objects.

Users can log in to the database and perform work. They can create and own objects such as views, tables, and stored programs. In general, any object a user creates is considered to be owned by that user. However, there are exceptions to this general rule, such as a user who is granted system privileges that allow him or her to create objects on behalf of another user.

From an Oracle perspective, the *schema* refers to all of the objects owned by a user. There is a CREATE SCHEMA statement, but on closer examination, you will find that the schema name used in this statement must be the same as the Oracle username.

The CREATE SCHEMA statement is used to create all user objects at one time in a single statement. But it allows only three operations:

- CREATE TABLE
- CREATE VIEW
- GRANT

If any part of the statement fails, the entire statement fails. Since there are many other operations, such as creating constraints, primary and foreign keys, indexes, and the like that cannot be done with the CREATE SCHEMA statement, the use of this statement is very limited.

In commands where the term "schema," "user," or "owner" is included, the *oracle* username is meant.

Security within Oracle begins with the concept that non-public objects are owned by the creator of those objects. Only the owner of an object or a user with DBA-type privileges can give access privileges to other users to enable them to interact with the objects. Careful consideration should be given before privileged access is granted to *any* user within the database system to *any* object.

About Quotas

In the last section, we mentioned that a *quota* had to be granted on a tablespace for a user to be able to create objects in a database. Quotas are used to control the amount of space a user will be allowed to "fill up" in the database. Quotas are one way you can monitor and control the allocation of resources in your development database. If you decide that you do not need to monitor the amount of space an application is using, you can set the quota to UNLIMITED for the tablespaces in which the user will be creating objects.

At one facility we're familiar with, the application manager requested that his developers be given fairly restrictive quotas on his application's tablespaces and no quota on the schema's default tablespace. He did this to force the developers to explicitly name the tablespace to which each created object would go. Since this was a conversion of an existing data warehouse over to an Oracle database, the manager also wanted to be able to trace the growth of the application data during conversion so he could gauge the size of the actual production data.

The bad news is that the day the developers exceeded their quotas on *all* of their tablespaces happened to be the day that both the application manager and the application DBA were out of the office on vacation. The decision made by the alternate DBA was to just go ahead and raise the quotas to UNLIMITED so the developers could continue working and to let the manager and application DBA address any issues when they both got back to the office.

Although the developers were temporarily impacted by not being able to continue working until their tablespace quotas were increased, the quota restrictions the manager imposed on the developers made sense for two reasons. The developers were forced to code more carefully to ensure that the proper tablespaces were used for each object, and the amount of space used for the objects could be more carefully monitored to help size the application for production.

In a production system, the use and amount of quota assigned to each application should be very carefully evaluated and monitored. In many cases, the decision for production has been made to allow the applications to grow as needed and to set quotas to UNLIMITED across the board.

Objects

Prior to Oracle8, the term "object" was used loosely to mean any entry in the data dictionary other than a user. Thus, an object could be a table, synonym, view, index, stored procedure, trigger, and so on. Oracle8 introduced the concepts of both an object-relational database and a user-created object type. Discussion about

Oracle8 new features becomes very confusing as soon as relational objects, database objects, and object types are mentioned.

In this book, the term "objects" will be used in the generic sense to mean any item created by a user and will include (but not be limited to) tables, synonyms, views, indexes, stored procedures, and triggers, and so on. "Object" references may include Oracle8 "object types" as well. We will try to make the distinction as clear as possible in all cases.

Tables

A table is the basic building block for storing data in the database. Conceptually, a table is a file that is created and maintained within the data files assigned to the database.

Table Parameters

When a user creates a table, he or she specifies parameters such as the table name, the column names, their data types, and their lengths. The tablespace is also usually specified in the CREATE statement to ensure that the table is created in the proper tablespace. If a tablespace name is not specified, the table will be created in the user's default tablespace. An initial amount of space is specified for the table's data using the INITIAL parameter of the STORAGE clause in the CREATE TABLE statement. When that amount of space is filled, more space will be allocated based on the value set by the NEXT parameter in the STORAGE clause. If no STORAGE clause is present in the CREATE TABLE statement, the default storage values of the tablespace in which the table has been created will be used. The kernel handles this allocation, and the space comes from the datafiles assigned to the tablespace in which the table was created.

What Happens When a Table Is Created

Suppose the database has a data01 tablespace and there are three datafiles named *persdata01.dbf*, *persdata02.dbf*, and *persdata03.dbf* associated with the data01 tablespace. User *mary* creates a table named "employee" and specifies the data01 tablespace. A command such as the following might be used while *mary* is logged into SQL*Plus:

```
CREATE TABLE employee
  (employee_num          NUMBER(6)    NOT NULL,
   employee_name         VARCHAR2(20),
   employee_location     VARCHAR2(10),
   manager_name          VARCHAR2(20),
   init_employment_date  DATE,
   title                 VARCHAR2(20))
```

```
TABLESPACE data01
STORAGE (INITIAL     275K
            NEXT     50K
      MAXEXTENTS     UNLIMITED
     PCTINCREASE     0);
```

The kernel will allocate 275 Kbytes in one of the three datafiles of the data01 tablespace. Generally, the space allocated will be the first contiguous space found that is greater than or equal to the size specified for the initial allocation. If many tables have already been created, this table may be in file *persdata03.dbf.* If the table is one of the first created in the tablespace, it will probably be built in *persdata01.dbf.* If prior tables that were created were allocated with very large amounts of space, there may not be enough space for the minimum size specified for this table. This situation would occur, for example, if the *persdata01.dbf* file were 1 megabyte in size and a table were created with an initial size of 800 Kbytes. There is only 200 Kbytes left in the *persdata01.dbf* file. This is not enough for the new table, so in this case, *mary*'s employee table will be created in *persdata02.dbf.* The 200 Kbytes left in *persdata01.dbf* will remain unused until an allocation request is made for an amount of space that is equal to or less than the 200 Kbytes remaining in *persdata01.dbf.* Should that space be available when the initial allocation for the employee table is filled, the NEXT allocation of 50 Kbytes could be taken from the remaining 200 Kbytes in *persdata01.dbf.*

As the Table Grows

When the initial 275 Kbytes allocated to the employee table are filled, an additional 50 Kbytes (the NEXT parameter) will be allocated. This will also come from any one of the three datafiles, but will not necessarily come from the same file as the first allocation. Each allocation is referred to as an *extent.* Since in our example this table is defined with the MAXEXTENTS parameter as UNLIMITED, the table can grow unbounded except by the space available in the three datafiles in the tablespace. If the datafiles fill up, any more attempts to allocate space will generate a "cannot allocate extent" error. In all cases, the space requested to build a table or perform an allocation of an extent must be "contiguous" space, that is, enough bytes located in a group together.

A tablespace may become fragmented. That happens when there is enough total space available within a tablespace to meet the allocation request, but the space is not contiguous. In this situation, the CREATE command or the attempt to allocate the NEXT extent will fail to complete.

Note that each field is defined by a data type and length. The kernel enforces the type and length restrictions during inserts and updates. An error will be returned when an INSERT or UPDATE statement contains data that does not fit the type defined for the field or when the data is too large to fit in the field.

Table Ownership

Tables are usually owned by the user who creates them. The exception is when a privileged user creates an object on behalf of another user. In that case, the specified user owns the object as though the specified user had created the object explicitly. For example, a user with the CREATE ANY TABLE privilege (such as the DBA) could specify the statement as:

```
CREATE TABLE mary.employee ...
```

and the resultant table would be owned by *mary*, and not by the user who actually entered the command.

Tables can have more complex characteristics than we have shown in this example, such as partitions and embedded objects, which are beyond the scope of our discussion. The general concept does not change.

Users can access other users' tables only if the owning user or a DBA grants privileges to them. These grants may be made directly to the users, to a special user named *public*, or to a role. These types of grants are discussed later in this chapter in the "Privileges" section.

Table Triggers

A trigger is a special stored program attached to a table. A trigger is executed when the event on which it is based occurs. There is a distinct difference between triggers and other types of stored programs. A trigger is directly associated with a table and always includes the event for which an action will occur. Since execution, or "firing of the trigger," is controlled only by this event, triggers cannot be executed directly by a user. In contrast, stored programs can be executed directly by an authorized user.

A trigger cannot be created unless the text of the command includes a table name. Consequently, if the table is dropped, the trigger will also be dropped automatically.

About Creating a Trigger

The statement that creates a trigger includes both the triggering event and the table name. You can specify that a trigger is to be fired either before or after the event, followed by one or more actions such as INSERT, UPDATE, or DELETE. Within Oracle8, you can also specify the INSTEAD OF condition. That is used to solve the problem of updating through complex views. All triggers are based on modification events. Triggers can be quite useful from a security standpoint to track or prevent activities that change the data.

For security and/or monitoring purposes, tables are frequently created with extra fields to capture the username, time, and modification action performed. These additional columns are intended to be used for auditing. However, such a scheme only retains the last event unless you take other precautions to preserve the history. The information is also available to any user with the SELECT privilege on the table. A trigger can be used instead of maintaining this auditing data within the table. The trigger would be set to execute before an INSERT, UPDATE, or DELETE for each row. The trigger body would write audit information to another table. This data could include the name of the table being modified, the date and time, the username, and any other pertinent information, including the actual data before and after the modification was made. The user performing the action does not have to have any privileges on the underlying "audit" table where this information is written.

The execution of the trigger is transparent to the user and, since most triggers become memory-resident through frequent usage, their execution is quite fast. See Chapter 11, *Developing a Sample Audit Application*, for an application that uses this approach to implement auditing of data at the column level.

An example of a trigger to capture audit type information follows:

```
CREATE OR REPLACE TRIGGER BIUDR_EMP
  BEFORE INSERT OR UPDATE OR DELETE
  ON employee
  FOR EACH ROW
/*  Capture the id of the user making the change, the type of action, and the
    date of the action. */
 DECLARE
  tyact   VARCHAR2(1);
 BEGIN
  IF INSERTING THEN
      tyact := 'I';
  ELSIF updating THEN
      tyact := 'U';
  ELSIF deleting THEN
      tyact := 'D';
  END IF;
 INSERT INTO private_audit
  (id_of_user, action_performed, table_name, primary_key, date_of_action)
 VALUES
  (user, tyact, 'EMP', :old.employee_num, sysdate);
 END;
/
```

Although we show the trigger name with the action representation (BIUDR—BEFORE INSERT UPDATE DELETE FOR EACH ROW) before the table name (EMP), many developers prefer to list the table name first and then the trigger actions for ease of maintainability. It doesn't matter how the trigger is named, but do use a standard naming convention.

How the Trigger Works

In the previous example, the user does not have to have any privileges on the table (private_audit) to which the trigger is writing. The trigger executes with the privileges of the trigger owner (who does not have to be the table owner). Assuming that the trigger owner either owns the target table or has appropriate permissions, the required entries will be made and the user performing the data manipulation will never know that anything happened. Also, if the user issues a ROLLBACK command, the trigger action is also rolled back so no misleading entries are made in the private_audit table.

Naming Triggers

Trigger names do not have to follow any special rules other than the usual "no blanks or special characters." The naming convention used in the previous example, however, is recommended. This convention combines the table name (or a shortened version if the table name is very long) with "style" abbreviations for the triggering event and action. The style indicates what the trigger is supposed to do: "B" for before, "I" for insert, "U" for update, "D" for delete, "R" for by-row. This naming convention allows the events that fire the trigger to be determined from the name.

What Cannot Be Trapped by a Trigger

Remember the actions that cause the trigger code to execute in the example? You will notice that SELECT is not mentioned. The exclusion of SELECT is not an oversight. A trigger cannot be written to execute on a SELECT statement. Triggers are usually used to enforce business rules and maintain data integrity during INSERT, UPDATE, and DELETE events.

Views

Oracle allows a definition to be stored in the data dictionary that describes how data is to be retrieved from one or more tables. This logical definition is called a view. A view may be thought of as a layer on top of the tables that actually contain the data. Views do not store any data themselves; they only define what data is to be retrieved and, in many cases, the restrictions for retrieving the data. Views are treated exactly like tables when data is being selected. In fact, in the sample statement below, there is no way to tell if the table emp_sal specified in the query is really a table or a view:

```
SELECT employee_name, current_salary
  FROM emp_sal;
```

Figure 3-1 shows how a user would access the view as though it were a table and how execution of the view causes required data to be retrieved from several tables.

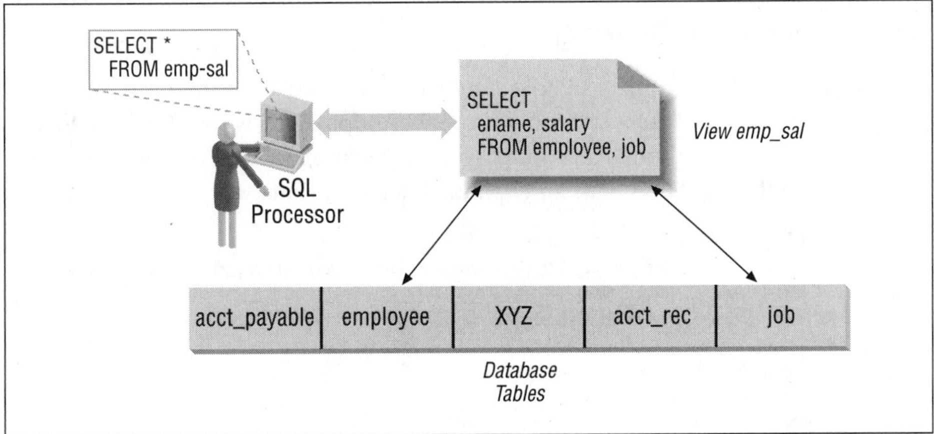

Figure 3-1. View implementation

Views can be used for several purposes relevant to security; for example, they can simplify user access by pre-joining tables and they can limit the data retrieved.

Using Views

Consider the two tables referenced in Figure 3-1: employee and salary. The employee table contains the constant employee information such as name, social security number, and other basic data which is not expected to change. The salary table contains the employee number along with the employee's job, when the job was started and ended, as well as the salary. This type of structure would be used to maintain a history of employment. To simplify access, a view could be written to join the two tables and provide salary data along with the employee's name so that an authorized user could write a simple query as shown in the SELECT statement. Using the employee and salary tables, the view could be created as follows.

```
CREATE OR REPLACE VIEW emp_sal AS
SELECT a.employee_num, a.employee_name, a.init_employment_date, b.salary
  FROM employee a, salary b
 WHERE a.employee_num = b.employee_num;
```

This view returns all rows with no limiting qualifications.

In addition to simplifying the query itself, a view can be used to limit the data in different ways so that, depending on who is performing the query, different information will be returned. For example, when an employee who is not a manager queries the data, he sees only his own records. A manager, on the other hand, would see his records and all of the records of the people in his group, but not the records of his own manager. This approach is frequently referred to as *row-level security.*

Using Views for Security

The employee table in this example could be modified to include an additional column: login_name. This column would be populated when the employee's account is created, or when the employee is given access to the database. The view can then be modified with an expanded WHERE clause:

```
CREATE OR REPLACE VIEW emp_sal AS
SELECT a.employee_num, a.employee_name, a.init_employment_date, b.salary
  FROM employee a, salary b
 WHERE a.employee_num = b.employee_num
   AND a.employee_num in
     (SELECT employee_num
        FROM employee
       WHERE login_name = user
       UNION
      SELECT b.employee_num
        FROM employee a, employee b
       WHERE a.login_name = user
         AND a.employee_name = b.manager_name);
```

The first-order row is the employee's own record. This is specified by the first part of the nested SELECT that has only the one limiting condition: WHERE login_name = user. Second-order rows are the people who report directly to a manager. These are returned when the second part of the nested SELECT (the part after the UNION) returns all of the employee numbers of people who report to the employee running the query. This view returns multiple rows when an employee has people who report directly to him, and always returns the employee's row. For instance, the president will only see the managers who report to her, not the clerks who report to the managers. This is one method for implementing data security through the use of a view.

About Using Views

on about views. The SQL that defines a view is executed and the assembled in a temporary table using the tablespace defined as the user. If the GROUP BY clause or a UNION statement is used in data is gathered in the temporary tablespace before any user-nditions are applied. If the view will return one million rows, and ERE conditions will reduce that million rows to 30, the one mil-bled in the temporary table within the user's tablespace, then the conditions are applied to select the 30 of interest. Enough space the user's defined temporary tablespace to support the largest irement to support the view.

radation of performance exists if a grouping function is used. load a temporary table with the initial data values before any nditions are applied, you may see a slower response time for a c more views than for a query based on the underlying tables. Y he view on a set of tables which have been joined together. Tl produce a slower response time. To determine whether a po gradation exists, create an EXPLAIN PLAN for the query. If the s in the plan, the potential for degradation *does* exist.

Up

There of a view you need to remember. When creating a view that c is, either columns can be updated or new rows created), TH CHECK OPTION clause at the end of the WHERE clause. causes the WHERE clause to be evaluated when updates or inserts are made. By adding the WHERE clause evaluation up front, a user will be prevented from updating a row or entering a value that would subsequently not be able to be retrieved because the data would not satisfy the WHERE clause.

Suppose you have a view being used by a user in department 20:

```
SELECT *
  FROM employee
 WHERE department_num =
     (SELECT department_num
        FROM employee
       WHERE employee_name = user) ;
```

where the assumption is that the employee_name column in the employee table contains the database login name. In this case, the user will only see records that match his own department. However, the user can insert a record into the view with a department of 30 and will not be able to retrieve the row later because of the "department_num = ... " clause.

If the view is modified to add checking during UPDATE or INSERT like this:

```
SELECT *
  FROM employee
 WHERE department_num =
     (SELECT department_num
        FROM employee
       WHERE employee_name = user)
  WITH CHECK OPTION;
```

then the user will be prevented from adding a record with a department other than 20 because the insert is validated against the "WHERE department_num = ..." clause. The record will not be retrievable by the user, so the transaction is rejected.

When the view is created, its definition specifies the columns (or fields) to be retrieved from each table. This approach provides column-level security. In the preceding examples, the login_name column was not included in the SELECT list for the view. Consequently, that column remains hidden from the users.

When you are using updateable views that join tables, you must also consider any primary or foreign keys present on the underlying tables. The views must preserve the keys or the views will fail during update.

Stored Programs

Programs written in PL/SQL can be stored in compiled form in the database. These programs are referred to as either *procedures* or *functions*. The only difference is that, by definition, a function must return a value, while a procedure does not have to return a value. However, there is no problem in coding a procedure to return a value. Stored programs can be executed by table triggers, applications, or users. In this book, we use the phrase "stored program" or "program" to refer to both procedures and functions.

Stored programs can be created using either of two methods. You can create the program simply as a program, or you can create it in two parts: a package that specifies the programs to be implemented, and a package body containing the actual code.

Executing a Procedure or Function

Users or applications can execute stored programs provided that EXECUTE permission on the program has been granted. Unlike table triggers, procedures and functions are executed by an explicit call. For example, suppose a procedure called give_raise has been written and requires an employee number and percentage of raise as arguments. The call might then look like this:

```
SQL> EXECUTE give_raise(8138, 23);

PL/SQL procedure successfully completed
```

Executing a function interactively is a bit more complex, as a function always returns a value and the calling statement structure must be able to receive the value. Stored functions can be included in SQL statements. The position in the SELECT statement satisfies the requirement for a place to receive the return value from the function. However, since only a single value is returned and not a set of values, this is generally useful only in SQL statements that are expected to return only one row.

Why Use Packages?

A package is a method of creating a program in two parts, the specification and the body. There are several advantages to using the package approach. One of these is *overloading*. Overloading means that one program name can be used more than once as long as the formal argument parameter list is different. So, if a program in a package is created as:

```
give_raise(empno IN NUMBER, pct IN NUMBER)
```

then it can be declared again as either of the following:

```
give_raise (empno IN NUMBER, pct IN NUMBER, effdate IN DATE)
give_raise (ename IN VARCHAR2, pct IN NUMBER).
```

Since the argument lists are all different, the three programs can exist with the same name in the package. The PL/SQL engine will figure out which program within the package to use based on the arguments provided in the call.

The second advantage to using packages is the ability to avoid dependent invalidation. If the give_raise stored procedure is called by other stored procedures and is then changed, the other stored procedures are invalidated and must be recompiled. However, if the package/package body approach has been used, then as long as the package is not recompiled the dependent programs will remain valid. This allows the package body to be developed and changed without the inconvenience of having to find and recompile all the dependent programs. The assumption here is that the specification in the package does not change. If the specification in the package does change, the dependent programs will of course have to be recompiled. That, however, does not happen as frequently as recompiling of the package body occurs.

Using the PL/SQL Wrapper

We have stressed the advantages to using PL/SQL procedures and packages but, until version 7.2, there was one very distinct disadvantage. You might need to deliver your application code outside of your own area or company. In order to install the PL/SQL code, the source code must CREATE OR REPLACE the programs. Anyone could see the source code by accessing the view ALL_SOURCE. Value-added resellers (VARs) registered their dissatisfaction at having their proprietary source code visible to customers and competitors. Oracle responded by adding a utility which can be used to effectively encrypt or "wrap" the PL/SQL source code. This utility is generally referred to as the PL/SQL Wrapper.*

When you run the utility, your readable ASCII text source code is converted into unreadable ASCII text source code. The unreadable code can then be delivered anywhere for creation in any Oracle version 7.2 or higher database, and its contents are secured. The code is treated in the database like normal PL/SQL code and is just as portable and usable as unencrypted code. The utility is actually an executable file which is usually located in the *$ORACLE_HOME/bin* directory on a UNIX system and in the *c:/orant/bin* directory on a Windows NT system. The executable file is named *wrapNN.exe* where the *NN* represents the RDBMS version number. For a version 7.3 database, the executable will be named *wrap73.exe*.

To run the utility to encrypt your PL/SQL code, you would type the following:

```
wrapNN iname=readable_filename [oname=encrypted_filename]
```

where *NN* is the version number of your RDBMS (72, 73, 80, etc.); the readable_filename points to your original source code file; and the encrypted_filename points to the output file name which you want the encrypted file to have. If you do not specify an extension, *.sql* is assumed, and if you do not supply an oname value, the original filename will be used for the output file with the extension *.plb* for "PL/SQL binary." Here is an example of using the *wrap73* utility to encrypt a file named *my_plsql.sql* on a Windows NT machine:

- Using all default values:

  ```
  c:\orant\bin\wrap73 iname=my_plsql
  ```

- Using explicit, overriding values:

  ```
  c:\orant\bin\wrap73 iname=my_plsql.sql oname=hideit.sec
  ```

Procedure Ownership and Privileges

It is very important for you to understand the relationship between the owner of a stored procedure and the user who executes the procedure. In general, stored procedures execute on behalf of the user, but use the privileges of the creator. Also, synonyms (described later in this chapter) are resolved by the owner of a stored

* For more detailed information about using the PL/SQL Wrapper, see Chapter 23 of Steven Feuerstein and Bill Pribyl's *Oracle PL/SQL Programming*, second edition (O'Reilly & Associates, 1997).

procedure, not by the user. For ease in maintenance, a good policy to follow would be to ensure that the schema owner also owns all stored procedures, including triggers associated with that schema's objects. There may, however, be some cases where it makes sense to have another owner for the stored procedure. For development purposes, this approach makes sense because each developer can make changes and test the same procedure without breaking the application.

If the creator does not own the tables that will be read or modified by the stored program, is there a problem? Well, let's take an example, walk through it, and see for ourselves. Suppose *mary* is the schema owner and has granted SELECT and UPDATE privileges on the employee table to *ralph*.

```
GRANT SELECT, UPDATE ON employee TO ralph;
```

User *ralph* then writes a stored program to update the employee number of an employee record that exists in *mary*'s table.

```
SQL> CREATE OR REPLACE PROCEDURE test AS
       e_no number;
     BEGIN
       SELECT employee_num
         INTO e_no
         FROM employee
        WHERE ename = 'MILLER';
       DBMS_OUTPUT.PUT_LINE ('e_no is '||e_no);
       UPDATE mary.employee
          SET employee_num = 1154
        WHERE employee_num = 7934;
       SELECT employee_num
         INTO e_no
         FROM employee
        WHERE employee_name = 'SUE';
       DBMS_OUTPUT.PUT_LINE ('e_no is '||e_no);
     END;
     /

Procedure created.
```

The concatenation of the numeric variable e_no with the character string "e_no is " will not produce an error as it does in some versions of PL/SQL used in Oracle Forms. The conversion of the numeric value to character is automatic.

Since this is not the real world, the procedure makes little sense. However, we have tested the code to verify that it works correctly, so we will assume here that *ralph* tests the stored program and everything works to his specifications.

The user *ed*, who does not have privileges on *mary*'s employee table, runs the application that will attempt to update a record in the employee table. The stored program will succeed!

```
SQL> GRANT EXECUTE ON test TO ed;
Grant succeeded.
SQL> connect ed/miok4u?
Connected.
SQL> set serveroutput on
SQL> execute ralph.test
e_no is 7934
e_no is 1154
PL/SQL procedure successfully completed.
```

Why did this happen? The user *mary* granted privileges to *ralph*. The stored program worked for *ralph* because he has the appropriate privileges on the employee tables. *ed*, on the other hand, has no privileges on the employee table, but the procedure still worked. When the program ran, even though *ed* was recognized as the user, the procedure was owned by *ralph*. The Oracle database knew that *ralph* could perform updates to the employee table and carried that privilege over to *ed*. This is a really cool feature of Oracle!

The user who runs a procedure takes on the privileges of the procedure, package, or function owner!

Privileges, Procedures, and Roles

There is one "gotcha." Privileges granted via roles are not understood by stored programs. You cannot grant privileges to a role, grant that role to a user, and have the user successfully run the stored program with access determined by the role privileges. This is yet another argument for the schema owner to own all programs.

There are two categories of stored programs: those supplied by Oracle and those which are custom-written. We recommend that both DBAs and developers look in the Oracle home directory under the *RDBMS/ADMIN* directory for the *DBMS_<NAME>.SQL* scripts. These scripts create most of the stored packages available in the database. One of these, *DBMSUTIL.SQL*, contains the DBMS_SESSION package that we will use in Chapter 9, *Developing a Simple Security Application*.

The DBA should take the time to carefully walk through the *DBMSUTIL.SQL* script since there are many utilities of interest within this file.

Synonyms

A synonym is another name for something. We use synonyms every day. Probably the most common synonym usage is a nickname or familiar name used in conversations. Few people named "William" are called by that name, except perhaps William the Conqueror. Most Williams prefer to be called "Bill." Margaret becomes Peg or Peggy, John becomes Jack (which doesn't make much sense. But then, most of the "synonyms" we describe in the following sections don't make much sense either!).

How Synonyms Are Used

Synonyms are used in the Oracle database to provide *location transparency* by concealing the owner and location of the object. (The next section explains why you might want to do this.) The object can be a table, view, stored procedure, package, function, snapshot, sequence, or even another synonym. Synonyms in the Oracle database are either public or private. If a synonym is public, then all users can reference the synonym even though they may not have privileges to access the underlying object itself. In that case, an error is returned. If a user creates a synonym without the PUBLIC keyword (a special privilege is required to do this), then the synonym is private and can be used only by the user who created the private synonym.

Why Synonyms Are Used

The primary reason for using synonyms is to avoid the requirement to know the owner of the object. If *mary* owns the employee table and *ralph* wants to select some data from it, then the command would look like this:

```
SQL> SELECT *
       FROM mary.employee;
```

If *ralph* does not know that *mary* owns the table, *ralph* will have a problem attempting to access that table. On the other hand, *mary* (a privileged user) creates a public synonym with the following command:

```
SQL> CREATE PUBLIC SYNONYM employee
        FOR mary.employee;
```

mary then grants access privileges by way of the synonym either to PUBLIC or to specific users. All of those users granted the privilege can refer to the synonym without adding *mary* as shown in the above example. Although the example shows the synonym with the same name as the table, this is not a requirement. Creating the synonym with the same name as the table is, however, a common implementation practice which makes object tracking easier.

By removing the need to specify the owner of a table, the use of a synonym provides location transparency. The syntax of the CREATE SYNONYM command allows reference to a remote database as well. The user not only does not have to know who actually owns the table, but also does not have to know on which database the table is located.

Synonyms are treated exactly like the tables they represent when referenced in SQL statements.

Privileges given on a synonym translate to the object itself. A user given the SELECT privilege on the public synonym "employee" could still use the mary.employee syntax. The use of synonyms helps to hide the underlying database structure, which helps to protect the database from curious or malicious actions.

If an underlying object is deleted from the database, the synonym that was created for it will *not* be deleted automatically.

Privileges

The DBA can create a user account but, until the CREATE SESSION system privilege is granted, that user cannot even log on or connect to the database. Once a minimum privilege of CREATE SESSION is granted, the user can connect, but cannot access any objects other than those granted explicitly to him or to the *public* user.

The *public* user is a special entry in the data dictionary. Privileges granted to *public* are automatically available to every user in the system who has been granted the CREATE SESSION privilege. Granting public access is commonly done with tables containing data that must be made generally available, or for objects where access by any user will not compromise anything within the database. A typical example of an area of information which can be made available to the public to view is a States lookup or reference table which contains state names and their respective abbreviations. There is no reason to prevent anyone from seeing the values in the States lookup table, although there would be good business reasons to prevent the general public from having INSERT, UPDATE, or DELETE privileges on this table.

About System and Object Privileges

Privileges fall into two general categories: system privileges and object privileges. System privileges allow the user to log on to the system and create or manipulate objects. Object privileges allow the user some sort of access to the data within an object, or allow the user to execute a stored program.

System privileges

Some examples of system privileges are:

CREATE SESSION
CREATE TABLE
ALTER SESSION
CREATE ANY VIEW

There are more than 80 system privileges available to Oracle users. The number of privileges will vary depending on the Oracle version being used. A complete list can be found in the data dictionary table called system_privilege_map. In the above list, the CREATE SESSION privilege is the only privilege required for a user to connect to a database. In a secure system, this might be the only privilege granted to a user. In general, when considered at the lowest level, the system privileges do not convey any rights for data access. The lowest-level system privileges are the ones like the first three items in the preceding list. However, note the word ANY in the fourth item. The CREATE ANY VIEW privilege allows exactly that. Any user given this privilege may create a view within any other user's area. For example, if user *ralph* has the CREATE ANY VIEW privilege, he can issue the following command:

```
SQL> CREATE VIEW mary.emp_dept
  2>   AS SELECT employee_name, department_num
  3>        FROM mary.emplyee;
```

A system privilege only conveys a specific right. In the example, *ralph* has created a view that is now owned by user *mary*, but *ralph* himself may not be able to select from that view. Only the right to create was given to *ralph*, not the right to use.

Object privileges

We've already looked at the most common object privileges:

SELECT
INSERT
UPDATE
DELETE

There are only 16 object privileges in an Oracle version 8.0.4 database. A complete list of object privileges can be found in the data dictionary table, table_privilege_map. Object privileges allow a user the right to manipulate the data within the object or, in the case of programs, to execute the program. These privileges are usually referred to as *grants* and are object-specific. A user granted INSERT on *mary*'s employee table does not automatically have any privileges on any other table owned by *mary* or anyone else. Following are the Oracle object privileges:

ALTER
: The structure of the table or sequence may be altered. For example, columns may be added or column data types may be changed.

AUDIT
: Auditing may be enabled or disabled on an object. For example, auditing could be enabled to capture each time data was inserted into a table.

COMMENT
: For each table in a database, an informational message about the table can be entered.

DELETE
: Allows rows to be removed from the table.

GRANT
: Allows the user receiving the grant option to grant privileges to other users.

INDEX
: Allows the user to create an index only on the table.

INSERT
: Allows new rows to be created in the table.

LOCK
: Allows the user to lock an object.

RENAME
: The table can be renamed—for example, RENAME TABLE emp AS old_emp;.

SELECT
: All data may be selected for viewing from the table.

UPDATE
: The data in columns may be modified; this is the only privilege that can be restricted to specific columns.

REFERENCES
: Allows the user to define foreign key integrity constraints only on the table.

EXECUTE
: Applies only to stored procedures and functions.

CREATE
: Allows the user to create a table.

READ
: Allows the user to read from a directory.

WRITE
: Allows the user to write to a directory.

As we've said, the most-used object privileges are SELECT, INSERT, UPDATE, and DELETE. These apply to tables and, in some instances, views. You will note that ALL is not included in the list. If you grant ALL on a table to a user, that user is granted all of the table privileges shown in the above list. The only privilege that can be granted on a stored program is EXECUTE. If the SELECT privilege is granted, the user will be allowed to look at all of the data in the specific table. The object privileges are "all or nothing" grants. They cannot be restricted to specific rows or records. The UPDATE privilege is somewhat different, though, in that this privilege can be granted on specific columns.

When you examine the GRANT command used to give system and object privileges, you should notice the striking absence of a limiting clause. You cannot grant SELECT where some condition is true. For example, you cannot attempt to grant access to the employee table WHERE manager_name = 'SMITHY'. The statement will fail. The object privileges SELECT, INSERT, UPDATE, and DELETE, specifically, are whole-table privileges.

The distinction between a system privilege and an object privilege becomes a little blurred in the case of the INDEX privilege. This privilege allows the user to create indexes on a specific table owned by another user. Compare this to the privilege conveyed by the CREATE ANY INDEX system privilege. With the system privilege, the user can create indexes on any table in the database. With the command:

```
GRANT INDEX ON employee TO mary
```

mary can only create indexes on the employee table.

Roles

A role is a named collection of privileges. A role may be assigned to a user, but a user cannot be assigned to a role. For example, users can log in to the database; roles cannot. A user can own objects while a role cannot. The function of a role is to group logically associated privileges and allow those privileges to be passed to a user by referencing the role. Consequently, when a user is assigned (granted) a role, that user inherits all the privileges assigned to the role. If the role's privileges are later changed, then the new privileges will be in effect the next time the user logs in to the database.

In an Oracle system, grants are issued on individual tables to individual users. This sounds very simple, but when hundreds of tables and users are involved, the implementation and management can be very complex. The usual situation is for a manager to ask the DBA to give *ralph* the same privileges that *mary* has. If grants have been made to individual users, the first task will be to find out what privileges *mary* has, and then create a script to duplicate those privileges, and finally to run that script to give *ralph* the privileges.

The action of giving an employee the same privileges as another employee is much easier if roles are used. The DBA creates a role and grants some privileges to it. These privileges can be a mix of system and object privileges. In a financial system, there might be a FINCLERK role. This role could include the CREATE SESSION privilege to allow the users to log on, and also some grants to enable table access. In turn, this role is granted to all the users who need the financial clerk privileges. In many systems, only one or two roles are needed by most users. The task of identifying the privileges held by a specific user now becomes a simple matter. The DBA can query the data dictionary view, DBA_ROLE_PRIVS, and specify the user of interest, as shown in the next section. (Chapter 4, *The Oracle Data Dictionary*, describes this view and other data dictionary views.)

Figure 3-2 shows the difference between assigning individual privileges to each user and assigning the privileges to a role and then assigning the role to each person.

Let's say that you are an application developer who works for a car dealership. You have developed an application to track the parts ordered, received, and used to make automobile repairs. The mechanics can access the application to enter the parts which they have put into a customer's car. The parts department manager can enter new part information, including the cost of the part, into the database through the same application. The parts department clerks can look up the parts information to verify if a part is currently in stock but cannot modify any of the parts information. You create three roles:

- The MECHANICS role, with SELECT and UPDATE privileges on the parts information tables
- The MANAGERS role, with SELECT, INSERT, and UPDATE privileges on the parts information tables
- The CLERKS role, with SELECT privileges on the parts information tables

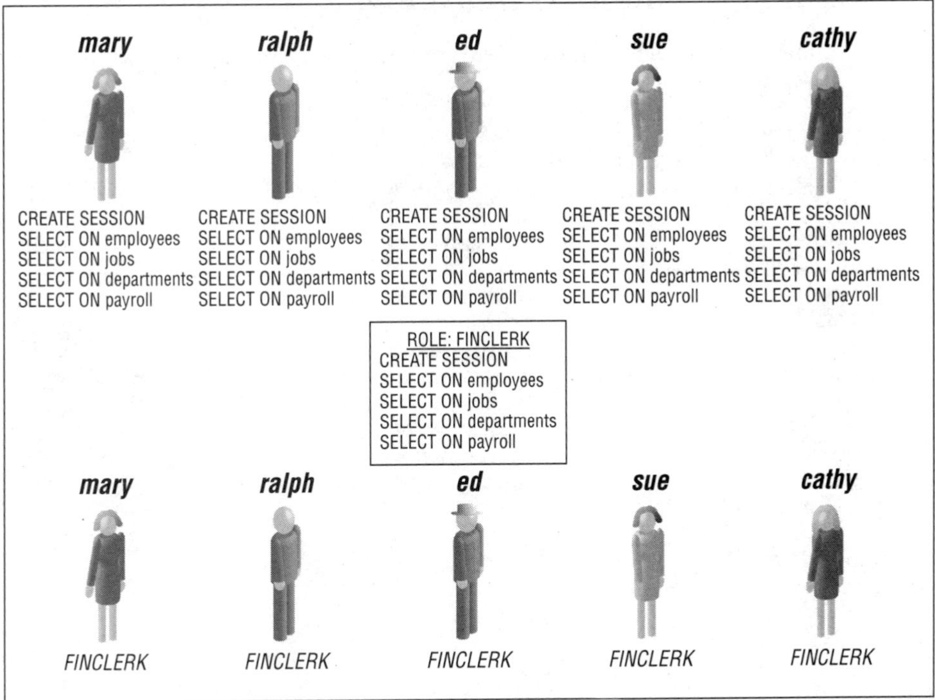

Figure 3-2. Role implementation

If the dealership later decides that clerks should be permitted to insert information on new parts into the database, you will just need to grant INSERT to the CLERKS role. The next time a clerk logs in to the database, she will be able to insert information to the parts tables.

Determining Privileges Granted to a User

To determine what privileges *mary* has, the DBA would issue the following command:

```
SQL> SELECT *
  2>   FROM dba_role_privs
  3>  WHERE grantee = 'MARY';

GRANTEE                        GRANTED_ROLE                   ADM DEF
------------------------------ ------------------------------ --- ---
MARY                           CONNECT                        NO  YES
MARY                           FINCLERK                       NO  YES
```

In this case, *mary* has two roles, CONNECT (the Oracle-supplied default role) and FINCLERK (an in-house-created role); see the "Oracle-Supplied Roles" section for information about CONNECT.

Determining Privileges Granted to a Role

To determine what privileges have been granted to a role, the DBA would issue the following commands:

```
SQL> SELECT *
  2>   FROM dba_sys_privs
  3>  WHERE grantee = 'CONNECT';

GRANTEE                        PRIVILEGE                                ADM
------------------------------ ---------------------------------------- ---
CONNECT                        ALTER SESSION                            NO
CONNECT                        CREATE CLUSTER                           NO
CONNECT                        CREATE DATABASE LINK                     NO
CONNECT                        CREATE SEQUENCE                          NO
CONNECT                        CREATE SESSION                           NO
CONNECT                        CREATE SYNONYM                           NO
CONNECT                        CREATE TABLE                             NO
CONNECT                        CREATE VIEW                              NO
8 rows selected.

SQL> SELECT *
  2>   FROM dba_tab_privs
  3>  WHERE grantee = 'CONNECT';
no rows selected
```

In this case, there were no object privileges granted to the CONNECT role. In other cases, there will be. Thus, both DBA views (DBA_SYS_PRIVS and DBA_TAB_PRIVS) should always be checked to determine the exact composition of the role of interest.

If new privileges are granted to a role, those privileges are inherited by all users who hold the role. Likewise, any privilege that is revoked is revoked from all users holding the role.

The "ADM" column shown in the output example indicates whether ADMIN OPTION was specified in the GRANT statement that granted the privilege. Chapter 4, *The Oracle Data Dictionary*, and Chapter 5, *Oracle Default Roles and User Accounts*, describe the ADMIN OPTION.

Establishing Classes of Users

Setting up roles is not difficult, but we highly recommend that you plan and document your roles carefully. As part of the system design, you must establish the various classes of users. As part of the audit plan, there should be a check to ensure that the permissions granted to roles have not changed. The classes of users identified will lead to the roles which are really required for the application. The classes can be expressed in standard English like "financial clerk," "accounts payable manager," "approving official," and so forth. The actual role names created in the database have to conform to the database naming restrictions regarding length and must contain no embedded spaces. So, as we've shown, "financial clerk" could be implemented as FINCLERK, FIN_CLERK, FINANCE_CLRK, or something like that.

After the classes and, hence, the role names have been established, you can create a matrix showing the roles and tables. Where the role and table rows and columns intersect, the privileges would typically be listed as S,I,U,D (for SELECT, INSERT, UPDATE, and DELETE) or a combination of these. Other terms in common use are CREATE (instead of INSERT) and READ (instead of SELECT). The options would then be R,C,U,D or, as most designers order the privileges, C,R,U,D. When this set of abbreviations is used, the chart is usually called a *CRUD matrix*.

Oracle-Supplied Roles

Oracle supplies several default roles with the installation of the database. These roles provide the same system privileges of earlier pre-role based versions of Oracle. The major default roles and a summary of privileges are shown in Table 3-1. The privileges associated with these roles are discussed in Chapter 5; that chapter also describes several additional roles that are used less frequently.

Table 3-1. Oracle Default Roles

Role Name	Type of Privileges
CONNECT	Allows login and ability to create tables, views, synonyms, and database links.
RESOURCE	Adds cluster, procedure, and trigger privileges.
DBA	Complete authority to manage database and users. Can create users.
SYSOPER	Ability to start up and shut down the database.
SYSDBA	All privileges available to the DBA role with the ability to create, start up, shut down, and recover a database.

We recommend that you do not use the CONNECT and RESOURCE roles for application users. These roles convey privileges that are not required by most of the users functioning within the bounds of an application. They also do not convey any indication of the purpose of the privilege by their names. We recommend that you create a standard logon role. This role should have only the CREATE SESSION system privileges. Grant the role to every user when the user account is created. Granting the role will allow the user to connect to the database and will make it much easier to disable an account by revoking the logon role but leaving the other privileges in place.

Do not use roles to assign privileges that will be required by a stored program. Because a role cannot own objects, programs do not recognize a role as a valid mechanism for granting privileges. This is usually not a problem if the schema owner also owns all of the stored programs.

Profiles

Oracle provides a way for you to control the allocation and use of resources in the database on a user-by-user basis. This mechanism is known as a *profile.* There are actually two different (and unrelated) types of profiles available in an Oracle database:

- Product profiles
- System resource profiles

Product profiles let you block access to specific commands or Oracle products. For several releases prior to Oracle7, you could control user access to almost any product by creating a record in the PRODUCT_USER_PROFILE table. For example, suppose that you did not want the user *mary* to be able to log on to SQL*Plus interactively. You would put an entry into the PRODUCT_USER_PROFILE table which indicated that *mary* was not to be granted access to SQL*Plus. In Oracle7, the PRODUCT_USER_PROFILE table was replaced with two tables: PRODUCT_PROFILE and USER_PROFILE.

Oracle 7 also introduced the concept of the system resource profile, which is used to limit the amount of database system resources available to each user; you limit resources by establishing a profile for each user. Oracle supplies a default profile for users who do not have custom profiles.

Chapter 6, *Profiles, Passwords, and Synonyms,* describes both product profiles and system resource profiles.

In this chapter:
- *Creating and Maintaining the Data Dictionary*
- *The Data Dictionary Views*
- *About SQL.BSQ*
- *Views Used for Security*
- *The Composition of the Views*

4
The Oracle Data Dictionary

When you want to find out the meaning of a word, how it is spelled, or its derivation, what do you do? Generally, you go to the nearest dictionary and look up the word. In the same way, when you want to find out the contents of your database, you go to the data dictionary to look up the information of interest. From a security perspective, you will use the data dictionary to gain information vital to your security implementation. If you are a DBA, you will spend a great deal of your time interacting with the data dictionary to gain information about the various objects with which you must interact. You will use the data dictionary to examine user accounts and user quota assignments, to look up the location of datafiles on your system, and to obtain the information you need to perform your job effectively. As a developer, you will use a different view of the data dictionary to keep track of the schema objects within your application. If you are a casual application user, you might never even see a data dictionary entry directly.

Oracle's data dictionary consists of two layers: the tables that make up the real data dictionary and a series of views that allow you to access the information in the data dictionary. Most of the data dictionary views are written to restrict your access to only the data appropriate for your specific level of privilege. The views have meaningful names along with equally meaningful attribute names. In this chapter, we will examine the following information about the Oracle data dictionary:

- What the data dictionary is
- How the data dictionary is created
- How the data dictionary is structured
- What type of information is available
- How that information may be used in a security system

For more detailed information, see the *Oracle8 Concepts Manual,* Release 8.0, Part A58227-01, Chapter 4, "The Data Dictionary."

Creating and Maintaining the Data Dictionary

The Oracle data dictionary is primarily an internal record of the state of all objects in the database. These objects include:

- Tables
- Users
- View definitions
- Indexes
- Triggers
- Sequences
- Constraints on tables and columns
- Database links
- Synonyms
- Stored programs

The data dictionary is created by the RDBMS when the database is initially created. The data dictionary is maintained by the RDBMS based on actions performed by the users, application developers, or database administrator. The data dictionary we use is actually a dictionary of the "metadata," the data that describes the objects in the database. These values are dynamic and are changed by the RDBMS as the objects change. For instance, when you create a table, the table name, along with the names of all the columns in the table and the column characteristics, are recorded in the data dictionary. If you drop the table or rename it, or if a column definition is modified, then the appropriate entry in the data dictionary is updated by the RDBMS on your behalf. In fact, you cannot directly make changes to the data dictionary—regardless of your privilege level.

Modification of a column definition does not mean there is a change in the data stored in the column—only that a change has occurred to some characteristic of the table's column such as the column name, data type, length, or other characteristic.

There is an audit function supported by the data dictionary. If you set it up properly, the data dictionary will also track, within a collection of audit tables, actions performed by users. From a security perspective, being able to keep track of users who have made modifications to a specific table can be very important. For example, you might want to keep track of who has modified salary information and when the updates were made. (Auditing is discussed more fully in Chapter 5, *Oracle Default Roles and User Accounts*, Chapter 10, *Developing an Audit Plan*, and Chapter 11, *Developing a Sample Audit Application*.) Finally, by learning how the views were constructed in the data dictionary, you will see how access to table data can be controlled down to the row level.

Usually a user's perspective on the data dictionary is somewhat different from its actual implementation. From the user's perspective, a *database* is the collection of objects (usually tables) that contain the data used by their applications. This is an acceptable definition from the user viewpoint. However, from the Oracle RDBMS viewpoint, there is only one database and only one data dictionary per instance or, at least, per database cluster. Some pertinent facts about the data dictionary are:

- The dictionary always encompasses *all* database objects regardless of the owner.
- Users are generally allowed to look at (query) the data dictionary.
- Users are only permitted to see data based on their job requirements or "need to know."
- Privileges are granted to users on the data dictionary views but not on the underlying tables.
- Users can only access the table data via the views.
- Users can see only information appropriate for their level of privilege, providing a horizontal look into the data.

We'll discuss some specific examples of how these points are accomplished later in this chapter.

The Data Dictionary Views

Data dictionary views may be grouped into four general categories:

- Those showing data about a user's own objects, labeled "USER_"
- Those showing data available to any user in the database, labeled "ALL_"
- Those showing data available to any DBA, labeled "DBA_"
- Everything else

The DICTIONARY View

Oracle provides, within the data dictionary, a view that you can access to see the composition of all of the data dictionary views. If you query the DICTIONARY view, you will find the specific names of data dictionary objects you have the privilege to access. You will not see any other objects. The DICTIONARY view is very simple, containing only two columns: table_name and comments. The column "table_name" is somewhat misleading because all of the "table" names are really views, synonyms, or other objects. None of the entities listed are actually tables. Here is a very small sample section of the DICTIONARY view, with minor formatting, so you can see what we are talking about:

```
SQL> COLUMN table_name FORMAT A20
SQL> COLUMN comments FORMAT A50 WORD
SQL> SELECT * FROM DICTIONARY;

TABLE_NAME           COMMENTS
-------------------- --------------------------------------------------
ALL_ALL_TABLES       Description of all object and relational tables
                     accessible to the user
ALL_ARGUMENTS        Arguments in object accessible to the user
ALL_CATALOG          All tables, views, synonyms, sequences accessible
                     to the user
```

If you create a user in a version 8.0.4 database and give that user just the ability to connect to the database (the CREATE SESSION privilege), the list of table names available to that user, as obtained from the DICTIONARY view, would total 242, distributed as follows:

- Personal object data with the prefix "USER_": 101
- All object data with the prefix "ALL_": 85
- DBA objects with the prefix "DBA_": 0
- Everything else: 56

As you can see from this list, there is no exact correspondence in terms of numbers among the "ALL," "DBA," and "USER" views. For each category of users, separate views are available. For example, USER_TABLES, ALL_TABLES, and DBA_TABLES each stores information about the tables in the database, but at different levels of privilege; despite their names, all of these entities are actually views on the same tables! The view names were selected to convey their general purpose. Here are comments from the data dictionary for these three views:

USER_TABLES
: Description of the user's own tables

ALL_TABLES
: Description of all tables accessible to the user

DBA_TABLES

Description of all tables in the database

If you look at the code the Oracle RDBMS uses to enable you to see the three types of TABLES views listed here, you will notice some interesting things:

- All three views contain the same SELECT list, except that the "owner" column is omitted from the USER_TABLES view. This makes sense since this view is expected to return only the names of tables owned by the user.
- All three views use the same list of data dictionary tables, except for the user$ table, which the USER_TABLES view does not use.
- The tables all three views use are: ts$, seg$, obj$, tab$, and obj$, which are all owned by *sys*.

We'll explain these internal ($) tables later in this chapter.

So, if the SELECT lists are essentially the same, and the FROM list of tables are essentially the same, what is the difference? The difference is in the WHERE clause, which contains the limiting conditions for the data to be retrieved. You will find many examples of Oracle using the same table with different restrictions in the data dictionary view creation statements.

A view's definition is stored in the data dictionary and is treated, in most cases, exactly like a table, but a view does not store any data. A view is merely a definition of what, and sometimes how, certain data should be retrieved. There is no distinction made in SQL DML statements between a "table" and a "view." For practical purposes, these terms are interchangeable. For example, in the following statement:

```
SELECT *
  FROM all_tables;
```

there is no qualifier to identify the object ALL_TABLES as either a view or a table; in fact, ALL_TABLES is a view.

Although you can think of tables and views as being interchangeable, don't overlook the potential impact on performance of using a view, as discussed in Chapter 3, *Oracle Database Objects*.

About Row-Level Security

The DICTIONARY view is a good example of how *row-level security* may be implemented. Data returned from the query will be controlled at the row level by the condition clause (WHERE ...) on the view definition. The DICTIONARY view is a three-part union query. We show the text of this view, as it appears in *CATALOG.SQL*, to give you an idea of how you can implement control over who sees what in your database:

```
remark  VIEW "DICTIONARY"
remark  Online documentation for data dictionary tables and views.
remark  This view exists outside of the family schema.
remark
/* Find the names of public synonyms for views owned by SYS that
have names different from the synonym name.  This allows the user
to see the short-hand synonyms we have created.
*/
create or replace view DICTIONARY
    (TABLE_NAME, COMMENTS)
as
select o.name, c.comment$
from sys.obj$ o, sys.com$ c
where o.obj# = c.obj#(+)
  and c.col# is null
  and o.owner# = 0
  and o.type = 4
  and (o.name like 'USER%'
       or o.name like 'ALL%'
       or (o.name like 'DBA%'
           and exists
                   (select null
                    from sys.v$enabledprivs
                    where priv_number = -47 /* SELECT ANY TABLE */)
           )
       )
union all
select o.name, c.comment$
from sys.obj$ o, sys.com$ c
where o.obj# = c.obj#(+)
  and o.owner# = 0
  and o.name in ('AUDIT_ACTIONS', 'COLUMN_PRIVILEGES', 'DICTIONARY',
        'DICT_COLUMNS', 'DUAL', 'GLOBAL_NAME', 'INDEX_HISTOGRAM',
        'INDEX_STATS', 'RESOURCE_COST', 'ROLE_ROLE_PRIVS', 'ROLE_SYS_PRIVS',
        'ROLE_TAB_PRIVS', 'SESSION_PRIVS', 'SESSION_ROLES',
        'TABLE_PRIVILEGES','NLS_SESSION_PARAMETERS',
        'NLS_INSTANCE_PARAMETERS',
        'NLS_DATABASE_PARAMETERS')
  and c.col# is null
union all
select so.name, 'Synonym for ' || sy.name
from sys.obj$ ro, sys.syn$ sy, sys.obj$ so
where so.type = 5
  and ro.linkname is null
  and so.owner# = 1
  and so.obj# = sy.obj#
  and so.name <> sy.name
  and sy.owner = 'SYS'
  and sy.name = ro.name
  and ro.owner# = 0
```

```
    and ro.type = 4
    and (ro.owner# = userenv('SCHEMAID')
         or ro.obj# in
            (select oa.obj#
             from sys.objauth$ oa
             where grantee# in (select kzsrorol from x$kzsro))
         or exists (select null from v$enabledprivs
              where priv_number in (-45 /* LOCK ANY TABLE */,
                     -47 /* SELECT ANY TABLE */,
                     -48 /* INSERT ANY TABLE */,
                     -49 /* UPDATE ANY TABLE */,
                     -50 /* DELETE ANY TABLE */)
                     ))
/
```

Examining the code for the first query

Let's take a closer look at the mechanism Oracle uses to control information access. In the first query of this three-part union, the two lines:

```
and o.owner#=0
and o.type = 4
```

ensure that only views (type = 4) owned by SYS (owner = 0) will be returned. The rows are further refined by the "and (o.name like 'USER%' ..." section so only the familiar data dictionary views will be returned. The nested SELECT ensures that this part of the union query will only return a row if the user has the specific system privilege, SELECT ANY TABLE. You can test this portion of the DICTIONARY view creation statement easily. Create a user (i.e., *mary*) and grant the user the CREATE SESSION privilege only. This is the minimum privilege required to access the database. Connect as *mary* and enter the following command:

```
SELECT COUNT(*)
  FROM dictionary
 WHERE table_name like 'DBA%';
```

On a Windows 95 Personal Oracle7 system, the count returned was 2. Connected as *system* to the same database with the DBA role enabled, the count was 93. On a Windows NT system running Oracle 8.0.3, the user *mary* with only the CREATE SESSION privilege showed no available rows in the DICTIONARY view for tables beginning with a "DBA" suffix, while the *system* user showed 117 available. From this exercise, you can learn two important points:

1. Users with different access privileges can see different objects.
2. With each new release of the Oracle RDBMS, new or different views are available.

When developing a security system, keep the second point in mind so you don't rely on objects that may change or disappear in later releases of the Oracle software.

Examining the code for the second and third queries

The second query of the DICTIONARY view returns descriptions of the specific views listed in the "in (...)" clause, and the third query returns synonyms owned by *system*. The DICTIONARY view will return to the user executing the query only all object names where the user created the object and has been granted some type of privilege on the object.

About CATALOG.SQL

On a Windows NT system, the Oracle version 7 *CATALOG.SQL* file is 234 Kbytes. On the same system, the Oracle8 *CATALOG.SQL* is 416 Kbytes. The differences in size are predominantly caused by the creation of "GV" global views and the new disaster recovery approach provided in Oracle8. In either version 7 or version 8, virtually every object defined in this script is either a view or a synonym. Additionally, most views are qualified in a manner similar to the DICTIONARY example to limit the rows returned to only those the user has the right to see. In order to accomplish this, the kernel must have two specific pieces of information about the user: the username and the user id. In addition, that information has to be available in the data dictionary tables. Since the username and user id are known from the login process, and since that data was verified against entries in the data dictionary, the kernel has the information available at all times to determine the levels of access that should be made available to each user.

Applying the Concepts

If you want to apply the approach Oracle uses within the data dictionary code, you will need some method of associating the users with data in the application tables. Typically, the information you will need is organizational in nature. A user whose real name is Mary Jane may be in division AB, department 4. If her userid of *mjane* is stored as part of her record in the employee table, along with her division and department, then you have captured the minimum amount of information your security system would need to limit data access.

Typically, when access to personnel data is allowed, there is a restriction that each user should only be able to see his or her own data unless that user is a department head or division chief. Here is an example of code you could use to implement the necessary restriction on the employee table:

```
/* return rows for division chiefs. */
SELECT *
  FROM employee a, employee e
 WHERE a.division = e.division
   AND e.job = 'DIVCHIEF'
/* return rows for department heads. */
```

```
 UNION
SELECT *
  FROM employee a, employee e
 WHERE a.division = e.division
   AND a.department = e.department
   AND e.job = 'DEPTHEAD'
/* return the employee's own record. */
 UNION
SELECT *
  FROM employee a
 WHERE emp_dbname = user;
```

The last query will return a duplicate row when either a division chief or department head uses this view. The UNION operator, however, automatically eliminates duplicate rows.

Are there other ways to do this? Absolutely, provided the structure is present in the database to support the approach.

About SQL.BSQ

Why would you want to know about the internal structure of the data dictionary of the database? Not only because some of the best examples of basic security implementation may be found within the Oracle data dictionary, but also because the more thoroughly you understand how the database is put together, the better you can protect it.

The data dictionary uses base tables for which nobody has implicit privileges, and many views, most of which are qualified so the user can see only those rows that are appropriate. Source code for the data dictionary is found in the *SQL.BSQ* file, which is read when the database instance is created. The views (with which many users are familiar) are created by *CATALOG.SQL*. There are other views created by other programs that are executed at database creation time, but we'll focus on these two scripts in our examples here.

In general, unless a user has been granted the DBA role, or comparable privileges, that user cannot access these base tables. These base tables are created when the *SQL.BSQ* file is executed at the time of database initialization and owned by a user known as *sys*. All of the views, including those that will be addressed later, are based on the base tables created from the statements in this file.

You must *not* modify the *SQL.BSQ* file or the *CATALOG.SQL* file, but you'll find the scripts within the files very educational. Therefore, we suggest that you copy the files to other file names and then walk through the copies. If either of these files is modified and something goes wrong with your database, Oracle Support may not be willing to assist in the repair efforts based on the modified files.

SQL.BSQ and CATALOG.SQL Locations

The Oracle-delivered scripts for these files can be found in the *.../rdbms/admin* directory on most systems. For a Windows NT database, the files will be found in:

<drive_designation>:\orant\rdbmsXX\admin\sql.bsq
<drive_designation>:\orant\rdbmsXX\admin\catalog.sql

where *XX* is the version of the RDBMS you have installed, such as *rdbms80.*

For UNIX installations, the files will be found in:

$ORACLE_HOME/dbs/sql.bsq or $ORACLE_HOME/rdbms/admin/sql.bsq
$ORACLE_HOME/dbs/catalog.sql or $ORACLE_HOME/rdbms/admin/catalog.sql

For an OpenVMS system, the files will be found in:

$ORACLE_HOME:[RDBMS]sql.bsq
$ORACLE_HOME:[RDBMS]catalog.sql

How SQL.BSQ Is Used

The *SQL.BSQ* file is read by the instance and is used to create the database system tablespace and all of the tables, clusters, indexes, sequences, and initial data required by the kernel code to store and maintain the metadata for user-created objects. No user, not even *sys* or *system,* ever directly manipulates the data in these tables. They are maintained as a result of Data Definition Language (DDL) commands. For example, executing the statement:

```
CREATE TABLE x
(col1  NUMBER);
```

will result in an entry in the tab$ table and will modify the contents of the fet$ table (free extent table), uet$ (used extent table), and so on. These "$" tables are a part of the internal Oracle data dictionary.

While it's true that the data dictionary offers a fascinating object study for data normalization, it has no inherent security aspects. What it does have is all of the characteristics that may be used to implement a security system. A security system that implements all aspects of the security plan will have several layers and will incorporate several components and features of the Oracle database, as we'll discuss in the sections that follow.

User and Role Names

User and role names must always be unique, not only within their individual category, but within the combined user and role set on your system. The reason can be explained by looking at the CREATE statement for the user$ table within *SQL.BSQ*. A portion of the CREATE statement is reproduced here:

```
create table user$                              /* user table */
( user#      number                not null,   /* user identified number */
  name       varchar2("M_IDEN") not null,   /* name of user */
  type       number                not null,   /* 0 = role, 1 = user */
...
```

Note the last attribute line, which defines the type of user. The comment indicates that there are only two options: zero (0) for a role, and one (1) for a user. Both user and role definitions will be stored in this table. Keep the following two facts in mind:

1. There is no command to create a role or user which specifies a value for "type". The value for "type" is inserted by the kernel when the appropriate DDL command is executed.
2. This table has an entry made when either of the following two DDL commands is used:

```
CREATE USER ...
CREATE ROLE ...
```

Later in the *SQL.BSQ* file, there is a relevant DDL command:

```
create unique index i_user1 on user$(name);
```

which further illustrates the duality of the use of the user$ table. Because this is a UNIQUE index, there cannot be duplicate entries in the user$ table that have the same value for name. Since this table is used to store both usernames and role names, each entry, regardless of type, must be unique.

SQL.BSQ and Database Creation

The *SQL.BSQ* file is never mentioned in any SQL statement. It is used by inference only once, at database creation time, when a script such as the following is executed:

```
rem  Create database script for the production database.
CREATE DATABASE prod1
     DATAFILE 'c:\orawin95\dataprod1\prod1sys01.dbf' SIZE 20m REUSE
```

```
    CONTROLFILE REUSE
        LOGFILE 'c:\orawin95\dataprod1\prod1log1.dbf' SIZE 500k REUSE,
                'c:\orawin95\dataprod1\prod1log2.dbf' SIZE 500k REUSE,
                'c:\orawin95\dataprod1\prod1log3.dbf' SIZE 500k REUSE
;

CREATE ROLLBACK SEGMENT tmprb
     TABLESPACE system
        STORAGE ( INITIAL 10K
                     NEXT 10K
              MINEXTENTS   2
              MAXEXTENTS UNLIMITED
                 OPTIMAL 30K
                )
;

ALTER ROLLBACK SEGMENT tmprb ONLINE;
```

This is a real statement that was used to create a real database. It is the first statement executed after performing a CONNECT INTERNAL command and issuing the STARTUP NOMOUNT command. Of course there are additional statements that create the remaining tablespaces that will be used for the data, indexes, and so on, but at this point, there is a functioning database. Note that in this statement, there is no explicit reference to *SQL.BSQ*. Note also that there is no reference to creating the *system* tablespace. In the initialization file (named *initprod1.ora* in this system) it will be seen that there is also no mention of the *system* tablespace, nor any mention of *SQL.BSQ*. The file is searched for by the kernel whenever the CREATE DATABASE statement is used. This file is used to create the internal objects of the data dictionary.

Inside SQL.BSQ

There are some rather unusual variable references in the *SQL.BSQ* file. For instance, the initial statement is:

```
create tablespace SYSTEM datafile "D_DBFN"
  default storage (initial 10K next 10K) online.
```

On the same page within the "create table tab$" is the column definition:

```
audit$ varchar2("S_OPFL") not null ...
```

The D_DBFN and S_OPFL terms again suggest the special nature of the *SQL.BSQ* file. Even though the file contains primarily SQL statements, it is clear it cannot be executed from a standard SQL*Plus or *svmgr* session. There are simply no provisions in the SQL syntax for these unusual parameters. They are replaced by the kernel at execution time with appropriate values and, if any of these statements are altered in any way, the results are unpredictable and there is a strong possibility that the database create will fail.

The objects created by *SQL.BSQ* are the internal data dictionary objects. Immediately after database creation, the status of the dictionary is as follows (comments are added for clarity):

```
SQL> SELECT type, count(*)
  2    FROM obj$
  3   GROUP BY type;
TYPE        COUNT(*)
---------- ----------
         0          1     -- Reference record for next object number
         1         65     -- Indexes
         2         68     -- Tables
         3          8     -- Clusters
         5          4     -- Synonyms
         6          8     -- Sequences
```

The values shown here are for version 7 of the RDBMS and may change from version to version.

Views Used for Security

Although the data dictionary views provide a wide range of information about the state of the database, the views shown in Table 4-1 are particularly important for providing security information. We've also listed the tables on which these views are built. We'll examine each of the views listed in this table later in this chapter.

Table 4-1. Data Dictionary Views for Security

View Name	Type of Information Available	Tables on Which View Is Built
DBA_PROFILES[a]	Profiles and their associated resource and time limits	profile$, profname$, resouce_map, obj$
DBA_ROLES[a]	All roles that exist in the database	user$
DBA_ROLE_PRIVS[a]	Roles granted to users and other roles	user$, sysauth$, defrole$
DBA_SYS_PRIVS[a]	System privileges granted to users and roles	user$, sysauth$, system_privilege_map
DBA_TAB_PRIVS	Privileges like SELECT, INSERT, UPDATE, etc. that each user or role has per object	user$, objauth$, obj$, table_privilege_map
DBA_USERS	Who has an account for the database; also, which profile is assigned to the user	user$, ts$, profname$, profile$, user_astatus_map
ROLE_ROLE_PRIVS	Roles granted to roles	user$, sysauth$

Table 4-1. Data Dictionary Views for Security (continued)

View Name	Type of Information Available	Tables on Which View Is Built
ROLE_SYS_PRIVS	System privileges granted to roles	user$, system_privilege_map, sysauth$
ROLE_TAB_PRIVS	Table privileges granted to roles	user$, table_privilege_map, objauth$, obj$, col$
USER_ROLE_PRIVS	Roles granted to the current user	user$, sysauth$, defrole$, and x$kzdos

[a] These views do not have an ALL_ counterpart.

The view composition shown here is for an Oracle8 database. The view composition will vary from version to version of Oracle. We recommend you check for changes in the composition of the views when you install a new Oracle version to determine what has changed.

Note that several of these views concern roles; roles were described briefly in Chapter 3.

Tables Used to Build the Views

Within the data dictionary, the ten views listed in Table 4-1 are used more heavily for security purposes. This section contains a description of each of the tables on which the views are built. Notice that most of the tables listed have names that end with $. Most of the views in the data dictionary are based on $ tables. There are comments within the *SQL.BSQ* file for most of the $ tables.

From a security standpoint, only thirteen of these tables are of interest. Note that not all of the tables listed have a $ in their names. However, they are shown because they're used to build the views we'll be examining next. The tables of interest are listed with some of the documentation as found in *SQL.BSQ*, or with documentation we've supplied. One of the views that uses the $ tables also uses a table named x$kzdos. (x$ tables are actually memory structures that are not documented by Oracle and only exist when the database is running.)

user$
: Users. Identifies users by name, type, and number.

col$
: Columns. References obj$.obj#.

defrole$
: Default roles. Two columns: user#, role#.

obj$
: Objects. Identifies objects by name, type, and owner number.

objauth$
: Table authorization. Grants, grantee, grantor, and options.

sysauth$
: System authorization. System privileges, grantee, options.

ts$
: Tablespaces. Identifies tablespaces by number, name, and owner.

profile$
: Crosswalk between profiles and resource privileges.

profname$
: Maps profile names to a number.

resource_map
: Description table for resources. Maps resource name to number.

system_privilege_map
: Maps a system privilege to a number. Two columns.

table_privilege_map
: Maps table auditing privileges to a number. Two columns.

User_astatus_map
: User account tracking of password and account status. Two columns.

You'll begin to understand the real meaning of "normalization" if you spend some time reviewing these tables and the views that incorporate them. Remember, this data dictionary is the same for a notebook installation and for a terabyte database in an international bank. The access has to be fast—and it is.

Views and Auditing

In addition to determining what privileges a user has within the database, the data dictionary also provides a minimal auditing capability. The information is limited in scope and is not available unless the DBA modifies the Oracle initialization file (*INIT.ORA*) to include the AUDIT_TRAIL parameter. The default for this parameter is "NONE." When the parameter is set to "DB," auditing is enabled and the results of audited actions are written to a table, SYS.AUD$, and maintained in the database.

Note that these are all "action" audits—that is, you may capture the fact that a user has logged on, has deleted from a table, or has updated a table, but the specifics about which row was affected are not trapped. To get this information, you must write custom code to put PL/SQL triggers on each table to be monitored. A sample application is provided in Chapter 10, showing examples of how to create and use triggers to capture row-level information.

A Closer Look at the Views for Security

Keep in mind that a user given the DBA role (or comparable privileges in another role) may access and possibly modify any object within the database. This section discusses all the views that are particularly relevant to security issues. Some of these views can only be seen by users with DBA privileges; you'll recognize these views by their prefix DBA_.

In the section "The Data Dictionary Views," early in this chapter, we explained that some of the views have equivalents with names like ALL_ and USER_. In those cases, while the explanation of the functionality will be consistent, the actual number of columns and rows returned by each privilege level of user will vary. For example, suppose that you have been granted the DBA role with its associated privileges. When you describe the view DBA_USERS, ALL_USERS, and USER_USERS, you will see a different number of columns and a different amount of column information for each view:

```
SQL> DESCRIBE dba_users
 Name                            Null?    Type
 ------------------------------- -------- ----
 USERNAME                        NOT NULL VARCHAR2(30)
 USER_ID                         NOT NULL NUMBER
 PASSWORD                                 VARCHAR2(30)
 ACCOUNT_STATUS                  NOT NULL VARCHAR2(32)
 LOCK_DATE                                DATE
 EXPIRY_DATE                              DATE
 DEFAULT_TABLESPACE              NOT NULL VARCHAR2(30)
 TEMPORARY_TABLESPACE            NOT NULL VARCHAR2(30)
 CREATED                         NOT NULL DATE
 PROFILE                         NOT NULL VARCHAR2(30)
 EXTERNAL_NAME                            VARCHAR2(4000)

SQL> DESCRIBE all_users
 Name                            Null?    Type
 ------------------------------- -------- ----
 USERNAME                        NOT NULL VARCHAR2(30)
 USER_ID                         NOT NULL NUMBER
 CREATED                         NOT NULL DATE

SQL> DESCRIBE user_users
 Name                            Null?    Type
 ------------------------------- -------- ----
 USERNAME                        NOT NULL VARCHAR2(30)
 USER_ID                         NOT NULL NUMBER
 ACCOUNT_STATUS                  NOT NULL VARCHAR2(32)
 LOCK_DATE                                DATE
 EXPIRY_DATE                              DATE
```

```
DEFAULT_TABLESPACE              NOT NULL VARCHAR2(30)
TEMPORARY_TABLESPACE            NOT NULL VARCHAR2(30)
CREATED                         NOT NULL DATE
EXTERNAL_NAME                            VARCHAR2(4000)
```

If you are a DBA, take a minute to really look at the descriptions of the _USER views here, because you will probably use these views frequently. For example, as a DBA, you will use the DBA_USERS view to check on the composition of a user account that you want to duplicate for another user. Among other things, you will use this view to determine the default tablespace and temporary tablespace assigned to each user.

The Composition of the Views

This section examines each of the views important for security. We will look at the information the view provides and whether the view has an ALL_ and/or USER_ counterpart. You will also find details on the composition (the columns) for each view and an explanation of why the view is important from a security perspective.

The DBA_PROFILES View

The DBA_PROFILES view lists all profiles and their limits. This view determines what profiles exist in your database, what resources have been limited, and what the limit is for each resource. The new password parameters are set by creating a profile. This view enables you to see the values to which the password limits have been set. The resources not marked as "PASSWORD" in the output below are parameters that are also available in a version 7 database. Columns include:

PROFILE
: Profile name. Limited to 30 characters

RESOURCE_NAME
: Name of resource controlled by profile

LIMIT
: Limit placed on this resource for this profile

RESOURCE_TYPE
: Added in Oracle8; indicates whether the profile is KERNEL or PASSWORD

If you never create a profile in an Oracle8 database, this view will contain the sixteen rows shown below. We have added formatting statements to be able to fit the information on one line for each row.

```
SQL> COLUMN profile FORMAT a10
SQL> COLUMN resource_name FORMAT a25
SQL> COLUMN limit FORMAT a10
SQL> SELECT *
```

```
  2   FROM dba_profiles
  3  ORDER by 1, 2;

PROFILE    RESOURCE_NAME              RESOURCE LIMIT
---------- ------------------------- -------- ----------
DEFAULT    COMPOSITE_LIMIT            KERNEL   UNLIMITED
DEFAULT    CONNECT_TIME               KERNEL   UNLIMITED
DEFAULT    CPU_PER_CALL               KERNEL   UNLIMITED
DEFAULT    CPU_PER_SESSION            KERNEL   UNLIMITED
DEFAULT    FAILED_LOGIN_ATTEMPTS      PASSWORD UNLIMITED
DEFAULT    IDLE_TIME                  KERNEL   UNLIMITED
DEFAULT    LOGICAL_READS_PER_CALL     KERNEL   UNLIMITED
DEFAULT    LOGICAL_READS_PER_SESSION KERNEL   UNLIMITED
DEFAULT    PASSWORD_GRACE_TIME        PASSWORD UNLIMITED
DEFAULT    PASSWORD_LIFE_TIME         PASSWORD UNLIMITED
DEFAULT    PASSWORD_LOCK_TIME         PASSWORD UNLIMITED
DEFAULT    PASSWORD_REUSE_MAX         PASSWORD UNLIMITED
DEFAULT    PASSWORD_REUSE_TIME        PASSWORD UNLIMITED
DEFAULT    PASSWORD_VERIFY_FUNCTION   PASSWORD UNLIMITED
DEFAULT    PRIVATE_SGA                KERNEL   UNLIMITED
DEFAULT    SESSIONS_PER_USER          KERNEL   UNLIMITED
16 rows selected.
```

If you create a profile and omit one of the parameters, the value specified in the DEFAULT for that parameter will be used. So, a profile named short_time could be created with one parameter, connect_time, specified. For that profile, the other resource parameters would be the same as the DEFAULT profile— that is, set to UNLIMITED.

The DBA_ROLE_PRIVS View

The DBA_ROLE_PRIVS view (also available in the form USER_ROLE_PRIVS) lists roles granted to users and roles. Columns include:

GRANTEE
: Grantee name, user, or role receiving the grant.

GRANTED_ROLE
: Granted role name.

ADMIN_OPTION
: GRANT was with ADMIN OPTION.

DEFAULT_ROLE
: Role is designated as a DEFAULT ROLE for the user.

This view shows the roles granted to each user. It is not necessary that a user have a role. As noted earlier, suppose that the user *mary* has been granted the system privilege CREATE SESSION. *mary*, however, has not been granted any roles, so in the following listing, *mary* does not appear. *ralph* is seen because that user was granted the CONNECT role.

The ADMIN_OPTION (which for space reasons, shows as ADM in the following output) indicates whether the privilege can be passed on with administrative privilege. This option may be specified for a user in the GRANT STATEMENT with the WITH ADMIN OPTION clause. If the entry in this column is "YES," then the grantee can grant the privilege to another user. If that privilege is later revoked from the grantee, the other user will still retain the privilege until it is explicitly revoked. See the further discussion of ADMIN OPTION in Chapter 5.

In this example, *ralph* also has been granted the FINMON role. In this system, this represents the "financial monitor" function and has the necessary privileges on tables to perform that function. This role, however, is not in effect when *ralph* logs in to the database; it must be manually set—as indicated by the "NO" in the DEFAULT column.

```
SQL> SELECT *
  2   FROM dba_role_privs
  3  ORDER BY 1,2;

GRANTEE              GRANTED_ROLE                   ADM DEF
-------------------- ------------------------------ --- ---
RALPH                CONNECT                        NO  YES
RALPH                FINMON                         NO  NO
DBA                  EXP_FULL_DATABASE              NO  YES
DBA                  IMP_FULL_DATABASE              NO  YES
SYS                  CONNECT                        YES YES
SYS                  DBA                            YES YES
SYS                  EXP_FULL_DATABASE              YES YES
SYS                  IMP_FULL_DATABASE              YES YES
SYS                  RESOURCE                       YES YES
SYSTEM               DBA                            YES YES

9 rows selected.
```

In the above example and all examples that follow, the output has been modified to group the GRANTEE entries for readability.

The FINMON role has been created with a password of *blah*. In order for *ralph* to enable this role, *ralph* must issue the following command:

```
SQL> SET ROLE finmon IDENTIFIED BY blah;
Role set.
```

In Chapter 14, *Maintaining User Accounts*, we will see how access to a password-protected role can be managed through the application so the user does not need to know the password, does not need to know that a role is being enabled, and does not need to hardcode the password in the application. All three of these actions are essential elements of a practical security system.

The DBA_ROLES View

The DBA_ROLES view lists all roles that exist in the database. You can use this view to easily see the roles available in the database. Columns include:

ROLE
Role name

PASSWORD_REQUIRED
"YES" indicates that the role requires a password to be enabled

This view is very straightforward. It lists roles (no users) and indicates whether a password is required before the role can be enabled. Remember, though, that if a password-protected role is granted to a user and made a default role for that user (the user can have several), then it is active when the user logs into the database. The user does not need to supply a password. In fact, the user may never be aware that the role exists or requires a password to be set.

In the listing that follows, all of the roles except FINMON are roles that will be found in a newly-created database. The standard roles do not have passwords, but the FINMON role does. That means that to enable the role, the user who has been granted the role must supply the password when enabling it. But, if this role is granted as a default role, it is set at login time and the user does not have to supply the password. Normally, password-protected roles are not set at login, as this defeats the benefit of having the password. The password-protected role is a key feature in establishing a controlled security environment.

```
SQL> SELECT role, password_required
  2    FROM dba_roles
  3   ORDER by role;

ROLE                           PASSWORD
------------------------------ --------
AQ_ADMINISTRATOR_ROLE          NO
AQ_USER_ROLE                   NO
CONNECT                        NO
CTXADMIN                       NO
CTXAPP                         NO
CTXUSER                        NO
DBA                            NO
DELETE_CATALOG_ROLE            NO
EXECUTE_CATALOG_ROLE           NO
EXP_FULL_DATABASE              NO
FINMON                         YES
IMP_FULL_DATABASE              NO
RECOVERY_CATALOG_OWNER         NO
```

```
RESOURCE                          NO
SELECT_CATALOG_ROLE               NO
SNMPAGENT                         NO

15 rows selected.
```

Other standard roles may exist after all available installation scripts are executed, but the roles shown here are the ones that exist after the *CATALOG.SQL* and *CATPROC.SQL* scripts have been executed.

The DBA_SYS_PRIVS View

The DBA_SYS_PRIVS view (also available in the form USER_SYS_PRIVS) lists the system privileges granted to users and roles. Use this view to determine what system privileges a particular user or role has granted to it. Columns include:

GRANTEE
: User or role receiving the grant.

PRIVILEGE
: System privilege granted.

ADMIN_OPTION
: Grant was with ADMIN OPTION.

System privileges differ from object privileges; system privileges are privileges to request system services, and object privileges are permissions to do something to an object. A short listing from this table is shown below:

```
SQL> SELECT grantee, privilege, admin_option
  2    FROM dba_sys_privs
  3   WHERE rownum < 6
  4   UNION
  5  SELECT grantee, privilege, admin_option
  6    FROM dba_sys_privs
  7   WHERE grantee = 'MARY
  8*  ORDER BY grantee, privilege

GRANTEE PRIVILEGE                                ADM
------- ---------------------------------------- ---
CONNECT ALTER SESSION                            NO
CONNECT CREATE CLUSTER                           NO
CONNECT CREATE DATABASE LINK                     NO
CONNECT CREATE SEQUENCE                          NO
CONNECT CREATE SESSION                           NO
MARY    CREATE SESSION                           NO

6 rows selected.
```

As with DBA_TAB_PRIVS (discussed next), this view shows the role or user receiving the privilege (GRANTEE in the output), but it does not show who issued the GRANT statement. In the list, you can see that the CONNECT role has several privileges, but *mary* only has the CREATE SESSION privilege (allows login to the database). As mentioned earlier, the ADM column indicates whether the privilege can be passed on with administrative privilege. If the entry in this column is "YES", the grantee can grant the privilege to another user. If that privilege is later revoked from the grantee, the other user will still retain the privilege.

The DBA_TAB_PRIVS View

The DBA_TAB_PRIVS view (also available in the form ALL_TAB_PRIVS and USER_TAB_PRIVS) lists privileges on objects in the database. Use this view to determine what privileges have been given to a particular user or role in the database. Columns include:

GRANTEE
: User or role granted the privilege

OWNER
: Owner of the object

TABLE_NAME
: Name of the object

GRANTOR
: Name of the user who performed the grant

PRIVILEGE
: Type of privilege granted

GRANTABLE
: Privilege is grantable

Note that these are object privileges; system privileges were covered in the DBA_SYS_PRIVS view earlier in this chapter.

The object grants

Object privileges enable a user to interact with data or perform work. If you GRANT SELECT on a table to *ralph*, for example, he will be able to look at the data contained in that table. Likewise, if you GRANT EXECUTE on a procedure to *ralph*, he will be able to activate that procedure.

The following object privileges are available via the GRANT command:

SELECT
: Gives the grantee the ability to look at the contents of an object.

INSERT
: Gives permission to add new rows to a table.

UPDATE

Gives permission to change existing rows. This permission may be further qualified to specific columns.

DELETE

Allows the user to delete any row.

EXECUTE

Allows stored programs to be run. This privilege only applies to stored programs, and cannot be granted on a table.

INDEX

Allows a user to create an index on a table, even one not owned by the user.

REFERENCES

Allows the grantee to create a foreign key reference to the named table.

ALL

Allows the user to perform all of the privileges on tables listed above. In addition, ALL allows the user to modify the structure of the table. This means that the user can change the length of a column, change the data type of a column, or add columns to the table. We strongly recommend that you never use GRANT ALL.

Note the slight contradiction in the view name and one of the privileges. EXECUTE cannot refer to a table, only to a stored program. So when EXECUTE on a stored program is granted to either a role or a user, that privilege will be found in the DBA_TAB_PRIVS view even though the name implies only tables.

Refer to the *Oracle SQL Language Reference Manual* for the correct syntax for the GRANT command, as there are several options for issuing object grants. An example of the data available from this view is shown below:

```
SQL> SELECT *
       FROM dba_tab_privs
      WHERE rownum < 6
      UNION
     SELECT *
       FROM dba_tab_privs
      WHERE grantee = 'MARY';

GRANTEE OWNER TABLE_NAME             GRANTOR PRIVILEGE       GRANTABLE
------- ----- ---------------------- ------- --------------- ---------
PUBLIC  SYS   DUAL                   SYS     SELECT          YES
PUBLIC  SYS   STMT_AUDIT_OPTION_MAP  SYS     SELECT          NO
PUBLIC  SYS   SYSTEM_PRIVILEGE_MAP   SYS     SELECT          YES
PUBLIC  SYS   TABLE_PRIVILEGE_MAP    SYS     SELECT          YES
PUBLIC  SYS   V_$NLS_PARAMETERS      SYS     SELECT          NO
MARY    SYS   EMP                    SYS     INSERT          NO
MARY    SYS   EMP                    SYS     SELECT          YES
MARY    SYS   DO_COMP                SYS     EXECUTE         NO

7 rows selected.
```

DO_COMP is a stored procedure, not a table, but the privilege is found in this view.

About the output

The output shown above is only a sample of the many records available in this view. The first query in the UNION uses the pseudo column rownum (number assigned as the rows are found) to limit the values to five rows, and the second part of the union specifies that only rows for *mary* will be returned. We did this simply to limit the amount of data returned for the example. Note that the GRANTEE shown in the output is the user to whom the privilege has been granted, and that there is one entry for each privilege granted. So, it can be determined that any user has the right to query (SELECT) the DUAL table owned by *sys*.

In the GRANTABLE column a "YES" indicates that the GRANTEE may give (GRANT) the same rights to any other user, although a public grant makes this capability meaningless since all users already have the right to the indicated privilege. As you can see for the three rows for user *mary*, the right to INSERT rows is restricted to *mary*, but *mary* may grant the SELECT privilege to any other user. In the third row, *mary* has been granted the ability to run the procedure DO_COMP.

If *mary* grants SELECT to *ralph* WITH GRANT OPTION, and *mary*'s privileges are later revoked, what will happen? Will *ralph* still be able to SELECT on the table? The answer is no! When *mary*'s privileges are revoked from the object, anyone to whom *mary* has granted privileges will also lose their privileges.

For DBA_TAB_PRIVS, there are no differences between the Oracle8 version and earlier versions.

The DBA_USERS View

The DBA_USERS view (also available in the form ALL_USERS and USER_USERS) will be queried frequently because the view provides account information about all users in the database. The DBA and/or security manager should be familiar with the information this view provides. Columns include:

USERNAME
Database login name of the user. Limit 30 characters

USER_ID
System-generated ID number of the user

PASSWORD
: 30-character encrypted version of the user password

DEFAULT_TABLESPACE
: Default tablespace where this user may create tables

TEMPORARY_TABLESPACE
: Tablespace used by the system for temporary tables

CREATED
: Date the user account was created

PROFILE
: Name of the profile assigned to the user

ACCOUNT_STATUS
: Added in Oracle8; shows whether an account is locked, expired, or unlocked

LOCK_DATA
: Added in Oracle8; if status is "locked," shows the date the account was locked

EXPIRY_DATE
: Added in Oracle8; date the account is set to expire

EXTERNAL_NAME
: Added in Oracle8; user's external name

Unless you have instituted customized profiles (described in Chapter 6, *Profiles, Passwords, and Synonyms*), the value of the PROFILE column will always read DEFAULT. The PASSWORD column is always a 16-character encrypted version of the password. There is no relationship between the length of the password and the value in this field. For instance, after creating user *mary* with a password of "y", a query on this view resulted in the output shown below. Note that in the example, the column names were shortened with the "column ... format" command, and the row for *mary* has been italicized for emphasis.

```
SQL> SELECT username, profile, password
  2    FROM dba_users;
USERNA PROFILE PASSWORD
------ ------- ------------------------------
SYS    DEFAULT D4C5016086B2DC6A
SYSTEM DEFAULT D4DF7931AB130E37
MARY   DEFAULT CCB9E1C39D4F9898
RALPH  DEFAULT 81B9E3D295699571
```

The ROLE_ROLE_PRIVS View

The ROLE_ROLE_PRIVS view lists roles which are granted to roles. Its columns are detailed in the following list.

ROLE

Role name

GRANTED_ROLE

Role that was granted

ADMIN_OPTION

GRANT was with ADMIN OPTION

The only difference between the ROLE_ROLE_PRIVS view and the DBA_ROLE_PRIVS view is that the ROLE_ROLE_PRIVS only shows roles granted to roles. The DBA_ROLE_PRIVS shows users as well as roles. This tends to be very confusing. The following example shows Oracle7 output:

```
SQL> SELECT *
  2    FROM role_role_privs
  3   ORDER BY role, granted_role;
ROLE                GRANTED_ROLE                       ADM
----------------    ------------------------------     ---
DBA                 EXP_FULL_DATABASE                  NO
DBA                 IMP_FULL_DATABASE                  NO
```

For Oracle8, the same SELECT statement yields the following:

```
ROLE                            GRANTED_ROLE                     ADM
------------------------------  ------------------------------   ---
DBA                             DELETE_CATALOG_ROLE              YES
DBA                             EXECUTE_CATALOG_ROLE             YES
DBA                             EXP_FULL_DATABASE                NO
DBA                             IMP_FULL_DATABASE                NO
DBA                             SELECT_CATALOG_ROLE              YES
EXP_FULL_DATABASE               EXECUTE_CATALOG_ROLE             NO
EXP_FULL_DATABASE               SELECT_CATALOG_ROLE              NO
IMP_FULL_DATABASE               EXECUTE_CATALOG_ROLE             NO
IMP_FULL_DATABASE               SELECT_CATALOG_ROLE              NO

9 rows selected.
```

The ROLE_SYS_PRIVS View

The ROLE_SYS_PRIVS view (also available in the form USER_SYS_PRIVS) lists system privileges granted to roles. Columns include:

ROLE

Role name

PRIVILEGE

System privilege

ADMIN_OPTION

Grant was with ADMIN OPTION

This view shows system privileges, not object privileges. There will not be any specific object names such as "employees," "salary," or the like mentioned here. Instead, you will see privileges such as SELECT ANY TABLE or CREATE TABLE. The number of privileges varies with the version of Oracle. Version 7.3.2.2 lists 86 in the system_privilege_map table. The number usually remains consistent within a major release. We have shortened the listing to illustrate the types of privileges available and the types of roles with which they are generally associated.

In Oracle version 8.0.3, there are 139 rows selected (shown in the following example):

```
SQL> SELECT *
  2    FROM role_sys_privs
  3   ORDER BY 1, 2;

ROLE                           PRIVILEGE                                ADM
------------------------------ ---------------------------------------- ---
DBA                            ALTER ANY CLUSTER                        YES
DBA                            ALTER ANY INDEX                          YES
DBA                            ALTER ANY LIBRARY                        YES
DBA                            ALTER ANY PROCEDURE                      YES
DBA                            ALTER ANY ROLE                           YES
DBA                            ALTER ANY SEQUENCE                       YES
DBA                            ALTER ANY SNAPSHOT                       YES
DBA                            ALTER ANY TABLE                          YES
DBA                            ALTER ANY TRIGGER                        YES
DBA                            ALTER ANY TYPE                           YES
DBA                            ALTER DATABASE                           YES
DBA                            ALTER PROFILE                            YES
DBA                            ALTER RESOURCE COST                      YES
DBA                            ALTER ROLLBACK SEGMENT                   YES
DBA                            ALTER SESSION                            YES
DBA                            ALTER SYSTEM                             YES
DBA                            ALTER TABLESPACE                         YES
DBA                            ALTER USER                               YES
DBA                            ANALYZE ANY                              YES
DBA                            AUDIT ANY                                YES
DBA                            AUDIT SYSTEM                             YES
DBA                            BACKUP ANY TABLE                         YES
DBA                            BECOME USER                              YES
DBA                            COMMENT ANY TABLE                        YES
DBA                            CREATE ANY CLUSTER                       YES
DBA                            CREATE ANY DIRECTORY                     YES
DBA                            CREATE ANY INDEX                         YES
DBA                            CREATE ANY LIBRARY                       YES
DBA                            CREATE ANY PROCEDURE                     YES
DBA                            CREATE ANY SEQUENCE                      YES
DBA                            CREATE ANY SNAPSHOT                      YES
DBA                            CREATE ANY SYNONYM                       YES
DBA                            CREATE ANY TABLE                         YES
DBA                            CREATE ANY TRIGGER                       YES
DBA                            CREATE ANY TYPE                          YES
```

```
DBA                    CREATE ANY VIEW                    YES
DBA                    CREATE CLUSTER                     YES
DBA                    CREATE DATABASE LINK               YES
DBA                    CREATE LIBRARY                     YES
DBA                    CREATE PROCEDURE                   YES
DBA                    CREATE PROFILE                     YES
DBA                    CREATE PUBLIC DATABASE LINK        YES
DBA                    CREATE PUBLIC SYNONYM              YES
DBA                    CREATE ROLE                        YES
DBA                    CREATE ROLLBACK SEGMENT            YES
DBA                    CREATE SEQUENCE                    YES
DBA                    CREATE SESSION                     YES
DBA                    CREATE SNAPSHOT                    YES
DBA                    CREATE SYNONYM                     YES
DBA                    CREATE TABLE                       YES
DBA                    CREATE TABLESPACE                  YES
DBA                    CREATE TRIGGER                     YES
DBA                    CREATE TYPE                        YES
DBA                    CREATE USER                        YES
DBA                    CREATE VIEW                        YES
DBA                    DELETE ANY TABLE                   YES
DBA                    DROP ANY CLUSTER                   YES
DBA                    DROP ANY DIRECTORY                 YES
DBA                    DROP ANY INDEX                     YES
DBA                    DROP ANY LIBRARY                   YES
DBA                    DROP ANY PROCEDURE                 YES
DBA                    DROP ANY ROLE                      YES
DBA                    DROP ANY SEQUENCE                  YES
DBA                    DROP ANY SNAPSHOT                  YES
DBA                    DROP ANY SYNONYM                   YES
DBA                    DROP ANY TABLE                     YES
DBA                    DROP ANY TRIGGER                   YES
DBA                    DROP ANY TYPE                      YES
DBA                    DROP ANY VIEW                      YES
DBA                    DROP PROFILE                       YES
DBA                    DROP PUBLIC DATABASE LINK          YES
DBA                    DROP PUBLIC SYNONYM                YES
DBA                    DROP ROLLBACK SEGMENT              YES
DBA                    DROP TABLESPACE                    YES
DBA                    DROP USER                          YES
DBA                    EXECUTE ANY LIBRARY                YES
DBA                    EXECUTE ANY PROCEDURE              YES
DBA                    EXECUTE ANY TYPE                   YES
DBA                    FORCE ANY TRANSACTION              YES
DBA                    FORCE TRANSACTION                  YES
DBA                    GRANT ANY PRIVILEGE                YES
DBA                    GRANT ANY ROLE                     YES
DBA                    INSERT ANY TABLE                   YES
DBA                    LOCK ANY TABLE                     YES
DBA                    MANAGE TABLESPACE                  YES
DBA                    RESTRICTED SESSION                 YES
DBA                    SELECT ANY SEQUENCE                YES
DBA                    SELECT ANY TABLE                   YES
DBA                    UPDATE ANY TABLE                   YES
```

```
EXP_FULL_DATABASE              BACKUP ANY TABLE                    NO
EXP_FULL_DATABASE              EXECUTE ANY PROCEDURE               NO
EXP_FULL_DATABASE              SELECT ANY TABLE                    NO
IMP_FULL_DATABASE              ALTER ANY TABLE                     NO
IMP_FULL_DATABASE              ALTER ANY TYPE                      NO
IMP_FULL_DATABASE              AUDIT ANY                           NO
IMP_FULL_DATABASE              BECOME USER                         NO
IMP_FULL_DATABASE              COMMENT ANY TABLE                   NO
IMP_FULL_DATABASE              CREATE ANY CLUSTER                  NO
IMP_FULL_DATABASE              CREATE ANY DIRECTORY                NO
IMP_FULL_DATABASE              CREATE ANY INDEX                    NO
IMP_FULL_DATABASE              CREATE ANY LIBRARY                  NO
IMP_FULL_DATABASE              CREATE ANY PROCEDURE                NO
IMP_FULL_DATABASE              CREATE ANY SEQUENCE                 NO
IMP_FULL_DATABASE              CREATE ANY SNAPSHOT                 NO
IMP_FULL_DATABASE              CREATE ANY SYNONYM                  NO
IMP_FULL_DATABASE              CREATE ANY TABLE                    NO
IMP_FULL_DATABASE              CREATE ANY TRIGGER                  NO
IMP_FULL_DATABASE              CREATE ANY TYPE                     NO
IMP_FULL_DATABASE              CREATE ANY VIEW                     NO
IMP_FULL_DATABASE              CREATE DATABASE LINK                NO
IMP_FULL_DATABASE              CREATE PROFILE                      NO
IMP_FULL_DATABASE              CREATE PUBLIC DATABASE LINK         NO
IMP_FULL_DATABASE              CREATE PUBLIC SYNONYM               NO
IMP_FULL_DATABASE              CREATE ROLE                         NO
IMP_FULL_DATABASE              CREATE ROLLBACK SEGMENT             NO
IMP_FULL_DATABASE              CREATE TABLESPACE                   NO
IMP_FULL_DATABASE              CREATE USER                         NO
IMP_FULL_DATABASE              DROP ANY CLUSTER                    NO
IMP_FULL_DATABASE              DROP ANY DIRECTORY                  NO
IMP_FULL_DATABASE              DROP ANY INDEX                      NO
IMP_FULL_DATABASE              DROP ANY LIBRARY                    NO
IMP_FULL_DATABASE              DROP ANY PROCEDURE                  NO
IMP_FULL_DATABASE              DROP ANY ROLE                       NO
IMP_FULL_DATABASE              DROP ANY SEQUENCE                   NO
IMP_FULL_DATABASE              DROP ANY SNAPSHOT                   NO
IMP_FULL_DATABASE              DROP ANY SYNONYM                    NO
IMP_FULL_DATABASE              DROP ANY TABLE                      NO
IMP_FULL_DATABASE              DROP ANY TRIGGER                    NO
IMP_FULL_DATABASE              DROP ANY TYPE                       NO
IMP_FULL_DATABASE              DROP ANY VIEW                       NO
IMP_FULL_DATABASE              DROP PROFILE                        NO
IMP_FULL_DATABASE              DROP PUBLIC DATABASE LINK           NO
IMP_FULL_DATABASE              DROP PUBLIC SYNONYM                 NO
IMP_FULL_DATABASE              DROP ROLLBACK SEGMENT               NO
IMP_FULL_DATABASE              DROP TABLESPACE                     NO
IMP_FULL_DATABASE              DROP USER                           NO
IMP_FULL_DATABASE              EXECUTE ANY PROCEDURE               NO
IMP_FULL_DATABASE              INSERT ANY TABLE                    NO
IMP_FULL_DATABASE              SELECT ANY TABLE                    NO
139 rows selected.
```

Note that there are no entries for CONNECT and RESOURCE in this list. The system privileges granted to the CONNECT and RESOURCE roles are not visible from this view. They are visible from the DBA_SYS_PRIVS view, however, and the grants follow:

```
SQL> SELECT *
  2    FROM dba_sys_privs
  3   WHERE grantee = 'CONNECT';
GRANTEE                        PRIVILEGE                                ADM
------------------------------ ---------------------------------------- ---
CONNECT                        ALTER SESSION                            NO
CONNECT                        CREATE CLUSTER                           NO
CONNECT                        CREATE DATABASE LINK                     NO
CONNECT                        CREATE SEQUENCE                          NO
CONNECT                        CREATE SESSION                           NO
CONNECT                        CREATE SYNONYM                           NO
CONNECT                        CREATE TABLE                             NO
CONNECT                        CREATE VIEW                              NO

8 rows selected.

SQL> SELECT *
  2    FROM dba_sys_privs
  3   WHERE grantee = 'RESOURCE';
GRANTEE                        PRIVILEGE                                ADM
------------------------------ ---------------------------------------- ---
RESOURCE                       CREATE CLUSTER                           NO
RESOURCE                       CREATE PROCEDURE                         NO
RESOURCE                       CREATE SEQUENCE                          NO
RESOURCE                       CREATE TABLE                             NO
RESOURCE                       CREATE TRIGGER                           NO
RESOURCE                       CREATE TYPE                              NO

6 rows selected.
```

The ROLE_TAB_PRIVS View

The ROLE_TAB_PRIVS view (also available in the form USER_TAB_PRIVS) lists table privileges granted to roles. Columns include:

ROLE
: Role name

OWNER
: Table owner

TABLE_NAME
: Table name or sequence name

COLUMN_NAME
: Column name if applicable

PRIVILEGE
: Table privilege

GRANTABLE
Role may be granted by holder

This view is a complement to the ROLE_SYS_PRIVS view. Whereas that view shows system privileges, this view shows privileges granted on objects such as tables, views, and stored programs. These privileges are shown as granted to roles, not users.

```
SQL> SELECT *
  2    FROM role_tab_privs
  3   ORDER BY 1, 3, 5;
ROLE              ONR TABLE_NAME   COLUMN_NAME     PRIVILEGE       GRANTABLE
----------------- --- ------------ --------------- --------------- ---
CONNECT           SYS TOTEXT                       EXECUTE         NO
EXP_FULL_DATABASE SYS INCEXP                       DELETE          NO
EXP_FULL_DATABASE SYS INCEXP                       INSERT          NO
EXP_FULL_DATABASE SYS INCEXP                       UPDATE          NO
EXP_FULL_DATABASE SYS INCFIL                       DELETE          NO
EXP_FULL_DATABASE SYS INCFIL                       INSERT          NO
EXP_FULL_DATABASE SYS INCFIL                       UPDATE          NO
EXP_FULL_DATABASE SYS INCVID                       DELETE          NO
EXP_FULL_DATABASE SYS INCVID                       INSERT          NO
EXP_FULL_DATABASE SYS INCVID                       UPDATE          NO
9 rows selected.
```

In Oracle8, there were no rows selected.

When stored procedures and functions were added to Oracle functionality, the decision was made to include them as a part of this view. As you can see, the CONNECT role has the EXECUTE privilege on the TOTEXT object. This is a stored function, not a table, so the view name and the column name are somewhat misleading.

5

Oracle Default Roles and User Accounts

In this chapter:

Okay, get your pencil and paper out. It's time for a pop quiz!

Question 1. You've just created an Oracle database. How many user accounts exist on your system?

1. 1
2. 2
3. 8
4. It depends on the version

Question 2. With the same database as above, how many roles exist in the database?

1. 1
2. 3
3. 6
4. It depends on the version

If you answered number 4—"It depends on the version"—for each of the questions, you are correct. Give yourself a gold star.

As we mentioned in Chapter 4, *The Oracle Data Dictionary*, when you create an Oracle database, Oracle performs many tasks in conjunction with the creation. There are several scripts that are run. Some of these scripts create default roles and default users in your database.

Chapter 3, *Oracle Database Objects*, explains that using roles can help you lighten your workload by letting you assign many privileges to many users quickly by performing the following tasks:

1. Create a role
2. Grant to the new role the privileges you want the set of users to have
3. Grant the role to each of the users

Oracle supplies several default ("canned") roles that you might use to quickly assign privileges to users. However, there are problems you need to be aware of when you use these Oracle-supplied default roles. In order to completely protect your database, you need to know what the default roles are and the advantages and disadvantages of using these roles.

Oracle also creates several default users within a database. Unfortunately, the usernames and passwords for these accounts are hardcoded into the scripts that reside in your operating system's Oracle directory structure. Many of the passwords are commonly known by most DBAs, and many are easy to guess.

For each new version of the RDBMS, default users and roles can change. Be sure to carefully examine the roles, users, and their assigned default privileges for your version.

In this chapter, we'll examine the default roles and users that exist in your newly-created database. We'll discuss the problems associated with these roles and users and look at why you might *not* want to take advantage of these constructs.

About the Defaults

Those of you who are familiar with earlier versions of Oracle (before version 6) will remember that three privilege levels were defined before the concept of roles was introduced in version 6. Oracle used the same names for the new roles that were used for the privilege levels. These are CONNECT, RESOURCE, and DBA. Four more roles were added in version 7.1.6: SYSDBA, SYSOPER, EXP_FULL_DATABASE, and IMP_FULL_DATABASE; these roles did not exist as privilege levels in earlier releases. Several more default roles have been added in Oracle8: DELETE_CATALOG_ROLE, EXECUTE_CATALOG_ROLE, and SELECT_CATALOG_ROLE. The following list briefly describes how the default roles are used.

There is one more default user group that exists in every database—*public*. *public* is a user group that is really a quasi-role; every user who is created belongs automatically to the *public* group. *public* does not have a password and cannot connect to the database, and, like a role, cannot own objects. See the section "Grants to public" later in this chapter.

CONNECT
: Allows users to log into the database, to create objects, and to perform exports.

RESOURCE
: Grants users the privileges necessary to create procedures, triggers, and (for Oracle8) types within the user's own schema area.

DBA
: Allows users virtually unlimited privileges.

SYSDBA
: Allows users to connect to the database and remotely perform privileged actions like starting up and shutting down the database (basically equivalent to the DBA role).

SYSOPER
: Allows users to connect to the database remotely and perform a limited set of privileged actions, including starting up and shutting down.

EXP_FULL_DATABASE
: Allows the user to perform export activities on any object within the database and record the export activities to the data dictionary.

IMP_FULL_DATABASE
: Allows the user to become a user so that the user's objects can be imported into the appropriate schema area.

For Oracle8, the default roles include:

DELETE_CATALOG_ROLE
: Allows the user to delete rows from the SYS.AUD$ table.

EXECUTE_CATALOG_ROLE
: Allows the user to execute any exported packages listed in the recovery catalog.*

* The recovery catalog is discussed in Chapter 12, *Backing Up and Recovering the Database*.

SELECT_CATALOG_ROLE

Allows the user to select rows from all exported recovery catalog views and tables. This role is granted to users who will not receive the DBA role but who must be able to view exported views and tables in the data dictionary.

At first glance, the Oracle-supplied default roles may seem to supply an appropriate range of privileges; for development environments, they may indeed be appropriate. For production systems, however, we recommend that you not use the CONNECT and RESOURCE roles. We make this recommendation for the following reasons:

- Oracle may change the privileges assigned to a default role from one major release of the software to another
- Some privileges may be created to give lower-level users more freedom than they should have
- Privileges on which an application may be relying may disappear

Any of these occurrences could create a dangerous situation for your site's security. We advise you to take the necessary time and effort from the beginning of system development to create roles and grant them only the access that is really required. In this way, you'll encounter fewer problems as future releases of the Oracle RDBMS are made available.

None of the default Oracle roles allows access to any database objects other than those granted to *public* and the data dictionary views. However, as we'll discuss later, the DBA role is quite powerful and should not be granted to anyone who is not in a direct database administration position.

The default Oracle roles convey only system privileges, not object privileges.

As we mentioned at the beginning of this chapter, Oracle also creates several default user accounts. Prior to version 7.3, the only user account (besides the standard *sys* and *system* accounts) that could be considered a "default" user was the account *scott*, which was always authenticated with the password *tiger*. The *scott* account (named after an early Oracle developer whose girlfriend owned a cat named Tiger) is intended for training purposes such as:

- Demonstrating new Oracle Forms and Reports products
- Teaching SQL and SQL*Plus
- Testing the database to verify that the installation was OK
- Testing SQL*Net connections

With the Oracle Enterprise Manager and Oracle8, several additional default user accounts are now created. The section "Default User Accounts" later in this chapter describes these accounts.

The CONNECT Role

The CONNECT role was originally intended to allow users to log in to the database. In versions of Oracle before version 6, the CONNECT *privilege* enabled a user to create a session in a database and allowed little else. In version 6, the CONNECT *role* was given the privileges shown in Table 5-1 and allowed the user to connect to the database, to create views, synonyms, and database links, and to perform table or user exports. The CONNECT role now conveys far more privileges than the original CONNECT privilege did. The most critical system privilege allowed by this role is CREATE SESSION; without this system privilege, the user cannot log on to the database.

System Privileges for the CONNECT Role

The system privileges for the CONNECT role, shown in Table 5-1, are the same for versions 7.X and 8.0 of the database.

Table 5-1. CONNECT Role System Privileges

Privilege
ALTER SESSION
CREATE CLUSTER
CREATE DATABASE LINK
CREATE SEQUENCE
CREATE SESSION
CREATE SYNONYM
CREATE TABLE
CREATE VIEW

Only the CREATE SESSION privilege is required for a user to log in to the database. The remaining privileges, except for CREATE SYNONYM, are generally not required by a user whose primary interface is through applications.

Problems with the CONNECT Role

A user who has been granted all of the privileges listed in Table 5-1 can actually create problems when using an interactive interface like SQL*Plus. Assume that user *mary* is the production schema owner. Also assume that user *ralph* has SELECT privilege on *mary*'s employee table, has enough quota granted to him on a tablespace to create a table, and does something like this:

```
SQL> CREATE TABLE employee
2     AS SELECT *
3          FROM mary.employee;

Table created
```

This creates *ralph*'s copy of the employee table and copies all of *mary*'s data into it.

The situation begins to compound

Next, *ralph* performs some analysis queries, perhaps even makes some "what if" changes to the data, and eventually logs off the system. Later, *ralph* runs an application that uses the employee table. The search precedence looks at the owner's objects first. Since *ralph* has an employee table, his table (rather than the mary.employee table), will be used by the application. Since *ralph* has changed the data in his private copy of the employee table, and also since no other user can get to that copy (yet), incorrect information will be returned if *ralph* attempts to do any work. The incorrect values will not be known to the application since all objects being used have the correct structure.

Getting further into trouble

To further complicate the issue, suppose that *ralph* tells *ed* he has explored some interesting "what if" situations and asks *ed* to take a look at the data. *ralph* grants access to his table with the command:

```
SQL> GRANT ALL ON employee
  2     TO public;

grant succeeded
```

ed now connects to his own account and issues the following command:

```
SQL> CREATE SYNONYM employee
  2     FOR ralph.employee;

synonym created
```

The plot thickens

Now there is a real problem. When both *ralph* and *ed* run applications that require the employee table, the ralph.employee copy, not mary.employee, will be used. Also, because *ralph* granted ALL to *public* on his employee table, *ed* or anyone else could physically alter the table structure, probably causing the application to fail. Finally, because *ralph* granted the privilege to public, any user on the system can access his employee table as well as create a synonym for it. So, unless these two object owners subsequently drop their objects (*ralph*'s table and *ed*'s synonym), the system could rapidly fall apart.

Name of the role

Another problem with the CONNECT role is its misleading name. In most implementations of roles, the role name conveys some intelligence regarding its usage within the system. The CONNECT role does not do this.

The RESOURCE Role

The RESOURCE role grants a user the privileges necessary to create procedures, triggers and, in Oracle8, types within the user's own schema area. Granting a user RESOURCE without CONNECT, while possible, does not allow the user to log in to the database. Therefore, if you really must grant a user RESOURCE, you have to grant CONNECT also—or, at least, CREATE SESSION—so the user can log in.

System Privileges for the RESOURCE Role

The system privileges for the RESOURCE role are shown in Table 5-2.

Table 5-2. RESOURCE Role System Privileges

Privilege
CREATE CLUSTER
CREATE PROCEDURE
CREATE SEQUENCE
CREATE TABLE
CREATE TRIGGER
CREATE TYPE (new in Oracle8)

Problems with the RESOURCE Role

There are several potential problems with the use of the RESOURCE role.

The Oracle-supplied roles can be moving targets

As we mentioned earlier in the section "About the Defaults," the system privileges of an Oracle-supplied role may change with a new version or upgrade release. For example, the privileges listed in Table 5-2 are from an Oracle8 RESOURCE role. Note that in an Oracle7 database, the CREATE TYPE privilege does not exist. There is another problem that has as much or more impact on your database security, which we examine next.

UNLIMITED TABLESPACE access

Another issue with the RESOURCE role is that the UNLIMITED TABLESPACE system privilege is explicitly granted. This privilege gives the user unlimited quotas on any tablespace in the database. Even if an explicit quota is specified for a user, if the user has been granted the RESOURCE role, the user may create objects on any tablespace, including the *system* tablespace.

For example, suppose that the user account *mary* is created and granted the RESOURCE role. Even if *mary* is altered and a quota of zero (0) is given on the *system* tablespace, *mary* can still create objects in the *system* tablespace because of the UNLIMITED TABLESPACE system privilege granted to the account.

About the CREATE TRIGGER privilege

Note that the RESOURCE role only adds three privileges to those provided by the CONNECT role: CREATE PROCEDURE, CREATE TRIGGER, and CREATE TYPE.

Use of the CREATE TRIGGER privilege may lead to an interesting situation. One of the most touchy aspects of a personnel system is salary. Suppose that the following situation exists:

- Employee Ralph Rotten (username *ralph*) has been granted the CONNECT and RESOURCE roles.
- Schema *mary* is the production schema owner. The employee table within *mary* contains salary information, which is sensitive data.
- *ralph* does not have any privileges on *mary*'s employee table.
- *ralph* is a bit of a hacker.

Now, user *ralph* finds out the structure of the employee table through the system documentation. User *ralph* then creates a script containing the following commands:

```
SQL>  CREATE TABLE private_audit
   2    (id_of_user            VARCHAR2(30),
   3    action_performed       VARCHAR2(5),
   4    tab_name               VARCHAR2(30),
   5    pkey                   VARCHAR2(20),
   6    salary                 NUMBER(10,2),
   7    date_of_action         DATE)
   8  ;

Table created.

SQL>  GRANT select, insert, update ON private_audit
  2       TO public;

Grant succeeded.
```

OK. User *ralph* then creates a trigger on the mary.employee table, a table that *ralph* cannot even describe!

```
SQL> CREATE OR REPLACE TRIGGER BIUDR_EMP
   2   BEFORE INSERT OR UPDATE OR DELETE
```

```
  ON mary.employee
  FOR EACH ROW
/* Capture the salary information and the user changing it!  */
DECLARE
  tyact   VARCHAR2(1);
  enam    VARCHAR2(20);
  sal     NUMBER(10,2) := :new.sal;
BEGIN
  IF INSERTING THEN
    tyact := 'I';
    enam  := :new.ename;
  ELSIF UPDATING THEN
    tyact := 'U';
    enam  := :old.ename;
    IF sal = 0 OR sal IS NULL THEN
       sal   := :old.sal;
    END IF;
  ELSIF DELETING THEN
    tyact := 'D';
    enam  := :old.ename;
    sal   := :old.sal;
  END IF;

INSERT INTO ralph.private_audit
    (id_of_user,action_performed,tab_name,pkey,date_of_action,salary)
 VALUES
    (user, tyact, 'EMP', enam, sysdate, sal)
;
/

Trigger created.
```

Having done this on the morning that new hires are registered or when raises are due, user *ralph* then waits. During the day, the payroll administrator runs the application to give the raises. About 4:00 p.m., *ralph* runs this query:

```
SQL> @qpaud1
SQL> COLUMN id_of_user FORMAT a8 HEADING uname
SQL> COLUMN action_performed FORMAT a3 HEADING act
SQL> COLUMN tab_name FORMAT a10
SQL> COLUMN salary FORMAT $99,999.90
SQL>
SQL> SELECT *
    FROM private_audit
   ORDER BY pkey;

uname    act TAB_NAME   PKEY                      SALARY DATE_OF_A
-------- --- ---------- -------------------- ----------- ---------
SYSTEM   U   EMPLOYEE   ALDER                  $1,149.50 01-MAR-98
SYSTEM   U   EMPLOYEE   ARDEN                  $1,660.80 01-MAR-98
SYSTEM   U   EMPLOYEE   BROWN                  $3,092.25 01-MAR-98
SYSTEM   U   EMPLOYEE   CLARY                  $2,658.25 01-MAR-98
SYSTEM   U   EMPLOYEE   JAMES                    $992.75 01-MAR-98
SYSTEM   U   EMPLOYEE   JOHNS                  $3,227.88 01-MAR-98
```

```
SYSTEM   U   EMPLOYEE    MARTIE                         $1,297.50 01-MAR-98
SYSTEM   U   EMPLOYEE    MIKERT                         $1,358.50 01-MAR-98
SYSTEM   U   EMPLOYEE    SAMUALS                        $3,000.00 01-MAR-98
SYSTEM   U   EMPLOYEE    SMYTHE                           $836.00 01-MAR-98
SYSTEM   U   EMPLOYEE    TANNER                         $1,557.00 01-MAR-98
SYSTEM   U   EMPLOYEE    WALTEN                         $1,297.50 01-MAR-98

12 rows selected.
```

Oops!

User *ralph* then drops the trigger and table to conceal what has been done, but retains the scripts to recreate the table and trigger when the next pay raises are due to be given.

The DBA Role

The role that literally has the "keys to the kingdom" is the DBA role. With few exceptions, this role will allow the granted user to do almost anything he wants within SQL*Plus or the Server Manager Utility. Well, almost anything. Unless the user has also been placed in the system group, which enables DBA access and the ability to CONNECT INTERNAL or CONNECT / AS SYSDBA, he will not be able to start up or shut down the database, or even completely destroy it by issuing a CREATE DATABASE statement on an existing database. However, he will be able to do tremendous damage to a database by adding or removing tablespaces or other objects—either maliciously or unintentionally.

System Privileges for the DBA Role

DBA role system privileges are shown in Table 5-3. There are 77 of these privileges in Oracle7, and 89 in Oracle8. The 12 new privileges in Oracle8 encompass actions with directory, library, and type.

A user who has been granted the DBA role has ADMIN OPTION and can therefore pass *any* of the associated privileges to other users with or without ADMIN OPTION if he chooses.

Table 5-3. DBA Role System Privileges

Privilege
ALTER ANY CLUSTER
ALTER ANY INDEX
ALTER ANY LIBRARY (new in Oracle8)

Table 5-3. DBA Role System Privileges (continued)

Privilege
ALTER ANY PROCEDURE
ALTER ANY ROLE
ALTER ANY SEQUENCE
ALTER ANY SNAPSHOT
ALTER ANY TABLE
ALTER ANY TRIGGER
ALTER ANY TYPE (new in Oracle8)
ALTER DATABASE
ALTER PROFILE
ALTER RESOURCE COST
ALTER ROLLBACK SEGMENT
ALTER SESSION
ALTER SYSTEM
ALTER TABLESPACE
ALTER USER
ANALYZE ANY
AUDIT ANY
AUDIT SYSTEM
BACKUP ANY TABLE
BECOME USER
COMMENT ANY TABLE
CREATE ANY CLUSTER
CREATE ANY DIRECTORY (new in Oracle8)
CREATE ANY INDEX
CREATE ANY LIBRARY (new in Oracle8)
CREATE ANY PROCEDURE
CREATE ANY SEQUENCE
CREATE ANY SNAPSHOT
CREATE ANY SYNONYM
CREATE ANY TABLE
CREATE ANY TRIGGER
CREATE ANY TYPE (new in Oracle8)
CREATE ANY VIEW
CREATE CLUSTER
CREATE DATABASE LINK
CREATE LIBRARY (new in Oracle8)

Table 5-3. DBA Role System Privileges (continued)

Privilege
CREATE PROCEDURE
CREATE PROFILE
CREATE PUBLIC DATABASE LINK
CREATE PUBLIC SYNONYM
CREATE ROLE
CREATE ROLLBACK SEGMENT
CREATE SEQUENCE
CREATE SESSION
CREATE SNAPSHOT
CREATE SYNONYM
CREATE TABLE
CREATE TABLESPACE
CREATE TRIGGER
CREATE TYPE (new in Oracle8)
CREATE USER
CREATE VIEW
DELETE ANY TABLE
DROP ANY CLUSTER
DROP ANY DIRECTORY (new in Oracle8)
DROP ANY INDEX
DROP ANY LIBRARY (new in Oracle8)
DROP ANY PROCEDURE
DROP ANY ROLE
DROP ANY SEQUENCE
DROP ANY SNAPSHOT
DROP ANY SYNONYM
DROP ANY TABLE
DROP ANY TRIGGER
DROP ANY TYPE (new in Oracle8)
DROP ANY VIEW
DROP PROFILE
DROP PUBLIC DATABASE LINK
DROP PUBLIC SYNONYM
DROP ROLLBACK SEGMENT
DROP TABLESPACE
DROP USER

Table 5-3. DBA Role System Privileges (continued)

Privilege
EXECUTE ANY LIBRARY (new in Oracle8)
EXECUTE ANY PROCEDURE
EXECUTE ANY TYPE (new in Oracle8)
FORCE ANY TRANSACTION
FORCE TRANSACTION
GRANT ANY PRIVILEGE
GRANT ANY ROLE
INSERT ANY TABLE
LOCK ANY TABLE
MANAGE TABLESPACE
RESTRICTED SESSION
SELECT ANY SEQUENCE
SELECT ANY TABLE
UPDATE ANY TABLE

As you can see, the DBA role has many system privileges attached to it, and many of these privileges include the ANY qualifier—for example, the CREATE ANY TABLE system privilege. The ANY qualifier allows just that—anything. The user with an ANY privilege can create the object under any schema or userid. Most of these privileges are rather self-explanatory, except, perhaps, for BECOME USER.

BECOME USER is there to allow a privileged user to perform *full* and *user* exports and imports. The user doing so must "become the user being exported or imported," and that is what the BECOME USER allows. The privilege does not allow a user to log in as another user without knowing that user's password.

Who Gets the DBA Role?

The DBA role conveys considerable privileges—essentially all of them. For that reason, this role (and most of the associated privileges) should never be given to any user other than a person who is to have full authority within the database. Restrictions on granting the DBA role should be strictly enforced. There is *never* any reason to grant developers the DBA role, even though many of them tend to ask for that privilege. In all cases, instruct those who request the DBA role to list the specific privileges needed for their particular application development, along with an explanation of why each individual privilege is needed. The DBA and appropriate managers can then arrange to meet the request (assuming that the needs are determined to be appropriate and justified). Often, a developer will demand quite forcibly the DBA role because he has not properly identified what specific privileges are really needed for his application.

Why is it so risky to grant the DBA role to a developer? When a developer is granted the DBA role and then moves his application into production, will you want to grant the production account the DBA role? Of course not. The potential for compromise of a production system through the DBA role would be far too great. Therefore, imposing the "no DBA role for non-DBAs" rule in development will force the developer to do the necessary up-front work to ensure that only the truly necessary privileges for the application move to production.

All too often, the development application *is* moved into production without a complete examination of the roles assigned to users. The users who have been created in development, for whatever reason, get carried along in an import and are not removed.

We recommend that you carefully examine every user who exists in your development database, and his or her roles and privileges, before and after that database is migrated to production.

The SYSDBA and SYSOPER Roles

In Chapter 8, *Installing and Starting Oracle*, we'll examine the use of operating system privileges for database access. One of the privileges used for authentication is the OSDBA operating system privilege. Another operating system privilege is OSOPER. Working hand in hand with these privileges is a mechanism known as the SYSDBA and SYSOPER roles, created in version 7.1.6 of the Oracle RDBMS.

Remote Database Administration

If a database account has been granted the SYSDBA or SYSOPER role, that account gains the ability to connect in any of the following ways:

```
CONNECT INTERNAL AS SYSDBA
CONNECT / AS SYSDBA
CONNECT INTERNAL AS SYSOPER
CONNECT / AS SYSOPER
```

The user can then perform privileged actions like starting up and shutting down the database. An account connected as SYSDBA can perform any function a user who has been granted the DBA role can perform. The SYSDBA privilege should be granted as cautiously as the normal DBA role. The SYSDBA role enables you to perform the following actions (as well as execute any of the privileges shown in Table 5-4):

- Create a database
- Start up a database
- Alter a database mount or open
- Alter a database for backup
- Enable archive logging
- Recover a database
- Restrict a session
- Shut down a database

System Privileges for the SYSDBA and SYSOPER Roles

SYSDBA role system privileges are shown in Table 5-4. There are 77 of these privileges in Oracle7, and 89 in Oracle8. The 12 new privileges in Oracle8 encompass actions with directory, library, and type. From a privilege perspective, the SYSDBA privileges are identical to the DBA privileges.

A user who has been granted the SYSDBA role or SYSOPER role has ADMIN OPTION and can pass *any* of the associated privileges on to other users with or without ADMIN OPTION if he chooses.

Table 5-4. SYSDBA Role System Privileges

Privilege
ALTER ANY CLUSTER
ALTER ANY INDEX
ALTER ANY LIBRARY (new in Oracle8)
ALTER ANY PROCEDURE
ALTER ANY ROLE
ALTER ANY SEQUENCE
ALTER ANY SNAPSHOT
ALTER ANY TABLE
ALTER ANY TRIGGER
ALTER ANY TYPE (new in Oracle8)
ALTER DATABASE

Table 5-4. SYSDBA Role System Privileges (continued)

Privilege
ALTER PROFILE
ALTER RESOURCE COST
ALTER ROLLBACK SEGMENT
ALTER SESSION
ALTER SYSTEM
ALTER TABLESPACE
ALTER USER
ANALYZE ANY
AUDIT ANY
AUDIT SYSTEM
BACKUP ANY TABLE
BECOME USER
COMMENT ANY TABLE
CREATE ANY CLUSTER
CREATE ANY DIRECTORY (new in Oracle8)
CREATE ANY INDEX
CREATE ANY LIBRARY (new in Oracle8)
CREATE ANY PROCEDURE
CREATE ANY SEQUENCE
CREATE ANY SNAPSHOT
CREATE ANY SYNONYM
CREATE ANY TABLE
CREATE ANY TRIGGER
CREATE ANY TYPE (new in Oracle8)
CREATE ANY VIEW
CREATE CLUSTER
CREATE DATABASE LINK
CREATE LIBRARY (new in Oracle8)
CREATE PROCEDURE
CREATE PROFILE
CREATE PUBLIC DATABASE LINK
CREATE PUBLIC SYNONYM
CREATE ROLE
CREATE ROLLBACK SEGMENT
CREATE SEQUENCE
CREATE SESSION

Table 5-4. SYSDBA Role System Privileges (continued)

Privilege
CREATE SNAPSHOT
CREATE SYNONYM
CREATE TABLE
CREATE TABLESPACE
CREATE TRIGGER
CREATE TYPE (new in Oracle8)
CREATE USER
CREATE VIEW
DELETE ANY TABLE
DROP ANY CLUSTER
DROP ANY DIRECTORY (new in Oracle8)
DROP ANY INDEX
DROP ANY LIBRARY (new in Oracle8)
DROP ANY PROCEDURE
DROP ANY ROLE
DROP ANY SEQUENCE
DROP ANY SNAPSHOT
DROP ANY SYNONYM
DROP ANY TABLE
DROP ANY TRIGGER
DROP ANY TYPE (new in Oracle8)
DROP ANY VIEW
DROP PROFILE
DROP PUBLIC DATABASE LINK
DROP PUBLIC SYNONYM
DROP ROLLBACK SEGMENT
DROP TABLESPACE
DROP USER
EXECUTE ANY LIBRARY (new in Oracle8)
EXECUTE ANY PROCEDURE
EXECUTE ANY TYPE (new in Oracle8)
FORCE ANY TRANSACTION
FORCE TRANSACTION
GRANT ANY PRIVILEGE
GRANT ANY ROLE
INSERT ANY TABLE

Table 5-4. SYSDBA Role System Privileges (continued)

Privilege
LOCK ANY TABLE
MANAGE TABLESPACE
RESTRICTED SESSION
SELECT ANY SEQUENCE
SELECT ANY TABLE
UPDATE ANY TABLE

The major difference between the SYSDBA and SYSOPER accounts is that the SYSOPER account cannot create or perform recovery of a database.

As you will see in Chapter 8, when an account is granted SYSDBA or SYSOPER, an entry is placed in an operating system password file. An account which has been granted SYSDBA or SYSOPER can access the database from a remote node and perform administrator duties. The connection convention of CONNECT / AS SYSDBA or CONNECT / AS SYSOPER has been created to replace the CONNECT INTERNAL convention, which has been around for several versions of the RDBMS. Currently, CONNECT INTERNAL has been retained for backward compatibility.

If your account has been granted the operating system privileges OSDBA or OSOPER, you do not need to be explicitly granted the SYSDBA or SYSOPER privilege to connect to the database and perform privileged tasks.

About OSOPER and SYSOPER

Generally, the OSOPER role has the ability to issue the following commands:

STARTUP
SHUTDOWN
ALTER DATABASE OPEN/MOUNT
ALTER DATABASE BACKUP
ARCHIVE LOG
RECOVER

This role also allows the user to enable RESTRICTED SESSION.

The SYSOPER role enables the same privileges as its operating system counterpart, OSOPER, but allows the account granted these privileges to perform the actions remotely, as well as directly from the local operating system account.

About OSDBA and SYSDBA

The OSDBA role encompasses all of the system privileges with ADMIN OPTION, the OSOPER role values, and the ability for the user to CREATE DATABASE and perform time-based recovery. Likewise, the SYSDBA role enables the same privileges as its operating system counterpart, OSDBA, but allows the account granted these privileges to perform the actions remotely, as well as directly from the local operating system account.

About CONNECT INTERNAL

In the previous sections, we briefly mentioned a new convention for connecting to the database through the Server Manager or SQLDBA. The reference was to CONNECT INTERNAL AS or CONNECT / AS a privilege set. Let's look at what happens when you perform a CONNECT / or CONNECT INTERNAL.

The only way a database can be created, started, or shut down is through a connection to the heart of the database. Some forms of recovery can only be performed from this connection. The connection is accomplished in one of two ways: either directly through the SQLDBA utility or Server Manager utility (*svrmgrl* or *svrmgrm*) or through a remote connection using the Oracle Enterprise Manager and an intelligent agent connection. Either way, when you CONNECT INTERNAL, you are connecting to the database as *sys* with much higher privilege levels. There are subtle differences between logging on to SQL*Plus as the user *sys* and connecting through the utilities as CONNECT INTERNAL.

The only accounts that have the ability to connect to the internal *sys* account are those which are either in the DBA operating system group or have been granted the SYSOPER or SYSDBA privilege. Care and thought must be given to allowing anyone but a trained DBA the ability to access the database using the CONNECT INTERNAL mechanism. Great harm can be inadvertently done to a database if a person who is not a skilled DBA attempts to perform work connected in this manner.

Using the Default Roles

As you've surely concluded by now, neither the CONNECT nor the RESOURCE role is appropriate for general users—those who will use the applications or will use an interactive query tool such as SQL*Plus. Not only are these roles far too permissive in terms of system privileges, but they also do not convey any intelligence about the user, as we'll discuss in the following section.

> ### *New Default Roles in Oracle8*
>
> As we mentioned, three new roles have been added in Oracle8. Why are these roles needed?
>
> Normally, users who have been granted explicit privileges on objects and users who have been granted the SYSDBA or DBA role can access the objects in the data dictionary. However, there may be times when you need to interact with objects to which you have not been granted access. In Oracle8, you can be granted one of the following roles to enable you to access these objects:
>
> *DELETE_CATALOG_ROLE*
> Grants DELETE on the SYS.AUD$ table.
>
> *EXECUTE_CATALOG_ROLE*
> Grants EXECUTE on all dictionary packages.
>
> *SELECT_CATALOG_ROLE*
> Grants SELECT on all dictionary packages.

Creating Roles with Meaningful Names

Suppose that we have Accounts Payable, Accounts Receivable, Personnel, and Organization logical databases, and a user has the CONNECT role. You would not be able to tell from the role which of these logical databases would be used. However, if you had defined roles such as AP_USER, AR_USER, PERS_USER, and ORG_USER, then you could tell rather quickly to which group the user belonged. These roles would only need one system privilege—CREATE SESSION—and any minimal table or procedure privileges required to get them started.

Advantages of Customized Roles

Another advantage of using roles in a specific manner is the ability to disable particular groups of users without impacting the remainder of the user community. Should it be necessary to block the personnel group, all the DBA would have to do would be revoke CREATE SESSION from the PERS_USER role. Since that role would be assigned to the personnel users as the default, the users would not be able to log in to the database. All other users would be unaffected and could continue their work. When the database or application work on the Personnel logical database was completed, granting CREATE SESSION to the PERS_USER role would re-enable the logins for those users.

The term "logical database" is used here to distinguish a group of objects (tables, views, etc.) that are associated with an application or schema area which is housed in a database. This is what the user generally means when referring to the "database." There may be many logical databases within a single physical database. The logical databases may be associated with only one application or may share tables between applications. For example, an employee table might be used by the HR application in its logical database as well as the Payroll application in its logical database.

Default User Accounts

In the various versions of Oracle, when you create a database, some user accounts are automatically created by default. In every version, *sys* and *system* are created. In the later versions of Oracle7 (beginning in version 7.1.6 or version 7.2), the user *dbsnmp* is created automatically to support the Oracle Enterprise Manager intelligent agent. As of Oracle8, *scott* (a standard account you can use for demonstrations, testing, and training users in a known environment) is automatically created and populated, as are other users based on the cartridges you have selected for installation. Let's take a closer look at the default user accounts that are created and their potential impacts on database security.

Default Users and Their Roles

When a Personal Oracle8 database is created using version 8.0.3, several users are created by default:

- *sys*
- *system*
- *dbsnmp*
- *scott*
- *demo*
- *po8* (for Personal Oracle8)

The *sys* user is always assigned the password *change_on_install*. *sys* is the heart of the Oracle system. You must work very carefully when logged on as *sys*, since you have the ability to do severe damage to the database from this account.

The *system* user always receives the password *manager*. Because the *sys* and *system* passwords are pre-set, the DBA always knows the initial passwords necessary to log on as either *system* or *sys* to begin interacting with the database. *system* is the account from which you initially create your tablespaces, rollback segments, and users.

Always be sure to change the *sys* and *system* passwords immediately after the database is created.

Scott and his tiger

As we mentioned at the beginning of this chapter, the user and associated schema area *scott* has been around as far back as version 2.0 of the RDBMS. In every release of the Oracle software, there has been a demonstration package included that you installed to create several tables and views. The standard tables are BONUS, EMP, DEPT, and SALGRADE. The user *scott* is always created with a password of *tiger* and is used as Oracle's default demonstration database. The *scott* account has always required the default Oracle roles CONNECT and RESOURCE.

As we mentioned in Chapter 4, the RESOURCE role enables the user to create objects in ANY tablespace of choice by granting the system privilege UNLIMITED TABLESPACE. This might not be viewed by the DBA as a particularly favorable action for any user to be able to casually perform, since a user having the UNLIMITED TABLESPACE privilege can create an object on any tablespace in the database. This privilege overrides any tablespace quotas that have been imposed on the user to help control the areas to which a user has access. A user with UNLIMITED TABLESPACE can even create objects in the *system* tablespace. The potential problem with this ability is that the *system* tablespace could become very fragmented, thus degrading performance. The only way to rebuild the *system* tablespace is to:

1. Export the database
2. Drop and recreate the tablespaces and primary users
3. Import the database

This process is time-consuming to perform and prevents users from accessing the system to perform work until the database is completely rebuilt. With the changes in the composition of the CONNECT and RESOURCE roles, we recommend that if you are going to maintain a *scott* account on your system you build the account with only CONNECT privilege.

In past releases, if a DBA wanted the *scott* account to be in his database, he'd have to explicitly create the account and assign privileges to it. You would then run the scripts to build the demonstration tables within your database. Along with the *scott* account, several other accounts were created. They were *adams, jones, clark*, and *blake*.

In the Oracle8 database, because *scott* is prebuilt, we suggest that you log on to SQL*Plus using a privileged account and issue the following:

```
REVOKE RESOURCE from scott;
```

The idea of having a known area in which users can learn to write SQL or PL/SQL scripts or gain insights into using various other Oracle products like Oracle Developer is very worthwhile in a development database. But we recommend having a noninvasive account that has been granted no more privilege than CREATE SESSION to test SQL*Net configurations, etc., in a production system under a username which is not known universally. We feel that there is no reason to have a *scott/tiger* account in a production environment and recommend strongly that you remove this account from your production environments. Access to this account will enable a user to see any objects on which privileges have been granted to *public* in your production system. This access could produce a security breach.

With the advent of the Oracle Enterprise Manager and the use of intelligent agents (see Chapter 13, *Using the Oracle Enterprise Manager*), the Oracle *CATSNMP.SQL* script was run from *CATALOG.SQL* to establish the environment in a new database to support the intelligent agent. The account *dbsnmp* is automatically created in databases from version 7.3.X through 8.0.X, as we describe in the next section.

Demo, dbsnmp, and po8

The next user of interest is *demo*. Can you guess *demo*'s password? If you guessed *demo*, you are correct. *demo* is also granted CONNECT and RESOURCE by default. *dbsnmp*'s password is equally predictable—*dbsnmp*. (*dbsnmp* is automatically created in version 8.0.X.) Not only is *dbsnmp* granted CONNECT and RESOURCE, but this user also receives the role SNMPAGENT to enable an intelligent agent to connect to the database to perform tasks which have been remotely issued through the Oracle Enterprise Manager utility. If you intend to use the Oracle Enterprise Manager to remotely administer your databases, you must leave this account available and intact.

Predictably, *po8*'s password also mirrors the username.

The *po8* account is granted the canned DBA role by default. We highly recommend that you revoke this privilege! Any user can gain access to your database using this account and immediately perform any actions he or she wants *as a DBA*. You can remove the DBA privilege by issuing the command:

```
REVOKE DBA from po8;
```

We don't believe that we are revealing anything sacred by telling you these passwords. We believe that Oracle has perhaps made these passwords too easy to figure out, and that, if you are aware that these accounts exist, you will be able to more effectively protect your database.

Example queries

We easily learned about these accounts by logging on to the newly created database and issuing three queries. The first query, used to determine what users had been created, was:

```
SELECT username FROM dba_users;
```

Once the usernames had been obtained, the next two queries issued for each username presented the roles and system privileges granted to each user. The queries for *scott* and their output are:

```
SQL> SELECT *
  2    FROM dba_role_privs
  3   WHERE grantee = 'SCOTT';
GRANTEE                        GRANTED_ROLE                   ADM DEF
------------------------------ ------------------------------ --- ---
SCOTT                          CONNECT                        NO  YES
SCOTT                          RESOURCE                       NO  YES

SQL> SELECT *
  2    FROM dba_sys_privs
  3   WHERE grantee = 'SCOTT';

GRANTEE                        PRIVILEGE                                ADM
------------------------------ ---------------------------------------- ---
SCOTT                          UNLIMITED TABLESPACE                     NO
```

The first Oracle database created in your environment for each new version of Oracle should be carefully examined to determine the users and schema areas created.

When to allow default users

In a learning environment, the access provided by Oracle for demonstration purposes is wonderful. However, the conscientious database administrator will most certainly want to change the *sys* and *system* passwords immediately to ensure the safety of the new database from anyone who has even a passing knowledge of the default Oracle database structure. If the database is to be used for development of applications, the decision might be made to leave the *scott* and *demo* accounts available for basic database verification purposes since each user schema contains basic Oracle demonstration tables. The *scott* user contains the BONUS, EMP, DEPT, and SALGRADE tables, while the *demo* area contains ten "company" tables for Forms and Reports demonstration purposes. The *dbsnmp* and *po8* users do not have any tables. A *scott*-like account, with the default roles removed and the CREATE SESSION privilege granted, is a very nice mechanism for the DBA to have available to determine unsuccessful and successful configuration of network connectivity without violating security.

For a production database, however, be sure to remove the demonstration accounts and all others not needed to support the application(s), except for the *dbsnmp* users. If remote database maintenance will not be performed on a production database, the *dbsnmp* user account may safely be removed. However, if, at a later date, the decision is made to enable an intelligent agent on the production node, this account will need to be rebuilt.

Checking on users and access

Periodically, the DBA should produce a report of all users and their granted access. The following script could be used to show who had access to the database and what roles and grants they have assigned to them. The formatting shown for this report is based on the known usernames in this database, and you should adjust it for your database.

This script eliminates the users *sys* and *system* from the report to conserve space and allow us to concentrate on the accounts whose accesses might have changed:

```
SQL> COLUMN username FORMAT a15
SQL> COLUMN granted_role FORMAT a30
SQL> COLUMN privilege FORMAT a30
SQL> SELECT username, granted_role privileges
  2    FROM dba_users, dba_role_privs
  3   WHERE grantee = username
  4     AND username NOT IN ('SYS','SYSTEM')
  5   UNION
  6  SELECT username, privilege privileges
  7    FROM dba_users, dba_sys_privs
  8   WHERE grantee = username
  9*    AND username NOT IN ('SYS','SYSTEM');

USERNAME        PRIVILEGES
--------------- ------------------------------
DBSNMP          CONNECT
DBSNMP          CREATE PUBLIC SYNONYM
DBSNMP          RESOURCE
DBSNMP          SNMPAGENT
DBSNMP          UNLIMITED TABLESPACE
DEMO            CONNECT
DEMO            RESOURCE
DEMO            UNLIMITED TABLESPACE
```

```
PO8             DBA
PO8             UNLIMITED TABLESPACE
SCOTT           CONNECT
SCOTT           RESOURCE
SCOTT           UNLIMITED TABLESPACE

13 rows selected.
```

Grants to "public"

Oracle supplies a convention that enables developers or the DBA to grant a specific access to the entire group of users who will access the database in one command. By granting the privilege to *public*, anyone who accesses the database will have that privilege just by virtue of having a database account. In the Personal Oracle8 database we have been using in examples in this chapter, the default number of accesses granted to *public* is 375 separate and distinct privileges. Of the privileges granted to *public*:

- 33 are EXECUTE on a database package or utility
- 3 allow the ability to insert into, update, and delete from a table called DEF$_TEMP$LOB
- 1 allows deletion from the PSTUBTBL table
- 338 enable selection from various other objects within the database

The DBA_TAB_PRIVS view (shown in Chapter 4) contains a list of all of the tables and views that exist in the database and who has access to them. The DBA should select the values from the DBA_TAB_PRIVS view that have been granted to *public* and evaluate their impact on the database's security.

There are times when a DBA may be placed in a pressure situation in which the solution might seem to be to grant to *public* a privilege in order to quickly give access to an object. Don't give in to the pressure! The use of the ability to sweepingly grant access to a database object to all users through the *public* mechanism should be carefully weighed and evaluated on a case-by-case basis to ensure that an access is not given to someone who should not be able to obtain the information. The general rule of thumb should be to *never* grant access to *public* unless you've thoroughly investigated the effects of this action. Database security is important. It is worth a little bit of time and trouble to be secure!

Segmenting Authority in the Database

In Chapter 7, *Developing a Database Security Plan*, we recommend that you use a spreadsheet approach to list the envisioned objects within an application. We tell you to identify the actions that would be permitted against each object and to group the actions together and assign them to a role. Let's look briefly here at how you might do this.

For example, let's look at a piece of an application that will be used in a car dealership. The departments follow:

- New and used car sales
- Customer vehicle servicing
- Car leasing
- Automobile parts
- General bookkeeping
- Automobile detailing
- Paint and body shop

When a new car is received, an entry is made into the database in the automobile information area detailing the car's vehicle identification number (VIN), make and model, color, wholesale price, accessories, etc., reflecting the information needed for the car's invoice. The dealership manager or sales manager might examine the car and decide to add a sunroof or other feature to improve the sales appeal. A work order will be written up and the body shop will perform the work. The car will go to the sales floor where it will be shown. A customer will come in, test-drive the vehicle, fall in love with it, and buy it. The sale will be finalized and the car delivered to the new owner. Assuming that the customer is loyal and stays in the dealership's area, the car will be returned to the dealership periodically for maintenance and repair work. Over the life of the car, several different areas of the dealership will interact with that car's records, but for different purposes. The body shop, parts department, and service department will need to be able to read the record and update it as work is performed on the car, while the sales force will only need to read it. The dealership manager might be the only person allowed to modify the price of the car.

From this scenario, we can see that there are six potential actions involved with the car's record:

- Read only, with possible areas hidden
- Read and update specific areas of the record
- Read the complete record
- Create, read, and update the entire record
- Archive the record
- Delete the record from the system

Since the management of security is easier and more effective with the use of roles, let's make a determination of how many roles are really needed in this situation. Since the deletion of the record will occur only once in the life of the car, a role to include this action is not necessary.

Now, what do we mean by "archive the record"? We mean that the car record is saved somewhere before the record is deleted from the system. (Note that "archiving" here does not constitute normal backups performed to protect the data.) In this sense, the action of archiving the record would be performed only once.

The other four action areas would be performed many times over the life of the car, so our list of actions of interest is down to four:

- Read only, with possible areas hidden
- Read and update specific areas of the record
- Read the complete record
- Create, read, and update the complete record

Since the sales force and repair staff will perform the first action—read only with possible areas hidden—the role to create might be called the WORK_FORCE role. To prevent the work force from viewing areas of the record that are to be kept private, a view would be created and that view would be granted to the WORK_FORCE role with the SELECT privilege.

The next set of actions is reserved for the department managers to perform and includes read and update to specific areas of the record. A DEPARTMENT_MANAGER role and views could be created and the SELECT and UPDATE privileges granted to the role DEPARTMENT_MANAGER.

Since the administrative staff would probably be the ones to enter the record and update the cost areas, an ADMIN_ASSISTANT role could be created with the SELECT, INSERT, and UPDATE privileges assigned.

Finally, a trigger could be created to ensure that specific areas of the record could not be modified except by the DEALERSHIP_MANAGER role. You could also accomplish the same thing through the use of views, grants, or triggers.

We've now identified the following:

- WORK_FORCE
- DEPARTMENT_MANAGER
- ADMIN_ASSISTANT
- DEALERSHIP_MANAGER

Without defining or formally creating any tables, we've outlined the roles and have made a start on tightening security for the application. You must strictly adhere to the naming conventions established in your organization's security policy as you define the roles. Since the security policy is a living document, these roles and the associated actions could now be placed in the appropriate area of the policy. (We'll say much more about security policies in Chapter 7.)

With a large application, as tables are defined and created, you can place them in a matrix with the identification of who will perform what actions against them. The matrix would contain the table name, envisioned actions, and role in which those actions would be permitted. Once the tables and roles have been identified and the actions established, you might want to add a column for a notation of the backup approach appropriate for the objects involved. In this way, you help ensure that backup criteria are established on an object-by-object basis. (See Chapter 12 for more information about backups.)

In the matrix, note that the heading of the first column, "Table Name/Role Name," is to be read as table names down and role names across.

For the piece of the car dealership application, a matrix might look like that in Table 5-5.

Table 5-5. Car Dealership Sample Matrix

Table Name/Role Name	dealership_ manager	department_ manager	admin_ assistant	work_ force
auto_info	S, I, U, D	S, U		
work_order	S, I, U	S, I, U	S, I, U	S, U
auto_parts	S, I, U, D	S, U		S

In this chapter:
- *Profiles*
- *Passwords*
- *Synonyms*

6

Profiles, Passwords, and Synonyms

Oracle provides many features that will help you secure your databases. Among these are the ability to create customized user profiles, the use of passwords and other forms of user account controls, and the use of object controls (i.e., views, roles, synonyms, and grants). This chapter describes profiles, passwords, and synonyms. You will find information on views, roles, and grants in earlier chapters.

There are two different forms of profiles available in an Oracle database: product profiles and system resource profiles. *Product profiles*, though the PRODUCT_PROFILE and USER_PROFILE tables, let you block access to individual Oracle products such as SQL, SQL*Plus, and PL/SQL; you can block by individual command, or you can block the entire product from access by a single user, a specific group of users, or everyone. *System resource profiles*, as the name implies, let you control the use of resources on your system. For example, through a system resource profile, you can limit the number of separate sessions a user can have at one time or the amount of CPU time which can be used on a per-session basis.

In Oracle8, passwords and password features have been enhanced substantially. The new password features include the ability to age and expire passwords, track password history, and lock accounts. Although these abilities have been around for years in many operating systems, they are new to Oracle databases and a very welcome addition to the stable of Oracle security measures. This chapter describes the new password features. It describes how to set password parameter values by creating or modifying a profile. It also discusses ways to avoid displaying a user's password in a command line when you need to perform work as a privileged user (for example, when testing an application).

This chapter also describes *synonyms*. We all use synonyms every day, but we may not even notice we're doing so. Nicknames, addresses, and telephone numbers are all synonyms that represent something else; given a telephone number or address, we may respond, "That is the number or address of XXX—a specific person, business, or place." Even an Internet address, the Uniform Resource Locator (URL), represents a physical machine's address. Synonyms are used in an Oracle database to represent other objects in the same way a telephone number, address, or URL identifies a person or physical location. The primary function of a synonym in the database is to provide location transparency—a nice buzzword to describe the fact that you don't know where the referenced object is located. For instance, by using synonyms, developers can write code that does not reference a specific schema. When the code moves into production, the objects can be placed in another schema and, as long as the synonyms point to the correct objects in the schema, the application will work as it did in development.

Profiles

As we mentioned earlier, Oracle provides two very different types of profile: product profiles and system resource profiles. The two have no relationship to each other, but both establish limits or restrictions of some kind. Product profiles limit user access to certain Oracle commands or products, while system resource profiles limit a particular user's use of certain system resources (e.g., sessions or CPU time).

When people talk about "profiles," they are usually referring to system resource profiles.

Product Profiles

With product profiles, you can block access to Oracle's SQL, SQL*Plus, and PL*SQL products. Any of the following can be blocked:

- One single command within any one of the product sets
- A group of commands within one or more of the product sets
- All of the commands within one or more of the product sets

PRODUCT_PROFILE and USER_PROFILE tables

The PRODUCT_PROFILE and USER_PROFILE tables provide the mechanism used to block commands. You create these tables by running the *PUPBLD.SQL* script while connected as user *system*. The script is used to establish tool resource limits on the Oracle tools. Product functions blocked in this table are not table-specific, they are system-wide, so you should carefully consider the impact of using this feature.

These PRODUCT_PROFILE and USER_PROFILE tables are not referenced directly by the users. The *PUPBLD.SQL* install script creates two views—PRODUCT_PRIVS on the PRODUCT_PROFILE table, and USER_PRIVS on the USER_PROFILE table. This latter view limits the records retrieved to those pertaining only to the user executing the query.

The *PUPBLD.SQL* script must be run by user *system*. If it has not been run, the tables will not exist. So when you log in with SQL*Plus, you will see a message before the "SQL>" prompt is displayed advising you that the script has not been created and telling you to run *PUPBLD.SQL* to build the table. The message appears because Oracle has attempted to verify, by looking in the PRODUCT_PROFILE table, that you are permitted to have access to the database via SQL*Plus. Since the table does not exist for Oracle to verify your access, an error message is generated but you will still be allowed to log in.

The *PUPBLD.SQL* can be found in one of several different directories, depending on your version of Oracle and your operating system. Look in the *$ORACLE_HOME/dbs* directory first. If the script is not there, check the *$ORACLE_HOME/plus80/demo* directory or, for databases prior to Oracle8, check the *$ORACLE_HOME/sqlplus/demo* directory.

Disabling SQL privileges

One of the characteristics of the SQL command processor is that it allows you to access the operating system by issuing either the HOST command or a symbolic equivalent. Depending on the operating system, the symbolic equivalent is usually $ or !. The point is that the user will be able to get to the operating system prompt. Now this is not generally a bad thing, but if there is no need for users to get to the operating system, the security requirements on the system administrator may be lessened if this access is disabled. For example, it may be that a particular application has files that must be accessible, but you don't want users to actually get to those files through the operating system. There are also users who love to save output files on disk; give these users access to the operating system and they will save everything—forever! By making the appropriate entry in the PRODUCT_PROFILE table to block usage of the HOST command (which includes the symbolic equivalents), you can prohibit access to the operating system. This won't eliminate users' ability to save files, but it will reduce it.

The SQL and SQL*Plus privileges and commands you can disable in the PRODUCT_PROFILE table are the following:

COPY
EDIT
EXECUTE
EXIT
GET
HOST (or your operating system's alias for HOST, such as $ on OpenVMS and ! on UNIX)
QUIT

PASSWORD
RUN
SAVE
SET (see the tip below)
SPOOL
START

If you disable the SQL*Plus SET command, the SQL SET ROLE and SET TRANSACTION commands will also be disabled. If you disable the SQL*Plus START command, the SQL*Plus @ and @@ commands will also be disabled.

The following SQL commands can be disabled:

ALTER
ANALYZE
AUDIT
CONNECT
CREATE
DELETE
DROP
GRANT
INSERT
LOCK
NOAUDIT
RENAME
REVOKE
SELECT
SET ROLE
SET TRANSACTION
TRUNCATE
UPDATE

The following PL/SQL commands can be disabled:

BEGIN
DECLARE
EXECUTE

If you disable the BEGIN and DECLARE commands through the PRODUCT_TABLE, the SQL*Plus EXECUTE command will not automatically be disabled. You must disable the EXECUTE command explicitly.

Using PRODUCT_PROFILE to enforce security

As we discussed in Chapter 3, *Oracle Database Objects*, roles are used in a database to enhance security. In theory, you create a role, give it privileges on tables, and set the role when running an application. The user, when logging on to the database, will have minimal privileges directly through SQL*Plus. However, a user could use the SET ROLE command from SQL*Plus to gain access to privileges normally enabled only when the application is used. The user could then issue SQL statements from SQL*Plus to change database tables in a way detrimental to the security of the system. You could disable the SET ROLE privilege for specific users to prevent this. But remember, this is a system-wide effect.

As indicated in the command list, the PRODUCT_PROFILE table can be used to disable the SET ROLE command. For each user whose access you want to block, an entry is made to the table listing that user's name in the USERID column, the word ROLES in the ATTRIBUTE column, and the specific role name to which you do not want to permit access in the CHAR_VALUE column. You can disable SQL*Plus access to a role for the entire user base by entering PUBLIC or "%" (the wild card symbol) in the USERID column. However, you should only use these values for roles granted to *public*. Disabling a role for a user who has not been granted that role will have no effect on the other roles the user holds.

The columns within the PRODUCT_PROFILE table that are actually used by SQL and can be populated are:

PRODUCT
: The product name, such as SQL*Plus or SQL*ReportWriter. Be sure to observe the case of the product name (upper/lower).

USERID
: The name of the user to disable. If the wildcard (%) character or the value PUBLIC is used, then all users are blocked.

ATTRIBUTE
: The product attribute to be disabled. If the product is SQL*Plus, any of the attributes from the previous list could be specified (e.g., ALTER, HOST, or GRANT). Only one attribute may be specified for each entry, so if these three were to be disabled, three records would be required.

CHAR_VALUE
: To disable an attribute for a product, enter DISABLED. This must be in uppercase. Wildcards (%) are not allowed.

The remaining columns, SCOPE, NUMERIC_VALUE, DATE_VALUE, and LONG_VALUE, are ignored by SQL, and may be omitted when adding rows to the table.

To re-enable a privilege that has been disabled for a user, simply remove the associated entry from the PRODUCT_PROFILE table.

System Resource Profiles

The second type of Oracle profile, the system resource profile, is a set of restrictions or limits that can be placed on a database resource—for example, the amount of time a process can be idle before the process will be disconnected. Here is a sample command you might use to create a system resource profile for a particular user:

```
CREATE PROFILE my_profile LIMIT
SESSIONS_PER_USER 3
CPU_PER_CALL 3000
CONNECT_TIME 60
FAILED_LOGIN_ATTEMPTS 3
PASSWORD_LOCK_TIME 1/12
```

In this example, we are creating a profile called "my_profile". The users to whom you assign this profile will have certain restrictions. They will only be allowed to establish a maximum of three sessions at one time. They can only use 3000 hundredths of a second per database transaction, and they can remain connected to the database for no longer than 60 minutes at a time. If they attempt to log on to their database account and fail more than three times in a row, they will be locked out of their account. They will remain locked out of their account for two hours (1/12 of a day).

Once you have created the profile, you can assign it to a user when you create the user's account. Alternatively, in the case of an already-existing account, you can modify the user's account (via the ALTER command) and assign the profile. Each user can be assigned to a specific profile. Once a profile has been assigned to an account, that account cannot exceed the specified limits. A profile is named when it is created and may be used to control the usage of a variety of system resources. Table 6-1 shows the resource controls of particular interest from a security standpoint.

Table 6-1. Security-Related Profile Parameters

Parameter	Characteristics
CPU_PER_SESSION and CPU_PER_CALL	The volume of CPU time used, both for a session and for individual calls such as parse, execute, and fetch. Both types of CPU limits are expressed in hundredths of a second.
CONNECT_TIME	The amount of total elapsed connection time an account may use, in minutes.
FAILED_LOGIN_ATTEMPTS	The number of failed login attempts before an account is locked.

Table 6-1. Security-Related Profile Parameters (continued)

Parameter	Characteristics
IDLE_TIME	The amount of allowable idle time before a process is disconnected. This value is expressed in minutes. Long-running queries and other operations are not subject to this limit since they are not actually viewed as idle.
PASSWORD_GRACE_TIME	The number of days after the grace period has begun during which a warning will be given that the password is going to expire.
PASSWORD_LIFE_TIME	The number of days the same password may be used before connections will be rejected.
PASSWORD_LOCK_TIME	The number of days an account will be locked after the specified number of failed login attempts.
PASSWORD_REUSE_MAX	An integer value for the number of password changes before a password can be reused. If you set PASSWORD_REUSE_MAX to a value, PASSWORD_REUSE_TIME must be set to "UNLIMITED."
PASSWORD_REUSE_TIME	The number of days before a password can be reused.
PASSWORD_VERIFY_FUNCTION	The complexity of a password; you must specify the name of a script to be called.
SESSIONS_PER_USER	The maximum number of allowable concurrent sessions on a per-user basis.

These password parameters are discussed in more detail later in this chapter.

There are several other possible resource control parameters that can be set for a user profile. Although these do not have as important an impact on security, they are listed in Table 6-2 for completeness.

Table 6-2. Remaining Profile Parameters

Parameter	Characteristics
COMPOSITE_LIMIT	Limits the total resources cost for a session in "service units" calculated by Oracle as a weighted sum of CPU_PER_SESSION + CONNECT_TIME + LOGICAL_READS_PER_SESSION + PRIVATE_SGA.
LOGICAL_READS_PER_CALL	An integer value (in blocks) of the number of data blocks read for a call to process a SQL statement (parse, execute, or fetch).
LOGICAL_READS_PER_SESSION	An integer value (in blocks) of the number of data blocks that can be read from memory and disk in a session.

Table 6-2. Remaining Profile Parameters (continued)

Parameter	Characteristics
PRIVATE_SGA	If you are using the multi-threaded server, this is used to limit the amount of private space a session can allocate in the shared pool in integer bytes. (You can express the value in "K" or "M" for kilobytes or megabytes.)
UNLIMITED	Allows a user unlimited resources on a database.
DEFAULT	Assigns the limits set in the DEFAULT profile to the specified user.

To create a profile, you must have the CREATE PROFILE system privilege granted to your account.

Where a parameter is specified in "number of days," you may use a fraction of a day expressed in the form x/y. For example, to specify one hour, you would use the form 1/24. Likewise, a minute would be expressed as 1/1440, and a second as 1/86400 of a day.

In the case of CPU session restrictions, if a user exceeds the limit set for CONNECT_TIME or IDLE_TIME, Oracle rolls back the current transaction and ends the session. However, the user does not realize the session has been ended because no notification is given until she issues a call. When the next call is issued from the affected session, Oracle will return an error message.

For other resource limits which are exceeded, Oracle aborts the operation, rolls back the current statement, and immediately returns an error message. At the point that an error message is received, the user has the choice of committing or rolling back the current transaction. Under these circumstances, after the user has issued either a COMMIT or a ROLLBACK statement, she must end the session.

If a single call has resource limits placed on it and the user attempts to exceed those limits, Oracle aborts the operation, rolls back the current statement, and returns an error message. In this case, the current transaction is left intact.

In order to enable the ability to set resource limits for a user, you must set the parameter RESOURCE_LIMIT equal to TRUE. You can do this either:

- By editing the *INIT.ORA* parameter file for the specific database in which you want to activate resource limits; you must set the parameter RESOURCE_LIMIT = TRUE.
- By issuing the following dynamic SQL statement:

```
ALTER SYSTEM SET RESOURCE_LIMIT = TRUE;
```

If you modify the *INIT.ORA* file, in order to have the change take effect you must shut down and restart the database. If you dynamically ALTER SYSTEM to set the RESOURCE_LIMIT to "TRUE," the change occurs immediately.

The DEFAULT profile

Oracle supplies a default profile, which is automatically imposed on each user who does not have a customized profile defined. You can display the default profile by examining the DBA_PROFILES view; Chapter 4 introduces this view and describes its columns. For an Oracle version 7.3 database, DBA_PROFILES looks like this:

```
SQL> SET PAGES 999
SQL> COLUMN profile format a9
SQL> COLUMN limit format a10
SQL> SELECT *
  2    FROM dba_profiles;

PROFILE   RESOURCE_NAME                    LIMIT
--------- -------------------------------- ----------
DEFAULT   COMPOSITE_LIMIT                  UNLIMITED
DEFAULT   SESSIONS_PER_USER                UNLIMITED
DEFAULT   CPU_PER_SESSION                  UNLIMITED
DEFAULT   CPU_PER_CALL                     UNLIMITED
DEFAULT   LOGICAL_READS_PER_SESSION        UNLIMITED
DEFAULT   LOGICAL_READS_PER_CALL           UNLIMITED
DEFAULT   IDLE_TIME                        UNLIMITED
DEFAULT   CONNECT_TIME                     UNLIMITED
DEFAULT   PRIVATE_SGA                      UNLIMITED

9 rows selected.
```

Note the absence of any password parameters in the default profile for version 7.3. Password parameters are not available until Oracle8.

The default profile for an Oracle version 8.0 database looks like this (Oracle8 additional parameters are emphasized in **bold**):

```
SQL> COLUMN profile format a9
SQL> COLUMN limit format a9
SQL> SELECT *
  2    FROM dba_profiles;

PROFILE   RESOURCE_NAME                    RESOURCE LIMIT
--------- -------------------------------- -------- ---------
DEFAULT   COMPOSITE_LIMIT                  KERNEL   UNLIMITED
DEFAULT   SESSIONS_PER_USER                KERNEL   UNLIMITED
DEFAULT   CPU_PER_SESSION                  KERNEL   UNLIMITED
```

```
DEFAULT   CPU_PER_CALL                     KERNEL   UNLIMITED
DEFAULT   LOGICAL_READS_PER_SESSION        KERNEL   UNLIMITED
DEFAULT   LOGICAL_READS_PER_CALL           KERNEL   UNLIMITED
DEFAULT   IDLE_TIME                        KERNEL   UNLIMITED
DEFAULT   CONNECT_TIME                     KERNEL   UNLIMITED
DEFAULT   PRIVATE_SGA                      KERNEL   UNLIMITED
DEFAULT   FAILED_LOGIN_ATTEMPTS            PASSWORD UNLIMITED
DEFAULT   PASSWORD_LIFE_TIME               PASSWORD UNLIMITED
DEFAULT   PASSWORD_REUSE_TIME              PASSWORD UNLIMITED
DEFAULT   PASSWORD_REUSE_MAX               PASSWORD UNLIMITED
DEFAULT   PASSWORD_VERIFY_FUNCTION         PASSWORD UNLIMITED
DEFAULT   PASSWORD_LOCK_TIME               PASSWORD UNLIMITED
DEFAULT   PASSWORD_GRACE_TIME              PASSWORD UNLIMITED

16 rows selected.
```

Imposing limits on a user

To impose resource limits on a specific user, you must create a profile in which you define the resource restrictions and then assign the profile to the user. For any parameters not defined in the customized profile, the values present in the DEFAULT profile will be used. If you want to be complete and explicitly define all of the parameters within your customized profile, you can specify the DEFAULT keyword to request the DEFAULT profile values.

Consider the following example of creating a user profile:

```
svrmgr> CREATE PROFILE std_user LIMIT
        SESSIONS_PER_USER            3
        CPU_PER_SESSION              UNLIMITED
        IDLE_TIME                    30
        FAILED_LOGIN_ATTEMPTS        5
        LOGICAL_READS_PER_SESSION    DEFAULT
        PASSWORD_LOCK_TIME           1/24
        PASSWORD_LIFE_TIME           90
        PASSWORD_REUSE_TIME          60
        PASSWORD_VERIFY_FUNCTION     my_password_funct
        PASSWORD_GRACE_TIME          15;
```

In this example, any user who is assigned "std_user" may not have more than three concurrent sessions. The CPU time is not limited, but each session cannot be idle for more than 30 minutes without being disconnected. The LOGICAL_READS_PER_SESSION will default to the value defined in the DEFAULT profile. After five unsuccessful attempts at logging in, the account will be locked. After one hour (1/24 day), the account will be unlocked automatically if it has been locked by failed attempts. The password will expire after 90 days, and there will be a 15-day grace period starting from the time at which the account is accessed after the 89th day. The same password cannot be used again within 60 days. The password complexity is established through the DBA-created function "my_password_funct," which we'll discuss later in this chapter.

In the following example, we see how the profile created in the last example is assigned to the user *mary*:

```
SVRMGR> CREATE USER          mary
        IDENTIFIED BY        abc75!d
        DEFAULT TABLESPACE   users
        TEMPORARY TABLESPACE temp
        PASSWORD             expire
        PROFILE              std_user
```

In this example, the user *mary* is created with a default password in keeping with the requirements to make the password at least four characters long with at least one numeric and one punctuation character. The password is set to pre-expire, and the password profile created in the previous example will be in effect for the user *mary*.

In the next section, we'll examine in much more detail the new password parameters used to control password management in an Oracle8 database.

Passwords

For years, many operating systems have supported the ability to define password composition, complexity, aging, expiration, history, and account locking. With past releases, Oracle has lagged behind. But with the advent of Oracle8, these features have now become available in an Oracle database. All the password functions mentioned here are defined using the CREATE PROFILE statement, as shown in the previous section. To enable password management in your Oracle system, the *UTLPWDMG.SQL* script must be run as *sys* from the *sysmgr* account. This script can be found in:

- The *$ORACLE_HOME/rdbms/admin* directory on a UNIX system
- The *$ORACLE_HOME/rdbms/admin* directory on a Windows NT system
- The *$ORACLE_HOME:[rdbms]* directory on an OpenVMS system

First, let's examine what each of these features lets the DBA accomplish.

Password Composition and Complexity

Oracle's password composition and complexity features enable the DBA to describe how a password must look (its physical composition). Oracle's new complexity verification mechanism checks each password to ensure that it is complex enough to provide reasonable protection from someone who might be trying to guess a password to break into the database. Since the complexity verification is provided by Oracle through a PL/SQL function, you can add even more complexity to the default mechanism by writing your own function. The function must be owned by *sys* in order to perform properly.

Basic rules

The basic rules enforced by the default PL/SQL function include a minimum length for the password and the requirement that one or more alphabetic, numeric, and punctuation marks must appear within the password. The default rules are that the password must:

- Contain a minimum of four characters
- Not be the same length as the userid
- Contain at least one alphabetic character, one numeric character, and one punctuation mark
- Differ from the previous password defined for this user by at least three characters

The first three rules are pretty easy to understand. The intent of the fourth rule is to try to keep you from changing your password by just one character at a time. For example, if you have used the password *my_1pass* previously, this rule would prevent you from changing your password to *my_2pass*. These two passwords do not differ by at least three characters.

A few passwords that would fulfill the complexity rules are:

du4_ck
qxrb21#
ruok4me?

As with system passwords, you should not use words or names that have a known meaning to you, like your birthday or your child's or pet's name.*

Writing your own function

If you decide to write your own function because you want to impose additional password complexity, you must use the format:

```
routine_name(
    userid_parameter IN VARCHAR(30),
    password_parameter IN VARCHAR(30),
    old_password_parameter IN VARCHAR(30))
    RETURN BOOLEAN
```

* Chapter 3 of *Practical UNIX & Internet Security*, by Simson Garfinkel and Gene Spafford, lists some excellent rules for choosing passwords.

Once you've created the function, you must assign the routine using either the user's profile or the system default profile by specifying the following CREATE PROFILE or ALTER PROFILE statement:

```
CREATE/ALTER PROFILE profile_name LIMIT (first line of statement)
PASSWORD_VERIFY_FUNCTION routine_name (parameter that names the routine)
```

The complexity function can be defined for a specific user or group through the CREATE PROFILE statement. Here are some suggestions you may want to keep in mind when creating your own complexity function:

- If the password verification routine raises an exception, an appropriate error message must be returned
- The routine is owned by *sys* and functions in system context
- If the routine becomes invalid, an appropriate error message must be returned

Password Aging and Expiration

Most operating systems have a mechanism to define how long a password can be used on the system before it expires. Oracle has not had this feature until Oracle8. The password lifetime can be set on either a group or an individual basis. By default, when password aging is enabled and the end of the life cycle for the password is reached, Oracle provides a grace period in which the user will be notified that the password must be changed. If the password is not changed during the grace period, the account will be locked and no logins will be permitted to the account until a DBA intercedes.

The DBA can explicitly set when passwords will be expired via the PASSWORD_LIFE_TIME parameter, and the grace period with the PASSWORD_GRACE_TIME parameter. This feature is useful both when the DBA wants every account to change passwords (for example, if a system break-in has occurred) and when a new account is created (so the user will be forced to change the password to something only that user knows).

With the advent of password expiration comes the necessity to provide users with a mechanism through which they can easily change their passwords. You may need to write a small, simple, possibly web-based application to perform this action. The utility could be as simple as an SQL script that:

- Prompts the user for the current password
- Prompts for a new password
- Prompts for a verification of the new password
- Performs a comparison of the new password and the verification presented

- Connects to the database
- Issues the command:

```
ALTER USER <username> IDENTIFIED BY <new_password>;
```

Note the use of ALTER USER instead of the older style:

```
GRANT <a_privilege> TO <username> IDENTIFIED BY <new_password>;
```

The DBA should make an effort to ensure that the ALTER USER command syntax is used since Oracle is moving away from supporting the "GRANT ... IDENTIFIED BY..." format.

If the users have access to the database via SQL*Plus, they can use the built-in *password* utility to change their passwords. That utility prompts for the old password, then the new one, and the new one again to verify it. We will discuss this utility later in this chapter.

Because there are so many approaches to enabling a user to change passwords, we won't provide a specific example here.

The Password Life Cycle

Let's look at the password life cycle (i.e., the length of time that a particular password remains valid) in a little more detail. Let us assume that the password life cycle has been set to 90 days (PASSWORD_LIFE_TIME 90) and the grace period has been set to 15 days (PASSWORD_GRACE_TIME 15). When the user logs in any time after the password reaches day 89, the expiration warning message will appear and the user will be notified of the 15-day grace period. If the user does not change passwords within the 15-day grace period, the account will be locked.

Oracle provides for a password history through the use of the parameters PASSWORD_REUSE_TIME and PASSWORD_REUSE_MAX. These parameters work together and define how long a period of time must elapse before a password can be reused (if ever). Some users like their passwords so much that they keep returning to them—this represents a security risk. PASSWORD_REUSE_TIME defines the number of days before a password can be reused, while PASSWORD_REUSE_MAX defines the maximum number of password changes before the password is allowed to be used again.

When one of the parameters (either PASSWORD_REUSE_TIME or PASSWORD_REUSE_MAX) is set to a value, the other parameter must be set to UNLIMITED.

You can specify an integer value for either PASSWORD_REUSE_TIME or PASSWORD_REUSE_MAX, but not both.

Both parameters can be set to UNLIMITED.

Account Locking

Until Oracle8, the only way to "lock" an account on an Oracle system was to revoke the role that had the CREATE SESSION privilege from the user or just revoke the CREATE SESSION privilege individually. In most cases, the role that was revoked was the CONNECT role. With Oracle8, the account can now be locked through several different approaches. The server will automatically lock an account:

- After a specific number of failed attempts have been made to access that account (set by the FAILED_LOGIN_ATTEMPTS parameter).
- When a password has expired and has not been reset during the allowed grace period or explicitly reset by the DBA (or, if your company has created the position, by the security manager). The account can be set to unlock after a specified period of time or by the DBA or security manager (PASSWORD_LOCK_TIME).

The number of attempts allowed before an account is locked can be set on a group or individual. When a user successfully logs in, the number of failed attempts is automatically reset to zero. Likewise, if an account is re-enabled after a period of time, the failed attempts will be reset to zero.

If a DBA or security manager locks an account, the account will not unlock automatically after a specified period of time.

If a user fails to log in successfully and is locked out, however, the account will be unlocked after the PASSWORD_LOCK_TIME has been reached.

If PASSWORD_LOCK_TIME is set to UNLIMITED, the account will never automatically unlock.

Even if resource limitations are disabled through RESOURCE_LIMIT or through the ALTER SYSTEM command, the behavior of the password manager features is still enforced. In other words, if you have activated the password facility by running the *UTLPWDMG.SQL* script, there is no "undo" script you can run, and when you set the profile variables back to DEFAULT, the default password values will become available again.

If you decide that you no longer want password features to be enabled, there is *no easy way to disable* these features once they have been enabled.

Password Enhancements in the Data Dictionary Views

The following columns have been added to the USER_USERS and DBA_USERS views in Oracle8 to support password features (see the description of these views in Chapter 4):

ACCOUNT_STATUS
: Tells whether the account is locked, expired, or open

GRACE_DATE
: Tells when the password will expire (the sum of the date when the password was changed and the password resource parameter, PASSWORD_LIFE_TIME)

LOCK_DATE
: Tells when the account was locked

EXPIRE_DATE
: Tells when the account will expire

The following new columns have been added to the DBA_PROFILES view in Oracle8:

RESOURCE_TYPE
: Is set to either KERNEL or PASSWORD

USER_PASSWORD_LIMITS
: Contains the column RESOURCE_NAME (the name of the password resource) and LIMIT (either a limit set by the DBA or the DEFAULT value)

Passwords and Data Encryption

When a user is created in the database, a password is assigned by the person creating the account—usually within the CREATE USER script. In this way, Oracle can verify that the user should be allowed access to the database. Oracle automatically encrypts the password and stores it in the data dictionary in a 16-character encrypted format so it's not easily readable by anyone examining the data dictionary views. In the same way, the user proves, by using the correct password, that access should be allowed.

When client/server networking is being used, Oracle also enables the encryption of passwords when connecting to a database over the network. If this feature is enabled through the use of the Advanced Networking Option (ANO), Oracle uses a modified Data Encryption Standard (DES) algorithm to encrypt the password before it is sent over the network.

Oracle8 also provides the ability to encrypt actual data and to produce checksums. Use of network data encryption and checksums ensures that the data cannot be read by intruders while it is in transit to the database. As with password encryption, DES is used to encrypt the data, but the RSA Data Security RC4 standard is used as well. Using the Advanced Networking Option available in Oracle8, a cryptographically secure message digest can be included in the header of each packet to ensure that data has not been intercepted, deleted, read, or in any way tampered with.

We'll describe DES, the RSA algorithms, cryptography, and data encryption more extensively in Chapter 15, *Using the Oracle Security Server*. In Chapter 17, *Using Extra-Cost Options*, we'll provide an overview of the Advanced Networking Option as well as Trusted Oracle and the Oracle Application Server.

Password Scripts and Commands

Have you ever wondered how the Oracle *import* utility accesses accounts to build the account's objects without ever knowing what the user's password really is? That utility uses an undocumented keyword, VALUES, to enable the use of the encrypted form of a password without ever knowing the unencrypted password. This section describes this facility, as well as the PASSWORD command available from SQL*Plus in Oracle8.

Swapping passwords

There are several situations in which you might want to be able to use an Oracle database account without knowing the user's actual password. In these cases, you want to be able to change a user's password temporarily and then change it back to its original value. For example, you might want to:

- Use a specific account to test something
- Run an application as a very privileged user without having the user's true password displayed in the operating system command (as a UNIX system would)
- Avoid the need to hard-code a *real* password in an operating system command file

How can you "swap" out the user's real password without knowing it and then, after you are finished using the account, replace the password you set with the user's original password? From a DBA account, you can take the following steps to use an account whose password you do not know (Oracle7 or higher).

1. Generate a SQL-generating SQL script by querying the DBA_USERS table to obtain the user's current encrypted password.
2. Alter the user's password to a value you know.
3. Perform the work you need to do.
4. Run the SQL script you created in Step 1 to replace the user's original password.

The section of script you can use to capture the encrypted password would look like the following:

```
SET TERMOUT OFF PAGESIZE 0 FEEDBACK OFF VERIFY OFF ECHO OFF
SPOOL redo.sql
SELECT 'ALTER USER &&1 IDENTIFIED BY VALUES '||''''||password||''''||';'
  FROM dba_users
 WHERE username = UPPER('&&1')
PROMPT '$<place your operating system command to delete the file here>'
PROMPT '$ EXIT'
 SPOOL OFF
```

In the first PROMPT line, place your specific operating system command to delete the *REDO.SQL* file. For example, on an OpenVMS system, the PROMPT line would look like the following:

```
PROMPT '$ DELETE/NOLOG/NOCONFIRM redo.sql;'
```

On a UNIX system, the command might look like the following:

```
PROMPT 'host rm -f redo.sql'
```

The output from the script, using the OpenVMS DELETE command, would look like the following:

```
ALTER USER mary IDENTIFIED BY VALUES '91B4B1F913D22B19';
$ DELETE/NOLOG/NOCONFIRM redo.sql;
$ EXIT
```

You then issue the following commands to modify the user account and connect to the modified account:

```
ALTER USER mary IDENTIFIED by abc75!d;
CONNECT mary/abc75!d
```

After performing the necessary work, simply reconnect to the system account and run the *REDO.SQL* script to reset the *mary* account to its original password.

This approach is very valuable to any DBA who has to perform work from a *cron* job as the *sys* user. The UNIX operating system has a command that will display the entire command line. If the username and password are used on the command line, they can be seen by other users. Using this approach will let you access the *sys* account with a benign password that will not compromise security if it is seen.

If you have enabled the password history feature on your Oracle8 database, this approach can be used only if you modify the user's profile values before you begin your work. If you do not modify the parameter PASSWORD_REUSE_TIME, you violate the restriction on the amount of time that must pass or the number of passwords that must be used before the current password can be reused.

The Oracle8 PASSWORD command

Beginning in Oracle8, there is a new SQL*Plus command, PASSWORD, which you can use to change your password. If you have DBA privileges on a database, you can also use this command from SQL*Plus to change another user's password. For security reasons, this utility echoes all password characters you type in as asterisks (*). In the example presented here, the PASSWORD command is used by *mary* to change her own password from one value to another. The transaction looks like the following:

```
SQL> PASSWORD
/* Changing password for mary */
Old password: *******
New password: *******
Retype new password: *******
Password changed
```

Before Oracle8, if you, working as the DBA, wanted to change a user's password, the ALTER command had to be used, as shown here:

```
ALTER USER <username> IDENTIFIED BY <new password>;
```

In Oracle8, you can now use the PASSWORD command to change a user's password by typing PASSWORD followed by the username as follows:

```
SQL> PASSWORD mary
Changing password for mary
New password: *******
Retype new password: *******
Password changed
```

When changing another user's password, you are not prompted for the user's old password. Users can take advantage of the PASSWORD command from SQL*Plus without having to know the syntax of the ALTER USER command.

Synonyms

This section looks at how and why we use synonyms in a database for security. As we said in Chapter 3, a synonym is really a nickname for something else. In an Oracle database, a synonym can represent one of several kinds of objects—a table, view, sequence, snapshot, program, procedure, function, or even another synonym. For our discussion, we will use a table as our reference object.

Normally, if you want to access an object, you have to know the owner of the object and the object name. If you want to look at something in the employee table owned by *mary*, you would say:

```
SELECT *
  FROM mary.employee;
```

The "mary.employee" reference is called a *fully qualified path name*. Because you have supplied all the information Oracle needs to locate the object, after verifying the statement's syntax for correctness and checking to see that you have privilege to access the mary.employee table, your query will be processed and the results returned to you.

Suppose, though, that you do not know the owner's name and you issue the following query:

```
SELECT *
  FROM employee;
```

Since you did not include the owner or schema name, the RDBMS will assume that you have a table called employee and will first look in your own object area and your list of private synonyms for the table. If Oracle does not find the table within your own area, it will look at publicly available objects and public synonyms that have been defined to include the location name (i.e., a synonym). If Oracle does not find an employee table reference in any of these areas, you will get an error message such as the following:

```
ORA-00942:  table or view does not exist
```

This is probably the most frequently encountered error message.

The solution then would seem to be to always code everything with fully qualified path names, right? Not really, since there is a problem with this approach. Such statements are usually embedded into applications, and if the owner of the table changes, all the applications have to be modified and recompiled.

So far, we've been talking about object ownership, but it is equally possible that the table name may be changed, and again the applications would have to be changed. It has never been a great idea to hardcode path names into applications. Oracle solved this problem by providing the ability to create a synonym that contains the object's location within its definition. All you have to do is use the synonym in your application and Oracle will resolve the object's true location.

About Public and Private Synonyms

There are two types of synonyms: public and private. A *private synonym* is owned by a specific user and is available for use only by that user, even if he or she issues privileges to other users. A *public synonym* is owned by a special user named *public* (which is really a role). Even though a public synonym exists for an object, you may not be able to see that object unless you have the SELECT privilege on that object. Figure 6-1 shows the contrast between private and public synonyms.

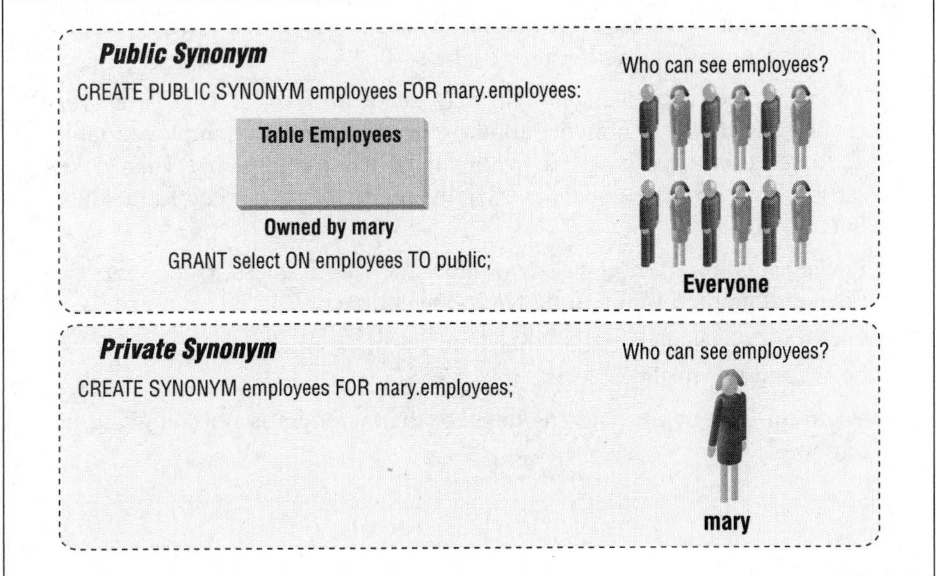

Figure 6-1. Public vs. private synonyms

Private synonyms are not unusual. They are frequently used by developers as a way to test stored programs, functions, snapshots, etc., without interfering with other developers. However, public synonyms are used more frequently in production systems. Only a user who has been granted the CREATE PUBLIC SYNONYM privilege can create a public synonym.

Assuming that *mary* has the appropriate privileges, the following command could be issued:

```
SQL> CREATE PUBLIC SYNONYM employee
  2*     FOR mary.employee;
```

The result is that the synonym "employee" will be found as an entry in the public list of objects. When found, it will be used as the target object. If permissions have been granted on it to the user, the system will navigate to the location of *mary*'s employee table.

Tips for Creating Synonyms

When you are using synonyms, note the following:

- Creating the public synonym or, for that matter, any synonym, does not convey any default ability to see the underlying object. There are no default privileges associated with a synonym.
- Any user with the CREATE PUBLIC SYNONYM privilege may create a public synonym on another user's tables.
- An instance of a public synonym may occur only once. That is, if *mary* creates the public synonym "admin_emp" for the mary.employee table, no other user may create a synonym of the same name. This makes sense because *public* covers everybody and there is no need for a subsequent definition.
- Privileges granted on a synonym allow the same access to the object as privileges granted to the underlying object directly.
- There are no checks made when you create a synonym. Synonyms can be created for invalid objects.
- When an underlying object is deleted, the synonym is not automatically removed.

Examples Using Public and Private Synonyms

In this section, you will find several practical examples of how public and private synonyms work.

Example 6-1: Hiding the tables and owner

This example demonstrates the ability to "hide" the underlying tables and owner from a user. The steps used to demonstrate this follow:

1. *mary* creates a table and a public synonym.
2. *mary* grants the SELECT privilege to *public* on the public synonym.
3. *ralph* examines the table through the synonym name.
4. *ralph* attempts to see the underlying object and owner but fails.
5. *ralph* can only see the underlying object if he knows the object name and the owner name.

A user whose name is *mary* creates a table with two columns:

```
SQL> CREATE TABLE employee
  2  (ssan       NUMBER(9),
  3   name       VARCHAR2(35));
Table created.
```

mary now creates a public synonym. The privilege to do so was previously granted.

```
SQL> CREATE PUBLIC SYNONYM empl
  2      FOR mary.employee;
Synonym created.
```

SELECT is granted to *public*, making the table accessible to all database users.

```
SQL> GRANT select ON empl TO public;
Grant succeeded.
```

Connect as a different user. Note that logout is not required.

```
SQL> CONNECT ralph/xyz_4u
Connected.
```

ralph describes the synonym and gets the structure of the real object: mary.employee.

```
SQL> DESCRIBE empl
 Name                            Null?    Type
 ------------------------------- -------- ----
 SSAN                                     NUMBER(9)
 NAME                                     VARCHAR2(35)
```

ralph attempts to describe the underlying object, but does *not* fully qualify the object. The system attempts to find the employee object, but as owned by *ralph*, not *mary*. An error message results since *ralph* does not own an employee table.

```
SQL> DESCRIBE employee
Object does not exist.
```

ralph now describes the object using the fully qualified name that includes the object's owner.

```
SQL> DESCRIBE mary.employee
 Name                            Null?    Type
 ------------------------------- -------- ----
 SSAN                                     NUMBER(9)
 NAME                                     VARCHAR2(35)
```

Example 6-2: Using private synonyms and path names

This example shows that, even though privilege is granted to everyone on a private synonym, no one will be able to see the object unless they use a fully qualified name. In the example, the following steps will be performed.

1. The original user, *mary*, creates a private synonym.
2. *mary* grants the SELECT privilege on the private synonym to *public.*
3. When another user attempts to use the private synonym, an error is returned. The user must use the fully qualified name as for the table in the first example.

Connect as *mary.*

```
SQL> CONNECT mary/abc75!d
Connected.
```

Create a private synonym for the employee table.

```
SQL> CREATE SYNONYM people
  2     FOR mary.employee;
Synonym created.
```

Grant SELECT on the private synonym to *public.*

```
SQL> GRANT select ON people TO public;
Grant succeeded.
```

Connect as another user and attempt to access the public synonym.

```
SQL> CONNECT ralph/xyz_4u
Connected.
SQL> DESCRIBE people
Object does not exist.
```

Now fully qualify the object with owner and name, as in the following.

```
SQL> DESCRIBE mary.people
 Name                            Null?    Type
 ------------------------------- -------- ----
 SSAN                                     NUMBER(9)
 NAME                                     VARCHAR2(35)
```

Example 6-3: Using public synonyms without user grants

This example demonstrates that if access is not given for a public synonym, a user will not be able to see that object.

1. *mary* will REVOKE SELECT on the private synonym (*people*) and then DROP the synonym.
2. *mary* will CREATE a new public synonym called *people.*
3. *mary* will not give any public access for the synonym.
4. *ralph* will try to "see" the synonym and will not be able to do so.

Connect as *mary* and fix the problem.

```
SQL> CONNECT mary/abc75!d
Connected.
```

```
SQL> REVOKE select ON people FROM public;
Revoke succeeded.
SQL> DROP SYNONYM people;
Synonym dropped.
SQL> CREATE PUBLIC SYNONYM people FOR mary.employee;
Synonym created.
```

Connect as *ralph* and attempt to use the public synonym "people."

```
SQL> CONNECT ralph/xyz_4u
Connected.
```

Just try "people" first.

```
SQL> DESCRIBE people
Object does not exist.
```

Now fully qualify the object. The following illustrates a public synonym without access privileges.

```
SQL> DESCRIBE mary.people
Object does not exist.
SQL> SELECT owner, object_name, object_type
  2    FROM all_objects
  3   WHERE object_name like 'PEO%';
OWNER                  OBJECT_NAME                    OBJECT_TYPE
---------------------- ------------------------------ ------------
PUBLIC                 PEOPLE                         SYNONYM
```

Example 6-4: Using no synonyms/user grants and private synonyms with no grants

This final example demonstrates that even though public synonyms exist for objects, the objects cannot be accessed unless privilege to do so is granted to the user. The steps used in this example are as follows:

1. *mary* drops the public synonym. (Remember that no access was granted to either the base table employee or the synonym "people.")
2. The SELECT privilege is then given on the employee table to *ralph*, but no public synonym is created.
3. When *ralph* attempts to access the employee table, he must use the fully qualified path.
4. *ralph* then creates a private synonym for the employee table.
5. Finally, a completely new user attempts to use both the mary.employee table, and the ralph.people synonym. Both efforts will be resoundingly unsuccessful.

Connect as user *mary*.

```
SQL> CONNECT mary/abc75!d
Connected.
```

Drop the public synonym.

```
SQL> DROP PUBLIC SYNONYM people;
Synonym dropped.
```

Grant SELECT on the employee table to *ralph* only:

```
SQL> GRANT select ON employee TO ralph;
Grant succeeded.
```

Connect as *ralph* and access the employee table.

```
SQL> CONNECT ralph/xyz_4u
Connected.
SQL> DESCRIBE employee
Object does not exist.
```

Try the fully qualified name.

```
SQL> DESCRIBE mary.employee
 Name                            Null?    Type
 ------------------------------- -------- ----
 SSAN                                     NUMBER(9)
 NAME                                     VARCHAR2(35)
```

Create a private synonym for *mary*'s employee table.

```
SQL> CREATE SYNONYM people FOR mary.employee;
Synonym created.
```

Describe the "people" table.

```
SQL> DESCRIBE people
 Name                            Null?    Type
 ------------------------------- -------- ----
 SSAN                                     NUMBER(9)
 NAME                                     VARCHAR2(35)
```

Connect as user *scott.*

```
SQL> CONNECT scott/tiger
Connected.
```

Try to use the *mary* employee table.

```
SQL> DESCRIBE employee
Object does not exist.
SQL> DESCRIBE mary.employee
Object does not exist.
```

Try to use the *ralph* private synonym "people."

```
SQL> DESCRIBE people
Object does not exist.
SQL> DESCRIBE ralph.people
Object does not exist.
```

See if the data dictionary has any information on either object. In the following, access is granted but no synonym exists:

```
SQL> SELECT owner, object_name, object_type
  2    FROM all_objects
  3   WHERE object_name IN ('EMPLOYEE','PEOPLE');
no rows selected
```

A public synonym can be used to provide access to an object while hiding the owner or schema location of that object. This is referred to as *location transparency*. However, a synonym does not prevent a user with privileges from accessing the object directly. Also, as illustrated in Example 6-3, a public synonym is always listed in the ALL_OBJECTS data dictionary view, and that view is available to every user in the database. Note that until access was granted, the synonym was as unavailable as the table.

II

Implementing Security

This part of the book describes the specific steps we recommend to make your Oracle system and database more secure. It explains the development of a security plan and an audit plan for your site. It presents a number of sample applications you might want to adapt for your own organization's use—a basic database security system, an audit application, and a user account maintenance application. It discusses specific strategies for starting up Oracle and backing up and restoring databases in the most secure manner. It also describes the use of the Oracle Enterprise Manager, a standard Oracle product you can use to simplify many security operations.

In this chapter:

- *About the Security Policy and Security Plan*
- *Types of Accounts*
- *Standards for Accounts*
- *Standards for Usernames*
- *Standards for Passwords*
- *Standards for Roles*
- *Standards for Views*
- *Standards for the Oracle Security Server*
- *Standards for Employees*
- *Sample Security Plan Index*
- *Sample Security Plan Checklist*

7

Developing a Database Security Plan

There are many steps to securing your system and its data. But one of the first—and one that too few organizations take—is the development of a security policy that outlines and maps out the enforcement of a security plan. We've included this chapter as the first one in the "Implementing Security" part of this book because we believe that the creation of security policies and the implementation of a security plan must precede the more operational steps of securing your system and database.

What's the difference between a security plan and a security policy? A *security policy* identifies the rules that will be followed to maintain security in a system, while a *security plan* details how those rules will be implemented. A security policy is generally included within a security plan. A security plan might be as simple as a verbal statement from the highest-level management that all accounts on a system must be protected by the use of a password. Or a security plan might be a thick document spelling out in great detail exactly how security will be implemented within the company's systems. Just as there are many individual needs and many different approaches to security, there are many types of database security policies. We'll present many aspects of these policies in this chapter; some may or may not apply to your specific organization. A checklist at the end of this chapter provides a resource you'll be able to use to evaluate which features of a security plan are important for your own particular environment. Also, bear in mind that, no matter how thorough a plan appears to be, changing environments can lead to holes in a security system. Therefore, you will need to re-examine your security plan on a regular basis to ensure its currency.

About the Security Policy and Security Plan

Why does a company need a security policy and plan? What's the point of having them? A security policy, included within a security plan, helps to ensure that everyone is in sync with the company's needs and requirements. With a firm policy in place, every employee knows what is expected—what the rules are—and how the requirements are to be implemented. The limits are clearly defined and consistent guidance is provided for everyone. Statements within a security plan can help to ensure that each employee knows the boundaries and what the penalties of overstepping those boundaries will be. For example, here are clear, concise rules employees can easily understand and follow:

- Always log off the system before going to lunch.
- Never share a password with anyone else.
- Never bring software from home to put on your machine at work.

In order to have a truly solid and meaningful policy defined, the highest level of management needs to be committed to ensuring that the security policy will be enforceable. The security policy might state:

- Any employee leaving a computer unsecured will be formally reprimanded.
- Any employee found sharing a password will be suspended for one day.
- Unlicensed software found on a personal computer will be removed and the personal computer user will be shot at sunrise. Survivors will be prosecuted.

Under certain circumstances, the requirement to have and enforce a security policy may come from an agency outside the company. In the case of banks, external agencies control and define what constitutes security for the databases within the bank. The company, however, might decide that even more rigid standards are necessary or that further definitions are required to ensure that no financial transactions become compromised and that confidentiality is maintained. The bank may implement a security plan that further defines exactly how the standards will be implemented, maintained, and audited.

Management Considerations

Once you've determined that a security plan is required for a company, a person or team of people will be needed to begin to define the policy. This chapter assumes a team of people.

Who's on the team?

Members of the team might include the person or people who will be administering the system, one or more application owners, and at least one management person who is high enough in the corporate structure to ensure that the policy—as written—will be enforceable. The system administrator may have a different perspective from the database administrator on what comprises security on a system, but the goals of both should be the same—to ensure that the system cannot be compromised. If the policy is to be in effect across divisions within a company, representatives from each division might be included to ensure "buy-in" across the entire corporate structure. The goal is to include enough people to ensure that all areas of corporate need are met, but to keep the group small enough that the team will be able to create an effective, workable policy.

Establishing overall requirements

After the team is assembled, you'll first need to identify the overall requirements of the organization in regard to system and database security. The requirements might include (but are not limited to) the following:

- A uniform approach to security across computer systems and databases
- Identification of the form and style of authorization required to initiate the creation of an account
- A determination of who will create user accounts on the operating system, within each application if necessary, and within the databases
- How those accounts will be created
- Whether a standard convention for usernames and passwords should be imposed and what it should be
- Whether password aging will be enabled and in what time frame
- A determination of access requirements on an application-by-application basis
- Identification of how users will be tracked to ensure that as an employee's job description or location changes, the access to applications remains correct
- Identification of sensitive information and an outline of steps to take for data protection
- A determination of penalties to be enforced as a result of different levels of security breaches

Operating System Security Mechanisms

In implementing a requirement for a uniform security approach across platforms, you need to take into consideration the native security mechanisms available on each platform. For example, most operating systems require each user who will be interacting with that system to have a unique username and password. Access by a user on a UNIX or OpenVMS system can be further restricted by placing users in specific groups. Group membership might enable a user to interact with specific directories on the system. The security plan could detail each of these requirements.

We don't describe the details of operating system security in this book, but see Appendix A, *References*, for references to books and other sources of information.

Identifying Key Components

We recommend that you use a spreadsheet approach to identify the components within your company that the security plan must encompass—for example:

- Each division within the corporation to be included in the policy
- Each platform within the division
- Each database housed on each platform along with its function (development, test, pre-production, or production)
- Each application supported within each database
- The "owner" of the application, or person responsible for authorization of users within the application
- Required security controls for each application, such as roles or grants required
- Username and password composition
- Type(s) of accessibility (Telnet, client server, external identification)
- What form of authorization will be accepted for that application (electronic authorization, verbal, email, hard-copy form, World Wide Web)
- Person authorized to create accounts for each application
- Forms of backup to be implemented
- Recovery procedures to be used
- Database availability
- Type of auditing required
- Who will perform the auditing
- How auditing will be performed

A possible spreadsheet might look like the one shown in Table 7-1.

Table 7-1. Sample Security Plan Spreadsheet

Component	Database A	Database B	Database C
Platform/Division	Windows NT (Div. X)	Digital UNIX (Div. Y)	OpenVMS (Div. Z)
Database/SID Name	*larry*/lar1	*curly*/cur2	*moe*/moe1
Database Function	Development/test	Production	Pre-production
Application(s)	Accounts Payable	Human Resources	Office Equipment Locations
Application Owner	H. Brown	Personnel Manager	Facilities Manager
Username	User-defined	First initial/last name	Three letters, two numbers
Password	User-defined	2 letters, 1 number, 1 punctuation mark, 3 letters (e.g., XX#(!)XXX)	Any combination of letters, numbers, and punctuation, up to 8 total
Access Type	Client Server	Log on to application and application connect to database	Telnet to platform and connect directly to database
Authorization Mode	Email	Paper form signed by head of HR	Phone call
Person to Create Account	Application DBA	HR Security Clerk	Database DBA
Auditing Type	Connections to database	Connections to database SELECT FROM salary table	None
Form(s) of Backup	Exports nightly No archivelog mode	File-level backups weekly Archivelog mode enabled Exports nightly	Exports nightly No archivelog mode
Recovery Procedure	Rebuild database and import	Recover per procedures in the System Recovery Document	Rebuild database and import
Database Availability	Mon–Fri 7:30–18:00	7 days a week, 24 hours a day	Mon–Fri 7:30–18:00
Auditor	Accounts Payable Manager	HR Security Clerk	N/A

Table 7-1. Sample Security Plan Spreadsheet (continued)

Component	Database A	Database B	Database C
Roles Required	ap_clerk ap_manager	hr_clerk hr_developer hr_manager	None
Grants Required	CREATE SESSION, SELECT FROM ap tables, INSERT/ UPDATE ON ap tables (clerk, manager) DELETE FROM ap tables (mgr only)	CREATE SESSION, SELECT on specific tables (clerk) INSERT/UPDATE specific tables (clerk) SELECT, INSERT, UPDATE, DELETE on all tables (manager) CREATE TABLEs, TRIGGERs, PROCEDUREs, etc. (developer)	CREATE SESSION, SELECT, INSERT, UPDATE, DELETE ON ANY TABLE

As you can see from this table, many different security requirements may be present in one environment.

Types of Accounts

From the earliest releases of the Oracle database, a mechanism has been provided to let users connect to the database in order to perform tasks via user accounts. There are several different types of Oracle user accounts—both operating system and database—that a company might implement:

- Although they are created with the CREATE USER command, some accounts are used to house application schemas. These accounts own objects like tables, views, indexes, triggers, procedures, etc.
- Another type of account is used by Oracle itself to enable the database engine work to be performed; these accounts are *sys* and *system*.
- In later versions of the RDBMS, an account to enable the intelligent agent to connect to each database is automatically created during database creation. This account is *dbsnmp* and carries full DBA privileges.
- Each application might need one or more accounts to enable work to be performed.
- Each user in your system may require an individual Oracle account with specific privileges to enable the user to work with an application.
- One or more accounts may be needed to enable one or more DBAs to perform database maintenance and duties.

Each account type must be considered and a decision reached on whether that account type will be used and how it will be set up and administered. In smaller organizations, there may be little need for some types of accounts discussed in this section. In very large organizations, there may be a need for more extensive divisions of database account types.

Administrator Accounts

The most obvious account type is the one used for database administration. A small company might have one person acting as system administrator, database administrator, and network administrator, while a larger company might have several people acting as administrators for specific areas. At your site, who will have access to the code area for installation and maintenance of the Oracle software? There may be one or more accounts that will need to be established for various administrative tasks as well as privilege sets—both operating system and database privileges—to perform the required tasks.

Security Manager

Who will serve as the security manager at your site? This person will be responsible for creating user accounts and monitoring user access and database security. In smaller organizations, the DBA will probably handle these tasks.

Application Manager

For each application, there will be developer accounts, application user accounts, and, possibly, application coordinator accounts. An application developer will need the ability to create objects and to code triggers, procedures, etc., while an application user might need only CREATE SESSION access. In larger companies, people are sometimes designated as "application coordinators." Their job is often to handle the administrative tasks for the specific database in which their application is housed. They may need all of the rights and privileges of a DBA—both at the operating system level and at the database level.

Network Manager

There may be a need for a network manager whose job is to administer the network products and oversee Names Servers and network configurations for Oracle databases. Will a separate person or people be needed for this task at your site? Again, in a small company, the individual DBA may be responsible for all Oracle database networking tasks.

Application Schema (User) Accounts

Oracle's mechanism for creating schemas in which application objects are stored is to actually create a form of "user" account, generally referred to as a "schema," which will probably require more privileges than a general user account. The security policy might state what specific system privileges an application account may or may not be permitted to have. In an Oracle version 8.0.3 database, there are 89 distinct system privileges available; these privileges are listed in Chapter 5, *Oracle Default Roles and User Accounts.* Few, if any, applications have a need to hold all 89 privileges. A security plan might list the privileges that are *never* to be given to any application. Almost all of the privileges that grant ANY should be carefully examined and evaluated for listing in the security plan. Here are a few very good examples of privileges that should never be granted to an application (without a really strong business case):

ALTER/CREATE/DROP ANY INDEX/PROCEDURE /TABLE /TRIGGER, etc.
BECOME USER
GRANT ANY PRIVILEGE /ROLE
EXECUTE ANY PROCEDURE
UNLIMITED TABLESPACE

General User Accounts

More and more, applications are being provided with user validation present in the application itself. In these cases, a user account is created in the application. The user connects to the application and the application connects to the database on the user's behalf. The user's privileges are determined within the application. In cases where the application provides the user access control, the security plan might simply list what those accesses are and what user type should be granted which privileges.

In applications that rely on database authentication, a careful examination of what privileges a general user should receive may need to be identified and detailed in the security plan. In both Oracle's Financials Applications and the PeopleSoft HR packages, control of user access to the database is performed through the application's own internal utilities. Regardless of whether an application's security relies on the Oracle RDBMS or the application's own code, the security plan should clearly state what type of user accounts will receive each level of privilege in the system.

Oracle's HR/Payroll product, in releases 9 and 10 of the application, allows "secure users." Oracle recommends that the "secure users" account be one created with CONNECT and RESOURCE privileges (described in Chapter 5). However, a tablespace quota is made available to these accounts. With the CONNECT and

RESOURCE roles both assigned to an account, the explicit UNLIMITED TABLESPACE privilege is given so a user with these roles can create objects in *any* tablespace—with *no* overt quota assigned. With the CONNECT role assigned to an account and without a tablespace quota being assigned, the account is unable to actually create objects.

Standards for Accounts

You need to determine the mechanism for the creation of new accounts. There are many possible mechanisms. One form of account creation that is gaining popularity is for a company to enable "restricted" access to their sites on the World Wide Web. A person who wants to access a more privileged area of a web site might be required to register with that site through electronic registration. The person is presented with a form requesting his name, company name, address, email address, and other information. He might be prompted to select a username and password. He submits the completed form and, within some space of time, receives in his email account an acknowledgment that he has registered, along with notification or verification of a username and a password for his use in accessing the site. At no time has the person seen or talked to a human being, but he has now been authorized as a user on a system.

In this example of web site access, we are not judging the procedure or security. (If we were, we might question sending a password via email.) We are merely outlining a general method of a request for an account in which the requester and the administrator have never seen or spoken with each other. Other forms of more anonymous account requests would be via telephone voice mail or electronic mail. On a more personal level, a meeting might be held between the administrator and the requester.

Possible Account Requests

The policy team or higher-level management must decide whether access to the database can be granted through an electronic request, or whether some level of management must physically sign a form acknowledging that the employee seeking entry into the system is a valid employee with a proven need to interact with a specific application area. The authorization required might even be as casual as a user picking up a telephone or walking into a designated person's office and saying, "I need access to xyz system" and receiving an account on that system. Thus, we see that account requests might be generated through a number of different venues (or a combination of several of the approaches listed here):

- Electronic requests via a web site or email
- Telephone

- Hardcopy form—with or without a signature of authorization
- Personal interaction with a verbal request
- Personal interaction with a hardcopy form

Contents of the Form

If a physical record must be made available for future auditing of the system, you need to create a form for that purpose. The security plan would include a copy of the form. A form might include the following information:

- The requester's full name
- Physical location
- Telephone number
- Employee number
- Username and initial password
- Access required
- Platform to access
- Database to access
- Type of work to be performed
- Signature of person authorized to approve the request
- Date by which the account is needed

A sample form might be as simple as the one shown in Figure 7-1.

Ways to Create an Account

There are several possible approaches to creating accounts; for example, you could develop a utility to be used by one or more people to create the accounts on one or more systems. An alternative would be for each system administrator and each database administrator to interactively create the requested accounts for their system. Some applications support registration of users within the application and then rely on a single logon to the database. Once a user has logged on to the application, the application connects to the database using a single "super user" account. In this scenario, each application administrator might be in charge of creating the user registrations within his application. The routine that could be activated through a command procedure might be quite simple. The SQL code might look like this:

```
PROMPT
PROMPT  You will be prompted for a username and password.
```

Request Form for XYZ Company Computing System Services

Your request will be processed in accordance with the standards that have been established for the Computing System Services. When your access has been established, you will be notified by the Security Manager and/or the Application Administrator.

In applying for access to the XYZ Company applications, I agree to exercise due care to protect the security and integrity of the company data.

Signature of Applicant ______________________ Date ____________

Please get the appropriate signature(s) for the application(s) below and forward the completed form to the Computing System Services Administrative office, Room 3124.

ORACLE Development

Application	Option	ADD/DELETE	Authorization
____________	Developer	____________	________________
____________	Test User	____________	________________

For Office Use Only

Date Received ________ Date Entered ____________ Userid __________

Remove User ________ Remove Project ___________ Date Closed ______

Figure 7-1. A simple user account request form

```
PROMPT
CREATE USER &&username
IDENTIFIED BY &password
DEFAULT TABLESPACE users
TEMPORARY TABLESPACE temp;
PROMPT
PROMPT You will be prompted to enter the list of privileges associated
PROMPT with this user
PROMPT
GRANT &privileges TO &&username;
EXIT;
```

This is obviously a very rudimentary routine, shown here only to convey the idea of a possible script. You will probably want a much more robust utility at your site.

Standards for Usernames

There are several different types of standards for usernames. What username standards will you enforce at your site?

Advantages and Disadvantages

Let's consider a uniform approach for usernames across systems within a company. Such an approach has several benefits:

- It is easier to administer than randomly generated usernames or usernames selected by the user.
- It ensures that the username will be the same for each operating system, each database, each application, and for email interaction.
- It can require the inclusion of specific characters or numbers within a username, so a standard makes it easier to ensure that those requirements are always met.

A possible disadvantage to having a username standard is that anyone who has been associated with the company may have enough information to be able to determine any employee's username easily.

Suggested Username Standards

In the case where a username is constructed using part or all of a person's actual name, the username is easy to remember; you only need to know what the standard is to determine what the composition of the username is or will be. An example of a standard using parts of a person's name as a username is:

- The first three letters of the person's first name
- Plus the first letter of the middle name
- Plus the first four letters of the last name
- Plus a designating number at the end to fulfill the requirement of some operating systems to include both alphabetic and numeric or special characters in a username

The name Mary Lou Janes would be translated to the username *marljane1.*

Following this standard would make all usernames a maximum of nine characters long. You could go one step further and give special significance to the number chosen. The number "1" could be used to indicate that this is the first employee to have a particular username. If more than one employee has the same first and last name, the first employee would receive the number "1," while the second employee would receive the number "2."

If more than one employee has the same first, middle, and last names, the standard would need to include exception handling. The final username for an employee named Ralph Kenmore Scott might be *ralkscot1*. A second employee named Ralph Kenneth Scott would end up with the username *ralkscot2*. A third employee whose name is Raldania Karen Scott would end up *ralkscot3*. Since this is a potential problem with username standards, we recommend including a further identification mechanism like a comment line designating which username has been assigned to which user. The publication of usernames within a company private phone book helps to distinguish who has which username.

In the case where a user's actual name is shorter than three letters for a first name or last name or where no middle name is present, the username would be shorter that the nine alphanumeric characters normally used. The standard would outline possible exceptions to be allowed. Thus, Ed Bin (no middle initial) would receive the username *edbin1*.

You might also want to consider having different standards for usernames for different types of accounts. Perhaps you could have one or more of the following types of standard formats:

- User accounts that do not own objects
- Accounts that do own objects (schema accounts)
- Accounts that belong to DBAs and/or security managers

Standards for Passwords

Many children have clubs in which a secret word is used to gain entry to the clubhouse. In my club, the password was *hobgoblin*. Since no one but our group knew the secret word, we could feel pretty confident that someone saying *hobgoblin* at our clubhouse door was a member to be allowed in. Operating systems and the Oracle database use passwords in much the same way.

Password Decisions

When you are developing your database security plan, you'll need to make a number of decisions about password use at your site:

- Whether a user will be permitted to create and change his own password
- How frequently the password will expire and how long a grace period will be allowed before the account is locked

- Whether a set standard for password composition is to be used, and what that composition will be
- Whether account lockout will be enabled, whether the account can be automatically unlocked, or whether a security manager will have to intervene to unlock a locked account
- Whether a password will be permitted to be reused, and what length of time must pass before a password can be reused
- How the user or designated account manager will actually change the password—through a created form, through a SQL script, etc.
- If users will not be permitted to change their own passwords, the mechanism by which users will be notified of password changes

The decision to enforce a specific pattern for passwords raises the question of just how secure the password will really be since anyone who knows the imposed template will know the form passwords for the system must take. A previous employee could pose a security threat because the username and password structures are known to him or her. If a template for passwords is to be used, we recommend you make the template complex enough to ensure greater difficulty in breaking the password security.

Oracle8 supports a number of new password features, described in Chapter 6. You need to consider all of the following when you set password standards:

Password aging and expiration
: To help ensure that a password will not be compromised, we suggest that passwords be changed on a system at least every three months. The decision of whether to enforce password aging and expiration should be identified in the security plan. The longer a password remains in effect for an account, the greater the possibility that the password can be compromised.

Password reuse
: If a password will be permitted to be reused, we recommend you consider restricting its use to no more frequently than every seventh password cycle. A better approach would to be to completely exclude a password that has been used from being used by that person again.

Failed login attempts
: The number of failed login attempts that will be tolerated on a system should be defined in the security plan. You must also determine the actions that should be taken when the number of failed login attempts has been exceeded.

Account locking and unlocking
: The decision might be made to never enable account locking or never enable automatic account unlocking. Either decision should be documented within

the security plan. If account locking is going to be enabled, you need to define the personnel who will be in charge of performing the account unlocking.

Changing Passwords

Since passwords in Oracle8 can now be aged and expired, the decision about whether users should be allowed to change their own passwords becomes a bit more complex. If the user is not going to be permitted to change his or her own password, then the use of password expiration might not make sense in the company's plan. Determining who can change passwords and how often the passwords must be changed becomes vital if the user is not permitted to change passwords. You must also identify in your plan the mechanism by which users will be notified of their password changes. If a large number of users' passwords are going to be changed at the same time, the only feasible way to notify them all quickly might be email. In some sites, the requirement has been to distribute new passwords via regular "snail" mail. Phone calls might be another less secure way to relay password changes when notification must occur very quickly. We do not recommend using telephones to relay password changes, since the person on the other end of the phone may not be the person to whom you think you are talking.

If a user will be permitted to change passwords, you must define the mechanism for changing those passwords. You might want to create a utility that enables the user to change passwords—especially if direct SQL access is not going to be permitted in the system. Something as elaborate as an Oracle Form or as simple as a SQL statement might be required for a password change. The ability to force the choosing of a password other than one that has already been used is now available (password history), so you will need to specify the length of time that must elapse before a password can be reused.

Standards for Roles

In the spreadsheet shown earlier in this chapter, references to "ap_clerk," "hr_manager," and "hr_developer," among others, were used in the "Roles" area of the chart. The convention displayed there was the application name coupled with a task nomenclature—for example, the Human Resources application (hr) coupled with the "clerk" tasks of entering or updating data within areas of the hr application. In this application, the ability to delete information was not a duty deemed appropriate for a clerk to perform. Only a manager can delete information.

The security plan team must decide on the naming conventions that will be used for role creations on a database-by-database and application-by-application basis. The composition of each role (who will be allowed to perform what actions) also needs to be identified, as well as the designation of who will create and assign roles for each application in each database.

Oracle-Supplied Roles

By default, until Oracle version 7.1.6, Oracle supplied three default roles within a database (CONNECT, RESOURCE, and DBA). From version 7.1.6 forward, Oracle supplies two additional roles (SYSDBA and SYSOPER). These are described in some detail in Chapter 5.

Because the composition of these roles has changed from version to version of the RDBMS, we recommend that DBAs define their own roles for user access. For example, in Oracle's version 6, the RESOURCE role was granted to users who were performing development tasks within a database because the RESOURCE role included the ability to create tables. In Oracle7, the ability to create tables appears in the CONNECT role. However, no tables or indexes can actually be created without a tablespace quota being granted to the user.

Granting Access to the Database

As we explained in Chapter 3, *Oracle Database Objects*, Oracle provides the ability to grant privileges directly either to specific users or to roles. The security team will need to decide whether privileges will ever be directly granted to a specific user or will be granted only through roles. If direct grants are allowed, you'll have to decide under what circumstances they will be used. During application development, for example, the developers will have access to the application schema and will have, through that account, many direct privileges.

Oracle provides the ability to grant privileges in the GRANT statement WITH GRANT OPTION, WITH ADMIN OPTION, or without any option. The security plan should designate whether these options will or will not be permitted within the databases being defined.

Standards for Views

Views are wonderful mechanisms for hiding data from different classes of users. For example, I would not want my salary to be visible to the majority of employees in my company. Suppose that my salary is resident in a table called EMPLOYEES. The table might be comprised of columns for the employee's name, location, telephone number, manager's name, department name, and salary. In this case, the only information in this table that might be considered sensitive is salary. Therefore, you might create a view called "emp_view" to display all of the columns except the salary column.

As with roles, the security plan needs to define any conventions for view names, a designation for who will be permitted to create views, a designation of who can grant access to which views, and an identification of who can say that a view is, in fact, necessary or unnecessary.

Standards for the Oracle Security Server

In Oracle8, a new Security Server facility is supplied to either stand alone or work in conjunction with several third-party vendor products for generating certificates of authentication. These certificates enable users to connect to various applications and databases without having to provide a username and password each time they want to change connections from one place to another. The Oracle Security Server is discussed in Chapter 15, *Using the Oracle Security Server*.

If a company is planning to implement, or has implemented, a single sign-on utility for user authorization, the security plan should detail who will administer the Oracle Security Server and how users will receive accounts and interact with the Security Server.

Standards for Employees

Within your organization, there will be many different interactions with employees. You need to determine how to deal with these interactions and add your organization's policies to the security plan. The driving force behind any security policy should be what an employee needs to know to perform his or her job effectively.

Employee Procedures

What privileges do particular employees need? What limitations should you place on these privileges? A major problem with trying to determine how employees will be able to access a database or application is the need to balance giving enough privilege to enable the employee to get the job done against the risk of allowing too much access to sensitive information. If a security plan becomes too rigid, employees may feel they are not trusted or may not be able to perform their jobs effectively.

Pre-employment tracking

Before an employee is ever hired, an employment application, resumé, or both, is usually submitted for consideration to a company. Many companies track their candidate submittals using computer programs that interact with a database. The information presented in a job application or resume is private and must be handled with care. Your security plan should include procedures for employment application and resumé handling.

New hires

Once an employee is hired for a position, the security plan should clearly state the steps to be followed for giving a new employee access to platforms and databases needed to perform his or her job effectively. If you've already determined the possible functions for an employee using a specific application, the task of knowing what accesses (roles and grants) are needed by that employee will be made much more easily.

Changing positions

Over a period of time, the employee will learn and (you hope) grow within your organization. He may find that the job he was hired for is no longer challenging enough, or he may receive one or more promotions. With promotions, the employee may require different privileges to perform his new duties. Or, an employee may take courses or receive in-house training and become proficient enough to apply for and obtain a position in another department or branch or division of the company. In each of these cases, the security plan should cover what actions should be taken as an employee changes positions within the company.

The disgruntled employee

No one likes to think about the possibility that a coworker may become so upset that he might take action to intentionally damage part or all of a database or system. Unfortunately, this possibility does exist and you must address it. Many years ago at a company in which Marlene Theriault worked, there was a Christmas office party where an employee enjoyed a little too much wine, went back to his office to do a little work before the holiday break, was unable to log on to his account because he mistyped his password repeatedly, decided that his boss had modified his account to deny him access, and relocated some of his boss's data files to another directory location as "payback" for the assumed insult. The good news is that the action was easily corrected and the boss was understanding enough to let the employee off with a mild reprimand. Under less amicable circumstances, however, major damage could have been done to the system since the employee involved had enough privileges to potentially cause real harm. You need to periodically review employee privileges. Be sure such issues are addressed as policies in the security plan.

When an Employee Leaves

Another threat to a system is the employee who either gives notice or is being terminated. Although there are many different philosophies on how to best handle a terminating employee, the security plan should outline exactly what actions are to be taken.

Termination types

The following are a few of the possible termination types to be addressed in a security plan:

- Immediate dismissal, including escorting the employee out of the building with or without severance pay in hand, because the employee has been involved in a major breach of conduct or ethics
- Giving the employee the option of working for a period of time—usually two weeks—before departing the organization; this is usually done in cases where an employee has voluntarily given notice to pursue other interests
- Giving the employee an extended amount of time to continue working and possibly even providing company assistance in a job search; this may be done when a large number of employees have been laid off (downsizing)

The policy should have clear directions on what steps are to be taken in each situation. For example, if an employee is being escorted out of the building immediately and both management and HR are in agreement about the dismissal, the policy might state that the company should revoke all access to all computer accounts and all databases before confronting the employee.

When an employee gives notice

When an employee gives notice, many different approaches may be appropriate. If the employee works directly with the systems or databases in a support capacity, the company might choose to offer two weeks severance pay and have the employee leave immediately rather than take the chance that the employee will do any of the following:

- Work himself to excess trying to clean up every possible task before departing and make careless, costly errors due to fatigue
- Develop a "short-timer" attitude and do little or nothing for the two weeks, which can be very demoralizing to those employees who are not leaving
- Cause damage to the system by inserting a time bomb or Trojan horse set to go off after his departure to sabotage the system or a specific manager's data area

On the other hand, in the situation where an employee has proven his trustworthiness, you might consider maintaining his accounts even after he has left—for a specified amount of time. If there is a chance that the employee might someday return to the company, access to accounts might be locked instead of explicitly revoked or deleted from the system. This approach is particularly useful for workers such as consultants, resident contractors, or temporary hires who may work sporadically with the databases or systems.

The curious employee

Many people are curious. Some have a desire to know as much as they can about their surroundings, while others just love to poke around and see how much information they can access that they are not supposed to know. The curious employee poses a difficult type of security challenge; there may be absolutely no malicious intent involved, but such an employee might nevertheless violate the privacy rights of others. The decision about what penalties should be imposed on an employee who stumbles into data areas to which he should not have access should be considered and clearly defined in the policy.

User Tracking

In the last several sections, we've shown that an employee does not necessarily spend his entire professional life in the same job or the same area of the company. There is, therefore, a need to keep track of each employee's location and current job requirements to ensure that the employee's system and database access rights remain appropriate as he moves around or changes jobs. Let's follow a bit of the employment history of our old friend, Ima Ticdoff.

When Ima came to work for her company, she started as a clerk in the mailroom. Initially, Ima needed access to only one database application to be able to look up employee locations. Ima was bright and learned quickly. Over a period of time, Ima attended night school, obtained other skills, and was eventually brought into the payroll area. At that point in time, Ima's computer access needs changed. She now required access to three different databases to perform her varied tasks.

As we mentioned in Chapter 1, Ima became unhappy with her boss. Her unhappiness grew to a point where she finally requested a transfer to the billing department. When she moved to her new department, it was no longer appropriate for her to have access to any payroll information but she now required access to the billing applications. What mechanism was used to ensure that Ima's access to payroll information stopped and her access to billing information began? How was a user tracked in Ima's company? How are users tracked in your company? What vehicle ensures that an employee does not have inappropriate access to sensitive data?

You can use your organization's security plan as the vehicle for specifying how users and their privileges and accesses will be tracked within your company. In one organization, a user tracking application was written to populate a database nightly with current employee information. The application includes each operating system and identifies the databases on each system. Each application manager, DBA, and all developers associated with each database are recorded within the user tracking application, as well as everyone who has an account on each system and database. All privileges and roles for each database are housed within the user tracking application, and each user who has been granted each role and/or privilege is recorded with the associated role or privilege information. Once each quarter, a report is generated and emailed to each manager showing who has access to their applications and what privileges are held. Before the user tracking application was written, the requirements for this application were carefully outlined in the company's security plan. Once the requirements were defined, the creation of the user tracking application became a simple task of implementing the requirements as specified. By basing the application on the security plan details, the finished user tracking application was both easy to create and completely in sync with the security plan.

Sample Security Plan Index

As mentioned at the beginning of this chapter, security policies differ greatly in how complex and specific they are. Some policies may be as simple as an electronic memorandum designating a particular employee as the point of contact to create accounts for anyone needing access to a database or system. For most companies, however, a more formal document may be in order. Here is a sample generic index of topics you might include in a security plan:

Topics
Corporate Philosophy on Security
Configuration of the Operating Systems by Divisions
Configuration of the Databases for each System by Division
Configuration of Applications by Database and System for Each Division
Configuration of Single Sign-on Utility
Composition of Certificates of Authority
USERID Guidelines for a Database Account
USERID Guidelines for an Operating System Account
Password Guidelines for a Database Account
Password Guidelines for an Operating System Account
Operating System Access Types
Database Access Types

Topics
Authorization for Establishment of User Accounts
Establishing a USERID for a Database
Establishing a USERID for an Operating System
User Administration—Accounts Creation
User Administration—Appropriate Roles by Application
User Administration—Appropriate Views by Application
User Administration—Administrator Privileges
User Administration—for Applications
Establishing Access to an Application
Revoking Access to an Application
Revoking Access to an Application for People Who Leave the Company
Removing Access to a USERID for an Operating System Account
Removing Access to a USERID for a Database Account
Notification of Termination
Revoking Access for Abruptly Terminated Employees
Transferring Staff to Another Group Within a Division
Transferring Staff to Another Group Outside of a Division
Reinstating a USERID
File Security Guidelines
Restricting Access to Systems
Restricting Access to Databases
Security Audits for Operating Systems
Security Audits for Databases
Time Schedule for Security Plan Reviews

Sample Security Plan Checklist

The following checklist is provided as an aid to ensure that you've identified and addressed all of the necessary areas of interest to your company. The checklist is designed to be a guide for you and your team to ensure that topics that need to be included in your security plan will not be overlooked.

Have You	Yes/No
Identified all of the key players?	
Obtained management buy-in (at all levels)?	
Collected all applicable system and database information?	
Identified the specific types of accounts required for each system—both operating system and database?	

Have You	Yes/No
Determined who will have authority to approve accounts?	
Determined who will create/delete/manage accounts?	
Determined a user tracking method and implementation?	
Decided how account approval will be performed: email, web site, hard-copy form, etc.?	
Identified all affected applications on each system?	
Identified a username and password structure?	
Determined what constitutes a security breach and the appropriate penalty for each breach?	
Identified all sensitive data on the system and created methods to protect that data?	
Determined what forms of monitoring will be used?	
Determined what forms of backup will be used?	
Created recovery procedures to be followed?	
Determined the required availability for the database?	
Established standards for views and roles?	

8

Installing and Starting Oracle

In this chapter:

- *Segmenting Application Processing*
- *Installing Oracle Securely*
- *Connecting to the Database Without a Password*
- *Installing and Configuring SQL*Net*
- *Setting Up Initialization Parameters for Security*

The best approach to doing anything is supposedly to begin at the beginning, proceed through to the end, and then stop. But how do you determine where the "beginning" is? When it comes to database security, you may feel that there are several different points of origin. However, it seems to us that you should first protect the Oracle source code. Before you begin to install the Oracle code, there are steps you should take to establish the environment for the source code installation. Since each platform Oracle has been ported to has different procedures for Oracle software installation, we won't cover detailed information on code installation in this book. However, we'll look briefly at the approaches you can use to protect your Oracle environment in the correct way "from the beginning."

To help you to understand the various ways you can set up your Oracle source code and applications code, we'll first present a discussion of alternative architectures: "dumb terminal," two-tier, and three-tier. We'll describe the system-level approaches you can use to secure your database and the methods you can use to enable connection to your database without the use of passwords—either directly from the operating system level or remotely through the use of SQL*Net. Because SQL*Net has become an integral part of the way you interact with the database from both a two-tier and three-tier architecture, we'll briefly explore the methods used to configure and interact with this product. Finally, we'll look at the initialization parameters used to configure the database at database startup.

Although we use the term SQL*Net throughout this chapter, in Oracle8 the product name has changed to Net8.

Segmenting Application Processing

Not that long ago, the common environment for performing computer-related tasks was to log on to an operating system from a terminal directly connected to that system. From your connection, you could interact with applications and, possibly, a database or two. Everything lived on the server:

- The operating system code
- The database software
- The applications code

As computing has evolved, additional ways of interacting with a computer and an RDBMS have also evolved. There are now three common approaches:

- A direct connection to a computer on which we perform all our work
- A client/server (two-tier) architecture
- A thin client (three-tier) architecture

We'll describe each of these architectures briefly in the following sections.

Direct Connection to a Database Server

Originally, the Oracle software, database(s), applications code, and everything else necessary to perform the required work was housed locally on one machine. You worked from a terminal directly connected to the computer to perform whatever tasks were required. Using this method of connection meant that you had to be in the same building as the computer—or at a distance limited by how far away from the computer the hardwiring would reach and still be usable. Figure 8-1 illustrates a direct connection to the database.

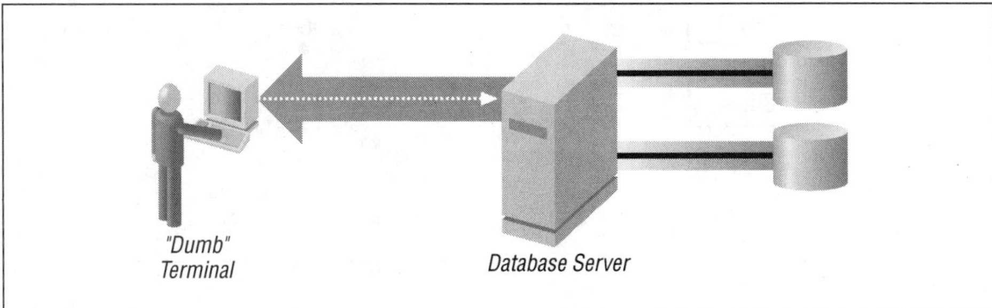

Figure 8-1. Direct connection to a database server

There were several common problems with this approach.

- You had to be in close proximity to the computer with which you were interacting
- If you were too far away from the central computer, line noise could cause interference with data transmission
- You could not send or receive information to or from another site easily

If you needed to send critical information to your boss halfway across the country, you would create a 9-track tape containing the information you wanted to send, package the tape, and ship it via a ground or air carrier. Your boss might not receive the tape until several days or a week later. Obviously, this method of information transmission was not very efficient or quick.

Client/Server (Two-Tier) Architecture

The next architectural advance was called *client/server* and placed the Oracle software and database(s) on one platform and the applications code on a client or personal computer (PC). In this scenario, Oracle's SQL*Net product was used to carry queries to the server and carry data back to the PC. The PC required substantial resources to support this environment, and the task of ensuring that all PC clients were current and secure has proved to be an administrative and security nightmare. This architecture is typically referred to as *two-tier* and can be seen in Figure 8-2.

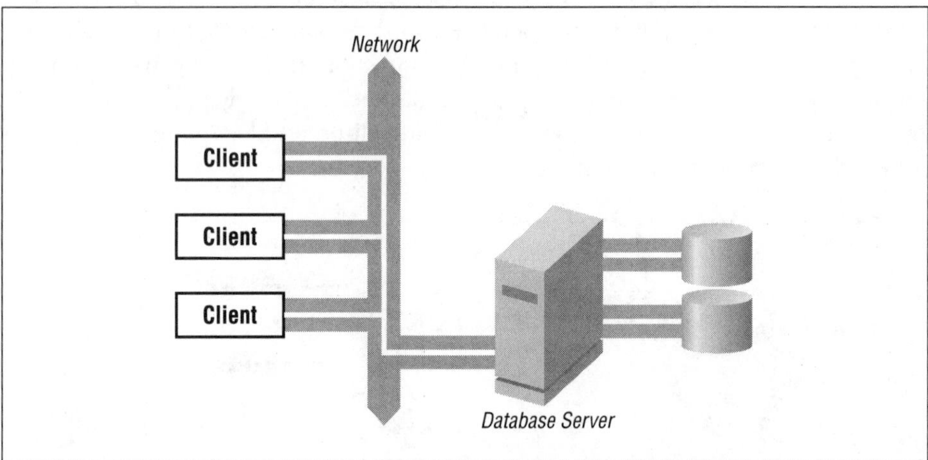

Figure 8-2. The client/server architecture

Client/server has the advantage of distributed processing. Part of the processing of the work is done on the database server, and part is done on the workstation. The latter mostly includes the display management, user interface, and application processing that is independent of the database. Not only is the total computing burden spread more evenly between the client machine and the host or server machine, but you can perform tasks independently from the server. You can perform these tasks in a room or building much farther away from the physical location of the server.

The client/server configuration requires a fairly robust workstation, typically having a 2-gigabyte hard disk (or larger) and 24 megabytes or more (frequently 64M or more) of RAM. Not too many years ago, the cost of such a computer would have been over $5,000. Even though workstation costs have declined, the cost of maintenance, primarily the software upgrades and configuration, has been estimated in excess of $10,000 per workstation per year as a recurring cost.

Because of some of the drawbacks of the two-tier architecture, a configuration was sought that would provide the distributed processing capability of the client/server implementation, but reduce the maintenance costs. If it also reduced the cost of the workstation, so much the better. One approach was to put the application executables on a network file server and let the workstation load the executables from there. This met with some success in reducing the maintenance effort, but still required a robust or *fat client* for a workstation. The term fat client comes from the need to store all the application code on each client in order for the client to perform the required work.

Thin Client (Three-Tier) Architecture

The next and newest level of architecture uses a low-capacity workstation, sometimes without a hard disk, as the first tier. This workstation does not actually run the application but performs the display management and more—after code is downloaded to the client. A second "application server" holds and executes the applications using a language such as Java to communicate with the workstation. The applications executing on this server communicate with the database server, the third tier, using the protocols of the database (in the context of this book, Oracle and SQL*Net).

A slightly different version of the second and third tier relationship is one in which the second tier performs *some* of the application processing and the rest is performed on the third tier. This is how the Oracle Application Server functions when dynamic HTML is used for the application.

In all cases, since there are now three computers continuously involved in the processing stream, this architecture is referred to as a *three-tier* architecture, shown in Figure 8-3. Because the workstation now has virtually nothing installed, and does not have to have a large disk or huge amounts of memory, it is frequently referred to as a *thin client*.

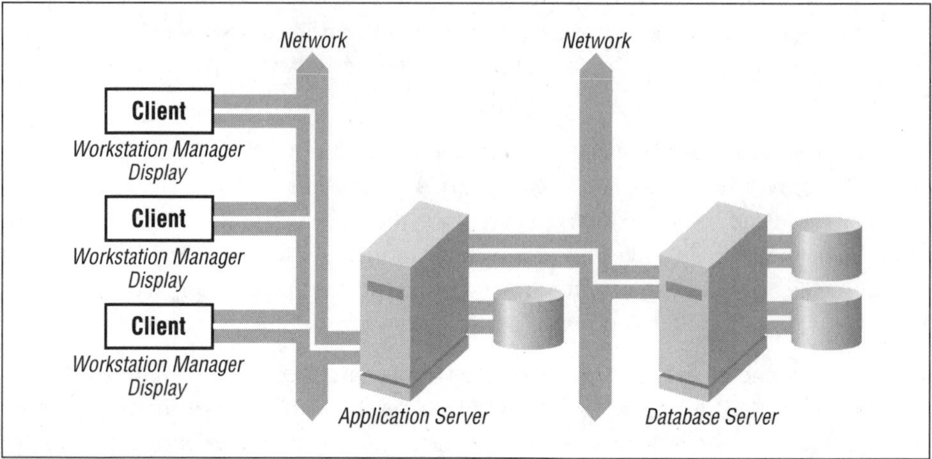

Figure 8-3. The thin client architecture

The three-tier architecture is useful in many ways. It enables:

- Low resources on the client side with potentially minimal security requirements
- Medium amounts of resources on the application server with higher security requirements
- High resources requirements for one or more back end servers with varying amounts of security required (based on the application which a particular database supports)

Installing Oracle Securely

There are many approaches you can take to securing an operating system and database and an equal number of views on what really fulfills the definition of a "secure operating system." In a systems administration class we attended many years ago, the instructor drew a picture on the board. The picture was of a large room in which a very large computer and operator's console had been placed. There was only one door leading into the room and in front of that door, he drew a picture of a guard with a gun. He explained that he had just drawn a system that was quite secure: the only truly secure system is the system that allows no one to ever interact with the computer inside. A friend of ours describes his vision of the truly secure computer as "a computer in a lead-lined vault (no EMF emissions to be sniffed) with no network connections and a Marine guard with 'shoot on sight' orders."

Okay, these are not real-world solutions. However, both descriptions do bring home the point that as long as there are people interacting with a system, there is always the potential for a security breach. One of the most formidable threats to any system's security is the user who does not log off the system at night and does not have password protection on his terminal or personal computer. In this section, we'll look at ways of protecting logins to the system.

Security and the Operating System

From the operating system perspective, security measures are used to protect access to files. On most operating systems, security is accomplished by creating specific groups of users with specific access rights defined for them. Each file within the directory can be granted different access restrictions. You might assign the ability to read from and write to one file while another file might receive read, write, and execute privileges or only read access, as you deem appropriate. For example, you might want the salesmen in your automobile dealership to be able to see what cars are in stock, so you give them read access to the car information. You might want your administrative assistants to enter information on the new cars as they arrive at your lot—so you give them read and write privileges.

Most database systems share this attribute with the Oracle database: no user has any need of any kind to directly access the database data files, or any of the installed database software (binaries, and in some cases, source code). The access to the database files is the responsibility and function of the database management system. Access to these files should always be severely restricted.

In the following sections, we examine the various considerations for installing the Oracle software and creating an Oracle database. Because each operating system Oracle installation is potentially different, this discussion is not platform-specific. Oracle Corporation delivers operating system-specific guides for product installation, and we recommend that you read the guides supplied with your software and become very familiar with them. (We do show examples to make the discussion more tangible, however.)

Oracle and Operating System Authentication

The standard Oracle access control mechanism is a database username and password combination, like the one you'd have with any computer system such as UNIX or with an Internet Service Provider (ISP). This allows access from any workstation that can successfully contact the computer running the database management system. In some implementations, however, identification and authentication at the point of access are more tightly controlled.

There are several options in Oracle for achieving tighter access control. From Oracle version 7.x forward, the DBA has had two ways to provide authentication to the Oracle RDBMS:

- Operating system authentication
- Password files

We'll discuss both of these in the sections that follow. If you use either one of these forms of access, you will not be prompted for a username or password when you go to access the system. To perform administration tasks as a DBA, if you want to administer one or more databases directly on the machine on which they reside, you will probably choose the operating system authentication approach. If you want to manage one or more databases from a remote client and you do not have a secure connection, you will probably use the password file approach. Either way, the use of the password file is reserved for highly privileged accounts to enable database tasks to be performed remotely.

The OSDBA and OSOPER roles

Depending on the operating system you're using, there are two groups that can be created during installation of the Oracle software to provide operating system authentication for DBAs and operators. These *groups* (referred to in Oracle documentation as *roles*), which are granted at the operating system level, are OSDBA (for DBAs) and OSOPER (for operators). They can have different names and different functionality depending on the operating system involved. We introduced these roles in Chapter 5, *Oracle Default Roles and User Accounts.*

OSDBA is obviously used in conjunction with the DBA functions. The OSOPER group is used to indicate a person performing more restricted privileged actions in the database. Do not confuse the OSOPER group with any casual database user.

In addition, don't confuse these operating system roles with the roles described in Chapter 5. These roles are not the same as the Oracle internal roles used to control access to various application objects. These operating system roles are used to enable a DBA or operator to perform database system functions.

From the operating system

On a UNIX operating system, placing a user account in the DBA group enables that user to interact with the database to perform any functions the OSDBA role enables. Likewise, assigning a user to the OPERATOR system group enables that user to perform any tasks allowed within the OSOPER role. On a Digital UNIX system, for example, you can use the *addgroup* utility to create a group named "DBA." Likewise, you can create a group for the OSOPER with the same utility.

By comparison, on an OpenVMS system, the operating system identifier *ORA_DBA* or *ORA_<SID>_DBA* is created and granted to any account that will perform DBA functions related to the OSDBA role. There does not seem to be an equivalent group for operators in an OpenVMS system. Any user who is placed in the operating system group, DBA, has the ability to connect to the database using the Server Manger Utility (*svrmgr*).

When you issue a CONNECT INTERNAL command using *svrmgrl* (or *svrmgrm* on a UNIX system), in essence, you are connecting to the heart of the RDBMS as *sys* and can perform actions that could potentially damage the database. If you were a very new DBA, you might think you were connecting to a new database you were about to build, but might accidentally connect to a development or production database. If you were to execute a CREATE DATABASE command from the *svrmgrl* utility, your current database would be destroyed. Assigning a user access to the DBA group should, therefore, be done carefully and only after building a good business case for granting someone privileges that could jeopardize your production systems.

If you want to limit the amount of privilege given to a user performing DBA tasks, you can create and customize your own roles. You do not need to make the decision at Oracle software installation time, and can take advantage of or disable these roles after installation.

OSOPER

Generally, the OSOPER role has the ability to perform the following commands:

STARTUP
SHUTDOWN
ALTER DATABASE OPEN/MOUNT
ALTER DATABASE BACKUP
ARCHIVE LOG
RECOVER

This role allows the user to enable RESTRICTED SESSION. The ability to perform any of these operations requires the user to have a much higher privilege level than the normal user or developer.

OSDBA

The OSDBA role encompasses all the system privileges with the DBA role (explained in Chapter 5), the OSOPER role values, and the ability for the user to CREATE DATABASE and perform time-based recovery.

The OSDBA and OSOPER groups can only be granted to a user through the operating system and cannot be granted, revoked, or dropped through the database. The method used for granting these groups is operating system-specific. If a user attempts to connect to the database from the operating system and the REMOTE_LOGIN_PASSWORD parameter in the database's *INIT.ORA* file is set to "NONE," Oracle will first attempt to connect using the OSDBA role. If that fails, Oracle will attempt to use the OSOPER role to connect. If both connection attempts fail, the connection will fail.

Operating System Accounts

As we discussed in Chapter 7, *Developing a Database Security Plan*, there are several types of accounts that might be required for your system. This section examines more closely the types of operating system access required by a DBA or operator to perform various database system jobs.

Using CONNECT INTERNAL and CONNECT /

In early versions of the Oracle RDBMS, in order to start up or shut down the database, you issued a command from the operating system command-line level. In a Windows NT environment, you can still start up or shut down the database by issuing the following commands:

```
Net Start OracleStart<db_name>
Net Stop OracleStart<db_name>
```

Beginning in Oracle version 6.0, a new convention was introduced to enable you to connect to the database and issue interactive commands to perform database system work. In the earlier versions of the Oracle RDBMS—version 6 and version 7.1.x—the method of attaching to the database to perform tasks such as STARTUP, SHUTDOWN, and CREATE DATABASE was through a utility called *SQLDBA*. You entered the command CONNECT INTERNAL to connect to the database at a much more privileged level. Using the CONNECT INTERNAL mechanism, you attached to the database as *sys* and could perform these duties successfully. The tasks of starting up, shutting down, or creating a database cannot be accomplished directly from SQL*Plus—even as the user *sys*.

For version 7.2 and higher, the utility Oracle uses to perform these functions has changed. The new utility used is the Server Manager line mode (*svrmgrl*) and the connect string is one of the following:

```
CONNECT INTERNAL AS SYSDBA
CONNECT / AS SYSDBA
CONNECT INTERNAL AS SYSOPER
CONNECT / AS SYSOPER
```

depending on the operating system group in which your account belongs. The unqualified command, CONNECT INTERNAL, is supported for backwards compatibility only and, on some operating systems, may cause errors to be written to the operating system console log. In version 7.2 or higher, in order to start a database, issue the following commands:

```
svrmgrl
CONNECT / AS SYSDBA
STARTUP OPEN <db_name>
EXIT
```

From most operating systems, you cannot successfully issue this set of commands unless you have the OSOPER or OSDBA or equivalent operating system privileges.

Connecting to the Database Without a Password

There are three approaches commonly used to enable a user to connect to a database without explicitly typing a password. All of the approaches take advantage of the OPS$ account.

With the first approach, the account is created with the actual prefix "OPS$" used in the account name, and a password is assigned to the user. The user can connect from the operating system level to a database by using just a "/" in place of the username/password string. The user does not have to type his username or password to gain access to the database. If, however, the user wants to connect to the database from a remote client, he can use his username and password and connect successfully. The advantage of this approach is that the user can hide both his username and password when using a command-line connection and still retain the ability to use SQL*Net to connect to the database from a client machine.

With the second approach, you set the *INIT.ORA* parameter OS_AUTHENT_PREFIX="", and the actual username without the "OPS$" prefix is used in creating the user account. No password is assigned to the account. Instead, the account is created with the IDENTIFIED EXTERNALLY option, as described later in this chapter. The user can connect to the database from the operating system level but has no password to enable remote connection from a client machine.

The only difference between the second and third approach is the use of the *INIT.ORA* parameter REMOTE_OS_AUTHENT set to "TRUE" to enable an "identified externally" account to connect to the database from a remote client. The disadvantage of this form of access is that database security could potentially be compromised by someone other than the intended user accessing the database without needing to know either a username or a password.

OPS$ Accounts

As we mentioned in the last section, Oracle provides the ability to access the database from the operating system level without providing a username and password. When this mechanism, set with the IDENTIFIED EXTERNALLY option, is used, Oracle views the operating system authentication as "good enough" and allows access to the database based on the operating system account name. The advantage of using an account that relies on operating system verification is that there is no need to type a password on the operating system command line. This is a great aid to a developer who is testing code from an operating system prompt and does not want his password to be exposed. This approach is also excellent for running a command procedure for an application without having to embed a password in the procedure and provide a possible security breach.

The down side to this approach is one that was cited earlier. If a developer has an "identified externally" account and does not lock his terminal when he walks away from his machine, anyone passing by has access to his database account without the need to know a password.

In most cases, the "identified externally" approach should only be used on development and test databases.

Identified externally accounts

The only way the "identified externally" approach may be safe to use on a production system is from an account created in a way that ensures that the user cannot get to the operating system level. In an OpenVMS system, for example, keeping users from reaching the operating system level can be accomplished by having the system administrator create a "captive" account. In an OpenVMS system, the operating system treats an account that has been flagged as "captive" as having no privilege at the operating system level. Thus, if a user attempts to break out of the application he or she is using and tries to get to the operating system level, the user's current process will be terminated. The user will be automatically logged off the account he or she is using.

In a UNIX environment, the user could be placed in a "trusted shell" (tsh). The login profile (*.profile* or *.cshrc/.login*) could include a START command for an application, followed by an EXIT command. In this manner, the user's application is started at login, and access to the operating system is controlled or eliminated. When the application exits, the login session also exits. The *.profile* for the account would have to be customized to capture all control characters so the user could not break out of the login process. In UNIX systems, this is easily done through the TRAP statement. Keeping a user from accessing the operating system level can also be accomplished from a normal shell, but you would have to trap all escape routes to keep the user from getting to a shell prompt. Even with tight controls on the application account, the roles and privileges for the account would have to be strictly evaluated to ensure the least possible jeopardy to the production system.

OS_AUTHENT_PREFIX and OPS$

Within the database initialization file (*INIT.ORA*), the OS_AUTHENT_PREFIX parameter can be set to the prefix, if any, that will be used to identify a database that will rely on operating system verification of the user alone. As delivered, the Oracle RDBMS default value for OS_AUTHENT_PREFIX is set to "OPS$". Therefore, the convention used to identify an account that is able to log on to the database without using a username and password is to precede the username with the value "OPS$". For example, if the operating system account name is *mary*, the database username would be *ops$mary*, and the CREATE statement for the database account would be:

```
CREATE USER ops$mary IDENTIFIED BY abc75!d...
```

Note the use of a password assignment in the above statement. The password is required by the syntax of the statement, but because this is an OPS$ account, the user will not have to supply the assigned password at login. By default, an account created with the OPS$ prefix can be used to access the database without presenting a username/password from an operating system account with the matching name (minus the OPS$ prefix). Therefore, if the DBA wants an account that can also be used from a client machine to SQL*Net to the database, and can be used from the operating system without using a username and password, this convention will work very nicely. When the user connects using SQL*Net, he types the username "OPS$<username>" and places his password in the requested "password" area. When the user is logged directly in to the operating system account, he uses just "/" as his username and password.

For example, from a client PC, the user *mary* would log on using:

```
username:  ops$mary
password:  abc75!d
```

From the operating system, the user would log on using:

```
sqlplus /
```

OPS$ in version 7

With version 7, the "OPS$" account took on two possible approaches with very different connotations. The DBA could create a user account and dub that account "identified externally" as follows:

```
CREATE USER mary IDENTIFIED EXTERNALLY...
```

The DBA would also have to modify the *INIT.ORA* file to include the following line:

```
OS_AUTHENT_PREFIX = ""
```

to let Oracle know that the operating system prefix was to be blank and that the default for authentication should be just the user's name without the "OPS$" prefix. By creating the user this way and declaring the operating system prefix to be blank, the DBA eliminates the ability to assign a password to the account since, if a password is assigned to the account, the ability to connect to the database and rely on the operating system authentication is negated. In all cases where an account is allowed to connect without a password, the syntax for connecting to the database is:

```
sqlplus /
```

If the account is set up as "identified externally," no password can be assigned and the user will not be able to use the account in a dual manner. He will not be able to use the account both as a SQL*Net account with a password and as an operating system account without a username and password.

Another approach

Another available approach is to use the "identified externally" account creation and set the *INIT.ORA* parameter REMOTE_OS_AUTHENT to "TRUE". This approach enables an account that has been created using the same name as the client account to connect to the database via SQL*Net without the use of a password. Let's say the account on a PC is identified with the name *mary* and an account is created in the SMOKE database for "mary identified externally." *mary* can now select SQL*Plus from her PC start/program menu and, at the username prompt, type "/@SMOKE" and connect to the SQL> command line in the SMOKE instance. If *mary* is logged on directly to the operating system on which SMOKE is running, she can still just type "sqlplus /" to access the database.

Two problems with REMOTE_OS_AUTHENT

In the scenario in the last section, the security danger is that *mary* will walk away from her PC without locking her terminal. Anyone would then be able to access the database without knowing *mary*'s username or password and have *mary*'s privileges on the system.

The second danger is that you are trusting a *remote* operating system over which you may have no control. All somebody needs to do is determine an Oracle user in your database who has the desired role—including DBA—with an account that has been IDENTIFIED EXTERNALLY. Then, the person creates an account with the same username as the privileged database account, fires up SQL*Plus, and WHAMMO! That person is in your database with the highest possible privileges and there is *nothing* you can do—except set REMOTE_OS_AUTHENT=FALSE.

An alternative method you can use in Oracle8 for account authorization—the *ORAPWD* utility—is described next.

The ORAPWD Utility

Another method Oracle uses for account authentication is the *ORAPWD* utility (named *ORAPWD80* under Oracle8). This utility is used to create a password file to enable accounts from SQL*Net clients to connect to an Oracle database without the use of a password. It's used by the Oracle Enterprise Manager (discussed in Chapter 13, *Using the Oracle Enterprise Manager*) to connect to remote databases to perform various DBA tasks.

Steps to setting up the password file

There are two steps involved in establishing the environment to use a password file. The actual file must be created using the *ORAPWD* utility, then a value must be assigned to the *INIT.ORA* variable REMOTE_LOGIN_PASSWORD.

To see the syntax for the *ORAPWD* utility on any operating system with version 7 or higher, type the command *ORAPWD* (in lowercase on a UNIX or Windows NT system) at the operating system prompt. You should see the following information:

```
Usage: orapwd file=<fname> password=<password> entries=<users>

  where
    file - name of password file (mand),
    password - password for SYS and INTERNAL (mand),
    entries - maximum number of distinct DBA and OPERs (opt),
  There are no spaces around the equal-to (=) character.
```

The syntax used to create the password file should be the same from operating system to operating system.*

Parameters have the following meanings:

FILE

Must be a fully qualified path name; (i.e., the name must include the disk name, directory name, and file name). The file parameter may have other

* We include the information on how to get the operating system to present the syntax here because we found that having the syntax available when we went to create the password file was very helpful and made the process easier.

requirements established for it within the operating system-specific installation guide.

PASSWORD
: Establishes the password used for the *sys* and *internal* users. If you alter the user to change the password established in the password file, the password will be changed both in the database and in the password file.

ENTRIES
: Used only when the REMOTE_LOGIN_PASSWORDFILE parameter in the *INIT.ORA* file is set to "EXCLUSIVE." This value is the maximum number of users that can connect to the database with SYSDBA or SYSOPER privileges. Since the file must be recreated if the maximum number of allowable users needs to be exceeded, the number might be set high on initial creation. However, the person creating this file may want to carefully examine the ramifications of allowing several people to have DBA authority within their databases.

To use the *ORAPWD* or *ORAPWD80* utility, you must first decide where you want the created password file to be placed for each database and what password(s) you will use. You must also decide whether you want to set up one shared password file or enable an exclusive file for each database available on your system.

If a shared file is used, the accounts that access the database(s) can only connect as *sys* or *internal*. This means you cannot restrict the actions the account can perform. If an exclusive file is used, the accounts that access the database can be defined by creating the users in that database and granting them SYSDBA or SYSOPER privileges. Thus, when you create an exclusive password file, you can control to a finer granularity the privileges available to the users granted access to the database. When you create an account that is granted SYSDBA and/or SYSOPER, the password assigned to the account is also recorded in an encrypted format in the password file.

The second step in establishing an environment in which an account can access the database using the password file is to assign a value to the *INIT.ORA* parameter, REMOTE_LOGIN_PASSWORDFILE. The three possible values are:

NONE
: No password file will be used

EXCLUSIVE
: The password file will be used by one specific database

SHARED
: The password file will be shared among more than one database

In order to make entries in the *ORAPWD* file, the value for REMOTE_OS_AUTHENT must be set to "EXCLUSIVE."

*Installing and Configuring SQL*Net*

The advent of a product to enable the interaction with the database from a remote client has been a boon to the computing world. For the Oracle RDBMS, that product was SQL*Net (Net8 for Oracle8). SQL*Net enables the ability to connect to a database in Tokyo from a database in New York and share information between the two. While this ability has been a benefit to industry, it carries with it the potential for security breaches.

Required Files

Connections via SQL*Net are controlled by three files, the *LISTENER.ORA* file, the *TNSNAMES.ORA* file, and the *SQLNET.ORA* file. If you do not define the database in these files (called "configuring the Listener"), connecting to your database from a remote client is virtually impossible. In an environment where the Oracle Names Server is used, the third file, *SQLNET.ORA*, defines the location of the Names Server and the order in which a database connection is determined. The *SQLNET.ORA* file indicates either that the Names Server is to be checked first for a database's connection information or that the *TNSNAMES.ORA* file is to be checked first.

You must configure these files if you are not going to use a Names Server, after installing the SQL*Net product on your system and in order to run a listener process on your system (see the section "About the Names Server" later in this chapter) as follows:

LISTENER.ORA

This is a *required file* on the database server, and it contains the configuration for the listener. If several listeners are to be used on a node, they will all share the same *LISTENER.ORA* file. The file contains three parts: the area that defines the listening addresses, the SID of each database it listens for, and parameters that define the listener's behavior.

TNSNAMES.ORA

This is a *required* file on the database server and may or may not be required on the client, depending on whether a Names Server is being used. The file contains a list of the service names of all databases to which you want to connect and information about the connection—for example, the protocol being used, the host location, the port, etc.

SQLNET.ORA

This file contains diagnostic parameters for the location of log and trace files for SQL*Net clients. If a Names Server is to be used, this file also contains information about the Names Server preferred server names and the Names Server directory path. This file will also designate whether the Names Server or the *TNSNAMES.ORA* file is to be checked first for connection information.

The listener not only listens for calls from other nodes, but also listens for Interprocess Calls (IPCs) from databases on the same node. Oracle Corporation provides fairly extensive information about configuring each of the files. The DBA is generally the person who configures the listener(s), Names Server(s), and all required support files for these utilities.

Installation is easy

The installation of the base SQL*Net product is very straightforward on all platforms. You simply select the product from the installation menu and accept it. You must know what protocols you are using in your environment and select the appropriate one(s) from the list presented. If you are installing a SQL*Net server, you must also identify a client directory location and a client group name.

The SQL*Net configuration may not be quite as straightforward as the installation of the product. In a Windows NT environment, the listener can be automatically configured and started using the installer and default values. To learn more about installing and configuring SQL*Net, see the networking documentation shipped with your Oracle product set.

About the Names Server

The first decision to make after installing the SQL*Net product set is whether you want to enable a Names Server to supply the connection information for your databases or whether you want to maintain the connection information yourself. Installing, maintaining, and interacting with the Names Server requires the use of a network manager utility. If you are planning to configure a Names Server to run with an Oracle7 database, you need to use the 16-bit Windows version of the Network Manager product. If you are going to use the Names Server with an Oracle8 database, you will use the Net8 Assistant to configure the Names Server. You can configure a Names Server with the Net8 Assistant for Oracle8 and serve connection information for an Oracle7 database from it. You can even save off the Names Server configuration from the Net8 Assistant to a version 7 database. However, because of the difference in composition of the rowids between Oracle8 and Oracle7, you cannot run an Oracle7 Names Server from an Oracle8 configuration.

Oracle Corporation provides a detailed explanation and instructions on how to configure a Names Server with your Oracle product set.

Generally, once you have configured your listener and it is up and running, your clients must install a client version of SQL*Net and create a *TNSNAMES.ORA* file using a product called Easy Net Config in order to connect to your databases. If you have many databases on your system or if the database names are changing fairly frequently, it will be very difficult for your users to keep track of what their *TNSNAMES.ORA* file should look like. Each time you upgrade your system, your users will need to upgrade their SQL*Net client software. If the software is distributed from a central network location, there is a very good chance that the user's current *TNSNAMES.ORA* file will be overwritten with an incorrect file.

The advantage of using a Names Server is that the only file that needs to be fielded to all of your client machines is a *SQLNET.ORA* file. All new databases are registered with the Names Server using the utility, and all required files are generated automatically through that utility. The disadvantage is that you must modify the configuration through the Network Manager utility to remain consistent; if you are storing your configuration in a database rather than a system file and your storage site database is not available, clients may not be able to obtain connection information and connect to their database. Another potential disadvantage may be the amount of time it takes for the connection lookup to occur. If several databases are used as Names Servers, each database must be updated to reflect each change in configuration, but you will have backup Names Servers available to serve database connection information if one of your Names Servers is unavailable.

The listener and passwords

The second decision that must be made is whether or not each network listener will have an associated password. The default password for a listener is *listener*, but the password can be changed, as shown in this line of code from a sample *LISTENER.ORA* file:

```
PASSWORDS_LISTENER = (oracle)
```

If a password is to be used for each listener, you must ensure that the *LISTENER.ORA* file that stores the password(s) is protected from being read by anyone who is not a DBA charged with supporting the SQL*Net configuration.

Setting Up Initialization Parameters for Security

As we described in Chapter 2, the initialization file is a list of parameters supplied by Oracle with your database. You can change the values of these parameters to configure the database system. The file is used to modify parameters that affect performance, set global defaults and limits, and establish file names and locations. This file is generally referred to as the *INIT.ORA* file even though its actual name might vary. By default, when a database is created, a file with the naming convention of *INIT<DATABASE SID>.ORA* is also created.

From version 7.3 on, some of the *INIT.ORA* parameters can be dynamically modified using the following commands:

ALTER SESSION
: When specified, the parameters are only changed for that session and will not remain in effect after the session ends.

ALTER SYSTEM
: When specified, the parameters will remain in effect until the database is shut down but may not affect the current session.

ALTER SYSTEM DEFFERED
: When specified, will not affect the current sessions but will affect all future sessions until the database is shut down.

Viewing the Parameters

There are more than 100 different parameters that can be set in the *INIT.ORA* file. When a value is changed in the *INIT.ORA* file, the value will not take effect until the database is "bounced," or shut down and then restarted using the modified *INIT.ORA* parameter file. Since the Oracle RDBMS has a default value for every parameter available, the absence of a value for a parameter in the file will signal that the default value is to be used. The Oracle-supplied default *INIT.ORA* file is a basic, sample file that gives information about database sizes in relation to parameter settings. The current values for parameters can be viewed by using the line mode of the Server Manager and issuing the command:

```
SVRMGR> SHOW PARAMETERS
```

There are parameters in Oracle that have minimum values. If these parameters are set too low, Oracle either will not start or will perform very badly. Take care when modifying *INIT.ORA* parameters.

Here is a list of the parameters available from the SHOW PARAMETERS command in an Oracle8 version 8.0.4 default database on a Windows NT system. A few of these parameters need some explanation. As we mentioned earlier in this chapter, if OS_AUTHENT_PREFIX is set to an empty string ("") and REMOTE_OS_AUTHENT is set to "TRUE," then if an "identified externally" account is created, the potential is there for a breach of database security.

In the list, you will notice that the parameter AUDIT_TRAIL is set to the value "db." See Chapter 10, *Developing an Audit Plan*, for more information about this parameter.

There are a number of parameters you'll want to evaluate for their effect on database security. Each of these parameters is identified by an asterisk (*) in the following list. We've also starred the parameters that represent an operating system directory to remind you that the operating system directories must be protected from casual user interaction and possible destruction.

```
NAME                                 TYPE    VALUE
------------------------------------ ------- ------------------------------
O7_DICTIONARY_ACCESSIBILITY          boolean TRUE
allow_partial_sn_results             boolean FALSE
always_anti_join                     string  NESTED_LOOPS
always_semi_join                     string  standard
aq_tm_processes                      integer 0
arch_io_slaves                       integer 0
*audit_trail                         string  DB
b_tree_bitmap_plans                  boolean FALSE
*background_dump_dest                string  %RDBMS80%\trace
backup_disk_io_slaves                integer 0
backup_tape_io_slaves                boolean FALSE
bitmap_merge_area_size               integer 1048576
blank_trimming                       boolean FALSE
buffer_pool_keep                     string
buffer_pool_recycle                  string
cache_size_threshold                 integer 20
cleanup_rollback_entries             integer 20
close_cached_open_cursors            boolean FALSE
commit_point_strength                integer 1
compatible                           string  8.0.0
compatible_no_recovery               string  0.0.0
complex_view_merging                 boolean FALSE
control_file_record_keep_time        integer 7
*control_files                       string  C:\orant\DATABASE\ctl1ORCL.ora
cpu_count                            integer 1
create_bitmap_area_size              integer 8388608
cursor_space_for_time                boolean FALSE
db_block_buffers                     integer 200
db_block_checkpoint_batch            integer 8
db_block_checksum                    boolean FALSE
db_block_lru_extended_statistics     integer 0
db_block_lru_latches                 integer 1
db_block_lru_statistics              boolean FALSE
db_block_max_dirty_target            integer 4294967294
db_block_size                        integer 2048
db_domain                            string  WORLD
db_file_direct_io_count              integer 64
```

```
db_file_multiblock_read_count        integer 8
db_file_name_convert                 string
db_file_simultaneous_writes          integer 4
db_files                             integer 1024
db_name                              string  ORCL
db_writer_processes                  integer 1
dblink_encrypt_login                 boolean FALSE
dbwr_io_slaves                       integer 0
delayed_logging_block_cleanouts      boolean TRUE
discrete_transactions_enabled        boolean FALSE
disk_asynch_io                       boolean TRUE
distributed_lock_timeout             integer 300
distributed_recovery_connection_hol integer 200
distributed_transactions             integer 5
dml_locks                            integer 300
enqueue_resources                    integer 320
event                                string
fast_full_scan_enabled               boolean FALSE
fixed_date                           string
freeze_DB_for_fast_instance_recover boolean FALSE
gc_defer_time                        integer 10
gc_files_to_locks                    string
gc_latches                           integer 2
gc_lck_procs                         integer 1
gc_releasable_locks                  integer 0
gc_rollback_locks                    string
*global_names                        boolean TRUE
hash_area_size                       integer 0
hash_join_enabled                    boolean TRUE
hash_multiblock_io_count             integer 1
hi_shared_memory_address             integer 0
ifile                                file
instance_groups                      string
instance_number                      integer 0
job_queue_interval                   integer 10
job_queue_keep_connections           boolean FALSE
job_queue_processes                  integer 2
large_pool_min_alloc                 string  16K
large_pool_size                      string  0
lgwr_io_slaves                       integer 0
license_max_sessions                 integer 0
license_max_users                    integer 0
license_sessions_warning             integer 0
lm_locks                             integer 12000
lm_procs                             integer 96
lm_ress                              integer 6000
local_listener                       string
lock_name_space                      string
lock_sga                             boolean FALSE
lock_sga_areas                       integer 0
log_archive_buffer_size              integer 127
log_archive_buffers                  integer 4
*log_archive_dest                    string  %RDBMS80%\
*log_archive_duplex_dest             string
```

```
log_archive_format                    string  ARC%s.%t
log_archive_min_succeed_dest          integer 1
log_archive_start                     boolean FALSE
log_block_checksum                    boolean FALSE
log_buffer                            integer 8192
log_checkpoint_interval               integer 10000
log_checkpoint_timeout                integer 0
log_checkpoints_to_alert              boolean FALSE
log_file_name_convert                 string
log_files                             integer 255
log_simultaneous_copies               integer 0
log_small_entry_max_size              integer 80
max_commit_propagation_delay          integer 90000
max_dump_file_size                    integer 10240
*max_enabled_roles                    integer 20
max_rollback_segments                 integer 30
max_transaction_branches              integer 8
mts_dispatchers                       string
mts_listener_address                  string
mts_max_dispatchers                   integer 5
mts_max_servers                       integer 20
mts_multiple_listeners                boolean FALSE
mts_rate_log_size                     string
mts_rate_scale                        string
mts_servers                           integer 0
mts_service                           string  ORCL
nls_calendar                          string
nls_currency                          string
nls_date_format                       string
nls_date_language                     string
nls_iso_currency                      string
nls_language                          string  AMERICAN
nls_numeric_characters                string
nls_sort                              string
nls_territory                         string  AMERICA
object_cache_max_size_percent         integer 10
object_cache_optimal_size             integer 102400
ogms_home                             string
open_cursors                          integer 50
open_links                            integer 4
open_links_per_instance               integer 4
*ops_admin_group                      string
optimizer_features_enable             string  8.0.0
optimizer_mode                        string  CHOOSE
optimizer_percent_parallel            integer 0
optimizer_search_limit                integer 5
oracle_trace_collection_name          string
oracle_trace_collection_path          string  %OTRACE80%\ADMIN\CDF\
oracle_trace_collection_size          integer 5242880
oracle_trace_enable                   boolean FALSE
oracle_trace_facility_name            string  oracled
oracle_trace_facility_path            string  %OTRACE80%\ADMIN\FDF\
*os_authent_prefix                    string  OPS$
*os_roles                             boolean FALSE
```

```
parallel_adaptive_multi_user          boolean FALSE
parallel_broadcast_enabled            boolean FALSE
parallel_default_max_instances        integer 0
parallel_execution_message_size       integer 2148
parallel_instance_group               string
parallel_max_servers                  integer 5
parallel_min_message_pool             integer 48330
parallel_min_percent                  integer 0
parallel_min_servers                  integer 0
parallel_server                       boolean FALSE
parallel_server_idle_time             integer 5
parallel_transaction_resource_timeo   integer 300
partition_view_enabled                boolean FALSE
plsql_v2_compatibility                boolean FALSE
pre_page_sga                          boolean FALSE
*processes                            integer 59
push_join_predicate                   boolean FALSE
read_only_open_delayed                boolean FALSE
recovery_parallelism                  integer 0
remote_dependencies_mode              string  TIMESTAMP
*remote_login_passwordfile            string  SHARED
*remote_os_authent                    boolean FALSE
*remote_os_roles                      boolean FALSE
replication_dependency_tracking       boolean TRUE
*resource_limit                       boolean FALSE
rollback_segments                     string
row_cache_cursors                     integer 10
row_locking                           string  always
sequence_cache_entries                integer 10
sequence_cache_hash_buckets           integer 10
serial_reuse                          string  DISABLE
serializable                          boolean FALSE
session_cached_cursors                integer 0
session_max_open_files                integer 0
sessions                              integer 69
shared_memory_address                 integer 0
shared_pool_reserved_min_alloc        string  4K
shared_pool_reserved_size             string  500000
shared_pool_size                      string  10000000
snapshot_refresh_interval             integer 60
snapshot_refresh_keep_connections     boolean FALSE
snapshot_refresh_processes            integer 0
sort_area_retained_size               integer 0
sort_area_size                        integer 65536
sort_direct_writes                    string  AUTO
sort_read_fac                         integer 20
sort_spacemap_size                    integer 512
sort_write_buffer_size                integer 32768
sort_write_buffers                    integer 2
spin_count                            integer 1
sql92_security                        boolean FALSE
sql_trace                             boolean FALSE
star_transformation_enabled           boolean FALSE
tape_asynch_io                        boolean TRUE
```

```
temporary_table_locks              integer 69
text_enable                        boolean TRUE
thread                             integer 0
timed_os_statistics                integer 0
timed_statistics                   boolean TRUE
transaction_auditing               boolean TRUE
transactions                       integer 75
transactions_per_rollback_segment  integer 11
use_indirect_data_buffers          boolean FALSE
use_ism                            boolean TRUE
*user_dump_dest                    string  %RDBMS80%\trace
utl_file_dir                       string
```

9

Developing a Simple Security Application

In this chapter:

- *The Application Overview*
- *Preparing the Role-Object Matrix*
- *Views*
- *Roles*
- *Grants*
- *Application Control of Access*

There are many approaches you can use to implement security on your system. In this chapter, we're going to show you a sample application demonstrating one such approach. We're not going to include every detail of every step that was taken to build the original application on which this example is based. Our goal is not to teach you how to implement only one security method. Instead, we'd like to provide you with ideas you can use to build your own system.

The sample application is a credit card review and certification system. To set the stage, we'll provide a brief overview of the system's functionality and present a discussion of the environment and requirements of the system. In Chapter 3, *Oracle Database Objects*, when we talked about database objects, we said that the tables in the database could be used by more than one application. This is the case with the credit card system. There will be references to objects (mostly tables) shared with other applications. We'll refer to these objects as *enterprise objects* and the entire database as the *enterprise database*. Access to each object is controlled by the privileges that you give (or don't give) to each user.

In this chapter we'll use these steps in describing how the application was built:

1. Define the functionality of the application.
2. Describe the portions of the security plan that pertain to the application.
3. Explain how to build a role-object matrix (generally referred to as "the matrix").
4. Show how to build the views defined in the matrix.
5. Describe how to build the roles that were defined in the matrix.
6. Show how to assign privileges to roles and users through the GRANT command.

7. Explain how to use password-protected roles to implement security on the system.
8. Discuss the way to use password-protected roles without the users needing to know the role's password.

As you can see from this list of steps, the key to building the sample application is to first define and then use the role-object matrix. The matrix is then used to guide you through your application development cycle so you do not miss a functional area or privilege set.

We'll use many of the terms and definitions that have been discussed elsewhere in this book (e.g., table, view, program, etc.). If you find you're unfamiliar with any of these terms, we suggest that you review Chapters 2 through 6.

The Application Overview

First, let's take a look at the credit card review and certification application to see its purpose in life. The XYZ Corporation has issued corporate credit cards to many of its employees for various reasons:

- Administrative assistants can order and pay for supplies for their areas.
- Consultants use their cards to cover their expenses when they travel to customer sites.
- Sales personnel entertain customers and hold business meetings outside of the corporate offices.
- Company purchase order personnel use their cards for purchases under a specific dollar amount.
- Many other employees have cards for other reasons.

As part of the corporate system of accountability, each employee with a card must review his or her statement electronically and certify that the changes are correct. This is the same action you probably take each month when you receive your personal statement. This application allows the certification to be done electronically. Once certified as accurate, the information can be posted to the corporate accounts payable tables. A manager might also want to verify her section's spending to ensure that her area is not going over budget. The highest-level managers might want to confirm that employees are not abusing the system. A salesman, out of town on business, may want to verify that he has not exceeded his card limit. Each of these employees will require different forms of access and different privilege levels within the system.

To accommodate all the different needs of the various employees in the system, a credit card review and certification system has been developed. Of course, there is much more to the complete credit card system than the areas we'll discuss. In the rest of the chapter, we'll present the general development steps for a portion of the application.

As we said at the beginning of this chapter, there are several tables the credit card system uses that are not specifically part of the credit card system but must be used by the application. Let's look at these tables first.

About Enterprise Tables

For our discussion, we'll first examine part of an enterprise database that has many public tables and views outside the credit card review and certification system. Some points of interest about the system are the following:

- Most of the reference, or lookup, data in the database is available to all the users.
- The use of various query tools by the users is encouraged.
- The credit card users are allowed to see their own credit purchase records, as well as many enterprise tables.
- Supervisors can see records of all employees they manage.

Although most of the credit card purchase data tables can be accessed only through the applications, some of them are to be accessible for query at all times. All table data updates are to be performed *only* through the application.

Enterprise Tables Used by the Credit Card System

The credit card system uses the following enterprise tables:

- EMPLOYEE
- POSITION
- EMP_POS
- Various lookup tables

A *lookup table*, otherwise referred to as a *list of values*, is used to simplify data storage. Say you have a set of job titles which cover the range of job possibilities for any employee. These titles might be fairly long. Wouldn't it be easier and take up less storage space in the database to be able to store a one or two-digit number instead of the same titles over and over again? To accomplish this, create a table we will call TITLE_LOV with two columns—a number column and a title column. Entries in the table might look like this:

TITLE_NUM	TITLE
1	Administrative Assistant
2	Salesman
3	Buyer

If you want to store employees' titles in the employee table, all you need to do is store the number in the table. When you want to display the title, look the title up in the lookup table. You would use a SELECT statement like the following:

```
SELECT title
  FROM title_lov
 WHERE title_num = 3;
```

The value that would be returned in this example would be "Buyer." In the enterprise system, the SELECT privilege has been granted to *public* on all lookup tables, so we won't discuss them further.

A record in the EMPLOYEE table includes the employee's database username and an employee number. The POSITION table contains all the jobs and the organizational entity to which each job belongs. An employee can be assigned to work in more than one area (i.e., organization). For this reason, we can't put the organization code in the employee record. Moreover, we can't put the employee's id in the organization record because it contains only one record for each position type, and many employees can be assigned to one position type. This relationship between the EMPLOYEE table and the POSITION table is commonly called *many-to-many.*

A many-to-many relationship is resolved by using another table, usually referred to as an *intersection* or *associative table,* that will hold the employee number and the organization position code to which the employee is assigned. With this type of table, there can be many entries for each employee number, each with a different organization position code. Conversely, the table can have many entries of the same organization position code, each associated with a different employee. In the enterprise system, this is the EMP_POS table in which an employee number may occur many times and a position code may appear many times. The combination, however, must be unique—it doesn't make sense to assign an employee to the same position more than once (even though we all work hard enough to deserve the extra pay)! For example, Mary Janes is listed as both a database administrator for Department A and a database designer for Department B. Mary occasionally does work for Department C as a systems administrator. To correctly show all Mary's different positions, you need three separate entries. Using the tables listed here, you would put Mary's personnel information in the EMPLOYEE table. You would have three entries in the EMP_POS table, one for each position Mary performs. The entries in the EMP_POS table would be numbers: Mary's employee number and a number to represent each position Mary holds. Finally, in the POSITION table, you would have each position available within the company and a number to represent it, just as we had in the lookup table discussed earlier.

The EMPLOYEE table includes three fields that will be used in this system:

Field	Description
emp_no	Employee number obtained from an enterprise-wide sequence generator when a record is created
emp_db_name	Database username for this employee. If blank, no access is allowed through this application
job_title	Employee job title (clerk, manager, department head, etc.). Validated against a standard list when a record is inserted or updated

The POSITION table contains one record for each position within the organization. Each position record specifies how many employees may be assigned to that position. For example, there are four department managers, so the max_emp field in the position record for that record has "4" in it. Application and database code ensure that no more than four employees are assigned as department managers.

The POSITION table includes the following fields that will be required by the credit card system:

Field	Description
pos_no	Position number obtained from an enterprise-wide sequence generator when a record is created
pos_type	Symbol for type of position (DH-department head, E-employee, etc.)

The EMP_POS table is an associative or intersection table used to resolve the many-to-many relationship we examined earlier in this section.

The EMP_POS table includes the following fields:

Field	Description
emp_no	Foreign key to the EMPLOYEE table emp_no field
pos_no	Foreign key to the POSITION table pos_no field

These three enterprise tables will all be involved at various times during the implementation of the application.

Preparing the Role-Object Matrix

To control the levels of access different users will have in your system, you have to identify the specific privileges for each object. Database roles will be used as part of the security system, and you must associate these privileges with specific roles.

It does not actually matter whether you determine the roles first or the table privileges first. However, we recommend you determine the roles first since that tends to make it easier to determine the privileges required for each objects.

Review the Security Plan

The security plan (introduced in Chapter 7, *Developing a Database Security Plan*) for your application will include the definitions of the types of access for the system. We recommend you write a security plan even if the system being designed is not complex. By creating a security plan, you document the security approach that was intended. Should all of the people involved in the project leave, there will still be a record of the thinking behind the application implementation. The security plan serves two purposes:

- It documents the system security approach and concepts.
- It defines the specific access requirements.

From the security plan and from interviews with the customers, you can determine what the user grouping will be, and you will be able to establish some role names to represent those groups. Once you have that, you can continue with the role-object access matrix.

Role-Object Access Matrix

Access definitions from the security plan are used to determine role names. You can develop a matrix showing which roles will be given which type of access to which tables. This is the part of implementing a security system that everybody hates. In every attempt to establish a security system, all the participants secretly know that specific access rights have to be determined, and everybody tries to avoid determining them because it is a tiresome job. Unfortunately, you cannot have a successful and secure system without clearly specifying the roles and access rights.

Table 9-1 illustrates one approach to building the matrix; this table is based on one used by an actual organization. If this type of approach works for your system, by all means use it. The specific format is not as important as the function. The objective is to determine the specific object grants to be given and which functional roles will be given these privileges. The matrix uses S for SELECT, I for INSERT, U for UPDATE, and D for DELETE; an X indicates EXECUTE and is only used for stored PL/SQL programs. The common name for these is "program units" (a term used in Oracle Developer Forms) since they may be created as packages or stand-alone procedures. There are no rules about how to put a matrix together. Do what works for you in your own matrix.

The matrix uses the following enterprise tables:

EMPLOYEE
EMP_POS
POSITION

The matrix in Table 9-1 is not complete; we show just enough of it to give you an idea of what one can look like. We've included a few tables not discussed in this chapter to show you the types of tables you might want in an application. Tables not specifically associated with the system are listed at the end of the matrix, simply to keep the matrix as small as possible and to help make it easier to read and use. Generally, tables that are publicly available are not shown.

In the matrix, note that the heading of the first column, "Table Name/Role Name," is to be read as table names down, and role names across.

Table 9-1. Sample (Partial) Role-Object Privilege Matrix

Table Name/Role Name	CDHOLDER	CDAPPR	CDSYSADM	CDFINMON
CARD_HOLDER_B	S	S,I,U	S,I,U	S
DISCREP	S,I,U	S	S	S
DISPUTE_CODE	S	S	S,I,U	S
DISPUTE_SUB_CODE	S	S	S,I,U	S
ERR_LOG			S	
COMMENT_LOG	S,I,U,D	S,I,U,D	S,I,U,D	S,I,U,D
CARD_TRANS_B	S	S	S	S
CARD_TRANS_ITEM_B[a]	S,U	S	S	S
DEF_COST_CENTER_B [b]	S	S	S,I,U,D	S

Table 9-1. Sample (Partial) Role-Object Privilege Matrix (continued)

Table Name/Role Name	CDHOLDER	CDAPPR	CDSYSADM	CDFINMON
Sequences				
CARD_SEQ	S		S	
TEMP_CARD_NBR_SEQ			S	
Views				
APPROVERS_V	S	S	S	S
CARD_HOLDER_V				
DEPT_DEF_CC_V	S	S		
Program Units (EXECUTE)				
TSEC.SROLE [c]	X			

[a] The UPDATE privilege on CARD_TRANS_ITEM_B is granted only on columns reconcile, receive_date, reconcile_date, parent_id, parent_item, and reconciled_by_emp.
[b] One row is required in DEF_COST_CENTER_B and it must have item_no = 1.
[c] The EXECUTE privilege on TSEC.SROLE is granted to the CDUSER role (described later in this chapter). This role will also have the CREATE_SESSION system privilege to allow the user to log in to the database. This role will never become disabled, so EXECUTE on the program is not granted to any other role. (The program is included in the matrix for documentation purposes.)

There is one table that does not appear in the security plan or in the role-object matrix but is vital to the functionality of the sample application. This table, APP_ROLE, holds the passwords for each role in the system. It is intentionally excluded from the documentation to ensure the security of the system, but we'll discuss it in the section "Using Password-Protected Roles."

Naming Conventions

The naming convention in the security plan for this application specifies that all tables will be named to indicate their contents. We recommend that you establish a naming convention before any applications are developed. It will be too late to try to implement changes in a naming convention after the application implementation has begun. The sample application adheres to the following conventions:

- A table accessed through an application or a view has a suffix of "_B", indicating that it is a base table.
- View names have a suffix of "_V".
- Sequences have a suffix of "_SEQ".
- All stored programs are created using packaged procedures and functions.

To comply with these conventions, the TSEC package is created containing the SROLE procedure even though this is the only program within the package.

Once you have completed the matrix, you can begin to create the views and roles and determine the appropriate privileges that will be granted to each role or to an individual user.

Views

To refresh your memory, a view is a description of how data is to be retrieved from the underlying tables. It does not store data but it is treated as though it were a table in SQL statements. Views can be used to perform the following actions:

- Limit the rows accessible to a user (row-level security)
- Limit specific columns accessible to a user (column-level security)
- Pre-join several tables (removing the requirement that the user understand the complexity of joining tables)

Most of the views we discuss here are used for row-level security. One way to achieve row-level security is to use views that include qualifying conditions based on some characteristic of the user login id. If the table is never to be accessed via a query tool, then application-implemented security can be used. Even this form of security usually relies on the same login id characteristics.

In this section we discuss the logic used to determine the structure of the views, and we provide examples of how the logic is incorporated into the view definitions.

View Syntax

The view definitions we provide all use the command "SELECT *" for clarity. The * means retrieve all columns. In a real system, however, you would replace the * with a list of specific column names. The columns in the view take their names from the columns in the tables from which they are selected, but you can provide aliases for these columns. There are two syntax constructs you can use to declare column aliases in a view: with one you declare the aliases first, with the other you embed the aliases in the SELECT list. The following code examples both create the emp_v view on the employee table (the FROM and WHERE clauses are omitted for clarity):

In this example you declare aliases first:

```
CREATE OR REPLACE VIEW emp_v (employee_number, last_name, first_name, ...)
   AS
SELECT emp_no, lname, fname, ...
```

In this example, employee_number is an alias for emp_no, last_name is an alias for lname, etc.

In this example you embed aliases within the clause:

```
CREATE OR REPLACE VIEW emp_v
    AS
SELECT emp_no employee_number, lname last_name, fname first_name,
    ...
```

The aliases become the column names of the view when you either DESCRIBE the view or SELECT from the view. In the first example, the aliases listed after the view name are associated with the columns in the order in which they were declared and selected. In the second example, the same aliases are stated after each column name as part of the SELECT section of the statement. This is done by adding one or more spaces after the column, then stating the alias.

There are three advantages to using the second method:

1. The source code is easier to read and immediately identifies the column associated with an alias.
2. Aliases only have to be provided for the columns that need them.
3. It is easier to retrieve the source code of the second version from the data dictionary.

Both approaches work, however, and create the same object.

Creating the Views

In this section, we describe how the APPROVERS_V and CARD_HOLDER_V views are created. The third view listed in the matrix in Table 9-1 requires some tables that we haven't discussed, but the approach is generally the same. Naturally, applications generally have many more views than are shown here.

The APPROVERS_V view

The APPROVERS_V view is used to provide a list of only the employees who have authority to approve purchases. Both credit card holder and approver data is stored in the CARD_HOLDER_B table. This view is simple but effective.

```
CREATE OR REPLACE VIEW approvers_v AS
SELECT *
  FROM card_holder_b
 WHERE card_holder_type = 'A';
```

As written here, this view will return all approvers. However, the requirement is that, for general usage, this view should show only the person who can approve purchases for a specific employee. Note that the person who provides the approver function will not necessarily be that employee's manager.

Therefore, the view needs more qualifiers so only the one appropriate row will be returned.

```
CREATE OR REPLACE VIEW approvers_v AS
SELECT *
  FROM card_holder_b
 WHERE card_holder_type = 'A'
   AND emp_no = (SELECT approver_no
                   FROM card_holder_b
                  WHERE emp_no = (SELECT emp_no
                                    FROM employee
                                   WHERE emp_db_name = user
                                 )
                )
;
```

The logic is to get the list of approvers, then only get the one whose employee number is registered to the user. To accomplish this, we have to get the user's employee number. This is done in the second (bottom) nested SELECT—the one that is indented rightmost. Note that the emp_db_name from the EMPLOYEE table is matched with the pseudo column "user". This is one of several virtual columns available for use by anybody. The value of "user" is always the database login name. Once that value is obtained, the first nested SELECT will retrieve the employee number of the approver for that employee, then the SELECT part of the view will retrieve the CARD_HOLDER_B records for that emp_no. Only one record is returned: the employee's approver.

Could this code have been written differently? Of course. Most SQL statements that use multiple tables and something other than a very simple WHERE clause can be written several ways. For example, the view could have been written as a join of the CARD_HOLDER_B and EMPLOYEE tables:

```
CREATE OR REPLACE VIEW APPROVERS_V as
SELECT ch.*
  FROM card_holder_b ch, employee e
 WHERE ch.card_holder_type = 'A'
   AND ch.emp_no = e.emp_no
   AND e.emp_no = (SELECT approver_no
                     FROM card_holder_b chi, employee ei
                    WHERE chi.emp_no = ei.emp_no
                      AND ei.emp_db_name = user
                  )
;
```

While both of these approaches will work, there is one more consideration. The view returns only one row, the user's approving manager. Administrators or other higher-level users will want to see all approvers. If either of the previous examples is used, another view similar to the first example will be needed. But, this will result in two pieces of code and additional maintenance. It would be easier to manage if the one view could provide one or more rows depending on the type of person using the view. This is the approach used in the Oracle data dictionary views. You can add an additional WHERE condition or a UNION, as shown in the following, to accomplish this goal:

```
/* This part returns only the user's row */
CREATE OR REPLACE VIEW APPROVERS_V AS
SELECT ch.*
  FROM card_holder_b ch, employee e
 WHERE ch.card_holder_type = 'A'
  AND ch.emp_no = e.emp_no
  AND e.emp_no = (SELECT approver_no
                    FROM card_holder_b chi, employee ei
                   WHERE chi.emp_no = ei.emp_no
                     AND ei.emp_db_name = user
                 )
UNION
/* This part returns all approvers rows for managers, dept heads, and
   the dba.  The UNION operator eliminates duplicate rows. */
SELECT ch.*
  FROM card_holder_b ch, employee e
 WHERE ch.card_holder_type = 'A'
   AND ch.emp_no = e.emp_no
   AND e.emp_no IN (SELECT approver_no
                      FROM card_holder_b chi, employee ei
                     WHERE chi.emp_no = ei.emp_no
                       AND ei.emp_db_name = user
                       AND UPPER(ei.job_title) IN
                          ('MANAGER','DEPARTMENT HEAD','DBA')
                   )
;
```

The type of syntax you should use is the one that performs best on your computer and database configuration. We suggest that before you decide on a production version, you perform timing tests to select the most efficient approach.

The CARD_HOLDER_V view

The CARD_HOLDER_V view uses an approach similar to that of the APPROVERS_V view. Each employee is only allowed to see his or her own record. Managers can see the records of all employees in their own cost center. Note that the employee's manager is not necessarily the same as the employee's supervisor. Because this is a credit card system, the manager is concerned about cost center charges, and not all employees working in their cost center may be assigned to the manager. For this reason, we must use the associative table EMP_POS and the POSITION table as follows.

```
CREATE OR REPLACE VIEW CARD_HOLDER_V AS
SELECT ch.*
  FROM card_holder_b ch, employee e
 WHERE ch.card_holder_type = 'C'
```

```
    AND ch.emp_no = e.emp_no
    AND e.emp_db_name = user
UNION
SELECT ch.*
  FROM card_holder_b ch
 WHERE emp_no IN
  (SELECT emp_no
     FROM emp_pos ep, position p
    WHERE ep.pos_no = p.pos_no
      AND p.pos_no IN (SELECT pos_no
                         FROM position pp, employee ee
                        WHERE pp.cost_center = ee.cost_center
                          AND ee.emp_db_name = user
                          AND UPPER(ee.job_title)
                           IN ('MANAGER','DEPARTMENT HEAD')
                      )
  )
  ;
```

Why is the base table called CARD_HOLDER_B instead of CARD_HOLDER? One reason is the security plan being followed. The naming conventions specify that tables accessed only through views or applications are to have the "_B" suffix to indicate that they are base tables. Only the administrator of the application and the DBA will use this table directly. Because the information in the table is quite sensitive, the users should not even know the name of the table. When privileges are granted on the view or on the view synonym, the privileges granted do not translate down to the underlying table. Thus, the view protects the name and structure of the underlying table.

Roles

Roles are actually rather easy. Assume for now that the TSEC package (discussed later in this chapter) has already been created. We will create a set of login roles with minimal privileges. For each role listed in the matrix, we create a set of functional roles with passwords. The statements for the functional roles are followed by an INSERT into the APP_ROLES table (whose purpose is described in the section "Using Password-Protected Roles"). Finally, we grant the object privileges to the functional roles.

The APP_ROLES table is not listed in the matrix for security reasons. It is not accessed directly by the users—they know nothing about it. However, this table is an integral part of the security approach and will be discussed later in this chapter.

Figure 9-1 shows two users: *sue* has been granted the *cdholder* role and thus has access to the application as a valid card holder; *cathy* has not been granted any of the available application roles and cannot see any application data.

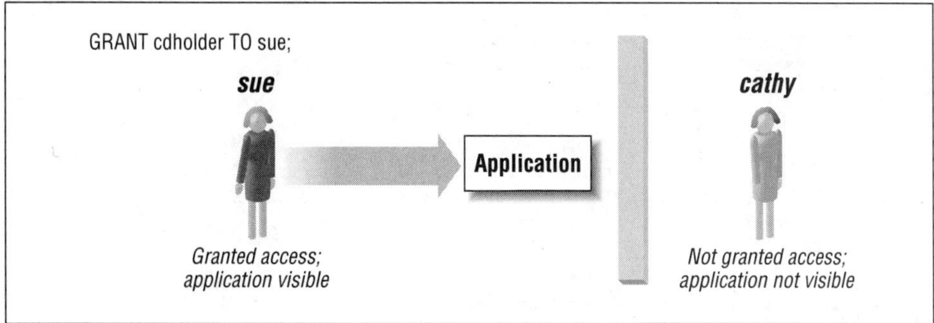

Figure 9-1. Levels of access control

In Figure 9-2, we see the steps involved when the user *sue* attempts to connect to the database. The database validates that *sue* has the appropriate privileges—granted through the CDHOLDER role—to interact with specific tables.

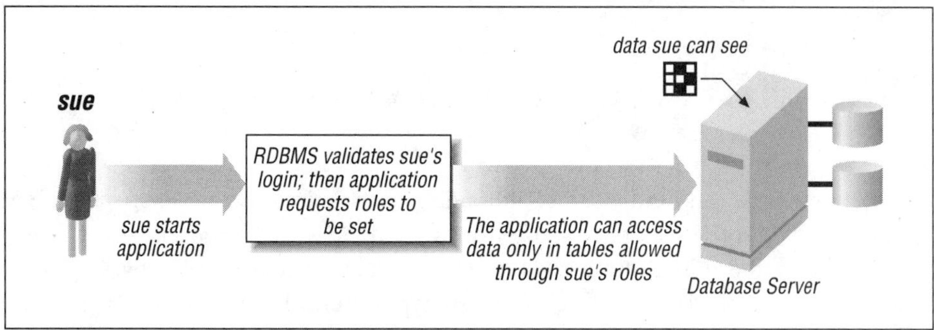

Figure 9-2. Row access control by application

```
doc

  Create one or more login roles.  These are not password protected and
  will be the user's only default role.  Note that execute privilege is
  granted on the package, and not the package.procedure.

#

CREATE ROLE cduser;
 GRANT create session TO cduser;
 GRANT execute ON tsec TO cduser;

CREATE ROLE cdappruser;
 GRANT create session TO cdappruser;
 GRANT execute ON TSEC TO cdappruser;

CREATE ROLE cdsysadmuser;
 GRANT create session TO cdsysadmuser;
 GRANT execute ON tsec TO cdsysadmuser;
```

```
CREATE ROLE cdfinmonuser;
 GRANT create session TO cdfinmONuser;
 GRANT execute ON tsec TO cdsysadmuser;

doc

  Create the functional roles with passwords.  Also insert a row
  into the app_roles table for each functional, passworded role that
  is created.

#
-- create a general role for the view access.

CREATE ROLE cdgenaccess;

-- functional roles.

CREATE ROLE cdholder IDENTIFIED BY apw_4u;
INSERT INTO app_roles
VALUES ('cdholder', 'orapgm', 'apw_4u', 'splash', null);

CREATE ROLE cdappr IDENTIFIED BY apw_4u;
INSERT INTO app_roles
VALUES ('cdappr', 'orapgm', 'apw_4u', 'splash', null);

etc.
```

All the passwords can be the same, although from a strict security perspective they should be different. These passwords will never be given to the users and will not be needed by the administrative users who must have these roles enabled at all times. The password is saved in clear, unencrypted form because it will be needed when the application runs the TSEC.SROLE program to enable the role. There is little risk in this approach since no users will have privileges on table APP_ROLES unless you grant SELECT ANY TABLE to a user. If this privilege is granted, the user can retrieve data from any table in the database even if that privilege has not been granted by the table owner.

Grants

Two types of grants will be made. First, we give table access to the roles; then the roles are granted to the users. Remember from the previous section that the login roles already have the CREATE SESSION privilege and EXECUTE privilege on the TSEC package. These grants follow the matrix, so we'll provide only a few examples here.

```
doc

  grant table and view access to the roles.
```

```
#
-- general access to the views.

GRANT select ON approvers_v TO cdgenaccess;
GRANT select ON card_holder_v TO cdgenaccess;
etc.

-- specific object grants.

PROMPT ************* cdholder *************
PROMPT
PROMPT s,i,u,d
PROMPT
GRANT select, insert, update, delete ON comment_log TO cdholder;
etc.

PROMPT s,i,u
PROMPT
GRANT select, insert, update ON discrep TO cdholder;
etc.

PROMPT s,i
PROMPT
PROMPT none

PROMPT s
PROMPT
GRANT select ON card_trans_b TO cdholder;
GRANT select ON dispute_code TO cdholder;
GRANT select ON dispute_sub_code TO cdholder;
GRANT select ON err_log TO cdholder;
GRANT select ON card_trans TO cdholder;
GRANT select ON def_cost_center TO cdholder;
GRANT select ON card_seq TO cdholder;
-- views
GRANT select ON dept_def_cc_v TO cdholder;

PROMPT other grants
PROMPT
GRANT select, update (reconcile, receive_date, reconcile_date,
      parent_id, parent_item, reconciled_by_emp)
   ON card_trans_item_b TO cdholder;

PROMPT ************* cdsysadm *************
PROMPT
PROMPT s,i,u,d
PROMPT
GRANT select, insert, update, delete ON def_cost_center TO cdsysadm;
etc.

PROMPT s,i,u
PROMPT
GRANT select, insert, update ON dispute_code TO cdsysadm;
GRANT select, insert, update ON dispute_sub_code TO cdsysadm;
```

```
etc.

PROMPT s,i
PROMPT
PROMPT none

PROMPT s
PROMPT
GRANT select ON dispute_code TO cdsysadm;
GRANT select ON dispute_sub_code TO cdsysadm;
GRANT select ON err_log TO cdsysadm;
GRANT select ON card_trans TO cdsysadm;
GRANT select ON def_cost_center TO cdsysadm;
GRANT select ON card_trans_item TO cdsysadm;
-- sequences
GRANT select ON card_seq TO cdsysadm;
GRANT select ON temp_card_nbr_seq TO cdsysadm;

PROMPT other grants
PROMPT none

etc.
```

Grant the Roles to the Users

The GRANT statement is simple, but like everything else, it should be scripted. (A script provides documentation of what you did and is repeatable.) When a role is granted to a user, it becomes one of that user's default roles and is enabled at login time even if a password is required. We do not want all of a user's roles enabled when he logs in, so after granting all of the roles, the login role is identified as the user's default. When you identify a set of roles as the default for a user, all other roles granted to the user that you do not name become non-default and are not automatically enabled at login time.

The following statements grant *mary* all of the roles she will need:

```
GRANT cdholder TO mary;
GRANT cdgenaccess TO mary;
GRANT cduser TO mary;
```

We only want the last two roles to be enabled at login time. The CDHOLDER role is a password-protected role and allows direct access to the CARD_TRANS_B and CARD_TRANS_ITEM_B tables for performance purposes. Those tables are to be accessed only through the application. By declaring only the last two roles as defaults for *mary*, the CDHOLDER role will become non-default.

Set the default roles as follows:

```
ALTER USER mary DEFAULT ROLE cduser, cdgenaccess;
```

Now only these two roles will be activated when *mary* logs into the database. The *CDHOLDER* role will have to be set manually and requires a password that *mary* does not know.

Limitation of Grants and Roles

By now it should be clear that the default Oracle access control mechanism is *object-based.* If a user is granted the SELECT privilege on a table, all rows of the table are available to that user. But most security plans specify that row access control must be implemented—that only certain parts of the table, a horizontal cut, should be accessible to the user, and that is to be based on characteristics of the user.

Thus far, row-level access has been controlled through the use of views. Some situations, however, require complex decisions to be made based on conditions at the moment, to determine what type of rows can be viewed or updated, or which columns may be updated. These situations are usually addressed by the applications.

The problem in these complex cases is controlling the moment that access is allowed. As we've noted, the access grants become effective when made and are in effect regardless of the tool being used. As previously illustrated with user *mary,* we have granted her a role that can only be enabled by providing a password—a password she does not know. If we give the user the passwords, then the user can enable the role at any time. That defeats the purpose of having passwords on the roles, and is not satisfactory. Some part of the application will have to pass the enabling command to the database. We can embed the command along with the password in the application, but hardcoding a password is never a good idea, and we recommend against it. In addition, if the application is being run in an environment where the password may be sent over a network, the possibility of compromise exists. The application is the only place where password access can, therefore, be done.

The next section describes one method of solving the problems we have identified here by:

- Embedding the command in the application
- Not hardcoding the password
- Keeping the password off the network

Application Control of Access

Access control really begins when the application is started and continues through the entire session. We have divided the control approach into the following three steps.

Restricting user startup of the application
: We want to prevent unauthorized users from even seeing the application display.

Row access control by the application
: The application can supplement the views. For performance reasons, we may have the application directly access the base table and we may restrict access to the rows in a manner similar to the view.

Enabling access through the application
: We have the application initiate a process that is completed entirely within the database. The approach will avoid hardcoding the password in the application and will not require the user to know the password.

Startup Control

Before you can control what the user can do, you must know something about the user. This is typically the user's login name. Through the login name, you should be able to obtain the user's organization information, the type of job the user performs, and so on. You must also know something about the application. This information should be complementary to the information you know about the user. In this application, we are able to get the user's information because the login names are part of the record in the EMPLOYEE table.

Because all access is role-based, the application can check the roles the user has and compare those to the roles assigned to the application in the APP_ROLES table. We describe this table more thoroughly later in the section "Using Password-Protected Roles."

The APP_ROLES table contains the application name and the roles that application will require. On startup, the application checks the roles in that table against the roles granted to the user. If there is no match, the application displays a generic login error message and exits without showing the first screen. Avoid messages that convey the nature of the failure such as "You do not have the xyz role," because the user may be clever enough to find someone who does have that role and steal the person's login password.

We recommend a very generic message such as "Insufficient privilege, access denied."

While logged in as the owner of the APP_ROLES security table, you can create a view to simplify the required logic.

```
CREATE OR REPLACE VIEW app_roles_auth AS
SELECT ar.role_name, ar.application
  FROM app_roles ar, user_role_privs urp
 WHERE ar.role_name = urp.granted_role
;
```

This view returns only the roles the user has that match those in the APP_ROLES table. Note that there is no qualification such as "user_name = user" in this view. That qualification occurs in USER_ROLE_PRIVS, a data dictionary view already restricted to the user (as described in Chapter 4, *The Oracle Data Dictionary*). Also, the view does not limit the roles to a specific application since the roles are not known until the view is accessed. Let's assume that the user is running the USER_REVIEW application. At startup, the application runs this query:

```
SELECT role_name
  FROM app_roles_auth
 WHERE UPPER(application) = 'USER_REVIEW';
```

Case is important because all entries in the data dictionary are uppercase. You might not know if the application field is from a data dictionary table, so the UPPER function guarantees the match will be done in uppercase. An alternative would be to specify SELECT COUNT(*), which returns a count of the roles. Using the count is acceptable if it is only important to know if there are matches, rather than which ones match.

Within the Oracle Forms tools (either Developer or Designer 2000), this query could be placed in one of several triggers such as:

WHEN-NEW-FORM-INSTANCE
WHEN-NEW-BLOCK-INSTANCE
WHEN-NEW-FORM-NAVIGATE
WHEN-WINDOW-ACTIVATED

You should use the most appropriate one for your own situation. In most cases, this is the WHEN_NEW_FORM_INSTANCE trigger.

Application Row Access Control

To control access to specific rows, you have to know (as you did for startup control) something about the user and what the access requirements are. If these access conditions are complex, perhaps you should create a table with an application name column, a block column, and a query_limits column. The application name and block are put into the first two columns, and the block WHERE conditions put into the query_limits column. If multiple conditions are required, there should be additional columns for matching with user- and application-related criteria so only one row will be retrieved.

Once the query limits are retrieved, the application has to modify the SELECT statement. Within the Oracle Forms tool, you can modify the SELECT the form builds to include your customized WHERE conditions. You would do this with the SET-BLOCK-PROPERTY built-in program. Also, within this tool, the UPDATE, INSERT, and DELETE statements do not have to be modified. Indeed, they cannot be modified since the form builds them on the fly, and there are no built-in functions to perform this task. UPDATE and DELETE use ROWID to ensure the proper record is being manipulated, and the form handles that. If a third-party tool is being used, the developer will have to handle these three statements in a way appropriate for the product.

Using Password-Protected Roles

One problem now remains: how to turn on the roles that require a password without hardcoding it into the application, passing it over a network, or requiring that the user know it. The latter will defeat the whole purpose of the password protection idea since we do not want the user to access this data directly. We want the user to access the data only via the application.

The method described here uses a special user account. The *security* user account will have very specific privileges. You could just use a general DBA account, but for security reasons, we recommend you create a separate *security* user account. If you use your normal DBA account and the password is compromised, serious damage is likely to occur. The impact is somewhat diminished if the *security* user account password is discovered.

The *security* user will have more to do than just facilitate the enabling of password-protected roles. The *security* user will maintain user accounts as well. For that reason, the scripts that follow have more privileges than may seem appropriate at this point in our discussion.

We create the APP_ROLES table to hold application and role information. The table may be owned by any user, including the *security* user. The script provided here to create the *security* user assumes the table is not owned by the *security* user. First we create the table; next, we create the *security* user; and finally, that user creates the TSEC package.

Create the APP_ROLES table

The first script creates the APP_ROLES table as follows:

```
doc

  mkaprole.sql

Create the app_roles table.  This table will be used with the
```

```
TSEC.SROLE procedure to set password protected roles during the execution
of an application.

#

DROP TABLE app_roles;

CREATE TABLE app_roles
  (role_name        VARCHAR2(30) NOT NULL , -- name of role
   program          VARCHAR2(48) NOT NULL ,
     -- tool program associated with role.  value found in v$session
   passwd           VARCHAR2(30) NOT NULL , -- password for role
   application      VARCHAR2(8) NOT NULL ,  -- application name of the
     -- application authorized to use role.
   role_desc        VARCHAR2(80) -- description
  )
TABLESPACE &1
STORAGE  (INITIAL   50K
             NEXT   24K
       MAXEXTENTS  100
      PCTINCREASE    0
          )
;

COMMENT ON TABLE app_roles IS
  'security table for role passwords.  read only by function TSEC.SROLE to
extract the passwords.';
COMMENT ON COLUMN app_roles.role_name IS
  'name of role as it was created.';
COMMENT ON COLUMN app_roles.program IS
  'tool program associated with the role.  value comes from v$session';
COMMENT ON COLUMN app_roles.passwd IS
  'password for role.  not encrypted.';
COMMENT ON COLUMN app_roles.application IS
  'name of application which should be running when role is enabled.';
COMMENT ON COLUMN app_roles.role_desc IS
  'comment or description of entry.';
```

The purpose of the columns is explained in the column documentation comments. These are stored in the data dictionary. A nice report can be generated to document the system if comments are created.

Create the security user

After the table is created, user *sys* creates the *security* user. The code provided here switches logins several times. It also employs substitution variables in a manner that is correct, but not common. There is a syntax oddity that we should explain.

When you use substitution variables in a SQL statement, you normally do not need a variable terminator unless the variable is to be used in conjunction with an additional value. You don't run into this very often, as most variables are used like this:

```
WHERE this_column_in_the_table = &1
```

However, if the substitution is part of a string—for example, the owner name in:

```
CREATE SYNONYM apple FOR &1.orange;
```

there is a problem.

As you know, the syntax to create a synonym is:

```
CREATE SYNONYM <synonym name> FOR <owner>.<table>;
```

In the syntax, the dot serves as a separator between the owner name and table name. When using the substitution variable, however, the dot becomes the variable terminator, so if *mary* were passed into the first CREATE statement, it would be resolved as:

```
CREATE SYNONYM apple FOR maryorange;
```

and that will not work. The dot separator between the owner, *mary*, and the table orange is missing. The one that was there became the variable terminator. Since it served that purpose, it could not also be used as the owner-table separator. Therefore, a second dot is needed. Thus the statement becomes:

```
CREATE SYNONYM apple FOR &1..orange;
```

When the variable is resolved, it is terminated by the first dot, and the second remains as the separator, so the statement is resolved as:

```
CREATE SYNONYM apple FOR mary.orange;
```

which is what is needed.

The following script creates the *security* user.

```
doc

    mksysadm.sql

    This script must be executed by user sys.

    arguments:  1 =  username for security user (password is the same)
                2 =  default tablespace for security user
                3 =  temporary tablespace for security user
                4 =  owner of app_roles table
                5 =  password for owner


    Create the privileges necessary for a system administrator
    role.  Create a system administration user.  This user must
    be able to create and drop users and roles and also update
    the app_roles table.  Access to certain system tables is also
    required.  Privileges required are checked in the user role
```

```
   maintenance forms and it will not start if the privileges
   specified here are not granted.

#
SET TERMOUT ON ECHO ON
SPOOL mksysadm.lis

-- attempt to drop the role.  error here is ok.

DROP ROLE admin_usr_role;

-- create the sysadmin role

CREATE ROLE admin_usr_role;

-- privilege to connect and establish a login session
GRANT create session TO admin_usr_role;

-- privileges for personal objects
GRANT create synonym TO admin_usr_role;
GRANT create procedure TO admin_usr_role;

-- privileges to administer users
GRANT create user TO admin_usr_role;
GRANT drop user TO admin_usr_role;
GRANT alter user TO admin_usr_role;

-- privileges to administer roles
GRANT create role TO admin_usr_role;
GRANT drop any role TO admin_usr_role;
GRANT alter any role TO admin_usr_role;
GRANT grant any role TO admin_usr_role;

-- privilege to grant privileges to roles or users
GRANT grant any privilege TO admin_usr_role;

-- create the security user, grant the role,
-- set default and temporary tablespaces.

create user &1 identified by &1;
GRANT admin_usr_role TO &1;

ALTER USER &1
  DEFAULT TABLESPACE &2
  TEMPORARY TABLESPACE &3
  DEFAULT ROLE admin_usr_role;

-- grant privileges on sys's views to the security user and
-- not the role.  this user will be executing pl/sql and that
-- engine does not recognize privileges granted through roles.

GRANT select ON &tab TO &1 WITH GRANT OPTION

DEFINE tab=sys.dba_roles
```

```
/
DEFINE tab=sys.dba_role_privs
/
DEFINE tab=sys.dba_users
/
DEFINE tab=sys.dba_sys_privs

DEFINE tab=sys.dba_tablespaces
/
DEFINE tab=sys.system_privilege_map

DEFINE tab=v_$session
/

-- create synonyms for the security user

CREATE SYNONYM &1..dba_roles FOR sys.dba_roles;
CREATE SYNONYM &1..dba_role_privs FOR sys.dba_role_privs;
CREATE SYNONYM &1..dba_users FOR sys.dba_users;
CREATE SYNONYM &1..dba_sys_privs FOR sys.dba_sys_privs;
CREATE SYNONYM &1..dba_tablespaces FOR sys.dba_tablespaces;
CREATE SYNONYM &1..system_privilege_map FOR sys.system_privilege_map;
CREATE SYNONYM &1..v$session FOR sys.v_$session;

-- connect as the app_roles table owner and grant privs to security

CONNECT &4/&5

GRANT select, insert, update, delete ON app_roles TO &1
 WITH GRANT OPTION;

-- connect as the security user and create a private synonym
-- for the role security table and the sys tables.  cannot
-- guarantee that public synonyms exist.

CONNECT &1/&1

CREATE SYNONYM app_roles FOR &4..app_roles;

SPOOL OFF
SET ECHO OFF
PROMPT
PROMPT spool file for mksysadm is:  mksysadm.lis
PROMPT
```

We did a lot in this script. The program is documented internally, but a short overview of the steps is in order:

1. A role is created and assigned the system privileges required by the *security* user.
2. The *security* user is created.

3. Privileges on *sys*'s objects are granted directly to the *security* user. This is because PL/SQL will be used and object privileges cannot be inherited through a role.
4. Synonyms for *sys*'s objects are created for the *security* user.
5. The APP_ROLES owner connects and grants privileges to the *security* user with GRANT OPTION. This is needed again because PL/SQL is being used and the package owner has to be able to temporarily allow the executing user access rights on the APP_ROLES table.
6. The script then connects as the *security* user. The *security* user creates a private synonym for the APP_ROLES table.

Create the PL/SQL program that sets roles

Next, the TSEC package and package body are created by the *security* user as follows:

```
doc

     File:  mkpwsec.sql

     This script creates the tsec package and package body.
The body contains one function:  SROLE.  The function is used as
an argument to the standard database procedure DBMS_SESSION.SET_ROLE.
This procedure requires a string of roles to be set.  For example,
suppose a user had been granted the finadmin (financial administrator)
and finpersadmin (financial personnel administrator) roles, and that
these roles were not set as defaults.  Then the command:

    DBMS_SESSION.SET_ROLE(finadmin,finpersadmin);

would activate the two roles.  If there were a password (apw_4u) for
the finadmin role, then the command would be:

    DBMS_SESSION.SET_ROLE(finadmin identified by apw_4u,finpersadmin);

    To avoid coding all the roles and passwords into applications,
the TSEC.SROLE function will assemble the string of roles and passwords
for use by DBMS_SESSION.SET_ROLE.  Function TSEC.SROLE is then used
as the argument to set_role thus:

      EXEC DBMS_SESSION.SET_ROLE(TSEC.SROLE('APPLICATION_NAME'));

    Since the function is embedded in the call to set_role, it
will be executed first and will be executed within the database.
The returned string becomes the argument list for set_role which
also executes within the database.  This means that the only argument
visible outside of the database when the call is made is the
application name required by function TSEC.SROLE.  The returned string
of roles and passwords never appears outside of the database,
nor is it ever seen by the application.
```

```
     The TSEC.SROLE function returns a string to enable all roles granted
to the user appropriate for the application when the appropriate tool
is running an appropriate application, as well as the user's default
roles (including those granted to public).

     Passwords for roles are maintained in the APP_ROLES table, which has
the following structure:

 Name            Null?    Type
 --------------- -------- ----
 ROLE_NAME       NOT NULL VARCHAR2(30) -- Name of role
 PROGRAM         NOT NULL VARCHAR2(48)
     /* TOOL Program associated with role.  Value found in v$session */
 PASSWD          NOT NULL VARCHAR2(30) -- Password for role
 APPLICATION     NOT NULL VARCHAR2(8)  -- Application name
    /* Application authorized to use role.  Argument 1 in function
tsec.srole. */
 ROLE_DESC                VARCHAR2(80) -- Description


Logic:

     The function checks V$SESSION to insure that the user is
running the correct tool for the role (like F45RUN.EXE).  If
the user is not running a registered tool and program, this function
returns only the default roles.

     Calling format:

      EXEC DBMS_SESSION.SET_ROLE(TSEC.SROLE('APPLICATION_NAME'));

     Returned value (assumes a standard role:  genselect):

     genselect, abc identified by xyz, def identified by uvw, ...

     Where:

          APPLICATION_NAME corresponds to the APPLICATION field
          in the table.  It is not case sensitive.

          abc and def are an example role names, and xyz and uvw
          are example role passwords.

     When creating users, grant all roles to the user, then alter
the user to make the role with "create session" the default role.
For example a standard select only role would be GENSELECT.
#

CREATE OR REPLACE PACKAGE tsec IS
  FUNCTION srole (arg1 IN VARCHAR2) RETURN VARCHAR2;
END;
/
```

```
CREATE OR REPLACE PACKAGE BODY tsec AS
FUNCTION srole (arg1 IN VARCHAR2) RETURN VARCHAR2 IS
  role_cmd  VARCHAR2(256);
  prog_name VARCHAR2(48);
  i INTEGER;
/* get the password protected roles then get the user's default role. */
  CURSOR c1 IS
    SELECT role_name ||
    DECODE (a.passwd, null, null, ' identified by '||a.passwd) result
      FROM app_roles a, dba_role_privs r,
           v$session v, dba_roles dr
     WHERE UPPER(a.application) = UPPER(arg1)
       AND a.role_name = r.granted_role
       AND a.role_name = dr.role
       AND r.grantee = user
       AND dr.password_required = 'YES'
       AND INSTR(v.program, a.program) > 0
       AND (INSTR(UPPER(nvl(v.module,'no module')),'sql') = 0
            OR
            UPPER(a.program) = 'ALL')
       AND v.audsid = USERENV('sessionid')
    UNION
    SELECT drp.granted_role
      FROM dba_role_privs drp, dba_roles dr
     WHERE drp.granted_role = dr.role
       AND dr.password_required = 'no'
       AND drp.default_role = 'YES'
       AND grantee IN (user, 'PUBLIC')
    ;

role_rec c1%ROWTYPE;

BEGIN

/* Following query will return only the users default role if the program in
   v$session does not match the program in app_roles table */
  i := 0;
  OPEN c1;
  LOOP
     FETCH c1 INTO role_rec;
     EXIT WHEN c1%NOTFOUND;
     i := i+1;
     IF (i = 1) THEN
        role_cmd := role_rec.result;
     ELSE
        role_cmd := role_cmd || ', ' || role_rec.result;
     END IF;
  END LOOP;
  CLOSE c1;
  RETURN role_cmd;
END;
END tsec;
/
```

Implementation logic

We want to enable the role without giving the user the password, hardcoding the password into the application, or having the password be transmitted over a network. The TSEC package will allow the application to retrieve the default roles and all roles requiring passwords. This solves the problem of giving the password to the user. Since the program also checks to make sure that the correct application is being run, the user is prevented from running the TSEC.SROLE function from the SQL*Plus command line and discovering the roles and passwords that are valid within the system. Now we need a way to execute this function without moving the roles and passwords outside the database.

Oracle supplies many PL/SQL procedures that are created when the database is first initialized. These procedures are available for general use. One procedure, found in the *DBMSUTIL.SQL* script, is the package DBMS_SESSION. Within the package body is the procedure called SET_ROLE. This is one of the few PL/SQL procedures that executes on behalf of the user—not the procedure owner—and it can be used by the database user to activate a role.

You are probably aware that in a SQL*Plus session, you (or any user) can issue the SET ROLE command, and you may wonder why a stored program is available to do the same thing. It is there to simplify the coding when a role needs to be set from an application or from PL/SQL. SET ROLE cannot be directly used in PL/SQL.

The calling syntax allows for multiple roles to be passed to the procedure. Some of these roles may have passwords, as in:

```
DBMS_SESSION.SET_ROLE(role1, role2, ..., role10 IDENTIFIED BY apw_4u, ... );
```

Procedure SET_ROLE uses the passed information and builds the following SQL statement:

```
SET ROLE role1, role2, role10 IDENTIFIED BY apw_4u;
```

Now that we have a program to retrieve the default roles and the roles with passwords, and a program that will issue the SET ROLE command, we can combine the two. But first, a little *algebra*!

Don't panic! Remember that expressions are resolved from the inside out, so if you have a formula with parentheses, you have to do the stuff inside the parentheses first. This makes sense because the outer operation has to use the results of the inner ones. For example, given the equation (4 * (6 + 2)), you first resolve the inner equation (6 + 2) = 8 and then resolve the outer equation, which becomes (4 * 8) or 32.

The same principle applies to programs. Many programs require arguments to be passed, but you can actually pass a function as well—if the function returns the type of information that the program needs. This is referred to as a nested procedure call. That is how the DBMS_SESSION.SET_ROLE and TSEC.SROLE programs are used.

We call the SET_ROLE procedure and pass it the TSEC.SROLE function in the following manner:

```
DBMS_SESSION.SET_ROLE(TSEC.SROLE('APPLICATION_NAME'));
```

This is a nested procedure call, and any nested call is always resolved from the lowest level first, or from the inside out. So, TSEC.SROLE will use the application name to query the APP_ROLES table and find users' default roles as well as the roles needed by the application. If any of the roles require passwords, the passwords will also be returned. TSEC.SROLE returns the user's default roles and the roles-identified-by-password strings separated by commas. After that, the DBMS_SESSION.SET_ROLE procedure uses the returned string to issue the SET ROLE command as previously shown.

All this activity takes place *inside the database*. The only thing transmitted over the communication media is the initial command. Neither the roles nor the passwords are returned to the application.

To refine the procedure, the SQL statement in TSEC.SROLE uses four tables:

APP_ROLES
DBA_ROLE_PRIVS
DBA_ROLES
V$SESSION

The application name must be in the APP_ROLES table, along with all required roles and their passwords. The user must have been granted those roles. Finally, the application must be running under the proper tool, as registered in the APP_ROLES table.

Values for the program column of APP_ROLES and also V$SESSION will vary depending on the system configuration; we cannot give every possible option here. If you are running the application in host mode (that is, while physically logged onto the same machine running the database), the real application name will be found in the program column. For example, if you are running SQL*Plus on a Windows95 host, the value is *PLUS33W.EXE*. If you are running Forms in same environment, the value is *F50RUN32.EXE*. These are the actual programs.

A client/server configuration, however, is not seen by the database in the same way. If you run SQL*Plus or Forms on the client workstation, the value in the program is "OraPgm." The program name will probably be the same if you are running a web-enabled form. If the Oracle Application Server is being used as a dynamic HTML processor, a different program name may be seen.

Execution

Having set all of this in place (the APP_ROLES table, the *security* user, the TSEC.SROLE function, and users with roles they cannot enable), what happens when you run an application? The following analysis assumes the user is running the VERIFY_CHG application:

1. The user starts the application and provides the username and password.
2. The application validates the user.
3. The application sends DBMS_SQL.SET_ROLE(TSEC.SROLE('VERIFY_CHG')) to the database.
4. The database executes TSEC.SROLE to determine roles for application VERIFY_CHG and the user.
5. TSEC.SROLE returns a string of roles and role-password combinations to DBMS_SQL.SET_ROLE.
6. DBMS_SQL.SET_ROLE executes the SET ROLE command to enable the required roles.
7. The user navigates through the application and does work.

It is important to understand that the role is set only for the current session. If the user, after starting the application, opens another window, goes to another workstation (or even a dumb terminal), and then logs into the database, that is a different session—nothing done in the first session (where the application is being run) will be in place for the user.

Throughout this and other chapters, we've discussed roles, privileges, and users. Not too much has been said about the number of roles, privileges, and users you may have to establish and manage. The task can be daunting if you do not have some sort of application to simplify your administration tasks. You might also find that you need additional tools to help you document what you have in place. In this context, "documentation" means a script that can be used to recreate the account and access structures you have created in the database. In Chapter 14, *Maintaining User Accounts*, we'll discuss an application that can assist you with the management of user accounts and role privileges.

In this chapter:

10

Developing an Audit Plan

Database auditing is the monitoring and recording of activities occurring within a database. You typically audit to ensure that no unauthorized users are removing data from the data dictionary or accessing tables they should not have the privileges to see. You might also want to audit specific tables that help you determine the volume of accesses occurring at peak times. This type of auditing is helpful in analyzing trends and evaluating system performance.

The Oracle RDBMS provides functions that let you audit most actions that can be taken within and against the database. These actions can include (but are not limited to) the following:

- Viewing, modifying, or removing information from tables
- Creating or removing objects like tables, indexes, views, procedures, triggers, etc.
- Executing programs

This standard Oracle functionality does not support auditing at the row level. In other words, through standard auditing, you can audit actions that have been performed against a table, but not what has changed in a specific row of that table. To gain the ability to monitor who has changed a specific row of a table or exactly what action was taken against a row of a table, custom code is required; we'll show you an example of such code in Chapter 11, *Developing a Sample Audit Application*.

This chapter mainly discusses the standard auditing functionality of Oracle. Where appropriate, we'll mention custom approaches that you might want to take to extend this capability.

There are many schools of thought about enabling auditing on a database. If your company has implemented firewalls or other isolating security measures, you might believe that your system is secure. You might feel there is no need to enable auditing. Often, the issue of whether to perform any kind of auditing is overlooked when a security plan is being written. If auditing has not been discussed by the people creating the security policy and plan, an auditing policy and auditing plan may not be created. There are some companies that have never seen a need to implement auditing within their database and have never had a problem—that they are aware of.

Many sites don't initially activate the auditing of a database. In fact, auditing might not be activated unless or until there has been a security breach either by an outside intruder or by an employee who has overstepped his or her bounds. Either you observe some suspicious activity, or you spot resource usage that seems inconsistent with the normal pattern of operation. You might then enable auditing to confirm that something is wrong. We don't recommend this after-the-fact approach. It's like closing the barn door after the horse has escaped. You stand the chance of a hacker breaking in and either damaging the data in your database or obtaining information that might compromise your company's competitive edge.

Other sites choose to audit—and audit heavily. But this approach isn't always the right one either. Since each object you audit carries with it a potential cost in performance and resource use, you need to carefully evaluate and choose the forms of auditing that make the most sense for your own company's environment.

Why Audit?

The first step in developing an audit plan is to determine why you need to audit. Not every site does. As we've mentioned, there are two main reasons for auditing:

- Security auditing—to determine if someone is attempting to break into your system
- Performance auditing—to determine why the system is so slow

Once you've figured out why you want to implement auditing, deciding which objects to audit will be easier. Determining the purpose will also help you narrow your scope to avoid gathering too much superfluous information.

Auditing to Confirm Suspicions

One good reason for auditing is to confirm your suspicions that something or someone is causing a problem. For example, you might suspect that data is being deleted from a table that should not be losing any records. In order to determine whether or not this is the case, you could enable auditing to track deletions from that specific table. By limiting the scope of the audit, you get a much clearer picture of the specific activity you want to track. Having said that, we'll admit there are times when the suspicious activity may be so subtle that you must first enable general auditing and then, after you evaluate the audit results, narrow the auditing to better pinpoint the source of the problem. There is no rule that says you cannot enable one form of auditing for a period of time and then disable that auditing and enable another type.

Auditing to Analyze Performance

If you are performing auditing to determine the volume of traffic interacting with specific areas of your database, we recommend you narrow the scope of your auditing to those specific areas that will provide you the information you are looking for. If you are interested in monitoring I/O, then enabling object monitoring will not accomplish your purpose. You should also audit over a set period of time to limit the volume of data collected. In this way, the information you've gathered will not get cluttered or overwhelmed with extra, unneeded data. Once you have gathered enough information to fulfill your auditing purposes, you can archive the audit information and purge it from the database audit history to free space in the *system* tablespace, as we describe in the next section.

Where to Audit

Once you've decided to enable some form of auditing, you next have to decide where the audit information will be stored. If the operating system supports an audit trail that's stored outside the database, you can write the audit trail either directly to an operating system file or to the database.

Two *INIT.ORA* parameters control the auditing actions:

AUDIT_FILE_DEST
: Tells Oracle the directory name in which the audit trail is to be written. The default value for this parameter is $ORACLE_HOME/RDBMS/AUDIT.

AUDIT_TRAIL
: Enables or disables auditing.

As a value for AUDIT_TRAIL, specify one of these values: "NONE," "OS," or "DB." If you specify "NONE" (the default), no non-default auditing will occur. If you specify "OS," system-wide auditing will be turned on and the results written to a file in the *AUDIT_FILE_DEST* directory. The information written to the operating system file will be encoded and is not readable. If you specify "DB," system-wide auditing will be enabled and the results stored in the SYS.AUD$ table in the *sys* schema in an unencoded, readable format.

Oracle supplies several views against the SYS.AUD$ table to make viewing of the audit information easier. Oracle-supplied tools, such as SQL*Plus, can be used to generate reports about the auditing outcome.

About the SYS.AUD$ Table

Because the SYS.AUD$ table is owned by *sys*, the values are stored in the *system* tablespace. High audit activity results in fragmentation of the *system* tablespace—not a good thing to have happen. Therefore, if you decide to use the database to hold the audit information, be sure to move the SYS.AUD$ table to another tablespace.

You only to need change the location of the SYS.AUD$ table *once* for each database—at the time you create the database or when you decide to enable auditing on a database.

To accomplish this, you must be logged on as *sys*. However, you can work from SQL*Plus if you wish. In other words, you do not have to be connected from the Server Manager utility to perform this work.

Create a new tablespace with a meaningful name like "audit_storage" or "audit_info." Sizing the tablespace to ensure that you can hold enough information for the period of time you require auditing to be enabled can get tricky. You may need to play around with the storage parameters; you might initially size the tablespace large and adjust it down later as you get a feel for just how much space is required for your particular auditing needs. Here are some things to consider in determining the size of the tablespace:

1. The volume of different activities you are auditing
2. The amount of information you need to retain online
3. The amount of time you want to spend maintaining this table; if the table is sized too small, you have to archive and/or delete from the table more often than you might really want

Once the tablespace is created, you create a temporary table in the new tablespace using the command AS SELECT * FROM SYS.AUD$, then drop the current SYS.AUD$ table, and rename the temporary table to AUD$. Here is an example of what your script will look like:

```
SQL> connect sys/<appropriate_sys_password>
Connected.
SQL> CREATE TABLESPACE audit_storage
  2            DATAFILE 'E:\ORANT\DATABASE\AUDSTOR01.ORA'
  3            SIZE 40M;

Tablespace created.

SQL> CREATE TABLE audit_temp
  2        TABLESPACE audit_storage
  3           STORAGE (INITIAL 10M
  4                       NEXT  1M
  5                 MINEXTENTS  1
  6                  MAXEXTENTS 10
  7                 PCTINCREASE 1)
  8        AS SELECT *
  9            FROM sys.aud$;

Table created.

SQL> DROP TABLE sys.aud$;
Table dropped.

SQL> RENAME audit_temp TO aud$;
Table renamed.

SQL> SELECT table_name, tablespace_name
  2    FROM user_tables
  3   WHERE table_name = 'AUD$';

TABLE_NAME                     TABLESPACE_NAME
------------------------------ ------------------------------
AUD$                           AUDIT_STORAGE
```

A Problem

There is one problem with the approach described in the last section. When you create the table as SELECT * from AUD$, you do not carry over any of the views based on the AUD$ table. When you drop the real AUD$ table, the views become invalid. After renaming the temporary table to AUD$, the views will still be invalid and must be recompiled. To manually recompile the views, use a command with the following syntax:

```
SQL> ALTER VIEW dba_audit_exists COMPILE;

View altered.
```

To determine the list of invalid views, you can perform the following query—logged on as the user *sys*. The results shown here are from an Oracle8 version 8.0.4 database:

```
SQL> COLUMN object_name FORMAT a30
SQL> SELECT object_name, status
```

```
  2   FROM user_objects
  3  WHERE status = 'INVALID';

OBJECT_NAME                     STATUS
------------------------------ -------
DBA_AUDIT_EXISTS                INVALID
DBA_AUDIT_OBJECT                INVALID
DBA_AUDIT_SESSION               INVALID
DBA_AUDIT_STATEMENT             INVALID
USER_AUDIT_OBJECT               INVALID
USER_AUDIT_SESSION              INVALID
USER_AUDIT_STATEMENT            INVALID
USER_AUDIT_TRAIL                INVALID

8 rows selected.
```

Recompiling the views with the new SYS.AUD$ table will result in the views becoming valid for the renamed table.

Default Auditing Privileges

Even if you enable the auditing parameters through the *INIT.ORA* parameter file, only those areas you specifically declare will actually be audited. In order for an account to be able to activate auditing, the AUDIT SYSTEM privilege must be granted to that account.

Even without privileges granted to any account, there are some actions that will be stored to operating system files whether auditing is enabled or not. When a database is created, a file, commonly referred to as the *alert log*, is created. The location and name of this file are operating system-dependent. On a Windows NT system running Oracle8 with a database named ORCL, for example, the alert log is called *orclALRT.LOG* and is found in the *C:\orant\RDBMS80\TRACE* directory. The security-related actions stored in the alert log for the database include:

- Database startup
- Database shutdown
- Any connection made by an account that has administrator privileges
- Any database structure changes that are performed, like creating a tablespace or adding a datafile

Note that when you use *sys* or *internal* to connect to the database, a record is not generated in the alert log. The only way you can connect to a database as *sys* or *internal* is through an operating system account that either belongs to the DBA group or has the OPSYS privilege. These accounts skirt the normal database security and, therefore, their connection to the database as privileged users is assumed to be normal and is not tracked.

With auditing enabled and the information being stored in either the database or the operating system (or both), disk space becomes a very real consideration. If the tablespace or disk to which Oracle is writing the audit trail becomes full, the audit trail will cease to be logged and information will be lost. Therefore, you must ensure that ample room exists on the tablespace or disk to which the audit information will be written.

We noted in Chapter 4, *The Oracle Data Dictionary*, that the only view from which Oracle permits data to be deleted is AUDIT_HISTORY. This is to let you periodically reduce the storage area required for auditing.

How Auditing Works

By default, from Oracle version 7.X on, the following sequence of events occurs when the database is created:

1. *CATALOG.SQL* is run and calls several other scripts.
2. *CATAUDIT.SQL* is run as one of the scripts called from *CATALOG.SQL*.
3. The auditing views are created.
4. A public synonym is created for each of the auditing views.
5. Public access is granted to enable SELECT on each of the auditing views.

Thus, from the point in time when the database is created, the ability for anyone to audit activities in the database exists. In the case of USER_ audit views, as opposed to DBA_ audit views, the user will only be permitted to view information in his own area and not be able to see information in another user's schema. The *CATAUDIT.SQL* script can be found in the *$ORACLE_HOME/RDMBS80/ADMIN* directory on most platforms. On an OpenVMS system, all of the "CAT" scripts (Oracle-delivered scripts with the first three letters of the script name "CAT") can be found in the *ORA_ROOT:[RDBMS]* directory.

The Auditing Views

The auditing views require few resources prior to being activated. However, since *public* is granted access to them, be sure to protect them from tampering. Running the *CATAUDIT.SQL* script will create the auditing views shown in Table 10-1.

Only the access to the DBA_ views for auditing is granted to the SELECT_CATALOG_ROLE.

Table 10-1. Oracle Standard Auditing Views (from CATAUDIT.SQL)

Auditing View	Description
AUDIT_ACTIONS	Description table for audit trail action type codes.
ALL_DEF-AUDIT_OPTS	Single-row view indicating the default auditing options remark for newly-created objects. This view has an ALL member only, since the default is system-wide and applies to all accessible objects.
DBA_OBJ_AUDIT_OPTS	These views indicate what kind of audit trail entries (none, session-level, or access-level) are generated by the success or failure of each possible operation on a table or view (e.g., SELECT, ALTER). All information will be visible to the DBA.
USER_OBJ_AUDIT_OPTS	These views indicate what kind of audit trail entries (none, session-level, or access-level) are generated by the success or failure of each possible operation on a table or view (e.g., SELECT, ALTER). Only the user's own information will be visible to him.
DBA_STMT_AUDIT_OPTS	This view is only accessible to DBAs. One row is kept for each system auditing option set system-wide, or for a particular user.
DBA_PRIV_AUDIT_OPTS	One row is kept for each system privilege auditing option set system-wide, or for a particular user.
DBA_AUDIT_TRAIL	The raw audit trail of all audit trail records in the system. Some columns are only filled in by certain statements. This view is accessible only to DBAs.
USER_AUDIT_TRAIL	The raw audit trail of all information related to the user or the objects owned by the user. Some columns are only filled in by certain statements. This view is created by selecting from the DBA_AUDIT_TRAIL view and restricting the rows.
DBA_AUDIT_SESSION	All audit trail records concerning CONNECT and DISCONNECT, based on DBA_AUDIT_TRAIL.
USER_AUDIT_SESSION	All audit trail records concerning CONNECT and DISCONNECT, based on USER_AUDIT_TRAIL.
DBA_AUDIT_STATEMENT	All audit trail records concerning the following statements: GRANT, REVOKE, AUDIT, NOAUDIT, and ALTER SYSTEM. Based on DBA_AUDIT_TRAIL.
USER_AUDIT_STATEMENT	Same as the DBA version, except that it is based on USER_AUDIT_TRAIL.

Table 10-1. Oracle Standard Auditing Views (from CATAUDIT.SQL) (continued)

Auditing View	Description
DBA_AUDIT_OBJECT	Audit trail records for statements concerning objects, such as table, cluster, view, index, sequence, [public] database link, [public] synonym, procedure, trigger, rollback segment, tablespace, role, or user. The audit trail records for AUDIT/NOAUDIT and GRANT/REVOKE operations on these objects can be seen through the DBA_AUDIT_STATEMENT view.
USER_AUDIT_OBJECT	Same as DBA_AUDIT_OBJECT, except that it is based on the USER_AUDIT_TRAIL.
DBA_AUDIT_EXISTS	Only DBAs can see audit information about objects that do not exist. Lists audit trail entries produced by AUDIT EXISTS/NOT EXISTS. This is all audit trail entries with return codes of 942, 943, 959, 1418, 1432, 1434, 1435, 1534, 1917, 1918, 1919, 2019, 2024, and 2289, and for Trusted Oracle 1, 951, 955, 957, 1430, 1433, 1452, 1471, 1535, 1543, 1758, 1920, 1921, 1922, 2239, 2264, 2266, 2273, 2292, 2297, 2378, 2379, 2382, 4081, 12006, and 12325. This view is accessible to DBAs only.

If a DML statement such as UPDATE is performed and then rolled back, the audit entry may also be removed from the audit table.

The DBA as a Clairvoyant

In the documentation of the last view, DBA_AUDIT_EXISTS, the Oracle documentation supplied in the script does not mean to imply that the DBA is really clairvoyant! The statement "Only DBAs can see audit trail information about objects that do not exist" is in reference to Oracle's error code return when a query requests an object the user does not have the privilege to access. For example, an error with a code of 942 is generated when a request is made for a table whose table name is not registered within the data dictionary. Sometimes, 942 errors don't indicate any actual wrongdoing. There are occasions when a user or developer may just have "fat fingered" or mistyped a table name and received this error as a result. The error tells the user that the "table or view does not exist." However, an employee who is repeatedly receiving this error may be attempting to gain information from the database about areas with which he should *not* have the ability to interact. If you suspect that someone is fishing around in the database trying to guess the names of tables, you might enable auditing to track occurrences of 942 errors (among others). In this way, you might be able to spot someone who is steadily receiving this error. Once you have confirmed that someone is attempting to obtain information about the tables, you can take further action as required.

Available Audit Actions

In an Oracle 8.0.4 database, there are 121 separate types of auditing that can be performed. Once the *CATAUDIT.SQL* script has been run, you can do a SELECT on AUDIT_ACTIONS to display the complete list of audit actions you can perform. The list contains the following:

```
SQL> SELECT * FROM audit_actions;
   ACTION NAME
--------- ---------------------------
        0 UNKNOWN
        1 CREATE TABLE
        2 INSERT
        3 SELECT
        4 CREATE CLUSTER
        5 ALTER CLUSTER
        6 UPDATE
        7 DELETE
        8 DROP CLUSTER
        9 CREATE INDEX
       10 DROP INDEX
       11 ALTER INDEX
       12 DROP TABLE
       13 CREATE SEQUENCE
       14 ALTER SEQUENCE
       15 ALTER TABLE
       16 DROP SEQUENCE
       17 GRANT OBJECT
       18 REVOKE OBJECT
       19 CREATE SYNONYM
       20 DROP SYNONYM
       21 CREATE VIEW
       22 DROP VIEW
       23 VALIDATE INDEX
       24 CREATE PROCEDURE
       25 ALTER PROCEDURE
       26 LOCK
       27 NO-OP
       28 RENAME
       29 COMMENT
       30 AUDIT OBJECT
       31 NOAUDIT OBJECT
       32 CREATE DATABASE LINK
       33 DROP DATABASE LINK
       34 CREATE DATABASE
       35 ALTER DATABASE
       36 CREATE ROLLBACK SEG
       37 ALTER ROLLBACK SEG
       38 DROP ROLLBACK SEG
```

```
39 CREATE TABLESPACE
40 ALTER TABLESPACE
41 DROP TABLESPACE
42 ALTER SESSION
43 ALTER USER
44 COMMIT
45 ROLLBACK
46 SAVEPOINT
47 PL/SQL EXECUTE
48 SET TRANSACTION
49 ALTER SYSTEM
50 EXPLAIN
51 CREATE USER
52 CREATE ROLE
53 DROP USER
54 DROP ROLE
55 SET ROLE
56 CREATE SCHEMA
57 CREATE CONTROL FILE
59 CREATE TRIGGER
60 ALTER TRIGGER
61 DROP TRIGGER
62 ANALYZE TABLE
63 ANALYZE INDEX
64 ANALYZE CLUSTER
65 CREATE PROFILE
66 DROP PROFILE
67 ALTER PROFILE
68 DROP PROCEDURE
70 ALTER RESOURCE COST
71 CREATE SNAPSHOT LOG
72 ALTER SNAPSHOT LOG
73 DROP SNAPSHOT LOG
74 CREATE SNAPSHOT
75 ALTER SNAPSHOT
76 DROP SNAPSHOT
77 CREATE TYPE
78 DROP TYPE
79 ALTER ROLE
80 ALTER TYPE
81 CREATE TYPE BODY
82 ALTER TYPE BODY
83 DROP TYPE BODY
84 DROP LIBRARY
85 TRUNCATE TABLE
86 TRUNCATE CLUSTER
91 CREATE FUNCTION
92 ALTER FUNCTION
93 DROP FUNCTION
94 CREATE PACKAGE
95 ALTER PACKAGE
96 DROP PACKAGE
97 CREATE PACKAGE BODY
98 ALTER PACKAGE BODY
```

```
       99 DROP PACKAGE BODY
      100 LOGON
      101 LOGOFF
      102 LOGOFF BY CLEANUP
      103 SESSION REC
      104 SYSTEM AUDIT
      105 SYSTEM NOAUDIT
      106 AUDIT DEFAULT
      107 NOAUDIT DEFAULT
      108 SYSTEM GRANT
      109 SYSTEM REVOKE
      110 CREATE PUBLIC SYNONYM
      111 DROP PUBLIC SYNONYM
      112 CREATE PUBLIC DATABASE LINK
      113 DROP PUBLIC DATABASE LINK
      114 GRANT ROLE
      115 REVOKE ROLE
      116 EXECUTE PROCEDURE
      117 USER COMMENT
      118 ENABLE TRIGGER
      119 DISABLE TRIGGER
      120 ENABLE ALL TRIGGERS
      121 DISABLE ALL TRIGGERS
      122 NETWORK ERROR
      123 EXECUTE TYPE
      157 CREATE DIRECTORY
      158 DROP DIRECTORY
      159 CREATE LIBRARY
121 rows selected.
```

The number and type of auditing actions you can enable may vary from version to version of the RDBMS. The numbers listed in the ACTION column are used internally by Oracle to reference the actions rather than reference the character NAME translation. Oracle views that contain numbers generally have sequence gaps to provide space for options to be added in later releases. Keep in mind that when you enable auditing on an action, you are just asking Oracle to report each time that action has occurred.

Auditing Options

The default auditing options that can be taken against an object are normally activated with the clause WHENEVER SUCCESSFUL or WHENEVER UNSUCCESSFUL. The command to enable auditing when the user *ralph* successfully modifies a value in a table would look like this:

```
AUDIT UPDATE BY ralph BY SESSION WHENEVER SUCCESSFUL;
```

The default auditing options and their abbreviations are:

Option	Abbreviation
ALTER	ALT
AUDIT	AUD
COMMENT	COM
CREATE	CRE
DELETE	DEL
EXECUTE	EXE
GRANT	GRA
INDEX	IND
INSERT	INS
LOCK	LOC
READ	REA
REFERENCE	REF
RENAME	REN
SELECT	SEL
UPDATE	UPD
WRITE	WRI

For the USER_OBJ_AUDIT_OPTS and DBA_OBJ_AUDIT_OPTS views (see Table 10-1 for a summary of these views), the values in each column of the view from the ALT (ALTER) column through the UPD (UPDATE) column are three-character strings that represent different levels of detail. The other columns in this view are OWNER, OBJECT_NAME, and OBJECT_TYPE. For every object a user owns, there will be an entry in the USER_OBJ_AUDIT_OPTS view and the DBA_OBJ_AUDIT_OPTS view. A table owner can enable auditing to capture each time someone removes data from his table.

Since you can enable auditing by each time a user accesses an object or, alternatively, by each user session, the levels of detail are Access (A), Session (S), or None (-). The values appear in sequences like "A/S", "A/-", etc. The value before the slash indicates the auditing level if the action was successful. The value after the slash indicates the auditing level if the action was not successful. The form of display was chosen to enable the listing of all the forms of audit on one line. This is also the reason for the columns having three-letter names. The view may be formatted for readability but the values (once you get used to what the information is presenting) eventually become very readable. A sample output of one line from the DBA_OBJ_AUDIT_OPTS view minus the OBJECT_NAME and OBJECT_TYPE columns—without any auditing enabled—would look like the following.

```
ALT AUD COM DEL GRA IND INS LOC REN SEL UPD REF EXE CRE REA WRI
--- --- --- --- --- --- --- --- --- --- --- --- --- --- --- ---
-/- -/- -/- -/- -/- -/- -/- -/- -/- -/- -/- -/- -/- -/- -/- -/-
```

There are no action levels displayed in this example, so there is a dash (-) on either side of each slash in the pairs. The object types of interest in this view are TABLE, VIEW, SEQUENCE, PROCEDURE, TYPE, and DIRECTORY.

From the DICTIONARY View

Earlier in this chapter, we looked at the documentation stored in the actual *CATAUD.SQL* script to see what the auditing views are and to gain a brief description of each view. A much easier way to see the auditing view descriptions is to do a SELECT from the view DICTIONARY and just look for entries that contain the word "AUDIT." In an version 8.0.3 database, you will see the following entries:

```
SQL> COLUMN table_name FORMAT a25
SQL> COLUMN comments FORMAT a45 WORD
SQL> SELECT table_name, comments
  2    FROM dictionary
  3   WHERE table_name LIKE '%_AUDIT%';

TABLE_NAME                COMMENTS
------------------------- ---------------------------------------------
ALL_DEF_AUDIT_OPTS        Auditing options for newly created objects
DBA_AUDIT_EXISTS          Lists audit trail entries produced by AUDIT
                          NOT EXISTS and AUDIT EXISTS
DBA_AUDIT_OBJECT          Audit trail records for statements concerning
                          objects, specifically: table, cluster, view,
                          index, sequence,  [public] database link,
                          [public] synonym, procedure, trigger, rollback
                          segment, tablespace, role, user
DBA_AUDIT_SESSION         All audit trail records concerning CONNECT and
                          DISCONNECT
DBA_AUDIT_STATEMENT       Audit trail records concerning  grant,
                          revoke, audit, noaudit and alter system
DBA_AUDIT_TRAIL           All audit trail entries
DBA_OBJ_AUDIT_OPTS        Auditing options for all tables and views
DBA_PRIV_AUDIT_OPTS       Describes current system privileges being
                          audited across the system and by user
DBA_STMT_AUDIT_OPTS       Describes current system auditing options
                          across the system and by user
USER_AUDIT_OBJECT         Audit trail records for statements concerning
                          objects, specifically: table, cluster, view,
                          index, sequence,  [public] database link,
                          [public] synonym, procedure, trigger, rollback
                          segment, tablespace, role, user
USER_AUDIT_SESSION        All audit trail records concerning CONNECT and
                          DISCONNECT
USER_AUDIT_STATEMENT      Audit trail records concerning  grant, revoke,
                          audit, noaudit and alter system
```

```
USER_AUDIT_TRAIL          Audit trail entries relevant to the user
USER_OBJ_AUDIT_OPTS       Auditing options for user's own tables and
                          views

14 rows selected.
```

There were actually 20 rows returned from the query, but 6 of the rows pertain to replication internal auditing, so we eliminated them from the output since they do not pertain to this discussion. (Some minor massaging of the output was also done for readability.)

Views Related to SYS.AUD$

All the audit information is stored to one table, SYS.AUD$. The view used most often to gain data about the results of audits is the DBA_AUDIT_TRAIL view. Because this view is used most often, we examine it more closely here. We are not presenting the actual SYS.AUD$ table, because you will generally not be dealing with this table directly.

The DBA_AUDIT_TRAIL view contains the following columns:

```
SQL> DESCRIBE dba_audit_trail
 Name                            Null?    Type
 ------------------------------- -------- ----
 OS_USERNAME                              VARCHAR2(255)
 USERNAME                                 VARCHAR2(30)
 USERHOST                                 VARCHAR2(128)
 TERMINAL                                 VARCHAR2(255)
 TIMESTAMP                       NOT NULL DATE
 OWNER                                    VARCHAR2(30)
 OBJ_NAME                                 VARCHAR2(128)
 ACTION                          NOT NULL NUMBER
 ACTION_NAME                              VARCHAR2(27)
 NEW_OWNER                                VARCHAR2(30)
 NEW_NAME                                 VARCHAR2(128)
 OBJ_PRIVILEGE                            VARCHAR2(16)
 SYS_PRIVILEGE                            VARCHAR2(40)
 ADMIN_OPTION                             VARCHAR2(1)
 GRANTEE                                  VARCHAR2(30)
 AUDIT_OPTION                             VARCHAR2(40)
 SES_ACTIONS                              VARCHAR2(19)
 LOGOFF_TIME                              DATE
 LOGOFF_LREAD                             NUMBER
 LOGOFF_PREAD                             NUMBER
 LOGOFF_LWRITE                            NUMBER
 LOGOFF_DLOCK                             VARCHAR2(40)
 COMMENT_TEXT                             VARCHAR2(4000)
 SESSIONID                       NOT NULL NUMBER
 ENTRYID                         NOT NULL NUMBER
 STATEMENTID                     NOT NULL NUMBER
 RETURNCODE                      NOT NULL NUMBER
 PRIV_USED                                VARCHAR2(40)
```

```
OBJECT_LABEL                                          RAW MLSLABEL
SESSION_LABEL                                         RAW MLSLABEL
```

What's stored in SYS.AUD$?

Of the columns within the SYS.AUD$ table (provided the information is meaningful for the auditing action), there will always be information filled in about the user's name, the session identifier, the terminal identifier, the name of the schema object accessed, the operation that was performed or attempted, the completion code of the operation, the date and timestamp, the system privilege used, and, for Trusted Oracle, the user session label and the schema object accessed label.

For each action being audited, there may be a large volume of information generated. For this reason, you might decide to create a summary table to separate and/or summarize the information of interest from the total volume of information collected.

Creating a summary table

In order to easily view the audit information you have collected, you may want to create a table of data that summarizes the information of interest. By creating a smaller table and populating it with a summary of information, you accomplish two very important things:

- You enable removal of information from the underlying SYS.AUD$ audit table to conserve storage space.
- You gain easier access to your trending data.

In other words, if you are interested in collecting the total number of failed logons to your database over a two-week period of time, you might create a table that contains only two columns: the day's date and the total count of unsuccessful logons for that day. On an automated basis, you could populate the summary table for failed logins and delete the associated rows from the SYS.AUD$ table.

You should be very careful in choosing the columns of information you want to summarize since you may find it difficult to change the summary data later on. Let's go back to the example we just used with two summary columns for the day's date and the total count of unsuccessful logins. Suppose you've spent several weeks summarizing data and you now delete the day's values from the SYS.AUD$ table. You may realize later that you really wanted to retain the usernames of the accounts on which the connection attempt had failed in order to evaluate whether there was a pattern to the unsuccessful login attempts. But the data already summarized and deleted would be gone. Thus, your ability to perform trending analysis would be delayed while you attempted to accumulate more data. The current summary table would either need to be modified, or a new summary table would need to be created to fulfill the newly-identified requirement to capture account names. New code would need to be written to populate the new table.

Although changing audit requirements and revising auditing plans is sometimes necessary to help you perform the most effective auditing of a system, the more thought you put into the original plan, the better chance you will have of capturing effective data from the start.

Of the information stored in the audit trail, the data you decide to summarize will vary based on what you were trying to find out by auditing. If you were looking for the number of times a specific user connected to the database, your summary table would probably contain two columns—one for the user's name and one for the total count of accesses by day. If you are auditing to find out several different pieces of information, you might have one large summary table or several small ones. Either way, the summary table(s) should be kept in a different tablespace from the *system* tablespace to help avoid fragmentation of the *system* tablespace. Growth of the summary table(s) should be monitored to ensure that they remain manageable and that you don't run out of space in the tablespace.

Eliminating the Audit Views

If you choose not to audit anything and want to eliminate the auditing views from the database system, you can run the script *CATNOAUD.SQL* while connected as *sys* to drop the views and synonyms for the auditing metadata areas. The *CATNOAUD.SQL* script can be found in the *$ORACLE-HOME/RDBMS/ADMIN* directory on most systems. Why would you want to remove the audit views from a database?

Two reasons come to mind:

- You are supporting a system where disk space is at a premium.
- Performance is a major issue on your system and you want to ensure auditing can't be enabled accidentally.

Auditing and Performance

Auditing is usually not an enormous drain on performance, but there is an impact. Generally, the cost to performance of auditing is under about 5 percent. Enabling auditing on various areas of the database can affect performance in two ways:

- It can fill up storage space.
- It can slow down query response time.

If you enable auditing on a table with which users interact heavily, an entry will be made to the audit trail each time the audited action occurs. The overhead of frequent writes to the audit trail can impede overall database performance. Inside a PL/SQL program, statements are individually audited. Therefore, if a PL/SQL script is being run with auditing enabled on a table that is accessed in a loop, each time the table is accessed a record will be written to the audit trail. This could present a potentially high performance cost if too many objects or audit types are enabled.

If you are auditing to the database, every row of audit data is written to the *system* tablespace by default. The more objects you audit, the greater the amount of storage space consumed and the more potential fragmentation to the tablespace. You must ensure that the amount of auditing enabled is sufficient for the purposes you have envisioned but is not excessive. Monitoring the amount of data being stored into the SYS.AUD$ table on a daily basis during the time in which auditing is enabled will help the DBA learn how frequently the SYS.AUD$ table needs to be archived and cleaned out. You must be willing to take a proactive stance when enabling auditing to ensure that the performance costs—of space used and system slowdown—will remain reasonable.

Once a user has connected to the database with either session or privilege auditing enabled (we'll describe these types in the "Types of Auditing" section later on), auditing will remain in effect for that user's session, even if auditing is disabled after the session has started. On the other hand, if modifications are made to schema object audit options, those options become available immediately and take effect in the current user's session.

Default Auditing

As we mentioned earlier in this chapter, some actions will be stored to operating system files whether auditing is enabled or not. These actions are:

- Database startup
- Database shutdown
- Connection to the database from a privileged account
- Structural changes made to the database, like adding a tablespace datafile, etc.

When the database is started up, a record is written automatically to an operating system file. If the database was started with either *sys* or *internal*, the user information will not be recorded. The information recorded is the operating system username of the process starting the database, the terminal identifier, the timestamp (date and time) when the database was started, and whether or not auditing was enabled. The purpose of writing this information is to create a record of anyone attempting to start the database and disable auditing in order to hide their actions. At the time of database startup, the database audit trail is not yet available, so the startup information is always written to an operating system audit file.

In all of the auditing situations listed above, the information is recorded to an operating system log. If the operating system does not enable Oracle to access its audit facility, Oracle will record the information in a log in the same directory in which the background processes record their activities.

Auditing During Database Startup

The first type of default auditing occurs during database startup. An example of operating system audit entries stored automatically for a Windows NT system running Oracle version 8.0.4 is shown here:

```
Audit trail: ACTION : 'startup' OS_AUTHENT_PREFIX : OPS$. (3:55:41 a.m.)
Audit trail: ACTION : 'startup' AUDIT_TRAIL : none. (3:55:40 a.m.)
Audit trail: ACTION : 'connect INTERNAL' OSPRIV : OPER CLIENT USER: SYSTEM
CLIENT TERMINAL: MLT-PC. (3:55:31 a.m.)
```

These three entries were found in the Event Viewer, at the Start → Programs → Administrative Tools → Event Viewer menu option on a Window NT system. There are three event logs—System, Security, and Application—into which anyone can insert an event. Oracle will log events in both the System and the Application event logs. The time notations in parentheses were added by us to show you more clearly the sequence of events.

The first entry in the sequence above is actually the one listed last. This entry shows the initial connection made to the database in order to start it. Of special interest in the third entry is the notation of the client terminal from which the database was started—MLT-PC—and the system privilege used—OSPRIV. The three audit notations were present in the Windows NT Administrative Tools Event Viewer, in the Application log, after the database was started. As each of the individual detached processes (PMON, SMON, DBWR, LGWR, CKPT, RECO) was started, an individual entry was inserted in the event log. There was also an entry for the time at which the SGA was initialized.

Auditing During Database Shutdown

The second form of default auditing that may occur is at the time of database shutdown. Each time the database is shut down, a record may be written to the audit trail indicating the operating system username, the user's terminal identifier, and the date and timestamp when the action occurred. The use of the words "may be" in the last sentence is intentional. Depending on the operating system involved, if a privileged user, like *SYSDBA* or *SYSOPER*, shuts the database down, the event might not be registered in the System event log. On a Windows NT version 4.0 system running Oracle8 version 8.0.4, if the database is shut down using the command:

```
net stop OracleStart<db_name>
```

no record of the database shutdown is made either to the Windows NT Application event log or to the database alert log.

If your operating system/database automatically records the shutdown attempts performed by non-privileged users, you will find this information very valuable if you are investigating why your database unexpectedly shut down. The absence of an event entry for the shutdown could help you eliminate the fear that your database had been intentionally shut down by an outsider.

Auditing During Database Connection with Privileges

The third default action recorded to the operating system audit trail occurs when a user connects to the database with administrative privileges. The operating system user information is recorded. This information is very valuable in helping you detect whether someone has managed to acquire privileges they should not have.

Auditing During Database Structure Modification

When a command is issued from the database to modify the structure of the database, the command and its outcome are captured to the alert log for that database. This is the fourth default action. Some examples of commands that will be captured in the alert log follow:

```
CREATE TABLESPACE <tablespace_name>
ALTER TABLESPACE <tablespace_name> ADD DATAFILE
ALTER TABLESPACE OFFLINE  DROP TABLESPACE <tablespace_name>
                          INCLUDING CONTENTS
CREATE ROLLBACK SEGMENT <rollback_segment_name>
```

In all of these commands, the successful completion of the command will in some way alter the structure of the database.

Types of Auditing

There are several different forms of auditing that can be enabled. Each form covers a different area of interest within the database:

- Statement-level auditing

- System-level or privilege auditing
- Object-level auditing

The general command syntax used to enable any form of auditing is shown in Figure 10-1.

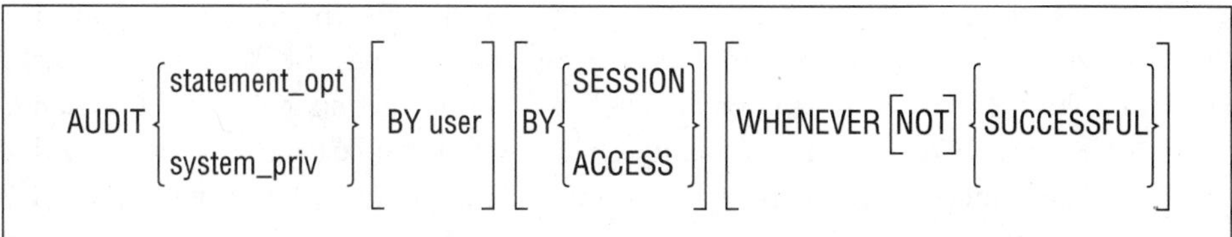

Figure 10-1. General command syntax

Statement-Level Auditing

Statement-level auditing falls into two categories: Data Definition Language (DDL) statements and Data Manipulation Language (DML) statements. This type of auditing can be very broad or very specific. The statement-level audits are based on the type of SQL statement presented. An example of a statement-level audit would be to audit any action performed on tables, such as CREATE TABLE, ALTER TABLE, DROP TABLE, TRUNCATE TABLE, etc. Another example of statement-level auditing would be to audit specific actions of one user on a session-by-session basis.

Enabling and viewing statement-level auditing

To view what statement-level auditing has been enabled in a database, you can issue the statement:

```
SQL> AUDIT SESSION BY mary;
Audit succeeded.
SQL> SELECT user_name, audit_option, success, failure
   2  FROM sys.dba_stmt_audit_opts;
USER_NAME   AUDIT_OPTION                             SUCCESS    FAILURE
----------- ---------------------------------------- ---------- ----------
MARY        CREATE SESSION                           BY ACCESS  BY ACCESS
```

In this example, we see that *mary* is being audited "by session." Whenever *mary* creates or fails to create a session, an entry will be placed in the audit trail.

Connect and disconnect auditing

One major area of concern in any computer system is whether someone is attempting to gain access to the database without authorization to do so. As we've mentioned previously, when an Oracle database is created, the default password for *system* is *MANAGER* and the default password for *sys* is *CHANGE_ON_INSTALL*. On some databases, default demonstration areas are created automatically with easily guessed passwords and very high privileges. An unknowledgeable DBA may neglect to change default passwords or not realize that the demonstration accounts can and should be deleted from a production system.

Alternatively, a user may attempt to "guess" his way into a system. Auditing is a way of helping you detect when someone is trying to break into your database. If a policy has been established that uses a very specific username convention and that convention is widely known, guessing usernames may be a very easy task. For example, suppose your company's policy is to have a six-character username using a person's first initial and as many characters of the last name as will yield a total of six characters. The employee whose name is Mary Janes will have the username *mjanes*. Any person who knows an employee well enough to know personal facts about that employee, and who knows your username convention, may be able to guess his way into your system based on this knowledge. They'll know Mary's username immediately. And if they know that Mary Janes loves fishing, they might try to guess her password by using names of fish or types of lures. The difficulty of the task of hacking into a system is reduced when the username is already known.

If you, as the DBA, have enabled auditing to watch for failures of a user to connect to the database, the hacker's attempts to guess the correct password for an account will be recorded as unsuccessful logons. You will be able to identify an unauthorized person's attempts to gain access to your system.

In looking through the list of command types that can be audited, note that command number 100 is "logon" and command 101 is "logoff." The action of attempting to connect to the database or disconnect from it can be audited by collecting data on the values "connect" and "disconnect." If you wanted to capture the number of times the database was accessed but the attempt to log on failed, the command you would issue would be:

```
SQL> AUDIT CONNECT WHENEVER UNSUCCESSFUL;
```

Your summary table for this audit might contain a count, by 24-hour period, of all of the failed attempts to connect to your database. A low number of failures to connect would be considered normal since not everyone successfully types his password every time they connect to a system. A higher than normal number of failures might indicate that someone was trying to break into the database by guessing account names and passwords.

Privilege Auditing

Recently, there was a news article about some teenagers who had successfully broken into a government system and managed to give themselves privileges on that system. Fortunately for the government agency involved, the teens did not do any overt damage to the system. They just wanted to prove they could compromise the system. There have also been numerous articles over time about employees who, while doing development work with higher than normal privileges enabled, have left "back doors" into systems so that they could re-enter the system after it had been "secured."

One such story involved a contractor who, when he did not receive payment for his services after repeatedly billing the company, re-entered the company's system, using the privileged account which he had left behind, and deleted a substantial amount of vital data. According to news reports about the incident, the loss of data to that company and the amount of time it will take them to recover the data far outweighs the amount of salary owed to the contractor. Criminal charges have been filed against the contractor, but that won't replace the data that was lost. How could this loss have been prevented? If you take the initiative to audit who has been granted specific privileges on your system, a developer will have a much harder time building "hidden" access to your database.

The audit plan you create should include both a definition of what privileges within the database will be audited and a statement of the interval at which the database will be reviewed to determine exactly which privileges have been assigned to which users and whether anyone has changed those privileges.

Enabling audit by privileges

You can enable auditing on specific privileges via the AUDIT command. The monitoring of who holds which privileges is a manual or automated task which is coded by creating SQL-generated SQL code something like the following:

```
SELECT grantee, privilege
  FROM dba_sys_privs
 WHERE GRANTEE NOT IN
       ('SYS','SYSTEM','CONNECT','RESOURCE','DBA','MDSYS',
        'RECOVERY_CATALOG_OWNER','IMP_FULL_DATABASE',
        'EXP_FULL_DATABASE')
 ORDER BY grantee
/
```

In this SELECT statement, the search has been narrowed on the users that will be returned. The WHERE clause has eliminated some usernames that are already known privileged users in the system. On a Windows NT database running Oracle8 version 8.0.4, the query produced the following results:

```
GRANTEE                        PRIVILEGE
------------------------------ ----------------------------------------
DBSNMP                         CREATE PUBLIC SYNONYM
DBSNMP                         UNLIMITED TABLESPACE
DEMO                           UNLIMITED TABLESPACE
ORACLE                         UNLIMITED TABLESPACE
```

```
ORACLE_SECURITY_SERVICE         CREATE SESSION
ORACLE_SECURITY_SERVICE         CREATE SYNONYM
ORACLE_SECURITY_SERVICE_ADMIN   CREATE ANY SYNONYM
ORACLE_SECURITY_SERVICE_ADMIN   CREATE PROCEDURE
ORACLE_SECURITY_SERVICE_ADMIN   CREATE SEQUENCE
ORACLE_SECURITY_SERVICE_ADMIN   CREATE SESSION
ORACLE_SECURITY_SERVICE_ADMIN   CREATE TABLE
ORACLE_SECURITY_SERVICE_ADMIN   CREATE TRIGGER
ORACLE_SECURITY_SERVICE_ADMIN   CREATE VIEW
ORACLE_SECURITY_SERVICE_ADMIN   DROP ANY SYNONYM
ORDSYS                          CREATE LIBRARY
ORDSYS                          GRANT ANY PRIVILEGE
ORDSYS                          UNLIMITED TABLESPACE
RECOV                           UNLIMITED TABLESPACE
ROGER                           UNLIMITED TABLESPACE
SCOTT                           ALTER SESSION
SCOTT                           CREATE TABLE
SCOTT                           UNLIMITED TABLESPACE
SNMPAGENT                       ANALYZE ANY
23 rows selected.
```

To enable auditing of a system privilege, identify the privilege, then issue the command to audit that privilege. The basic syntax used to enable auditing of a system privilege was shown earlier under "Types of Auditing." The command syntax shown below is presented in a slightly different form so we can further examine this code:

```
AUDIT <statement_opt or system_priv> BY <user> BY <SESSION or ACCESS>
       WHENEVER <SUCCESSFUL or UNSUCCESSFUL>;
```

Only the AUDIT <statement_opt or system_priv> portion is required. The other clauses:

```
BY user
BY SESSION
BY ACCESS
WHENEVER SUCCESSFUL
WHENEVER UNSUCCESSFUL
```

are optional and enable the audit to be performed in a narrower fashion.

If you are concerned about who might be creating tables in the database, you want to audit the use of the CREATE TABLE command as follows:

```
SQL> AUDIT create table
  2      WHENEVER SUCCESSFUL;

Audit succeeded.
```

After the general privilege for a period of time (i.e., all occurrences of "create table"), you might use a narrower audit scope. For example, you might issue a command like:

```
SQL> AUDIT create table
  2      BY mary
```

```
BY SESSION
WHENEVER SUCCESSFUL;
```

to capture only the tables *mary* created.

Object-Level Auditing

Auditing can also be used to aid in tuning a database. An easy way to determine how many times a table was accessed is to enable general auditing on all tables for a brief period of time and then generate a report showing the number of times each table was accessed. You would quickly be able to determine which tables were being used most heavily.

Enabling audit by object

To audit all table accesses for *all* tables, first issue the statement:

```
AUDIT select table, update table, delete table;
```

The command, in this form, tells the audit utility to audit all SELECT, UPDATE, and DELETE actions on all tables. If you want to audit only the SELECT actions on all tables, issue the statement:

```
AUDIT select table;
```

The summary table for the command to audit all SELECT, INSERT, and DELETE accesses includes the sum of the table accesses by date. A narrower audit might be tied to how many times a specific user accessed tables. Of particular interest might be an audit of how many tables were deleted from the system.

Capturing "before" data

As we mentioned earlier, when table auditing is enabled, the entire table is audited. You can audit for inserts to a table, updates to a table, deletions of rows in a table, or the viewing of information contained in the table. Auditing individual columns of a table becomes more problematic, and auditing specific data changes becomes very difficult. In the next chapter, we will present an audit trail application, written by Christopher Hamilton, that will show you a way to audit individual columns of a table.

In some applications, the ability to capture pieces of data before any changes have occurred may be of interest. Let's say you have an application from which you can change employee vacation and sick leave accrual. If 100 employees' amounts of vacation available were changed in error, either intentionally or accidentally, having the values that originally appeared in the "vacation available" column could help you correct the error more rapidly without having to perform extra computations.

The auditing capabilities delivered with the Oracle RDBMS do not include an easy way to accomplish tracking the "before image" appearance of the data. However, there are ways to accomplish this task. One effective approach is to create a separate audit table for the area of interest and create a "before update" trigger to capture the appearance of the data prior to allowing the change to occur. For example, let's say you have a table with many columns of employee information. One of these columns contains salary data, which should not change very often. Company policy states that no employee should have access to modify salary information unless that employee is a member of the timekeeping_supervisor group. In our payroll application, we want to be able to track exactly who has accessed the employee table and made any modifications to the salary column. We want to capture not only the value of the salary before the change occurred but who made the change and on what date. We have created views of the commonly-viewed columns of the employee table and have ensured that no direct access to the table can be accomplished unless the salary data is to be changed.

Enabling auditing to track updates on the table will show us any changes to the table but won't tell us what the salary column looked like prior to a change being made. A new table, sal_chg, could be created with five columns: old_salary, new_salary, user_changed, mod_user, and mod_date. A "before update" trigger could be created, which would fire each time a salary value was modified. The trigger would insert the values for the current salary, the new salary value, the employee whose salary was being changed, the employee who was making the change, and the date on which the change was made. In this way, if a salary was changed—whether maliciously or in error—a complete record of the transaction would be captured and an audit path enabled. The audit trail application shown in the next chapter will show you more fully how to implement this form of auditing.

Although implementing this approach is easy, use it with caution because it may have an impact on both data storage and performance. Each time a trigger fires, there is a minor amount of time used to write the information to the secondary table. If many tables are audited in this manner, you may observe a slowing down of the entire system. As with any other form of auditing, use this approach sparingly and with great forethought and care.

Capturing "after" data

As with capturing "before" values of interest, capturing modifications to data *after* they have occurred is difficult using normal Oracle auditing features. The fact that the data is present and observable does not give us any ability to tell exactly what progression of changes have occurred against the data. There is an internal timestamp Oracle maintains on each row of data in the database, but not on each individual value within the row. If it is critical to know exactly what values have changed, when, and by whom, the use of secondary tables and triggers may, again, provide a possible solution.

Auditing Shortcuts

Oracle provides the ability to audit groups of privileges by using the shortcuts CONNECT, RESOURCE, and DBA (the Oracle-supplied default role values), described in Chapter 5, *Oracle Default Roles and User Accounts.* If you need to audit the group of privileges associated with one of the default roles, you will find it easier to enable auditing on CONNECT than on each individual privilege within this role. Rather than enabling auditing on CREATE SESSION, you could enable auditing on CONNECT. If you enable auditing on RESOURCE, the privileges that would be audited are:

ALTER SESSION
CREATE CLUSTER
CREATE DATABASE LINK
CREATE PROCEDURE
CREATE ROLLBACK SEGMENT
CREATE SEQUENCE
CREATE SYNONYM
CREATE TABLE
CREATE TABLESPACE
CREATE VIEW

If you enable auditing on DBA, the privileges associated with "SYSTEM GRANT" and the following privileges would be included:

AUDIT SYSTEM
CREATE PUBLIC DATABASE LINK
CREATE PUBLIC SYNONYM
CREATE ROLE
CREATE USER

There are also shortcuts to audit "ALL" and "ALL PRIVILEGES." However, the overhead of enabling auditing on privileges by using these shortcuts may be high because of the volume of audit information you will be gathering in the SYS$AUD table. Give careful consideration before you enable auditing using any of these shortcuts, and be sure you have enough space in the tablespace in which your SYS$AUD table is stored.

Purging Audit Information

As we've mentioned several times in this chapter, you need to closely monitor the SYS.AUD$ table as long as any form of auditing is occurring in the database. This is the only data dictionary table from which Oracle permits DBAs to delete information. The wise DBA will archive the information from this table before removing the data. One way to archive data is to create a summary table and move the information of interest into the summary table before removing the data from the SYS.AUD$ table. Since the auditing views rely on information from the SYS.AUD$ table, remember that when you remove data from this table, the data will disappear from the audit views as well. Another way to archive the data from this table is to create a copy of the table in another schema and then export that schema. Figure 10-2 shows a possible purge cycle.

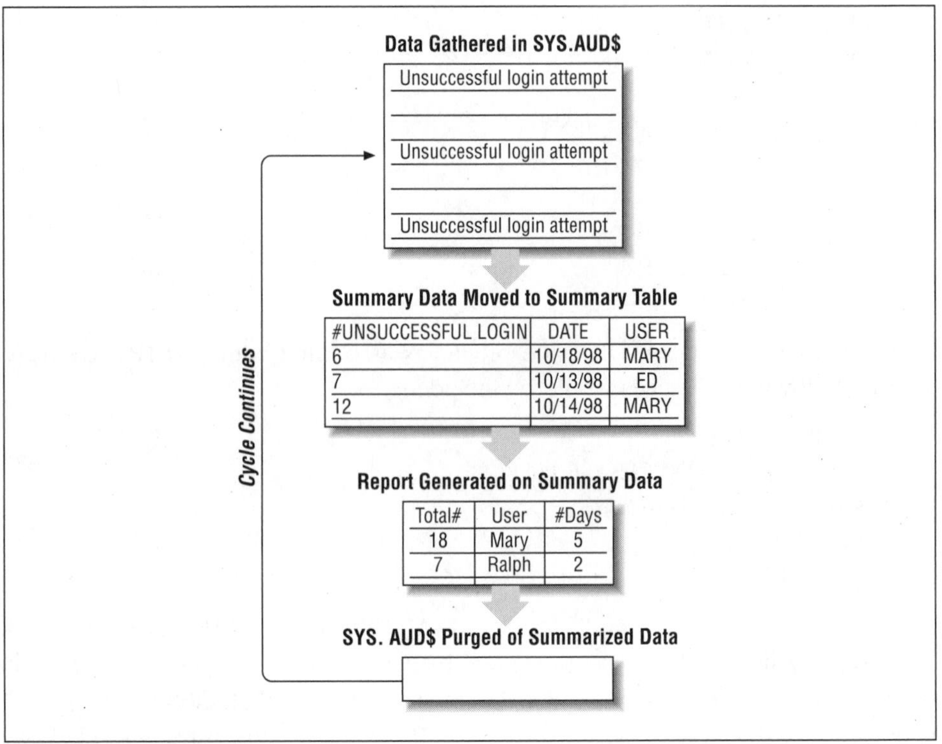

Figure 10-2. Data collection and summary cycle

Removing All the Data from SYS.AUD$

You can remove *all* the data from the SYS.AUD$ table by issuing the statement:

```
TRUNCATE TABLE sys.aud$;
```

or alternatively:

```
DELETE FROM sys.aud$;
```

Why would you use DELETE rather than TRUNCATE? As rows of information are inserted into a table, Oracle uses a mechanism called the "high-water mark" to indicate the location of the last row of data in the table. This mark tells Oracle how many blocks to examine during a full table scan. When you issue a DELETE statement, Oracle marks the row or rows you have specified as deleted but does not actually erase the rows from the table. From a performance perspective, if you merely delete all the rows from the audit table, you will not reset the high-water mark for the table. If a full table scan is required to obtain data from the table, performance might slow down substantially as Oracle examines every block of the table—even the "empty" blocks (those blocks containing rows marked as deleted).

If you issue the TRUNCATE command, on the other hand, the high-water mark is reset to the first block in the table and performance will be improved.

Removing Selected Data from SYS.AUD$

If you want to retain specific data in the table but want to ensure that the table is kept to a manageable size, you can create a script to delete only selected rows from the SYS.AUD$ table. You might base the deletions on a specific range of dates or by a specific group of actions or users.

As we described in the earlier "Creating a summary table" section, you may want to retain the information from the SYS.AUD$ table into a summary table before you delete any rows.

11

Developing a Sample Audit Application

In this chapter:

In business, you sometimes need to maintain detailed records about people, places, and things. You may feel that the information you are maintaining is so important to your company that more detailed data is needed to track:

- Who created the information
- Who has modified the information
- What was changed

As you saw in Chapter 10, *Developing an Audit Plan,* Oracle provides ways to track information about modifications that have been made to a table—at the table level. However, Oracle does not provide an easy way to keep track of actions that have been performed on specific rows within a table. For that information, you need to develop a customized application.

In this chapter, we will show you a simple, but effective, application* you can use for implementing transparent audit trails. Depending on how much auditing you implement, this application may not overly impact your database's performance, and it does not require a lot of complex maintenance. This sample trigger-based application can give you an idea of how you can implement your own audit trail application, or you can use this application either in part or as a complete application to perform whatever auditing you need.

About the Audit Trail Application

To implement the audit trail application described in this chapter, you need to create the following:

* Our thanks to Christopher Hamilton for developing the code and parts of the text included in this chapter.

- Three tables
- Two sequences
- One PL/SQL package (with two stored procedures)
- Three database triggers per audited table
- Three additional columns in each audited table

After that, the application runs itself.

Developers who are writing or modifying applications do not need to be concerned with the audit trail application, except when a new column is added to a table. The performance impact must be assessed on your own system, but can be minimized by selectively implementing some of the components that comprise the audit trail application. Note that you can implement only the components you want, for example:

- Only INSERT tracking
- Only a record of the fact that the transaction occurred (i.e., only the AUDIT_ROW table)
- Full UPDATE and DELETE tracking

You do this by commenting out the relevant lines in the trigger code included in the application. The triggers need only be written for the specific tables and columns you want to audit. You need to determine your desired level of detail, acceptable performance impact, and business requirements, and implement the audit trail application accordingly. For more detailed information, see the "About Performance" section later in this chapter.

The approach presented is very effective and easy to implement because:

- Each table needs triggers that are written only once.
- The triggers call stored procedures to do the actual auditing.
- Everything is handled by the Oracle kernel, so the audit trail cannot be bypassed during normal use except by rollback.
- Developers can develop applications without worrying about (or even knowing about) the triggers.
- The auditing triggers can be selectively disabled for certain functions like bulk updates or deletions.

As you did when you created an audit plan (see Chapter 10), you must first decide what you want to audit. So we can show you the full audit tracking implementation in this example, we assume here that you want full auditing—tracking inserts, updates down to the column level, and deletions, including deletion recovery capability. Because the application is written in a modular manner (several separate pieces), you will find it easy to implement only the parts you decide you actually need for your own facility.

A Few Limitations

There are ramifications to consider when implementing any application. If you choose to implement part or all of the application we present here, you must keep the following points in mind:

- If any of the auditing triggers fail for any reason, the SQL statement that caused the trigger to fire will also fail. This is very important to know if the application is being run in a production environment.
- The size of the fields in the application tables—particularly the username and data in the delete table—must be chosen very carefully. Any data overflow will raise a VALUE_ERROR and the triggering statement will fail.
- The trigger generation scripts do not handle LONG columns and the like when building triggers to store values.

Tracking Inserts

To track inserts, you need to add three columns to each table you wish to track. The columns are called rid, creator, and timestamp. Their definitions are listed in Table 11-1.

Table 11-1. Additional Table Columns for Inserts

Column Name	Definition	Default	Description
rid	NUMBER(10)		Record ID—unique in database
creator	VARCHAR2(12)	RTRIM(user)	User that created the record
timestamp	DATE	SYSDATE	Date/time of record creation

The creator and timestamp columns can be defined as nullable if your existing tables do not have any information to populate them. However, the rid column is essential and *must* be backfilled after you have added it to a table.

The creator and timestamp columns are defined as defaults so they will always be automatically populated when an INSERT is performed. For the creator column, 12 characters seems to be enough for "OPS$" plus eight characters. However, you can expand or shrink this column to meet your needs. The timestamp column includes the full time, so you may want to apply a TO_CHAR mask of "DD-MON-YYYY HH:MI:SS am" to it when displaying or selecting it, or use the TRUNC() function if you are searching for a specific day.

The First Sequence Creation Script (SEQ-RID)

You also need to define a new sequence, SEQ_RID, which is used to generate record IDs when a row is inserted. The sequence is used for the rid column in all tables, so the rid is unique in the entire database. It is *not* a replacement for your normal primary key column (although it can serve as one if you want), and need not be indexed.

```
REM This sequence is used to generate unique record IDs for each row in the
REM data tables.  Recommended to fill in via before-insert trigger. You'll
REM need to add the appropriate RID column to each audit table.

CREATE SEQUENCE seq_rid
  START WITH 1          /* starting number */
  INCREMENT BY 1        /* in increments of 1 */
  ORDER                 /* generate them in order */
  NOCYCLE               /* do not recycle numbers */
  CACHE 100             /* keep lots of them in RAM for speed! */
  MINVALUE 1            /* 1 is the minimum */
  NOMAXVALUE            /* no practical limit on high # */
/
GRANT select ON seq_rid TO public;
```

The First Trigger Creation Script (Before-Insert)

You need to create the before-insert database trigger (below) on each table you want to audit to ensure that the rid is filled in at insert time.

```
REM  Trigger to fill in the RID (Record ID) for the EMP table
REM  if not supplied by the application.

CREATE OR REPLACE TRIGGER emp_bi0
  BEFORE INSERT
      ON employee
     FOR EACH ROW
    WHEN (new.rid IS NULL)
BEGIN
  SELECT TRUNC(seq_rid.nextval)
         /* Use TRUNC() to avoid ORA-01438 errors - which you should
            not get, but ORACLE doesn't seem to know that. */
    INTO :new.rid
    FROM dual;
END;
/
```

Tracking Updates and Deletions

To track updates and deletions, you need to add (at a minimum) the RID column (described earlier under "Tracking Inserts") to each audited table. This provides an absolute method of uniquely identifying any record from any table. Then you need to create several objects (depending on the level of detail desired), listed in Table 11-2.

Table 11-2. Additional Table Columns for Updates and Deletes

Object Name	Object Type	Description
audit_row	Table	Holds record of transaction (UPDATE/ DELETE)
audit_column	Table	Holds old/new values of updated columns
audit_delete	Table	Holds image of deleted row data
seq_rid	Sequence	Generates unique record ID (as above)
seq_audit	Sequence	Generates unique audit transaction numbers
audit_trail	PL/SQL package	Contains stored procedures to write data to the AUDIT_<table> tables
record_transaction	Stored procedure	Writes the record to the AUDIT_ROW table
column_update	Stored procedure	Writes the data to the AUDIT_COLUMN table
<tablename>_bi0	Before-insert trigger	Populates the rid column of the table
<tablename_au0	After-update trigger	Determines which columns have been changed
<tablename>_ad0	After-delete trigger	Writes the deleted data to the AUDIT_ DELETE table

The three triggers are required for each audited table if you want to capture information about information that has been inserted, updated, or deleted. Substitute your table name for the <tablename> notation. The "0" on the end of the trigger name is used to avoid naming conflicts with possible existing triggers.

The Three Table Creation Scripts

The three tables we need to create for the audit trail application are AUDIT_ROW, AUDIT_COLUMN, and AUDIT_DELETE. The scripts used to create these tables, along with an explanation of each column, are presented in the following sections.

The AUDIT_ROW table

The AUDIT_ROW table contains information about the table that was changed, the type of change that was performed, the date and time when the change occurred, and who made the change. The timestamp is obtained by capturing the system time when the change was made, and, since Oracle stores the user's name in a variable called "user", we can obtain the information about who has made the change directly from Oracle and can store the value into the user_name column.

In Oracle8 you can make the old_value, new_value, and row_data columns up to 4000 bytes long.

```
REM AUDIT_ROW - one row per transaction.
CREATE TABLE audit_row
  (raid        NUMBER(10)    NOT NULL,         /* Row audit ID */
   table_name  VARCHAR2(30) NOT NULL,          /* Table name */
   rid         NUMBER(10)    NOT NULL,         /* Record ID (from table) */
   action      VARCHAR2(1)   NOT NULL,         /* Action (I, U, D) */
   REM use defaults to populate these columns - less overhead
   timestamp   DATE DEFAULT SYSDATE NOT NULL, /* Time of action */
   user_name   VARCHAR2(12) DEFAULT RTRIM(USER) NOT NULL) /* User */
   TABLESPACE audit_ts
   PCTFREE 0
   PCTUSED 90
   STORAGE (INITIAL 100k
            NEXT 100k
      MAXEXTENTS UNLIMITED
     PCTINCREASE 0);
```

The AUDIT_COLUMN table

The AUDIT_COLUMN table holds the record of what data was changed. The column OLD_VALUE holds the value prior to the change, and the column NEW_VALUE holds the value after the change has occurred. There is one row inserted in the table per changed column. The RAID (Row Audit ID) column is used as the foreign key link to the AUDIT_ROW table. The primary key is the CAID (Column Audit ID) column, which is also generated by the SEQ_AUDIT sequence generator.

The AUDIT_COLUMN table has the following columns:

RAID
: Row Audit ID. Number identifying the transaction. Foreign key link to the AUDIT_ROW table.

CAID
: Column Audit ID. Sequence-generated number (from SEQ_AUDIT) uniquely identifying each row in the table. Primary key.

COLUMN_NAME
: Name of the column involved in the transaction.

OLD_VALUE

Pre-transaction data value of the column.

NEW_VALUE

Post-transaction data value of the column.

```
REM AUDIT_COLUMN - one row per changed column.
CREATE TABLE audit_column
   (raid        NUMBER(10)     NOT NULL,     /* Row audit ID */
    caid        NUMBER(10)     NOT NULL,     /* Column audit ID */
    column_name VARCHAR2(30) NOT NULL   ,  /* Column name */
    old_value   VARCHAR2(2000),              /* Old data value */
    new_value   VARCHAR2(2000))              /* New data value */
TABLESPACE audit_ts
    PCTFREE 0
    PCTUSED 90
    STORAGE (INITIAL 100k
               NEXT 100k
          MAXEXTENTS UNLIMITED
         PCTINCREASE 0);
```

The AUDIT_DELETE table

The AUDIT_DELETE table holds the data (separated by "pipes") of a row that was deleted. The primary key and foreign key link to the AUDIT_ROW table is the RAID column. The AUDIT_DELETE columns are as follows:

RAID

Row Audit ID. Number identifying the transaction. Foreign key link to the AUDIT_ROW table.

ROW_DATA

Column data values of deleted row, separated by the pipe symbol, "|".

```
REM AUDIT_DELETE - one row per deleted row.
CREATE TABLE audit_delete
   (raid      NUMBER(10)     NOT NULL,      /* Row audit ID */
    row_data  VARCHAR2(2000) NOT NULL)      /* Data from row */
TABLESPACE audit_ts
    PCTFREE 0
    PCTUSED 90
    STORAGE (INITIAL 100k
               NEXT 100k
          MAXEXTENTS UNLIMITED
         PCTINCREASE 0);
```

For better security, grant privileges to the audit tables only to users who need to examine them. Since the audit tables are populated by database procedures, the normal user does not need *any* privileges to the audit tables. The procedure executes with the security level of the schema owner.

For better performance, use appropriate INITIAL and NEXT values. PCTINCREASE should be 0, since the tables will not be updated, and a 0 value will enable the most rows to be packed into each block. Also, *do not* index these tables (unless you're querying them) to avoid index update overhead on each audit row INSERT. A separate tablespace (separate disk if possible) is recommended for easy administration and optimum performance.

The Second Sequence Creation Script (SEQ_AUDIT)

A sequence generator is used to supply a unique, usually numeric, value for a column. In this script, a sequence generator is built to supply a unique, primary key value for the Row Audit ID (RAID) and the Column Audit ID (CAID). The SEQ_AUDIT sequence generator is called from the before-delete and after-update triggers. The same sequence generator is used for both triggers because there is no need to ensure that the RAID values are sequential. There is only a need to ensure that the RAID values are unique in the entire system.

```
CREATE SEQUENCE seq_audit
  START WITH 1          /* starting number */
  INCREMENT BY 1        /* in increments of 1 */
  ORDER                 /* generate them in order */
  NOCYCLE               /* do not recycle numbers */
  CACHE 100             /* keep lots of them in RAM for speed! */
  MINVALUE 1            /* 1 is the minimum */
  NOMAXVALUE            /* no practical limit on high # */
/

GRANT select ON seq_audit TO public;
```

The Second Trigger Creation Script (After-Update)

The after-update trigger (EMP_AU0) is used to populate two separate tables: the AUDIT_ROW table and, if a change has actually occurred in the table, the AUDIT_COLUMN table. Here's the way the second trigger works.

The trigger fires after the update has occurred, but before it is committed to the database. First it calls the procedure audit_trail.RECORD_TRANSACTION to record that this transaction occurred and set up a master audit record in the AUDIT_ROW table. Then it compares the pre- and post-update values of the columns to each other (old.column versus new.column). If they differ, the procedure audit_trail.COLUMN_UPDATE is called to record the data into the AUDIT_COLUMN table. Remember to NVL the comparisons, because a null is never equal to (or not equal to) a null, which will create false audit records. The dates are compared to a standard value of 9595 AD.* One record is written for each column changed in the UPDATE statement.

You don't need to audit all of the columns; simply name the ones you want in the AFTER UPDATE OF clause in the trigger definition. If you add columns to the table, add them to this clause and to the comparison clauses, or re-run the generation script (*gen_au.sql*).

Unfortunately, you cannot reliably use the PL/SQL "IF UPDATING column_name THEN..." structure to test old versus new values. It works for SQL*Plus, but SQL*Forms, Oracle Forms, and other development tools construct an UPDATE statement containing every column in the block, whether it has actually changed or not, which creates scads of false audit records and incurs enormous overhead. Trust me, I learned this the hard way! In Oracle Forms 4.x and above, however, you can select whether the block should pass all columns or only changed columns to the database.

```
REM AFTER UPDATE trigger to write a record of the UPDATE transaction and
REM the pre- and post-change values of the affected data.  The sample
REM trigger is for the EMPLOYEE table.

CREATE OR REPLACE TRIGGER emp_au0
 AFTER UPDATE OF
       empno, ename, job, mgr, hiredate, sal, comm, deptno, rid
    ON employee
   FOR EACH ROW

DECLARE
  raid NUMBER(10);

BEGIN

-- Get next RAID (Row Audit ID).

  SELECT seq_audit.nextval
    INTO raid
    FROM dual;

-- Record transaction into the AUDIT_ROW table.
```

* Surely this is all we'll need.

```
    audit_trail.record_transaction
      (raid, 'EMP', :old.rid, 'U');

-- Test columns to see what is updated and write to AUDIT_COLUMN.
-- You must use the NVL function, otherwise old nulls will not
-- compare properly to new nulls, and results will be unpredicable.

  IF NVL(:old.empno,0) != NVL(:new.empno,0) THEN
    audit_trail.column_update (raid, 'EMPNO', :old.empno, :new.empno);
  END IF;

  IF NVL(:old.ename,' ') != NVL(:new.ename,' ') THEN
    audit_trail.column_update (raid, 'ENAME', :old.ename, :new.ename);
  END IF;

  IF NVL(:old.job,' ') != NVL(:new.job,' ') THEN
    audit_trail.column_update (raid, 'JOB', :old.job, :new.job);
  END IF;

  IF NVL(:old.mgr,0) != NVL(:new.mgr,0) THEN
    audit_trail.column_update (raid, 'MGR', :old.mgr, :new.mgr);
  END IF;

  IF NVL(TO_CHAR(:old.hiredate,'dd-mon-yyyy'),'31-dec-9595') !=
     NVL(TO_CHAR(:new.hiredate,'dd-mon-yyyy'),'31-dec-9595') THEN
    audit_trail.column_update (raid, 'HIREDATE',
      TO_CHAR(:old.hiredate,'DD-MON-YYYY'),
      TO_CHAR(:new.hiredate,'DD-MON-YYYY');
  END IF;

  IF NVL(:old.sal,0) != NVL(:new.sal,0) THEN
    audit_trail.column_update (raid, 'SAL', :old.sal, :new.sal);
  END IF;

  IF NVL(:old.comm,0) != NVL(:new.comm,0) THEN
    audit_trail.column_update (raid, 'COMM', :old.comm, :new.comm);
  END IF;

  IF NVL(:old.rid,0) != NVL(:new.rid,0) THEN
    audit_trail.column_update (raid, 'RID', :old.rid, :new.rid);
  END IF;

END;
/
```

The Third Trigger Creation Script (After-Delete)

The after-delete trigger (EMP_AD0) fires after the deletion has occurred, but before it is committed to the database. First, it calls the procedure audit_trail.RECORD_TRANSACTION to record that this transaction has occurred and to set up a master audit record in the AUDIT_ROW table. Then it concatenates the data from each (desired) column together into a variable, and writes a record containing that data into the AUDIT_DELETE table. If a future "undelete" is desired, you can print out the record and reconstruct the data, or write a script to do it.

```
REM This script creates a trigger to track deletions made to the EMP table.

CREATE OR REPLACE TRIGGER emp_ad0
  AFTER DELETE
  ON emp
  FOR EACH ROW

DECLARE
  raid NUMBER(10);
  deleted_data VARCHAR2(2000);

BEGIN

-- Get the next RAID (Row Audit ID).

  SELECT seq_audit.nextval
    INTO raid
    FROM dual;

-- Record transaction in audit_row table and write data to
-- audit_delete table.

  audit_trail.record_transaction
    (raid, 'EMP', :old.rid, 'D');

  deleted_data :=
  TO_CHAR(:old.empno) || '|' ||
  :old.ename || '|' ||
  :old.job || '|' ||
  TO_CHAR(:old.mgr) || '|' ||
  TO_CHAR(:old.hiredate,'DD-MON-YYYY') || '|' ||
  TO_CHAR(:old.sal) || '|' ||
  TO_CHAR(:old.comm) || '|' ||
  TO_CHAR(:old.deptno) || '|' ||
  TO_CHAR(:old.rid) || '|' ||
  :old.creator || '|' ||
  TO_CHAR(:old.timestamp,'DD-MON-YYYY') || '|';

  INSERT INTO audit_delete
  VALUES (raid, deleted_data);

END;
/
```

A ROLLBACK statement will cause the audit trail records to be rolled back as well as the actual UPDATE/DELETE statement, so you won't end up with a lot of false audit records.

The Package and Procedure Creation Scripts

The procedures used in this application simply take input from the three triggers we've defined and actually create the audit records. Read the documentation included in the script for details.

```
/*
Definition of Parameters received from the calling trigger...
  raid    = Row Audit ID.
  tabname = Name of table involved in the transaction.
  erid    = Existing RID (Record ID) of row being audited.
  act     = Action that has occurred (Update or Delete).
  colname = Name of the column involved in the update.
  oldval  = Pre-Update (old) value of the column data.
  newval  = Post-Update (new) value of the column data.
*/

CREATE OR REPLACE PACKAGE audit_trail IS

  PROCEDURE record_transaction
    (raid IN NUMBER,
     tabname IN VARCHAR2,
     erid IN NUMBER,
     act IN VARCHAR2);

  PROCEDURE column_update
    (raid IN NUMBER,
     colname IN VARCHAR2,
     oldval IN VARCHAR2,
     newval IN VARCHAR2);

END audit_trail;
/

CREATE OR REPLACE PACKAGE BODY audit_trail IS

  PROCEDURE record_transaction

   (raid IN NUMBER,
     tabname IN VARCHAR2,
     erid IN NUMBER,
     act IN VARCHAR2) IS

  BEGIN

  -- Write a record of the transaction to the master audit trail
  -- table.  Timestamp and User_Name are not included here -
  -- they are filled in by column defaults defined at the table
  -- level (should be faster).

    INSERT INTO audit_row
      (raid, table_name, rid, action, timestamp, user_name)
      VALUES
```

```
      (raid, tabname, erid, act, sysdate, user);

  -- Return a scary message if for some reason the statement failed.

     IF sql%NOTFOUND THEN
       RAISE_APPLICATION_ERROR
         (-20000, 'Error creating Row Audit record. Contact DBA.');
     END IF;
  END;

  PROCEDURE column_update

     (raid IN NUMBER,
      colname IN VARCHAR2,
      oldval IN VARCHAR2,
      newval IN VARCHAR2) IS

  BEGIN

  -- Record the column names and old/new data values of individual
  -- columns altered in the transaction to the AUDIT_COLUMN table.

     INSERT INTO audit_column
       (raid, caid, column_name, old_value, new_value)
       VALUES
       (raid, seq_audit.nextval, colname, oldval, newval);

  -- Return a scary message if for some reason the statement fails.

     IF sql%NOTFOUND THEN
       RAISE_APPLICATION_ERROR
         (-20000, 'Error creating Column Audit record. Contact DBA.');
     END IF;
  END;
END audit_trail;
/
```

About Performance and Storage

Unquestionably, each of the audit trails you activate in your database add overhead to your system and consume disk space. The following sections provide suggestions you can implement to reduce the amount of overhead to your database performance.

Storage Suggestions

Ideally, you should create a separate tablespace for the audit data. Having the audit data on a separate tablespace will make administration considerably easier. Performance can be improved if you can put the audit data on a separate disk or filesystem from "real" data.

Make sure that you size the INITIAL and NEXT extents properly to:

- Avoid excessive dynamic space management and extension
- Not run out of extents (MAXEXTENTS)
- Avoid fragmentation

You may want to use the parameter AUTOEXTEND on the tablespace datafile for the audit trail storage to minimize the possibility of having a transaction hang due to lack of audit trail space. The AUTOEXTEND parameter enables the tablespace datafile to continue to extend automatically until it reaches a maximum space limit you have declared in the MAXSIZE parameter. The syntax you use to create a tablespace with AUTOEXEND enabled is:

```
CREATE TABLESPACE audit_data_ts
  DATAFILE '/my_disk/my_dir/audit_data_ts01.dbf'
   AUTOEXTEND ON NEXT 10m
   MAXSIZE UNLIMITED
  DEFAULT STORAGE (INITIAL 100K
                      NEXT 100K
               MINEXTENTS 1
               MAXEXTENTS UNLIMITED
              PCTINCREASE 10)
ONLINE;
```

You will want to purge the audit trail tables on a regular basis. Keep a close watch on the growth of the tables over a period of time to get a feeling for how often you need to clean the tables out. Remember that the goal with the DELETE audits is to be able to recover the deleted information, if necessary. Be sure to export from the audit tables often and keep the exports of the deletion information in a safe place!

Performance Suggestions

Because performance is almost always an issue in a production database, you want to carefully map out how you are going to use this auditing tool. Here are some suggestions you can follow to help avoid degradation of performance on your system if you use this application:

- Do not index the AUDIT_ROW, AUDIT_COLUMN, and AUDIT_DELETE tables. Since you will rarely select from them, the index is not usually necessary. Having to update the index on each transaction will bog things down.
- If you are doing bulk updates or deletions and you don't need to audit the transactions, disable these triggers before the run by using the following command with the appropriate trigger name:

  ```
  ALTER TRIGGER triggername DISABLE;
  ```

and enable the triggers when the large data load is completed. This will save a lot of audit writing, rollback allocation, and redo logging.

- Try to keep the trigger code as short as possible. Prior to Oracle version 7.3, triggers were not stored in compiled form in the database. In versions earlier than 7.3, the triggers must be compiled and parsed upon execution. However, once they have been compiled and parsed, they will be retained in the Shared Pool of the System Global Area (SGA). Thus, after the initial execution, the trigger performance will be better. Procedures, packages, and triggers (in version 7.3 and above) are stored in compiled form and will also be cached in the Shared Pool and can be pinned.
- Track only to the level of detail you need. For instance, if you don't care about the old or new values of updated columns, omit that portion of the system.

Using the Audit Data in Reports

This audit trail will be only an intellectual exercise unless you can use the data collected. At one company we're familiar with, the audit trail application literally saved the day more than once by making deleted data from a critical table recoverable. On one occasion, a new employee, trying to show how quickly she could perform her work, deleted several values from a vital requirements tracking system. Using the information stored in the audit trail application, the deleted information was restored to the appropriate tables almost as quickly as she had deleted the data from them. Since her actions were very random, replacing only the deleted data would have been extremely time-consuming and tedious without this application.

The Audit Trail Data Display

Here is a sample set of SQL*ReportWriter code used to display the complete set of audit trail data. The same queries will work with Oracle Reports.

```
REM This is the SQL code used in SQL*ReportWriter or Oracle Reports to make
REM an Audit Report.

REM The first query is the parent to the second and third queries.
REM The second and third queries are joined to it by the "raid"
REM field (raid1=raid2, raid1=raid3).

REM Query1
SELECT raid raid1, table_name, rid,
       DECODE(action, 'U','UPDATE', 'D','DELETE') action, user_name,
       TO_CHAR(timestamp, 'DD-MON-YYYY HH24:MM:SS') timestamp
  FROM audit_row
 WHERE user_name LIKE NVL(UPPER(:username),'%')
```

```
      AND table_name LIKE NVL(UPPER(:tabname),'%')
      AND action LIKE NVL(UPPER(:act),'%')
      AND rid BETWEEN NVL(:lo_rid,1)
      AND NVL(:hi_rid,999999999999)
      AND timestamp BETWEEN NVL(:lowdate,'01-JAN-80')
      AND NVL(:highdate,SYSDATE)
    ORDER BY user_name, table_name, timestamp;

REM Query 2
SELECT raid raid2, column_name, old_value, new_value
  FROM audit_column
 ORDER BY raid, caid;

REM Query 3
SELECT raid raid3, row_data
  FROM audit_delete
 ORDER BY raid;
```

Figure 11-1 shows a screen shot of the SQL*ReportWriter Parameter Form customized for use with the report.

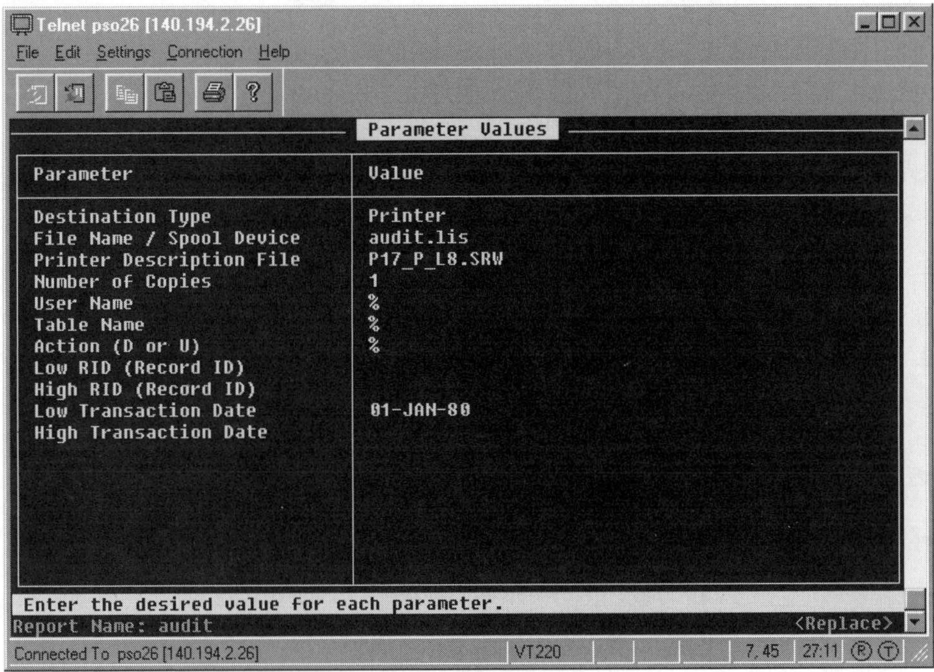

Figure 11-1. The Customized Report Parameter Screen

The AUDIT_ROW Table Report

To view the contents of the AUDIT_ROW table, you can use the following script in SQL*Plus.

```
SET LINESIZE 80;
SET PAGESIZE 22;
SET TRIMSPOOL ON;

COLUMN table_name FORMAT a10 HEADING "Table Name";
COLUMN rid FORMAT 9990 HEADING "RID";
COLUMN raid FORMAT 9990 HEADING "RAID";
COLUMN action FORMAT a3 HEADING "Act";
COLUMN user_name FORMAT a8 HEADING "User Name";
COLUMN timestamp FORMAT a20 HEADING "Timestamp";

SELECT ar.table_name, ar.rid, ar.raid, ar.action, ar.user_name,
       TO_CHAR(ar.timestamp,'DD-Mon-YYYY HH24:MI:SS') timestamp
  FROM audit_row ar
 ORDER BY ar.table_name, ar.rid, ar.raid;
```

SQL Scripts to Generate Scripts

Creating one or more of the three triggers presented in this chapter on each table you'd like to audit can be very tedious. The following three scripts can be used to generate SQL-generating SQL code to create the before-insert, after-update, and after-delete triggers for any table you would like to audit. By running these scripts, you can automate the process of script creation for all of the tables for which you want to implement auditing.

At the beginning of each script, you will find a brief purpose statement and any comments about what the script will not handle (if applicable).

The script presented here uses the DUAL table. Heavy use of the DUAL table can lead to serialization in the SGA. You might want to create multiple DUAL tables to spread the load.

Generating a Before-Insert Trigger Script

The following example generates a before_insert trigger script.

```
REM Purpose: Audit trail before-insert trigger generator.
REM          This script creates a BEFORE-INSERT trigger script for
REM          a given table for auditing.

SET SPACE 0;
SET VERIFY OFF;
SET NUMWIDTH 4;
SET HEADING OFF;
SET LINESIZE 80;
SET PAGESIZE 0;
SET FEEDBACK OFF;
```

```
SET RECSEP OFF;
SET LONG 255;
SET ECHO OFF;
SET TRIMSPOOL ON;

PROMPT -----------------------------------------------------------;
PROMPT Audit Trail BEFORE-INSERT Trigger Creation Script Generator;
PROMPT -----------------------------------------------------------;
-- accept tabowner char PROMPT 'Table Owner:  ';
ACCEPT tabname  char PROMPT 'Table Name:  ';
-- accept filename char PROMPT 'Spool to <filename>:  ';
PROMPT Spool File Name:  &&tabname._bi0.trg;
PROMPT -------------------------------------------------------;
PROMPT Working...;

COLUMN remarks FORMAT a80;
COLUMN col0 FORMAT 999999990 NOPRINT;
COLUMN col1 FORMAT a80;

DEFINE spoolfile = &&tabname._bi0.trg

SPOOL &&spoolfile;

REM -----------------------------------------------------------------
REM This query generates a file header.
REM -----------------------------------------------------------------

SELECT RPAD('rem ' || '&&spoolfile',80,' ') ||
       RPAD('rem ' || 'Generated on ' || sysdate || ' by ' ||
       user || '.',80,' ') ||
       RPAD('rem ' || 'Script to create BI audit trigger for the ' ||
       UPPER('&&tabname') || ' table.',80,' ') || RPAD(' ',80,' ') remarks
FROM dual;

REM -----------------------------------------------------------------
REM This query generates the trigger text.
REM -----------------------------------------------------------------

SELECT RPAD('create or replace trigger ' || table_name || '_BI0',80,' ') ||
       RPAD('  before insert',80,' ') ||
       RPAD('  on ' || lower(table_name),80,' ') ||
       RPAD('  for each row',80,' ') ||
       RPAD('  when (new.rid is null or new.rid = 0)',80,' ') ||
       RPAD(' ',80,' ') ||
       RPAD('begin',80,' ') ||
       RPAD('  select trunc(' || 'seq_rid.nextval)',80,' ') ||
       RPAD('  into :new.rid',80,' ') ||
       RPAD('  from dual;',80,' ') ||
       RPAD('end;',80,' ') ||
         '/' col1
 FROM user_tables
WHERE table_name = UPPER('&&tabname');

SELECT 0 col0,
```

```
       null col1
  FROM dual
 UNION
SELECT 1 col0,
       'exit;' col1
  FROM dual
 ORDER BY 1;

SPOOL OFF;

SET SPACE 1;
SET VERIFY ON;
SET NUMWIDTH 10;
SET HEADING ON;
SET PAGESIZE 14;
SET FEEDBACK ON;
```

Generating an After-Update Trigger Script

The following example generates an after_update trigger script.

```
REM Purpose: Audit Trail After-Update Trigger Generator.
REM          This script creates a AFTER-UPDATE trigger script for
REM          a given table for auditing.
REM Notes:   Does not handle LONG or similar columns at all!
REM          Chr(39) is the code representation of a single quote sign

SET SPACE 0;
SET VERIFY OFF;
SET NUMWIDTH 4;
SET HEADING OFF;
SET LINESIZE 80;
SET PAGESIZE 0;
SET FEEDBACK OFF;
SET RECSEP OFF;
SET LONG 255;
SET ECHO OFF;
SET TRIMSPOOL ON;

PROMPT -----------------------------------------------------------;
PROMPT Audit Trail AFTER-UPDATE Trigger Creation Script Generator;
PROMPT -----------------------------------------------------------;
ACCEPT tabname  char PROMPT 'Table Name:  ';
PROMPT Spool File Name:  &&tabname._au0.trg;
PROMPT -----------------------------------------------------------;
PROMPT Working...;

COLUMN remarks FORMAT a80;
COLUMN col0 FORMAT 999999990 noprint;
COLUMN col1 FORMAT a80;
COLUMN col2 FORMAT a80;
COLUMN col3 FORMAT a10;
COLUMN col4 FORMAT a80;
COLUMN col5 FORMAT a80;
```

```
COLUMN col6 FORMAT a80;
COLUMN col7 FORMAT a80;
COLUMN col8 FORMAT a80;

SPOOL &&tabname._au0.trg;

REM -----------------------------------------------------------------------
REM This query generates a file header.
REM -----------------------------------------------------------------------

SELECT RPAD('-- ' || '&&tabname._au0.trg',80,' ') ||
       RPAD('-- ' || 'Generated on ' || SYSDATE||' by ' ||
       user || '.', 80, ' ') ||
       RPAD('-- ' || 'Script to create AFTER-UPDATE audit trigger ' ||
       'for the ' || UPPER('&&tabname') || ' table.',80,' ') ||
       RPAD(' ',80,' ') remarks
  FROM dual;

REM -----------------------------------------------------------------------
REM These queries generate the trigger text.
REM -----------------------------------------------------------------------

SELECT RPAD('create or replace trigger ' ||
       table_name || '_AU0', 80, ' ') ||
       RPAD('  after update of', 80, ' ') col1
  FROM user_tables
 WHERE table_name = UPPER('&&tabname');

SELECT '   ' || LOWER(utc.column_name) || ',' col1
  FROM user_tab_columns utc
 WHERE utc.table_name = UPPER('&&tabname')
   AND tc.data_type in ('CHAR', 'VARCHAR', 'VARCHAR2', 'DATE', 'NUMBER')
   AND utc.column_name not in ('RID', 'CREATOR', 'TIMESTAMP')
 ORDER BY utc.column_id;

SELECT '   ' || LOWER(utc.column_name) col1
  FROM user_tab_columns utc
 WHERE utc.table_name = UPPER('&&tabname')
   AND utc.column_name = 'RID';

SELECT RPAD('  on ' || LOWER(table_name),80,' ') ||
       RPAD('  for each row',80,' ') ||
       RPAD(' ',80,' ') ||
       RPAD('declare',80,' ') ||
       RPAD('  raid number(10);',80,' ') ||
       RPAD(' ',80,' ') ||
       RPAD('begin',80,' ') ||
       RPAD('  select ' ||
       'seq_audit.nextval into raid from dual;',80,' ') ||
       RPAD(' ',80,' ') ||
       RPAD('  audit_trail.record_transaction',80,' ') ||
       RPAD('    (raid, ' || CHR(39) || table_name || CHR(39) ||
       ', :' || 'old.rid, ' || CHR(39) || 'U' || CHR(39) || ');',80,' ') ||
       RPAD(' ',80,' ') col1
```

```
  FROM user_tables
 WHERE table_name = upper('&&tabname');

REM -----------------------------------------------------------------
REM This section builds the column comparison section.
REM -----------------------------------------------------------------

SELECT RPAD('  if nvl(:old.' || LOWER(a.column_name) || ',' ||
       DECODE(a.data_type, 'NUMBER','0',
       'DATE', CHR(39) || '31-dec-9595' || CHR(39),
       CHR(39) || ' ' || CHR(39) ) ||
       ') != ',80,' ') col4,
       RPAD('     NVL(:new.'||LOWER(a.column_name)||',' ||
       DECODE(a.data_type, 'NUMBER','0',
       'DATE', CHR(39) || '31-dec-9595' || CHR(39),
       CHR(39) || ' ' || CHR(39) ) ||
       ') then',80,' ') col5,
       RPAD('     audit_trail.column_update',80,' ') col6,
       RPAD('       (raid, ' || chr(39) || a.column_name || CHR(39) ||
       ',',80,' ') col7,
       RPAD('       :old.' || LOWER(a.column_name) ||
       ', :new.' || lower(a.column_name) || ');',80,' ') col8,
       '  end if;' col3
  FROM user_tab_columns a
 WHERE a.table_name = upper('&&tabname')
   AND a.data_type IN ('CHAR', 'VARCHAR', 'VARCHAR2', 'DATE', 'NUMBER')
   AND a.column_name NOT IN ('CREATOR', 'TIMESTAMP')
 ORDER BY a.column_id;

REM -----------------------------------------------------------------
REM This section finishes up the trigger.
REM -----------------------------------------------------------------

SELECT null
  FROM dual;

SELECT 0 col0,
       'end;' col1
  FROM dual
 UNION
SELECT 1 col0,
       '/' col1
  FROM dual
 ORDER BY 1;

-- Optional:  If you want "exit" at the end of your script.
-- SELECT 0 col0,
--        null col1
--   FROM dual
--  UNION
-- SELECT 1 col0,
--        'exit;' col1
--   FROM dual
--  ORDER BY 1;
```

```
SPOOL OFF;

SET SPACE 1;
SET VERIFY ON;
SET NUMWIDTH 10;
SET HEADING ON;
SET PAGESIZE 14;
SET FEEDBACK ON;
```

Generating an After-Delete Trigger Script

The following example generates an after_delete trigger script.

```
REM Purpose: Audit Trail After Delete Trigger Generator.
REM          This script creates a AFTER-DELETE trigger script for
REM          a given table for auditing.
REM Notes:   Does not handle LONG or similar columns at all!

SET SPACE 0;
SET VERIFY OFF;
SET NUMWIDTH 4;
SET HEADING OFF;
SET LINESIZE 80;
SET PAGESIZE 0;
SET FEEDBACK OFF;
SET RECSEP OFF;
SET LONG 255;
SET ECHO OFF;
SET TRIMSPOOL ON;

PROMPT ---------------------------------------------------------;
PROMPT Audit Trail AFTER-DELETE Trigger Creation Script Generator;
PROMPT ---------------------------------------------------------;
ACCEPT tabname  char PROMPT 'Table Name:  ';
PROMPT Spool File Name:  &&tabname._ad0.trg;
PROMPT -----------------------------------------------------;
PROMPT Working...;

COLUMN remarks FORMAT a80;
COLUMN col0 FORMAT 999999990 noprint;
COLUMN col1 FORMAT a80;
COLUMN col2 FORMAT a80;
COLUMN col3 FORMAT a80;

SPOOL &&tabname._ad0.trg;

REM -----------------------------------------------------------------
REM This query generates a file header.
REM -----------------------------------------------------------------

SELECT RPAD('-- ' || '&&tabname._ad0.trg',80,' ') ||
       RPAD('-- ' || 'Generated on ' || sysdate || ' by ' ||
       user || '.', 80, ' ') ||
```

```
       RPAD('-- ' || 'Script to create AFTER-DELETE audit trigger ' ||
       'for the ' || UPPER('&&tabname') || ' table.',80,' ') ||
       RPAD(' ',80,' ') remarks
  FROM dual;

REM -------------------------------------------------------------------------
REM These queries generate the trigger text.
REM -------------------------------------------------------------------------

SELECT RPAD('create or replace trigger ' ||
       table_name || '_AD0',80,' ') ||
       RPAD('  after delete',80,' ') ||
       RPAD('  on ' || lower(table_name),80,' ') ||
       RPAD('  for each row',80,' ') ||
       RPAD(' ',80,' ') ||
       RPAD('declare',80,' ') ||
       RPAD('  raid number(10);',80,' ') ||
       RPAD('  deleted_data varchar2(2000);',80,' ') ||
       RPAD(' ',80,' ') ||
       RPAD('begin',80,' ') ||
       RPAD('  select seq_audit.nextval into raid from dual;',80,' ') ||
       RPAD(' ',80,' ') ||
       RPAD('  audit_trail.record_transaction',80,' ') ||
       RPAD('    (raid, ' || chr(39) || table_name || chr(39) ||
       ', :old.rid, ' || chr(39) || 'D' || chr(39) || ');',80,' ') ||
       RPAD(' ',80,' ') ||
       RPAD('  deleted_data :=',80,' ') col1
  FROM user_tables
 WHERE table_name = upper('&&tabname');

SELECT column_id col0,
       RPAD('  ' ||
       DECODE(a.data_type, 'NUMBER','to_char(',
       'DATE','to_char(', null) || ':old.' ||
       LOWER(a.column_name) ||
       DECODE(a.data_type, 'NUMBER',')',
       'DATE',')', null) || ' ' ||
       CHR(124) || CHR(124) || ' ' ||
       CHR(39) || CHR(124) || CHR(39) || ' ' ||
       CHR(124) || CHR(124), 80, ' ') col1
  FROM user_tab_columns a
 WHERE a.table_name = UPPER('&&tabname')
   AND a.data_type IN ('CHAR', 'VARCHAR', 'VARCHAR2', 'DATE', 'NUMBER')
   AND column_id <
        (SELECT MAX(a2.column_id)
           FROM   user_tab_columns a2
          WHERE  a2.table_name = UPPER('&&tabname')
            AND    a2.data_type IN ('CHAR', 'VARCHAR',
               'VARCHAR2', 'DATE', 'NUMBER'))
 UNION
SELECT column_id col0,
       RPAD('  ' ||
       DECODE(a.data_type, 'NUMBER','to_char(',
       'DATE','to_char(', null) || ':old.' ||
```

```
       LOWER(a.column_name) ||
       DECODE(a.data_type, 'NUMBER',')',
       'DATE',')', null) || ';', 80, ' ') col1
  FROM user_tab_columns a
 WHERE a.table_name = UPPER('&&tabname')
   AND a.data_type IN ('CHAR', 'VARCHAR', 'VARCHAR2', 'DATE', 'NUMBER')
   AND column_id =
       (SELECT MAX(a2.column_id)
          FROM   user_tab_columns a2
         WHERE  a2.table_name = UPPER('&&tabname')
           AND    a2.data_type IN ('CHAR', 'VARCHAR',
                  'VARCHAR2', 'DATE', 'NUMBER'))
 ORDER BY 1;

REM ------------------------------------------------------------------
REM This section finishes up the trigger.
REM ------------------------------------------------------------------

SELECT null
  FROM dual;

SELECT RPAD('insert into ' || 'audit_delete',80,' ') ||
       RPAD('(raid, row_data) values (raid, deleted_data);',80,' ') col1
  FROM dual;

SELECT 0 col0,
       'end;' col1
  FROM dual
 UNION
SELECT 1 col0,
       '/' col1
  FROM dual
 ORDER BY 1;

-- Optional - if you want 'exit' at the end of your script.
-- SELECT 0 col0,
--        null col1
--   FROM dual
--  UNION
-- SELECT 1 col0,
--        'exit;' col1
--   FROM dual
--  ORDER BY 1;

SPOOL OFF;

SET SPACE 1;
SET VERIFY ON;
SET NUMWIDTH 10;
SET HEADING ON;
SET PAGESIZE 14;
SET FEEDBACK ON;
```

12

In this chapter:
- *What Are the Backup Options?*
- *What's New for Oracle8?*
- *What Are the Recovery Options?*

Backing Up and Recovering the Database

A recent news story reported that a company suffered grave financial losses because a disgruntled employee destroyed the entire company's information system. The company spent many weeks and millions of dollars to recover their system. The company had viewed their backup strategies as "adequate" but had not tested their recovery plans thoroughly. When disaster occurred and they tried to recover their data, they found they could not recover all the files they needed. Their standard procedure had been to keep their backup data for one month and then reuse the tapes for new backups. In attempting to recover their data, though, they found that they had to go back further than one month. The data they needed was no longer available.

Even with rigorous security, a company can be vulnerable to data loss. One of the best policies a company can follow is to take a proactive stance in determining what forms of backup will be used to help ensure that the system can be successfully recovered. No matter what form of backups you choose to implement, we recommend you thoroughly *test* your recovery procedures to ensure that:

- You know how to perform all forms of recovery with confidence.
- You have completely analyzed your backup and recovery strategies.
- You can successfully read your tapes on different tape drives from those used to make them.

The third point is very important. If you have created your backup tapes on one type of tape drive, you might not be able to read them from any other tape drive. One DBA we know intentionally "loses" a tablespace datafile from his system about once a month and has his data center recover that file to ensure that random files can be recovered successfully—he insists they test recovery on the same type of drive and also a different one from the one on which the files were created. If the file can only be recovered from one specific tape drive (perhaps because the tape heads are slightly out of alignment), you may not be able to recover your system when you really need to.

Backup and recovery aren't only technical operations. Corporate management, as well as all systems support staff, must be made to understand the various forms of backup and recovery available. Since there are significant tradeoffs both in time and in the amount of data that can be recovered from the various forms of backup and recovery discussed here, you need to paint a clear picture to ensure that everyone understands the ramifications of choosing one form of backup over another.

In this chapter we'll briefly present an overview of the backup and recovery options available to the DBA. Because Oracle8 is new to many DBAs and because it presents some different backup and recovery choices, we'll first examine the various forms of backup available to the Oracle DBA, then follow with a discussion of what has been changed or is being provided in a different way for Oracle8.

What Are the Backup Options?

There are several different forms of backups that can be performed to ensure the recovery of data to a database. With the release of Oracle8, even more options become available. The backup options now available are:

- Cold backups—performed with the database shut down
- Hot backups (available for Oracle version 7 forward)—performed with the database up and available
- Logical backups (exports)—a snapshot in time, performed with the database up and available
- The Enterprise Backup Utility (EBU)—for UNIX version 7 users only
- Backup set (new with Oracle8)—performed using the Recovery Manager—with the database up and available
- Image copy (new with Oracle8)—performed using the Recovery Manager—with the database up and available

Hot and cold backups capture an image of the database by making a copy of the files comprising the database and saving the copy of the files to another disk on your system or to tape. If you use a file-level hot or cold backup, you'll be able to recover your database to the point in time at which the copies of the files were made. You replace the damaged datafiles on your system with the copies of the files you have made.

Logical backups are created using an Oracle-supplied utility called *EXPORT*. The utility enables you to capture a snapshot of the database as it appears at the time when you performed the export. Using an export, you can recover just a table or two if you need to, without having to restore the entire database, or you can recover an entire tablespace.

For UNIX platforms using version 7 databases, Oracle provides the Enterprise Backup Utility. This utility is configured to work with a media management product to provide a high-performance, robust backup and restore solution for large database managers. One of the key features of the EBU is its ability to perform online recovery to only the affected areas while enabling unaffected areas to remain available.

Backup sets and image copies are new with the Oracle8 RDBMS and are created using the new Oracle-supplied Recovery Manager utility. Like hot and cold backups, backup sets are copies of the database files. The difference is that the Recovery Manager controls the making of the copies and keeps track of when the copies were made and where they are stored. As the name implies, you use the Recovery Manager not only to create the backups automatically, but also to perform database recovery in an automated manner.

We'll discuss each of these backup mechanisms in more detail and look at the recovery options available to you.

About Archivelog Mode

As we mentioned earlier in Chapter 2, *Oracle System Files*, Oracle uses redo log files to capture changes made to the database. The redo log files are written to in a circular manner and, when all of the available redo log files have been filled up, the log writer (LGWR) begins to overwrite the first redo log file, thus destroying the old changes stored there. Oracle provides you with the ability to save off the redo log files before they are reused and overwritten with new data. The mechanism used to save off the redo log files is called *archivelog mode*. When you have enabled archivelog mode, the redo log file information is saved off to separate archive log files—either on a disk on your system or to a tape. If you enable archivelog mode, you can recover your database to a point in time other than the time at which your backups were created.

Archivelog mode is enabled using a two-step process. The default *INIT.ORA* file contains several archivelog mode parameters commented out. The first step in enabling archivelog mode is to uncomment the parameters:

```
log_archive_start = true
log_archive_dest = %ORACLE_HOME%\database\archive
log_archive_format = "%%ORACLE_SID%%T%S.ARC"
```

LOG_ARCHIVE_START

Tells Oracle to logically begin the archivelog mode process. However, just uncommenting these parameters and "bouncing" the database will *not* completely enable archivelog mode. You must set the other archivelog parameters as well.

LOG_ARCHIVE_DEST

Tells Oracle where to write the archive logs. This value can be either a disk on the operating system or a tape drive and is operating system-dependent.

LOG_ARCHIVE_FORMAT

Tells Oracle what format the archive log file names should be (i.e., what the names should look like). The "%T" is the thread number while the "%S" is the log sequence number. A capital "S" tells Oracle that the log sequence number should be a fixed length and padded with zeros.

The three parameters shown above are the basic archive log parameters already present in the *INIT.ORA* parameter file. There are other parameters available for the archivelog mode, but these three are the ones you must set in order to successfully enable archivelog mode on your database.

The second step, using *svrmgrl*, is to STARTUP MOUNT your database—but do not OPEN it. From *svrmgrl*, issue the command:

```
ALTER SYSTEM ARCHIVE LOG START;
```

After you have issued this command, specify:

```
ALTER DATABASE OPEN;
```

Your database is now in archivelog mode. Each time a redo log is filled or a checkpoint is reached, the data from the redo log file is saved to an archive log file by the ARCH process. You can use the archive log files to recover your database to a point in time later than the time the last hot or cold backup was taken.

Cold Database Backups

A *cold database backup*, also referred to at times as an *image backup*, derives its name from the fact that the database is shut down to perform this action. You must ensure that no processes are active within the database when the attempt is made to shut the database down. A good shutdown procedure includes verification that all processes have been stopped before a SHUTDOWN NORMAL command (the Oracle recommended shutdown) is issued to shut the database down. If there are any connected users, the database cannot be shut down with the NORMAL option.

After the database is shut down, each file that makes up the database is copied either to another disk or to tape. This process is referred to as a *file-level copy*. The files copied should include all datafiles, redo logs, control files, and the *INIT.ORA* file. There are many different system-dependent utilities that can be used to perform the actual backing up of the files. Among them are the following:

- UNIX: *obackup*, *tar*, *dd*, *fbackup*, or *cpio*
- VMS: BACKUP
- Windows NT: Backup Manager or OCOPY
- MAC: GUI Finder to copy to disk, third-party software such as Dantz Retrospect
- OS/2: Standard DOS/OS2 copy
- NetWare: NetWare NBACKUP utility, third-party software
- MVS: DFDSS or IDCAMS using EXPORT (not REPRO)

After the file-level copy is completed, the database is restarted. When the copy is completed, if a disaster occurs, the database can be recovered to the condition it was in when the copy was made. The disadvantage of performing a file-level copy is that it is very difficult, though not impossible, to recover one or more individual tables easily.

When a cold backup is used in conjunction with archive logging, the database can be recovered to a "point in time" or "until cancel." For example, suppose that the database is backed up at midnight on Sunday and archive logging is enabled. The system suffers a catastrophic event on Tuesday at 2:30 P.M. The DBA would first save off the current redo log files and control files to a separate area and then restore the files from the backup. The DBA would then replace the older log files with the current saved ones and roll forward through the archive log files until 2:29 P.M. on Tuesday just prior to the disaster. The result is that the organization would lose only the uncommitted transactions in process at the time the recovery was discontinued.

Hot Database Backups

Hot database backups are essential for a 24-hour-a-day, 7-day-a-week environment. They derive their name from the fact that the database remains up and running while the backup is performed. Essentially, file-level copies are made of the datafiles (as with the cold database backups). Archivelog mode must be enabled to ensure that effective backups are captured. To begin a hot backup of a tablespace's datafile(s), issue the command:

```
ALTER TABLESPACE <ts_name> BEGIN BACKUP
```

where ts_name is the tablespace name. Once you have issued this command from *svrmgrl* or SQL*Plus, return to the operating system level and copy the datafiles corresponding to the tablespace to another disk or to tape just as you would for a cold database backup.

There are some procedures that must be followed if effective hot backups are to be made. You must:

- Be sure to use ALTER TABLESPACE ts_name END BACKUP after completing each tablespace's file copies
- Capture the current log file by using ALTER SYSTEM SWITCH LOGFILE;
- Capture all archive logs from the time the backup was started until the backup is completed
- Back up the controlfile using the ALTER DATABASE BACKUP CONTROLFILE TO 'filespec'; command

As with cold backups, individual tables cannot easily be recovered but the database can be recovered to a "point in time" or until cancel. Oracle recommends doing hot backups during periods when less DML is occurring on the system.

Logical Database Backups (Exports)

An export is actually a "snapshot in time." There are several forms of export you can perform:

- A full database export
- An export by user or a full schema export
- An export by individual table or set of tables

A full database export captures a snapshot of the entire database at a particular point in time. Every object within the database is captured, including all tablespace definitions, users, tables, views, etc. You can perform an export to capture all of the objects owned by one or more particular users or schemas, or you can export a specific table or set of tables owned by a particular user or schema. Unlike a hot or cold backup, which captures complete datafiles and their contents, an export captures random pieces of the database or a complete copy of the entire database to one compressed file.

To perform an export of a database, the database must be up and running. One advantage of having an export is that it allows you to easily recover a single table or set of tables. If a full database export has been performed, you can subsequently produce a file containing the complete documentation of the composition of the database by issuing the *import* command in conjunction with the parameters "show=y log=<filename>".

Since anyone who has a privileged account in a database can run the import command and view the composition of the database that has been exported, you must ensure that the export files are kept in a restricted-access area of the operating system. Although the *show* command used in conjunction with a log file name produces what appears to be a usable SQL script, the output generated is *not* formatted properly to enable running the commands directly from the log file output.

Using an export file, the database can only be recovered to the time at which the export was performed. The database cannot be recovered to a specific point in time. Although archive logging can be used with any database if enough disk or tape storage is available for that system, archive logs cannot be used in conjunction with an export to restore a database. Export files are very portable and can be used to move or copy a database from one system to another. However, the process of exporting can be very slow and may not be feasible for very large databases. An interesting characteristic of the export process is that it identifies any data block corruption; it does so by failing.

There are several different forms of export that can be performed using the parameter "INC_TYPE="; you can specify:

COMPLETE
: For a full database export

INCREMENTAL
: Captures what has changed from the last increment (but can't be specified as read-consistent)

CUMULATIVE
: Captures what has changed since the last full export

In all of these cases, you must also specify the "FULL=Y" parameter.

The information about an export that has been performed using "INC_TYPE=" can be seen from SQL*Plus by performing a SELECT from:

SYS.INCEXP
: For objects in specific exports

SYS.INCFIL
: For incremental and cumulative exports

SYS.INCVID
: EXPID—used to determine next EXPID

To see the full list of the available export parameters, specify the command "EXP HELP=Y" at the operating system command prompt.

Enterprise Backup Utility

As we mentioned earlier. Oracle began providing a utility with version 7 for UNIX platforms. This utility, the Enterprise Backup Utility, is intended to solve the problem of providing backup and restore functions for a very large database in a timely and effective manner. EBU works with several media management products, including:

- Epoch EpochBackup
- IBM Adstar Distributed Storage Manager
- Legato Systems NetWorker
- Hewlett-Packard Omniback II
- SprectraLogic Alexandria
- StorageTek REEL Backup and REEL Librarian
- Open Vision NetBackup

Not all products listed here work on all platforms for which EBU is available. The EBU consists of software programs and a Backup Catalog. Oracle recommends that the EBU software and Backup Catalog be placed on a disk separate from the systems to be backed up. That way, if a media failure occurs, you can recover using the product from a separate area. If you have placed the software and Backup Catalog in a separate area and you have more than one database to back up, you can use this central area as the location for all your database backups.

The utility creates and runs processes for each backup or recovery job and requires a separate set of executables for each database to be protected. There are several processes that run for each database being backed up:

BRD (Instance Manager)
: This is a daemon process that monitors the Backup Catalog and *obackup*. The Instance Manager handles the cleanup work for all backup and restore operations which terminate abnormally.

obackup
: Monitors all the other processes and communicates with both the database being backed up and the Backup Catalog. *obackup* will spawn the Instance Manager process if it terminates abnormally.

BRDK
: Handles reads and writes of disk files. There is one BRDK process per file.

BRTP
: Handles the reads and writes to tape files. There is one BRTP per I/O stream.

BRIO

Coordinates between the *obackup*, BRDK, and BRTP processes. There is one BRIO process per parallel I/O stream.

During backups, BRDK reads the database files into a backup buffer area. After the BRDK process puts the backup information into the backup buffer area, the BRTP process writes the backup information to tape using the third-party media management system. During restoration operations, the BRTP process reads the information from tape via the third-party media management system and places the information in a restoration buffer area. The BRDK process takes the buffered information and writes it back to the database file. The other processes act in a managerial capacity, performing cleanup and processing errors.

The Backup Catalog tracks state information about each backup and restore job. The Backup Catalog also retains history information for browsing and reporting functions. When you run the EBU, the first thing the utility does is verify your current database configuration against the Backup Catalog information. If your database configuration has changed—you've added a new tablespace with two datafiles, for example—the Backup Catalog will be updated to reflect the changes and then the backup will be run.

The EBU supports both raw devices and file systems. You can perform partial or complete backups, and EBU will use whatever files it needs from both partial and full backups to restore the database files. You can even restore files to a point in time.

The EBU is really a forerunner of the Oracle8 Recovery Manager, which we will discuss next.

What's New for Oracle8?

Oracle8 provides several new table types, including partitioned tables and indexes, nested tables, advanced queue tables, and index-organized tables. Another new feature in Oracle8 is the ability to define object types. Oracle8 also provides the ability to back up all the different objects that can now be created.

The Oracle8 Recovery Manager

Within an Oracle8 environment, there is a new facility known as the Recovery Manager (RMAN). The Recovery Manager provides flexibility by allowing you to back up an entire database, individual tablespaces, or individual datafiles. The Recovery Manager starts Oracle server processes for the database to be backed up or restored and can write the backups directly to a storage device, as long as you have your media management software integrated with your Oracle software. The

Recovery Manager uses a *recovery catalog* to store information about its tasks and enables automated restore and recovery operations—in parallel, if desired. Reports can be generated of all backup and recovery actions. The Recovery Manager can be accessed either interactively or through batch mode using its command language interpreter (CLI) or through the Oracle Enterprise Manager (see Chapter 13, *Using the Oracle Enterprise Manager*).

The Recovery Catalog

The recovery catalog is a repository in which is stored the information about datafile and archive log backup sets and backup pieces, datafile copies, archive redo logs and copies, tablespaces and datafiles, and stored scripts that define sequences of Recovery Manager and SQL scripts.

The information within the catalog for archive logs should be refreshed (referred to as "resynchronization") frequently. In a situation requiring media recovery, the archive logs that have not been cataloged since the last resynchronization prior to the failure must be cataloged before any recovery can be performed. See the Oracle-supplied documentation for more information on resynchronization of archive logs.

The Recovery Manager stores information in, and gleans information about, the database backups from their control files. If, for whatever reason, the catalog is destroyed or is otherwise unavailable, you can construct a partial catalog from the control file for a database. If you are using the Recovery Manager to perform backups, you must set the parameter CONTROL_FILE_RECORD_KEEP_TIME in the *INIT.ORA* parameter file. This parameter contains the number of days a backup entry in the control file should be retained before it is overwritten with new information. The DBA must ensure that the catalog has been resynchronized within that time period to avoid losing backup information. The DBA should also be aware that the control file will grow in size up to the amount of space necessary to store "x" number of days information (where x is the number of days set in the CONTROL_FILE_RECORD_KEEP_TIME parameter). The maximum size allowable for your control file is operating system-dependent.

The information about the backups is stored in a Recovery Manager catalog within a database. Therefore, you must ensure that the Recovery Manager repository is also protected, and you must create a backup plan to ensure recovery of the catalog. We suggest that, if you have the resources, you use a separate database to back up the recovery catalog and use the Recovery Manager database to back up the database in which you are storing the recovery catalog backup.

You do not have to maintain a recovery catalog, but Oracle recommends that one be kept. Since the backup information is kept in the control file for each database, there is an "operational mode," which can be used for small databases where a recovery catalog would be burdensome. However, this mode does not support point-in-time recovery, stored scripts, and restore and recovery when the control file is lost or damaged. If you choose to not use a recovery catalog, you should maintain more than one control file on separate disks and keep very complete records of your backup activities.

Backups Supported by Recovery Manager

Two types of backup are supported using the Recovery Manager: a backup set and an image copy.

A backup set can contain either datafiles (a datafile backup set) or archive logs (an archive log backup set). Only one type of file can be stored in a backup set, but many files of that type can be stored within each set. Often, the backup sets are written to tape. One set may not fit completely on one tape. Thus, if backup sets are going to be made and written directly to tape, several tapes will need to be made available for the backup. Backup sets can be created on disk and later stored to tape. The DBA could keep the latest copy of the database backup sets on disk and the older sets on tape. If recovery is required, files must be extracted from the backup sets through restore operations.

An image copy is a copy of a single file. This copy can be used in a restore scenario or can be used directly by renaming a datafile within the database to the image copy. However, an image copy must be performed to disk, so be sure to take the amount of disk space required into consideration if you use this form of backup. Image copies can be made from archive logs, datafiles, or controlfiles, but each image copy can contain only one individual file.

We recommend that you perform image copies of files to different disks (preferably on different controllers) from the location of the file you are copying. For example, if you are making an image copy of the *temp* tablespace datafile located on my_disk01, put the image copy on another disk—like my_disk02.

Types of datafile backups

There are two possible types of datafile backups provided with the Oracle8 Recovery Manager—full and incremental—and four allowable levels of backup storage (discussed in the next section). The difference in the backups is the number of database blocks that are saved off. In a full datafile backup, every block that has ever been changed within a datafile is backed up. Blocks that have never been changed in the datafile are not captured. (Note that this is a different form of backup from the full, file-level backups we discussed in the section "Cold Database Backups.") In a full, file-level backup, *all* of the blocks in the datafiles are captured—not just the changed blocks. From the Recovery Manager, you can make full backups of the following files:

- Datafile
- Datafile copy
- Tablespace
- Control file
- Database
- Archived redo log files

An incremental backup captures the blocks in a datafile that have changed since the last backup performed at the same or a lower level. You can perform incremental backups, which only capture the changed blocks, on the following:

- Datafile
- Tablespace
- Database

You can also include control files in an incremental backup set, but the control files are always saved in their entirety.

Until Oracle8, when a change occurred to a row in a table and a backup was performed, the entire table's worth of data was captured. The new incremental feature available in Oracle8 enables only the actual changed blocks of a table to be saved. The use of this facility will reduce the amount of storage space required for backups, but may take longer to restore.

Using backup levels

We said that you could have up to four levels of backup storage. What does that mean exactly? With the new backup utility, you can have multi-level incremental backups. This means you can make a backup of every block that has changed in the database as a baseline starting point. This backup would be termed a *level 0* incremental backup. The next backup you would perform would be a *level 1* incremental backup. In this backup, only the blocks that changed since the last backup at the same or a lower level would be captured. Thus, in the level 1 backup, you would capture the blocks that had changed since the level 0 backup was performed.

You also have the option to make cumulative incremental backups at level 1 and higher. A cumulative incremental backup captures all the blocks that have changed since the last backup at the last *lower* level was performed. This means you would duplicate the work your incremental backups had done, but you would combine all of the "accumulated" changes into one file. The use of cumulative incremental backups makes the recovery process run more quickly.

During a recovery, the Recovery Manager can restore the backup set from tape back to disk. The assumption is, of course, that there will be enough space to support the restoration of files, so it is up to the DBA to ensure that there will be enough empty disk space to accomplish this task.

The Recovery Manager allows the DBA to use the different backup levels for different purposes. For example, level 0 (full) could be performed monthly while level 1 (cumulative) could be weekly and level 2 (incremental) could be daily, and so on. Each set of weekly incremental backups would replace the other six daily backups, and each level 1 monthly would replace the four weekly backups. If the backups were being stored on disk, the disk space could be reused on a rotating basis. The DBA is free to decide what each level of backup will contain and how frequently each level is replaced. Figure 12-1 shows a typical backup cycle.

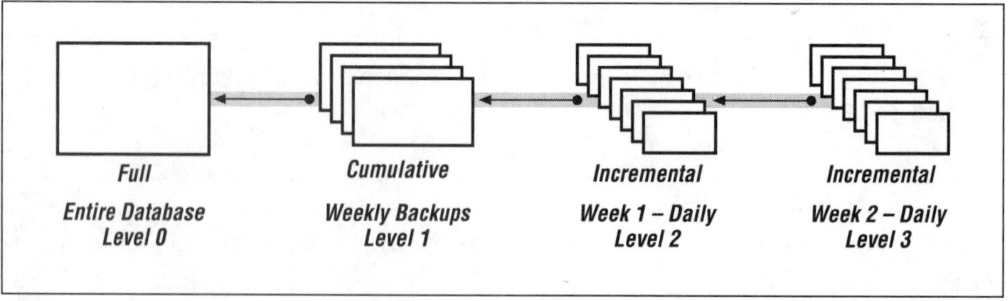

Figure 12-1. Using backup levels

What Are the Recovery Options?

There are many different ways in which a database can be recovered:

- As a snapshot in time (from export or file-level backups without archive logging enabled)
- To a point in time (from file-level backups plus archive logs)
- Until cancel (from file-level backups plus archive logs)

For an entire tablespace, you can restore one or more datafiles from file-level backups. From an export, you can restore an entire schema, a table, or a set of tables. Using the import option "INDEXFILE=<file_name>", you can obtain a script to build an index or set of indexes from an export file.

Backup and Recovery Reminders

Here are a few reminders about the behavior of different types of backup and recovery.

Cold file-level backups performed for Oracle7 or Oracle8 databases without the Recovery Manager, and backup sets created using the Oracle8 Recovery Manager without archivelog mode enabled, allow recovery of tablespaces or the entire database to the point in time when the backup was made. If a backup was made on Monday at 1:00 A.M. and the recovery was performed on Thursday, all data entries, DDL statements, and other modifications to the database done from 1:00 A.M. Monday morning until Thursday, when the recovery was required, would be lost.

Cold file-level backups, hot backups, backup sets, and full image copies, with archivelog mode enabled, enable recovery to be performed to a point in time or until cancel. If a backup was made on Monday at 1:00 A.M. and the recovery was desired to Thursday at 2:00 P.M., the database recovery can be performed to the time desired, as long as archive logging is enabled and the archive logs are available.

Exports enable the recovery of individual tables or groups of tables but can only be performed to recover to the point in time at which the export was done. Exports are only a snapshot in time. You cannot use archive logs with an export to recover to a point in time beyond the time when the export was performed.

There are two types of database recovery:

- Online—with the database open
- Offline—with the database closed

Online Recovery

For an online recovery from within the database, use the commands RECOVER TABLESPACE... and/or RECOVER DATAFILE... in tablespace recovery. From outside of the database, use the *import* utility to recover tables, schemas, or the entire database from an export file.

Offline Recovery

From an offline recovery from SQLDBA or the Server Manager line mode option (*svrmgrl*) with the database mounted but not opened, you can recover the *system* tablespace as well as an entire database. Using this method, if a tablespace has been corrupted and the DBA is absolutely sure that the tablespace can be rebuilt, the datafiles associated with that tablespace can be altered with the OFFLINE

DROP option and the database opened. In such a case, the tablespace will be "untouchable" and must be dropped immediately. Use great caution when applying this technique, and contact Oracle World-Wide Support before proceeding with this plan since there are possible repercussions that could result in still more severe database corruption.

In this chapter:
- *What Is the OEM?*
- *The DBA Toolkit and Security*
- *OEM and the Job Scheduler*
- *OEM and the Event Management System*

13

Using the Oracle Enterprise Manager

In early versions of the Oracle RDBMS, a very limited utility called the Oracle Diagnostic System (ODS) was used to help DBAs get some insight into what was happening within their databases. At that time, there was very little a DBA could do to improve performance or easily maintain or replicate a database. As time passed and the Oracle versions presented more and more sophisticated systems, the tool evolved into SQLDBA and then the Server Manager Utility (*svrmgr*). Today, Oracle packages a personal computer-based, graphical user interface (GUI) toolset called the Oracle Enterprise Manager (OEM) to aid the DBA in managing multiple databases on remote nodes throughout the world via networks.

This chapter examines the ways you can use the OEM to help enforce security in your system. We will look at how the OEM can aid you in performing your job more easily and efficiently by providing:

- A way to easily create users, roles, and grants
- The ability to create and examine views
- An easy way to use the Backup and Recovery Managers

We also pinpoint possible security breaches the OEM might both present and prevent through the CHANGE ROLE function and remote DBA connections.

Oracle Corporation has released a different version of the OEM with each release of the RDBMS since the early versions of 7.3. Since each released version of the OEM varies from the other released versions in several ways, we'll focus here only on release 1.5.0 for Oracle8 version 8.0.4.

What Is the OEM?

The Oracle Enterprise Manager lets DBAs manage one or more databases on one or more platforms in one or more locations—all from the same console. You can easily view all of the objects associated with a particular database or group of databases, and you can perform day-to-day tasks from the central console screen. In the following sections, we'll first examine the general composition of the OEM, then we'll discuss how the OEM can assist you in performing the tasks which will help secure the database.

The OEM Components

The OEM is made up of the following components:

- A set of console screens from which you can manage databases and software distribution
- A database repository in which information for the tool's use is stored
- A set of database tools for performing DBA tasks
- A job scheduler
- An event management system
- A graphical interface to the Recovery Manager tools (not available in Oracle7)
- One intelligent agent per node to support communication between the databases on that node and the OEM

From the console, you can:

- View the makeup of, and administer to, several databases on one or more nodes at once
- Access the various database administration tool manager options
- Schedule jobs to run on one or more nodes against one or more databases
- Monitor one or more databases for various events and notify designated people by displaying a message back to the OEM console, sending email, and/or paging a specific person or group of people

Along with the tasks listed above, you can also customize your view of the network using the graphical maps provided by Oracle with the tool, or you can create personalized representations of meaningful backgrounds on which to place icons of the databases being managed in a specific group. For example, you might take an organizational chart drawn as a bitmap and place icons of the databases that belong to each of your departments in that department's area of the chart.

Using the OEM, you can also distribute Oracle software to multiple servers in a coordinated manner. You can even configure the tool to launch other Oracle "cartridges" or third-party tools.

The DBA Toolkit

The database administration toolkit provided with the OEM consists of several different components you can access in any of the following ways:

- From the pull-down menu at the top of the OEM console screen
- From the manager icons just below the pull-down menu
- From the navigator object display by clicking the right mouse button
- From the Start → Program → Oracle Enterprise Manager → Administrator Toolbar Window menu
- From the stand-alone Database Administrator Toolbar which you can configure to be displayed at system boot time

Figure 13-1 shows the "floating" Database Administrator Toolbar for OEM release 1.5.0.

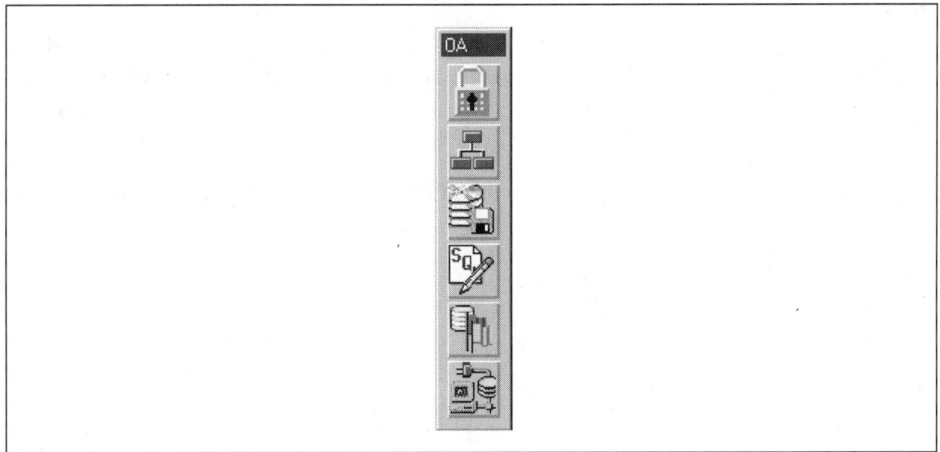

Figure 13-1. The Database Administrator Toolbar for release 1.5.0

The icons shown in this figure represent the following pieces of manager software (we'll describe each manager below):

- Lock icon—the Security Manager
- Tree icon—the Schema Manager
- Disk icon—the Storage Manager

- SQL icon—the Work Sheet
- Flags icon—the Instance Manager
- PC icon—the Net8 Assistant

Not all of the managers in the OEM are accessible from the Administrator Toolbar.

In later sections, we'll show you the ways you can use each manager to help make your database more secure.

For Oracle's version 8.0.4 with OEM release 1.5.0, the available components are:

Backup Manager
: Used to back up, recover, and restore a database. In Oracle8, the Enterprise Manager uses the new Recovery Manager to provide these utilities.

Data Manager
: Used to export, import, and load data.

Instance Manager
: Provides the ability to start up and shut down the database, modify initialization file (*INIT.ORA*) parameters, and manage in-doubt transactions and user sessions.

Replication Manager
: Enables you to create and manage both simple and complex database replication.

Schema Manager
: Used to create, edit, and examine schema objects like tables, indexes, triggers, procedures, packages, etc.

Security Manger
: Used to administer users, privileges, and profiles.

SQL Worksheet
: Used to create and run your SQL statements and PL/SQL code, and "canned" Oracle-provided scripts for environment establishment (e.g., the *CATALOG.SQL* and *CATPROC.SQL* scripts).

Storage Manager
: Used to administer tablespaces, rollback segments, and datafiles.

Software Manager
: Enables you to distribute Oracle software from one central place.

In Oracle8, the Backup Manager uses the Recovery Manager utility to perform any backup or recovery work from the OEM. See Chapter 12, *Backing Up and Recovering the Database*, for more information on the Recovery Manager.

For an additional fee, the Oracle Performance Packs are available to assist you with database performance tuning. In the Oracle7 versions of the OEM, there is only one performance pack. For Oracle8, the product has been divided and is being marketed as several separate packs.

Specifying the Database Repository

There are several considerations and decisions you need to resolve before you start the OEM for the first time. As you configure and run the OEM, the information is gathered and the configuration work you do is stored within a central repository. Each time you log on to the OEM, you are prompted with the name, password, and network location of the database in which the OEM has stored or will store repository data.

Therefore, you need to decide what database you will use to house the console repository and what user/schema area you will create for the name and password for the repository. Since the repository can reside in a database by itself or in a database on one of the servers that will be administered from the console, be sure to choose an easily recognized and meaningful name. For example, you might decide to use a name like OEM_REP for the repository schema.

Once you've decided on a meaningful name, you need to take the following steps:

1. Create the account for the user/schema area.
2. Grant the Oracle-supplied DBA default role to this account.
3. Create a tablespace with enough space to support the repository.
4. Assign the tablespace to the repository user/schema area as the "default tablespace."
5. Decide what form of backup(s) you will use to ensure that you can recover your OEM console repository.
6. Determine where your backups will be stored and how often you will back up the repository.

A Potential Security Problem

Because the OEM gives you the ability to perform major database administration tasks like starting up and shutting down a database from a remote console, the machine from which the OEM console is run must be protected from casual user access. From almost every DBA toolkit option, the OEM provides the person using the utilities the ability to "change roles." If the console is not protected and the console screen is available to casual users, a user could potentially access the "change role" option, enable a privileged role like SYSDBA, and access the database with much greater privileges than he or she would normally be entitled to.

Remember that the curious user can do as much or more damage accidentally than a person who is bent on sabotaging a system. For example, a curious user could access the *system* tables and modify either the structure or data within a privileged area without realizing the damage he or she is actually doing.

Running the Oracle Enterprise Manager

When you start the OEM, the first thing you see is the tool's splash screen. Once the splash screen has been displayed, you see the normal Oracle logon screen superimposed on the logo (see Figure 13-2). You are prompted for the username, password, and platform on which the repository is located. If you are using the default database on your Windows NT or Windows 95 machine as the site for the repository and are logging on from that machine, you do not have to enter a value in the Service area.

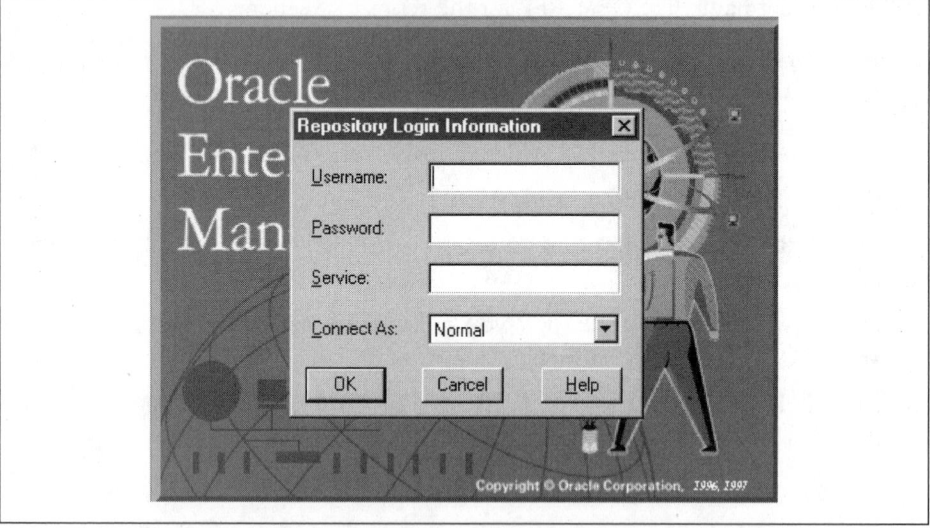

Figure 13-2. The Oracle Enterprise Manager logon screen with logo

The window displayed when you first connect to the OEM consists of four sections (see Figure 13-3).

The Navigator section (top left) enables you to:

- Connect to various databases
- Determine what is in a database
- Perform DBA duties
- Copy information from one database to another
- Perform quick edits of anything

The Map section (top right) enables you to:

- Create, delete, and modify locations of databases on a visual map
- Start up or shut down a database
- View and administer to the databases of interest as one group

The Job Scheduler section (bottom left) is a multi-threaded communications daemon that enables you to:

- Schedule jobs to perform tasks at remote sites
- Save jobs in a jobs library to submit against multiple sites

The Event Scheduler section (bottom right) enables you to:

- Define an event
- View the outcome of an event
- Handle events in remote databases

After you have begun to interact with the OEM console, if you leave the console screen with, say, only the navigation section visible, when you restart the OEM, the tool will remember and redisplay the last configuration of the console's appearance. However, if you resize a display from one of the utilities, the resized configuration will not be retained and you will either have to resize it each time you access that particular display or live with the default display.

The DBA Toolkit and Security

The OEM contains a set of database administration tools you can use to perform the normal, day-to-day tasks required of a DBA. As we said at the beginning of this chapter, the OEM is a GUI tool which will help you perform database administration tasks. Although it communicates with the databases using SQL commands (everything communicates with the database through SQL commands), the OEM is not a replacement for SQL*Plus—SQL never goes away.

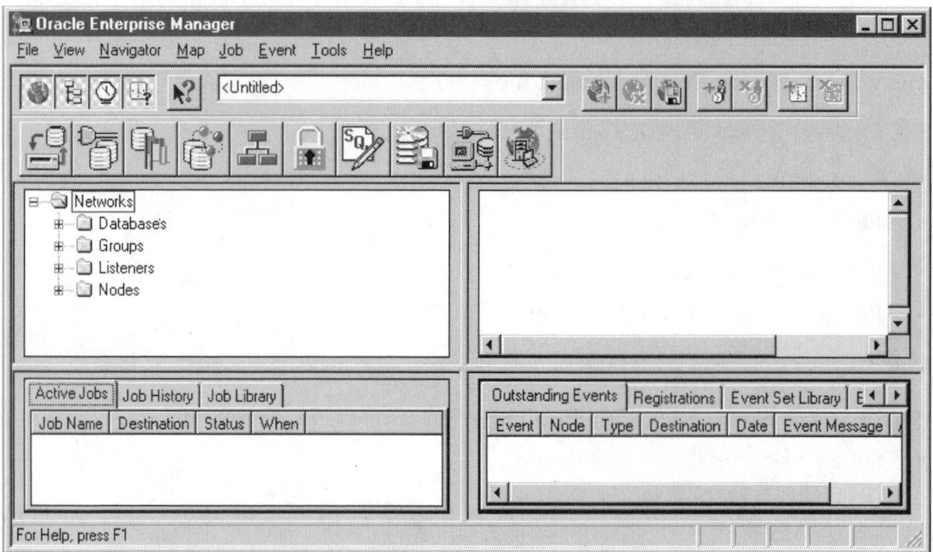

Figure 13-3. The Oracle Enterprise Manager control panel

If you are a new DBA, you will find tools within the OEM toolkit to help you perform your job more efficiently and effectively. If you are a seasoned DBA, you will still find many tools within the product set to help you be a better DBA. We recommend that, if you are a new DBA, you take advantage of the "Show SQL" option available from most of the tool screens to help you learn the SQL commands used to execute the various tasks you will perform with the OEM.

Do not rely solely on the OEM to perform your tasks. If, for whatever reasons, the OEM console becomes unavailable to you, you will have to be able to issue SQL commands explicitly and you'll need a thorough knowledge of those commands so you can administer your databases.

The following sections will examine each utility provided within the DBA toolkit and focus on what options, if any, are provided to aid you in implementing and maintaining database security.

The Oracle Backup Manager

The Backup Manager enables you to perform the backups necessary to protect your system. If you ever have a damaging security breach, sound backups will ensure your ability to recover to an undamaged version of the database.

The latest version of the Oracle Backup Manager provides the ability to:

- Use the new Recovery Manager option as well as the backup tasks available in earlier versions of the OEM
- Perform online or offline backups of a database
- Switch from database to database
- View the status of your tablespaces and log files
- Enable roles interactively
- Perform tablespace, control file, or redo log file backups (a "backup wizard" is provided)
- Shut down, start up, restrict sessions, and allow all sessions in a database
- Enable, disable, and examine archive logs
- Manually archive or switch log files
- Force checkpointing, add log members, and add group members
- Keep a log of your actions
- Quickly check the status of the database to see if it is up or down
- View the current size of the database's SGA and whether archive logging is enabled
- See the resource limits in effect for the database

The Oracle Data Manager

The Oracle Data Manager enables you to perform exports, imports, and data loads. For exports, you can:

- List the type of export to perform (tables, users, or full database)
- List the table names and select which ones you want to export
- Specify whether you want grants, indexes, rows, and/or constraints exported

Under the "Advanced" option, you are able to:

- Specify record length, buffer size, whether to generate a log file, and its name
- Specify whether to export a read-consistent view of the data
- Designate what export type to perform (Complete, Cumulative, Incremental, or None)
- Designate a statistics type (Estimate, Compute, or None)
- Specify whether to "Merge Extents for Import" (compress extents)

For imports, you can specify:

- The file to import

- The type of import (tables, users, or full database)
- Whether you want rows, indexes, and/or grants imported
- Whether to ignore errors when trying to create objects

Under the "Advanced" option, you can specify:

- Record length and buffer size
- Whether to generate a log file and its name
- Increment type (Restore, System, or None)
- Whether to write an index creation script to a file and the file name
- Whether to commit after each array
- Whether to overwrite existing data files

For the Load option, which invokes SQL*Loader, you can specify the names for the following entities:

- The control file
- The data file
- The log file
- The bad file
- The discard file

Under the "Advanced" option, you can specify:

- Records to skip and records to load
- Rows per commit and maximum errors
- Maximum discards
- Maximum bind array
- Whether the data path can be conventional or direct

For all of these options, there are areas in which default values have been placed, so if you are going to perform an export, import, or data load, for example, be sure to check the defaults under the "Advanced" option so a parameter that is set very small won't "bite" you.

As with the Backup Manager, the Data Manager helps you establish a fallback position for data recovery so you are prepared if anything happens to damage your database. See Chapter 12 for more information.

The Oracle Instance Manager

The Oracle Instance Manager enables you to:

- View the *INIT.ORA* parameters, sessions, and in-doubt transactions
- Start up, shut down, mount, or open a database
- Disconnect, restrict, or allow all sessions
- Force commit or rollback of transactions
- Import initialization parameters from a database or file, and export initialization parameters to a file

Since version 7.3 of the RDBMS, the Instance Manager has provided the ability to change many parameters dynamically. This tool enables you to change parameters interactively.

The ability to perform any of the actions available from the Instance Manager poses a very real security threat to your databases. As we mentioned earlier in this chapter, since you can start up the database both in normal and restricted mode and can shut down the database with this manager, be sure the console is protected from interaction by casual users.

The Oracle Replication Manager

The Oracle Replication Manager enables you to:

- Create database connections for master, snapshot, refresh, destination link, or job
- Add objects to master groups, snapshot groups, or refresh groups
- Modify default values for a master group, snapshot group, schedule database links, or refresh group
- Modify job parameters, show options, date options, row query limits, or fonts
- Record scripts

Note that under the default option, there are many changeable parameters under each area and many defaults to verify. Before submitting a job or taking an action, be sure to check all default parameters to ensure that what you want is really what you get.

Snapshots provide a way to replicate only a portion of data from one database to another. The use of both simple snapshot replication and more complex symmetric replication can help you implement applications with more secure data access.

The Oracle Schema Manager

The Oracle Schema Manager first displays a list of all available objects in the database to which you are connected. These include clusters, database links, functions, indexes, package bodies, packages, procedures, refresh groups, sequences, snapshot logs, snapshots, synonyms, tables, triggers, and views.

This manager enables you to create objects or, once you have selected an existing object, "CREATE objects LIKE" the object you have selected. The beauty of being able to create a new object like an existing one, but with minor modifications, is the speed and ease with which you can perform these tasks. Once you have selected an object, you can:

- Remove the object
- Grant privileges to the object
- Create synonyms for the object
- Create indexes on the object

Since database security can be enforced through views, triggers, synonyms, snapshots, packages, and procedures, the Schema Manager provides a utility through which these objects can be managed easily.

The Oracle Security Manger

Within the Oracle toolkits, there are two different products with very similar names:

- The Oracle Security Manager, which resides in the OEM
- The Oracle Security Server (OSS), which exists as a separate utility

The Oracle Security Manager, accessed through the OEM, is used to create and control users, roles, and profiles. The options to create, create like, and remove from each of these types is available. In addition, under users and roles, you can add and revoke privileges. Under profiles, the option to assign a profile to users exists. The Oracle Security Manager lets you administer and enforce basic database security.

The Oracle Security Server, accessed through its own option from the Start → Program windows menu, is discussed in detail in Chapter 15, *Using the Oracle Security Server*. This product is used to provide single sign-on access to databases by users through the generation and tracking of certificates of authority.

The windows displayed for both of these products are very similar, adding to the confusion. For the Oracle Security Manager, the initial window is shown in Figure 13-4.

The ability to create users, roles, and profiles through the Security Manager will help you implement some of the most powerful Oracle security features available.

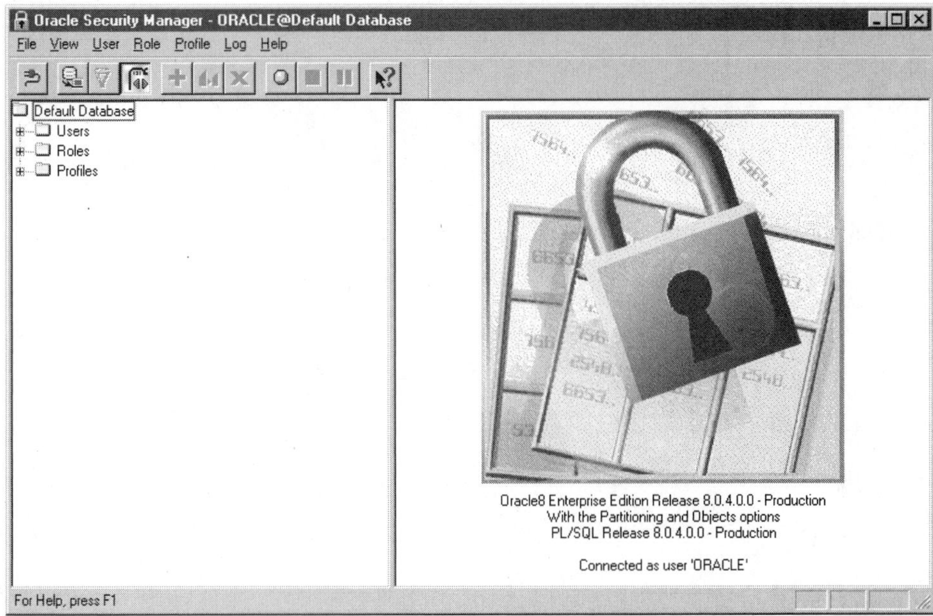

Figure 13-4. The Oracle Security Manager

The Oracle SQL Worksheet

The Oracle SQL Worksheet lets you:

- Create SQL and PL/SQL scripts
- Edit SQL and PL/SQL scripts
- Run SQL and PL/SQL scripts
- Save SQL and PL/SQL scripts to a file or to disk (when saving the work)

Through the SQL Worksheet, you can test your code easily and quickly, make modifications to the code, and retest it. You can also run Oracle-supplied environment scripts like *CATALOG.SQL* and *CATPROC.SQL* from the SQL Worksheet.

For security, you can use the SQL Worksheet option to run SQL statements to enable or disable auditing or to monitor who is currently accessing your database.

The Oracle Storage Manager

The Oracle Storage Manager enables the management of tablespaces, datafiles, and rollback segments. For a tablespace, you can:

- Create, remove, add a datafile to, or add a rollback segment to a tablespace
- Place a tablespace on or off line

- Make a tablespace read-only or writeable
- Use the backup wizard

For a datafile, you can:

- Create
- Create like
- Place online or offline

For a rollback segment, you can:

- Create
- Create like
- Remove
- Shrink
- Place online or offline

The interactive ability to shrink a rollback segment became available as of version 7.2. If you are using an earlier version of the database, the command to shrink a rollback segment will not work.

From a security point of view, the only significant feature of the Storage Manager is the ability to back up the database from this option.

The Oracle Software Manager

The Oracle Software Manager is an option that seems to change complexion with each new release of the OEM. The tool enables you to manage software and installations from the console for any distribution host in your OEM network. The Software Manager window initially consists of two sections. The first section is the Navigator list, which displays a World folder. Below the World folder are Hosts and a Hosts Folder folders. The second section is a Catalog—Software Packages section.

With the current version of the Software Manager, you can:

- Configure a customized installation of Oracle software from the OEM console
- Perform the installation across the network to the platform you have specified
- Easily see which versions of software have been fielded to which platforms

This feature gives you the ability to control and implement several software installations on various machines from a central location. As we mentioned, with any software installation, be sure to protect the operating system files from casual user interactions.

OEM and the Job Scheduler

The OEM provides you with the ability to configure a set of jobs to be automatically run on one or more of your databases. You can set up the jobs to run at the same time on each database or at different times. Oracle supplies a list of commonly used jobs to choose from. You can also write your own customized scripts and schedule them to run automatically.

As with all the OEM utilities, the OEM Job Scheduler uses the intelligent agent on each computer node to perform the actual work that has been scheduled. There is only one intelligent agent per node, regardless of how many databases are on that node or how many jobs have been scheduled to be run against those databases.

The default tasks provided with the OEM Job Scheduler utility can be run either one time or on a scheduled basis:

- Back up tablespace
- Export
- Import
- Load
- Run DBA script
- Run SQL*Plus
- Shut down database
- Start up database
- Broadcast message
- Run OS command
- Run TCL
- Deinstall product
- Delete package
- Distribute package
- Install package

Many of these tasks help protect your databases, as we describe in the following sections.

Back Up Tablespaces, Export, Import, and Load Data

The ability to back up tablespaces on a scheduled basis is a wonderful option that helps ensure you can recover your database to either the last time the tablespaces were backed up or to a point in time after the last backup (if archivelog mode has been enabled). However, if you are going to schedule automatic tablespace backups, you must be sure to also perform a log switch and capture the associated redo log files and control files to be included with the tablespace backup so you can perform an effective recovery.

Scheduled exports can help ensure that you can recover one or more tables, views, or indexes successfully and easily. Performing imports and data loads automatically can help you perform long-running tasks late at night. However, these abilities, when used by an unauthorized person, could potentially enable someone to introduce data to your system without your knowledge. You must ensure that the computer used as the OEM console is not accessible to anyone but your organization's DBAs.

For information about overall backup features and strategies, see Chapter 12.

Run SQL Scripts and SQL*Plus

By creating customized scripts, running them on a daily basis, and reading the output, you can monitor who has been accessing your systems. You might want to create a script to verify on an nightly basis who has been granted access to the database and what privileges each user possesses.

Start Up and Shut Down Your Database

As we have seen in other sections of the OEM, there are many options that include the ability to shut down and start up a database. In order to perform a cold, file-level backup, the database must be shut down. In order to perform an export of the database and ensure that only DBAs can interact with the database while the export is going on, you might want to start up the database in restricted mode and then perform the export.

Broadcast Messages

If you are performing a scheduled job on a database, the ability to warn users that the database is about to be shut down is very helpful. Although this option normally has little value from a security perspective, it is still a nice option to communicate information to all users of a system.

Run OS Commands and Tcl Commands

The OEM Job Scheduler gives you the ability to run command scripts to control operating system actions. For example, you might want to run an operating system command procedure to gather information about who is currently on that system. The OS command script might be as simple as the following command in UNIX, which shows all of the users on the system and redirects the output to a file called *users.txt*:

```
ps -ef > users.txt
```

The Tool Command Language (Tcl) is used with Oracle enhancements (Ora Tcl) to enable you to write command scripts in a language the OEM intelligent agents can understand. Tcl scripts, provided by Oracle through the OEM Job and Event Schedulers, are used to control intelligent agent actions and enable monitoring of your databases on one or more platforms.

Deinstall, Delete, Distribute, and Install Products

The final set of Oracle-supplied tasks available for the Job Scheduler through the OEM deal with Oracle software products. Through the Job Scheduler, you can deinstall products which are installed in your databases and install, delete, or distribute Oracle software to your various platforms through a scheduled job.

OEM and the Event Management System

The Event Management System provided by OEM enables you to define events you want the intelligent agent on a platform to watch for within one or more of your databases on that machine. For example, perhaps you would like to catch a high volume of I/O contention occurring within a specific database. The Event Manager can perform that activity.

The Event Management System provides you with a way to proactively monitor for specific events on each of your databases. Many of the monitoring options, like the database UpDown (indicating whether the database is up or down), the alert log being written to, and the number of processes or users exceeded, can be used to help ensure that your database is better protected and more secure.

There are several categories of event types Oracle has predefined and made available; these are broken down by the system events they will affect as follows:

- Fault Management events
- Space Management events
- Resource Management events

- Performance Management events

The following sections examine each category, and the events within, to see which events might either enhance or endanger your security system.

Fault Management events

You can configure the Event Management System to monitor for the following Fault Management events:

- New values being written to the alert log (Alert option)
- Cases where a user is being blocked from being able to perform an action (User Blocks)
- Whether the database is up or down (UpDown)
- The inability of a new database connection to be made (Probe)

From a security perspective, the most significant Fault Management events are:

- New entries to the alert log that might indicate that someone is modifying the database structure
- The database unexpectedly being started up or shut down
- A database connection failing to be made

Space Management events

You can configure the Event Management System to monitor for the following Space Management events:

- The archive log area being too full for another log to be written (the database will stop until space is obtained)
- The USER_DUMP_DEST or BACKGROUND_DUMP_DEST (*INIT.ORA* parameters) space used exceeding a threshold limit
- A table or tablespace approaching its maximum extent limit
- A tablespace becoming so fragmented that the largest contiguous chunk available is too small

Although each of these events can impact the ability of the database or a user task to continue to run, none of these events are of great interest to you from a security point of view.

Resource Management events

You can configure the Event Management System to monitor for the following Resource Management events:

- The addition of a datafile that exceeds the stated limit
- Exceeding an established lock resource limit
- Exceeding the established process limit
- Exceeding the session limit
- Having more users connect to the database than the LICENSE_MAX_SESSIONS value threshold you set

Of these possible events, exceeding either session or user limits is of special security significance. Too many sessions and too many users might indicate that someone is attempting to snoop around for information or hack into your system.

Performance Management events

You can configure the Event Management System to establish thresholds and monitor for the following Performance Management events:

- Buffer cache hit ratio (Buffer Cache)
- Chained Row
- Data Dictionary cache miss ratio (Data Dictionary Cache)
- The real-time, physical disk I/O rates (Disk I/O)
- Library cache miss ratio (Library Cache)
- Network I/O rates (Net I/O)
- Any selected value in the V$SYSSTAT view (SysStat Table)
- The change in any selected value from the last value obtained (SysStat Table Delta)

As with the Space Management events, although exceeding the thresholds established for these events can impact the performance of your database, sometimes quite dramatically, these Performance Management events do not ordinarily indicate security problems within your database.

14

In this chapter:

- *Application Design Requirements*
- *Running the Application*
- *Documenting the User State*
- *A Sample Script*

Maintaining User Accounts

If you've read this far, you've probably concluded that maintaining user accounts can be a tiresome job. Well, you are absolutely correct! Creating a user is easy. Creating a role is easy. Giving grants to roles is easy. Deciding how to mix all of these is sometimes tedious, but it gets done. Doing all of this once or twice is interesting. Doing it a third time is work, and on the fourth request, you will probably be ready to strangle your client. Without some interface to implement small changes, the maintenance of scripts will drive you crazy. You need a tool to help with the management of users and their privileges, and some tools to document what you have done. You really don't want to do it all over from scratch every time!

This chapter discusses an application that was developed for a client to help solve the maintenance problem. Toward the end of the chapter we provide a sample script to illustrate how the information to create the user and role scripts can be extracted from the data dictionary. You really do need scripts of these kinds in order to recover from catastrophic failure.

There are vendor-supplied tools available to do the type of work we describe in this chapter, but often they are too powerful or complex to turn over to the typical user. A simple custom application of the kind we show in this chapter has the advantage of doing exactly what is needed—and nothing more.

Application Design Requirements

What do we want from this application?

- The application must allow user accounts to be created and maintained.
- It must support the creation of roles and the assignment or removal of privileges to these roles.

- It must allow multiple roles to be assigned to a user.
- When a role is assigned, the application must allow the *security* user to designate if that role is to be a default role.
- In the process of assigning the role, the previously assigned roles must be preserved, and those that are default roles must remain in that state.
- In addition to creating the users, roles, and assignments, the application must allow you to review these assignments.

Running the Application

The security maintenance form we discuss in this chapter was developed using the Oracle Developer 2000 product. It was originally developed in version 4.5 of the Forms module of Developer 2000, and has been migrated to version 5.0. This form works only on users, roles, and system privileges, not on table grants. The use of grants was not a requirement for this particular application.

This application uses data dictionary tables and the APP_ROLES table. This table and its function were described in Chapter 9, *Developing a Simple Security Application*. This table is one that you create, and it is not part of the data dictionary. This is the only table used by the form whose contents you can modify directly. Changes in all of the other sections of the form are handled by PL/SQL procedures.

Initial Display

Figure 14-1 shows the startup display. There are three sections to the form: user maintenance, role maintenance, and role assignment. The latter also has a part in the role maintenance function.

The top four fields are the user maintenance section. Here a user may be created or dropped and the password changed if (when) the user forgets it. The default and temporary tablespace assignments are also made here. You may think from looking at the initial display format that there's no way to drop a user, but that depends on the status of the username entered in the first field. We'll explain more about this in the next section.

Selecting or Creating a User

If a username is entered that does not exist, a message to that effect appears to the right of the "User to create or modify" field. Let's take an existing user for this example. You can enter the name in the field, or the field may be queried. If you

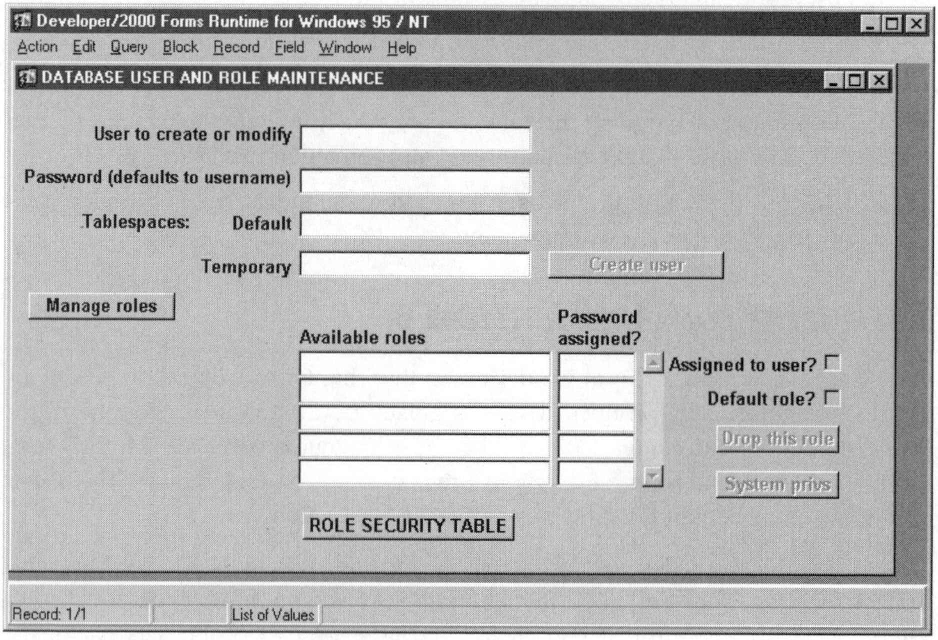

Figure 14-1. Maintenance form initial display

query the field, a pop-up window appears in the upper left corner of the form, as shown in Figure 14-2.

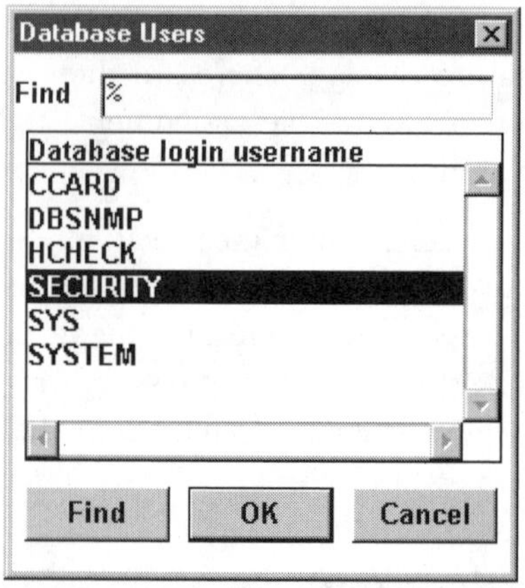

Figure 14-2. Username query pop-up

Here we select the *security* username. Pressing the "OK" button will move this name into the first field. At this time the form display changes to indicate that this is an existing user, and it now looks like Figure 14-3. Had we just entered an existing username, the same check would have occurred and the message would still have been displayed.

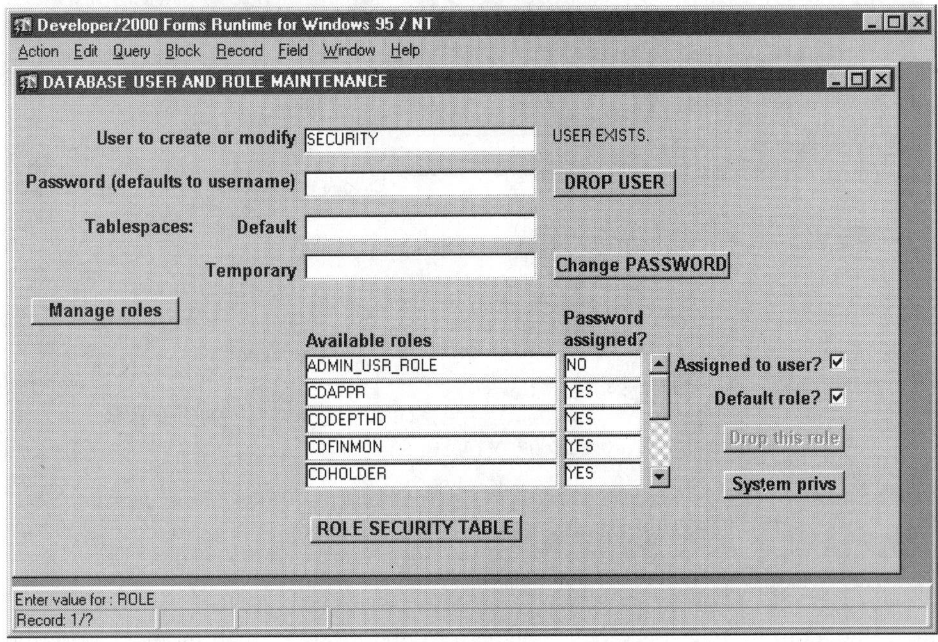

Figure 14-3. After selecting or entering an existing username

As you can see, now the form advises you that the user exists, and a new button appears that will allow you to drop the user. Also note that the button previously labeled "Create user" now says "Change PASSWORD." In addition, after you navigate into the "Available roles" block, that block is automatically populated with all the roles in the data dictionary. Finally, the two checkboxes to the right of the roles fields indicate the status of the role with respect to the username. It may be assigned to the user, may be the user's default role, or may be both. As you move through the "Available roles" records, the checkboxes change to indicate the relationship of the role to the user.

Assigning Roles

If a role is not assigned to the user, the "Assigned to user?" checkbox will be blank but functional while the "Default role?" checkbox will be dimmed, indicating it is disabled (similar to the "Drop this role" button below it). This is illustrated in Figure 14-4, where we have moved the cursor to the CONNECT role.

The "Default role?" checkbox is disabled because if a role is not assigned, it cannot possibly be made a default role. If you check the "Assigned to user?" check-

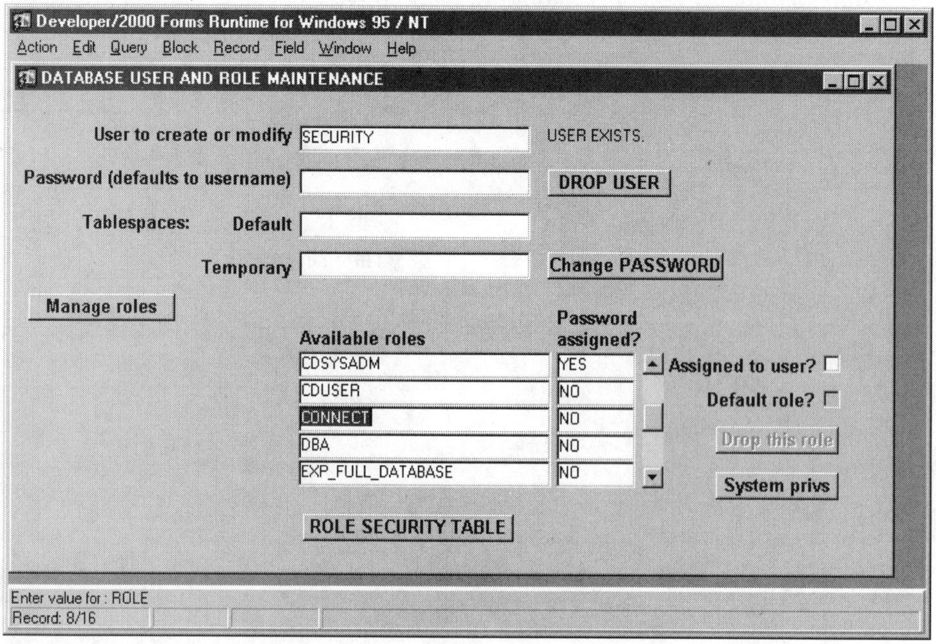

Figure 14-4. Status of the CONNECT role relative to the security user

box, the current role becomes assigned to the user at that moment and the "Default role?" checkbox becomes enabled. Checking the "Default role?" checkbox will cause the role to be designated as a default role while preserving all existing default roles since a user can have more than one. The opposite action occurs if a box is checked and you uncheck it. The role is then either removed from being a default, or removed from the user altogether.

There is a limit to the maximum number of roles a user can have enabled at one time. This limit is set by the MAX_ENABLED_ROLES parameter in the *INIT.ORA* file, and it defaults to 20 if you do not set it. You can assign more than this maximum value, but if you make more than the maximum as the default, then the user will not be able to log in. Few users ever need more than two or three default roles; most do not need more than five or six total.

Creating a New Role

In Figure 14-5, we decided to create the CDDEPTHD role. The window is accessed by pressing the "Manage roles" button. After entering the role name, we have the option of entering a password.

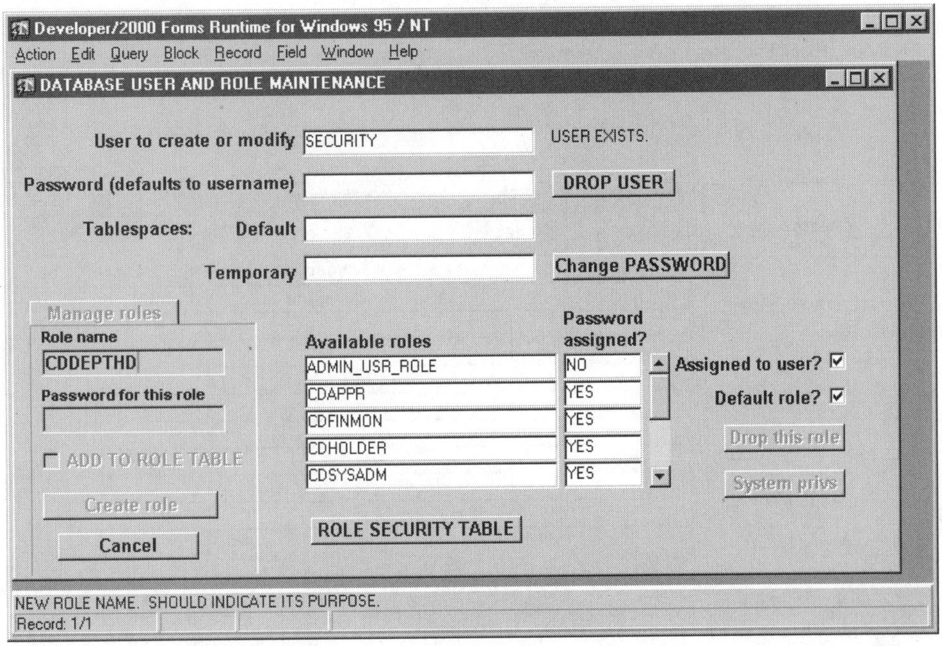

Figure 14-5. Creating a new role

When we enter a password for the role and move out of the field, the "ADD TO ROLE TABLE" checkbox becomes enabled. If we check this box, the Role Security Table screen will be displayed as shown in Figure 14-6. You can see in Figure 14-6 that the role name and password are already pre-populated with the values we just entered. Notice that these fields are disabled (dimmed) and the values cannot be changed at this time. If the password has to be changed, that can be done later by using the "ROLE SECURITY TABLE" button to navigate directly to the Application Role Security screen. This part of the form uses the APP_ROLES table. A PL/SQL procedure is executed when the password is changed to apply the change to the data dictionary.

All we have to do is add is the "Program" and "Application" information. (Remember that we mentioned these in Chapter 9, *Developing a Simple Security Application.*) When completed, we press the "Create role" button to the left on the main screen to create the role and add it to the APP_ROLES table.

Adding System Privileges to Roles

After returning to the initial form, we navigate into the "Available roles" block and move to the "ADMIN_USR_ROLE" role. By pressing the "System privs" button, the form shown in Figure 14-7 is displayed. This shows all of the available system

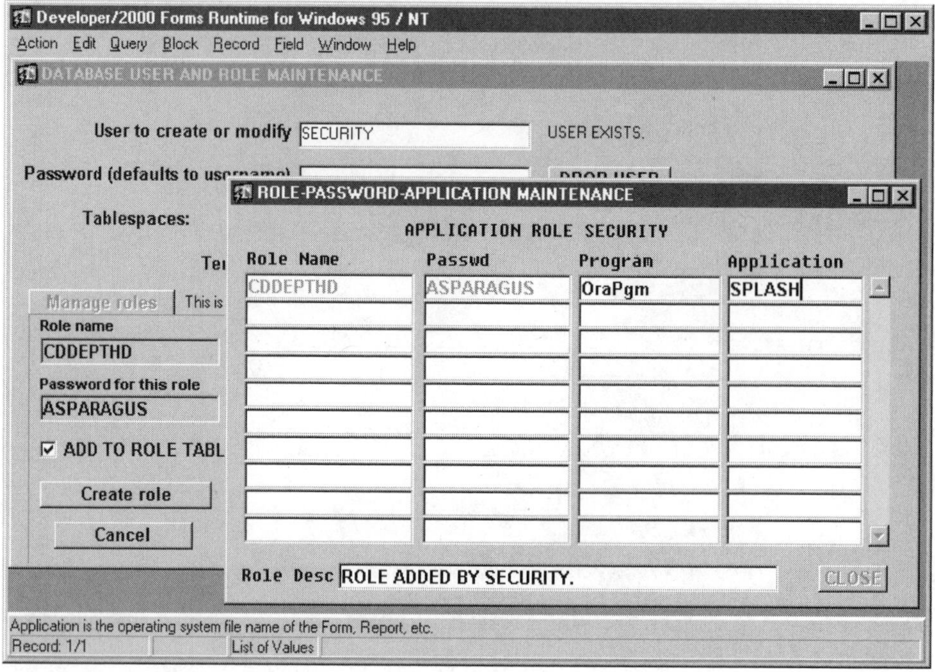

Figure 14-6. Adding role to the Role Security Table

privileges. These may be assigned or de-assigned to the currently selected role by checking or unchecking the checkbox to the right of the privilege.

Reserving the Security of the Security Maintenance Form

There is a funny thing about the Security Maintenance form: the user has privileges to grant anything to anybody, but cannot grant anything to himself. How did this happen? This user has no privileges on any of the tables in the system other than the APP_ROLES table, but this user can create any user and grant any privilege to that user or any existing user. For this reason, if you implement an application such as the one we describe in this chapter, there should be only one person who uses it. If you want more than one, you must create another *security* user with a different password.

We have a recommendation for how to ensure the security of the passwords used for this application while making sure there is a contingency plan. The user given the job of using this application should immediately change his or her account password and write the new password on a paper, put that into an envelope, seal it, and sign across the seal. Then that person should give the envelope to the security manager for safekeeping. This way, there is only one person who knows the

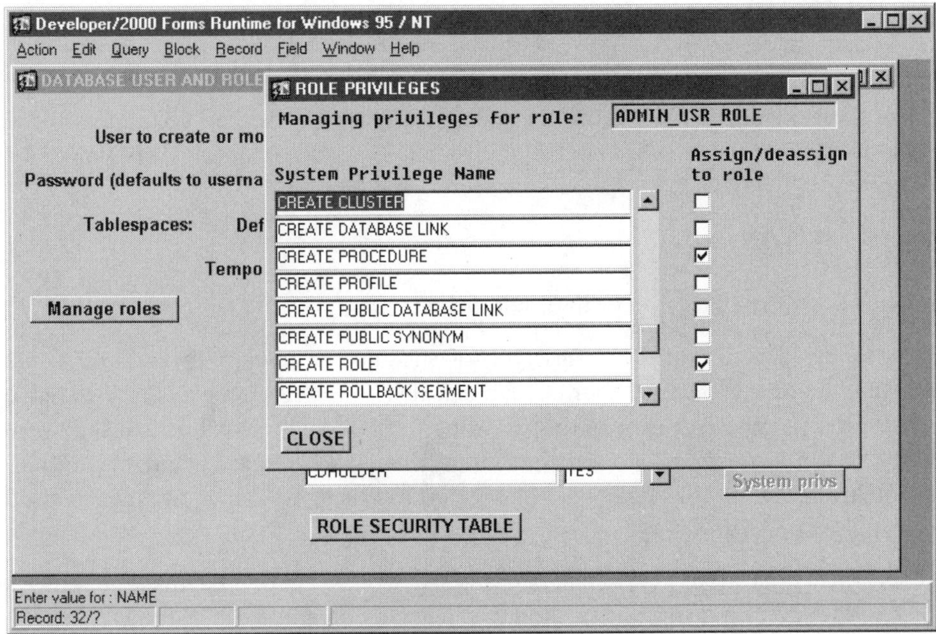

Figure 14-7. Adding system privileges to a role

password. If some grants are made that should not have been made, and you have an audit trail implemented behind this application (not hard to do), then you will know who did it.

Security books usually tell you never to write down your password, but that rule really applies to keeping the password in your wallet or purse, or on the back of a favorite photograph. The approach we've suggested allows the password to be available if an emergency arises and the person who knows the password is not available. Of course, if the envelope is opened, then the *security* user must change the password as soon as possible and prepare another envelope.

How Does the Code Work?

You might be wondering how the application does its work, since most of the fields on the form are from data dictionary tables, and we cannot modify those directly with conventional INSERT, UPDATE, or DELETE SQL statements. The changes are made by dynamically building SQL statements using the CREATE and ALTER USER commands. But this causes another problem within PL/SQL. Most of you may be familiar with the SQL substitution variables as are frequently used in "canned" program. Let's assume you have a program, *SHODEPTS.SQL*, with the following code.

```
SELECT deptno
  FROM &1
 GROUP BY deptno
;
```

Since there are at least two tables in the schema with the deptno column, you can run this program and pass the table to be used as argument 1. This would be either of the following:

```
@shodepts emp
@shodepts dept
```

Or you can let the program prompt you for the value of &1.

Unfortunately, you cannot do this type of substitution directly in PL/SQL. While you can build the statement string dynamically, the ability to execute a variable does not exist. But you can do this by using the DBMS_SQL built-in package provided in the standard database installation. This package allows dynamic SQL to be built and executed within PL/SQL. We will explain how that package is used within the application.

When the application was initially developed it was discovered that the various pieces of code to manage the user all had much in common when the DBMS_SQL package was being used. Because of this, it was decided to put all of these code pieces into a package. This package was called MG_USR, a shorthand name for "manage user."

About the mg_usr package

There are three actions to be performed on a user:

- Create the user
- Drop the user
- Change the user

Although the CREATE USER command can be quite complex, it was decided to use the simplest part of the CREATE USER command in one function and use the ALTER USER command in another function. Dropping a user requires some decision logic since a user can simply be dropped or the user and all of his or her objects can be dropped. Finally, changing a user could involve the password or the default and temporary tablespaces. Because all user access to objects was to be controlled by roles, object granting was not included. Also, role assignment is handled by another part of the application.

The mg_usr package is created in two parts: the package declaration and the package body declaration. A package declaration identifies the procedures and functions that will be available for calling. The mg_usr package has three functions, as shown below, and as you can see, the package declaration is quite small:

```
PACKAGE mg_usr
IS
  FUNCTION cr_usr (un IN VARCHAR2, pw IN VARCHAR2)
     RETURN NUMBER;
  FUNCTION dr_usr (un IN VARCHAR2, casc IN BOOLEAN DEFAULT FALSE)
     RETURN NUMBER;
  FUNCTION cg_usr (un IN VARCHAR2, action IN VARCHAR2, value IN VARCHAR2)
     RETURN NUMBER;
END mg_usr;
```

The three actions we identified are all implemented as function:

- cr_usr—creates the user
- dr_usr—drops the user
- cg_usr—changes the user

These functions will return a status code so the program that calls them can determine if they were successful or not. By placing the test for success in the calling code, error handling can be made specific to the event under which the call was made. This, as you will see, isn't really necessary here, but it is considered to be best practice and was followed for consistency in the application.

The cr_usr function requires a username and password to work. These are passed as the un and pw arguments. The function returns a 0 if it was successful, and a 1 if it failed.

Function dr_usr requires the username to be dropped, and a TRUE or FALSE for the casc argument that is a BOOLEAN datatype. This argument defaults to FALSE if it is not provided. The value of casc will be used to determine if the CASCADE option should be used when the user is dropped.

Finally, the cg_usr function is used to change the user. The three arguments are: un, representing the username of the user to be changed; action, representing what is to be done to the user; and value, representing the particular attribute that is to be applied to the user.

About the mg_usr package body

The package body supplies the code to be executed. The body of mg_usr has some variables declared before the functions are defined. These cannot be used by an external program, so they are said to be private to the package body. The code for the package body is shown here:

```
PACKAGE BODY mg_usr
IS
  cid     INTEGER;
```

```
  stmt     VARCHAR2(200);

FUNCTION cr_usr (un IN VARCHAR2, pw IN VARCHAR2)
   RETURN NUMBER
IS
BEGIN
   cid   := DMBS_SQL.OPEN_CURSOR;
   stmt  := 'create user '||un||' identified by '||pw;
   DBMS_SQL.PARSE(cid, stmt, 2);
   DBMS_SQL.CLOSE_CURSOR(cid);  RETURN 0;
EXCEPTION
   WHEN OTHERS
   THEN
     RETURN 1;
END cr_usr;


FUNCTION dr_usr (un IN VARCHAR2, casc IN BOOLEAN DEFAULT FALSE)
   RETURN NUMBER
IS
BEGIN
   cid   := DMBS_SQL.OPEN_CURSOR;
   stmt  :=  'drop user '||un;
   IF casc
   THEN
      stmt := stmt||' cascade';
   END IF;
   DBMS_SQL.PARSE(cid, stmt, 2);
   DBMS_SQL.CLOSE_CURSOR(cid);  RETURN 0;
EXCEPTION
   WHEN OTHERS
   THEN
     RETURN 1;
END dr_usr;

FUNCTION cg_usr (un IN VARCHAR2, action IN VARCHAR2, value IN VARCHAR2)
   RETURN NUMBER
IS
BEGIN
   cid   := DMBS_SQL.OPEN_CURSOR;
   stmt  :=  'alter user '||un;
   IF UPPER(action) = 'PWD'
   THEN
      stmt  :=  stmt||' identified by '||value;
   ELSIF UPPER(action) = 'DEFTS'
   THEN
      stmt  :=  stmt||' default tablespace '||value;
   ELSIF UPPER(action) = 'TMPTS'
   THEN
      stmt  :=  stmt||' temporary tablespace '||value;
   ELSIF UPPER(action) = 'DROP'
   THEN
      stmt  := 'drop user '||un||' cascade';
   ELSE
```

```
            MESSAGE('Unknown action:  '||action); RETURN 1;
        END IF;
        DBMS_SQL.PARSE(cid, stmt, 2);
        DBMS_SQL.CLOSE_CURSOR(cid);  RETURN 0;
    EXCEPTION
        WHEN OTHERS
        THEN
            RETURN 1;
    END cg_usr;

    END;
```

You can see that each function repeats the same name, argument list, and return value as declared in the package specification. The critical parts of code in each of the functions are the following four lines that appear in the cr_usr function:

```
cid   := DMBS_SQL.OPEN_CURSOR;
stmt  :=  'create user '||un||' identified by '||pw;
DBMS_SQL.PARSE(cid, stmt, 2);
DBMS_SQL.CLOSE_CURSOR(cid);
```

These appear in various forms in each of the other functions. The first line uses the DBMS_SQL.OPEN_CURSOR function to open a cursor or memory area that will be used to execute the SQL statement. The variable cid is used as a reference to this cursor. The SQL statement to be executed is then assembled and saved in the stmt variable. This is not necessary, but is considered best practice as it makes subsequent statements easier to read.

Having obtained the cursor and stored the SQL in a variable, the database package DBMS_SQL.PARSE procedure is called. This procedure is given the cursor, the statement, and the constant "2" that identifies which version of the database is in use—in this case, version 7 or 8.

The constant value "2" was used in the original version of this program that used the Oracle7 database. It did not have to be changed for use with an Oracle8 database.

The call to PARSE causes the statement contained in stmt to be executed. Because we are executing what amounts to Data Definition Language (DDL), no further action is necessary since the action completes. Had we used a SELECT, however, additional code would have been required to return the column values.

Although the cursor will be automatically closed when the function completes, it is considered best practice to explicitly close it, and that is done with the DBMS_SQL.CLOSE_CURSOR procedure.

In the dr_usr and cg_usr functions, there is some IF...THEN...ELSE logic to determine just how the SQL to be stored in the stmt variable is to be built. The execution, however, is the same in all functions.

If any part of the function should fail, the code will branch to the exception handler. Because this application was intended for use by an extremely small user group (at most two users), it was decided to only use a return code of "1" if the function failed. However, it would be possible to capture the actual code of the error and return that instead.

Now that the code to do the work has been defined, what type of code is needed in the form to call this package and its functions? This code is written behind a button.

Create user button code

The application code is associated with the BTN_CREATE_USER using the WHEN-BUTTON-PRESSED trigger. This is an Oracle Forms built-in trigger that executes the code associated with it. First we will show the code, then discuss it.

```
DECLARE
   stat    NUMBER  := 1;
   pwd     VARCHAR2(35);
BEGIN
   IF :global.usr_exists = 'F'            -- User  does not exist.
   THEN
      IF :ctl_usr_block.ndi_password IS NULL -- No password provided
      THEN
         pwd := :ctl_usr_block.ndi_username;  -- Use username
         :ctl_usr_block.ndi_password := pwd;
      ELSE
         pwd := :ctl_usr_block.ndi_password;  -- Password provided, use it.
      END IF;
      stat := mg_usr.cr_usr(:ctl_usr_block.ndi_username, pwd); -- Create user
      IF stat!= 0                                -- Failure.  STOP PROCESSING!
      THEN
         MESSAGE('Error creating user.  Notify DBA.');
         RAISE FORM_TRIGGER_FAILURE;
      END IF;

     -- Alter the new user and assign the DEFAULT tablespace.

      stat := mg_usr.cg_usr(:ctl_usr_block.ndi_username, 'DEFTS',
         :ctl_usr_block.ndi_def_ts);
      IF stat!= 0
      THEN
         MESSAGE('Error assigning default tablespace.  Notify DBA.');
         stat := mg_usr.cg_usr(:ctl_usr_block.ndi_username, 'DROP', 'dummy');
        RAISE FORM_TRIGGER_FAILURE;
      END IF;
```

```
        -- Alter the new user and assign the TEMPORARY tablespace.

        stat := mg_usr.cg_usr(:ctl_usr_block.ndi_username, 'TMPTS',
           :ctl_usr_block.ndi_temp_ts);
        IF stat!= 0
        THEN
           MESSAGE('Error assigning temporary tablespace.  Notify DBA.');
           stat := mg_usr.cg_usr(:ctl_usr_block.ndi_username, 'DROP', 'dummy');
           RAISE FORM_TRIGGER_FAILURE;
        END IF;
        pop_user_status(TRUE);  -- Do some screen maintenance.

        -- Advise operator that user must be assigned a role to be able to
login.

        MESSAGE('User created.  You must assign a role.');
     ELSIF :global.usr_exists = 'T' THEN  -- User exists, change the password.
     stat := mg_usr.cg_usr(:ctl_usr_block.ndi_username, 'PWD',
        :ctl_usr_block.ndi_password);
     END IF;
END;
```

When the button is pressed, this code block is executed. The logic determines what is to be done. For example, the memory variable :global.usr_exists will contain either an "F" or a "T". If it is a "T", the user exists and all that is being done is to change the user's password. That happens at the bottom of the code in the ELSIF statement. Here you can see the package.function call in the line beginning with stat. Remember that functions return values so you have to have somewhere for the returned value to be captured. Variable stat serves that purpose. The function call identifies both the package and the function separated by a period as shown below (emphasis added):

```
stat := mg_usr.cg_usr(:ctl_usr_block.ndi_username, 'PWD',
   :ctl_usr_block.ndi_password);
```

Here you can see the package name: mg_usr, separated by a period from the cg_usr function that is being called. The arguments are provided within the parentheses. Fields from the form are represented using the :block.field_name syntax. The :ctl_usr_block.ndi_username and :ctl_usr_block.ndi_password are both fields on the form. The :ctl_usr_block is the block name (a section of the form), and the ndi_... is the field name. We used the convention of prefixing all fields that don't belong to a table with "ndi" to mean non-database-item. This convention is considered best practice and helps programmers understand the nature of the items on the form.

If the variable :global.usr_exists contains an "F", there is more work to be done. We have to create the user and assign both the default and temporary tablespaces. If the password field is empty, the form takes the username and uses that as the password. The assumption is that the database will force the user to change it on the first login. After that is done, several calls are made to create the user and assign tablespaces:

Create the user
: Calls cr_usr, passing the username and password

Change the user to add the default tablespace
: Calls cg_usr, passing the username, the tablespace name, and the DEFTS constant to indicate that this is for the DEFAULT tablespace

Change the user to add the temporary tablespace
: Calls cg_usr, passing the username, the tablespace name, and the TMPTS constant to indicate that this is for the TEMPORARY tablespace

You may notice that the drop user function in the package is used if the change user actions fail. It is not necessary to drop the user, but the design decision was made that the entire process should succeed or none of the work should remain.

Documenting the User State

An application such as the one we've just discussed—one that simplifies the task of maintaining users and roles—does not necessarily help with the documentation of what has been done. That function could be built into the application, but it is not advised. People do make mistakes during development, and documenting the finished product is easier. The term "documentation" in this context means the creation of script files that will recreate the architecture of the database—particularly the assignment of roles to users and the declaration of the user default roles. This documentation is useful for several purposes, but the primary one is to assist with database recovery. If backups are done regularly, these scripts will probably never be used. Murphy, however, seems to work in every computer shop.

Most of the information in the data dictionary is already documented by the scripts the DBA creates. The assignment of roles to users is rather dynamic, particularly in the early phases of development of a system. A script to extract that information from the data dictionary would be handy; we provide one in the following section.

A Sample Script

Here we provide a script that will create a file. This file will contain the commands to grant roles to users and define their default roles. All this information is extracted from the data dictionary. The script file *CRUSRGRT.SQL* is provided as one example of how to create this file. It is a SQL script that writes another SQL script. This one is a little unusual because it combines conventional SQL with PL/SQL code:

```
doc

  crusrgrt.sql

  Arguments:  None

  Combination SQL and PL/SQL script.  Creates SQL script
  to grant roles to users and define user default roles.

  Output file is mkrolgrt.sql

#
SET TERMOUT OFF ECHO OFF FEEDBACK OFF PAGESIZE 0 VERIFY OFF
SPOOL mkrolgrt.sql

-- Get the granted roles and output a grant ... to ... string.

SELECT 'grant '||granted_role||' to '||grantee||
        DECODE(UPPER(admin_option), 'YES',
        ' with grant option', null)||';'
  FROM dba_role_privs
 WHERE grantee NOT IN ('SYS','SYSTEM','SCOTT','DBA','DBSNMP')
 ORDER BY grantee;

-- Default roles are tricky.  They must all be declared at once, so use a
-- PL/SQL loop to find all of them before writing out the string.

SET SERVEROUTPUT ON
DECLARE
   usrname      varchar2(35);
   lastusr      varchar2(35)  := 'START VALUE';
   cmd          varchar2(400) :=  null;
   CURSOR udr
   IS
    SELECT grantee, granted_role FROM dba_role_privs
     WHERE grantee NOT IN ('SYS','SYSTEM','SCOTT','DBA','DBSNMP')
       AND UPPER(default_role) = 'YES'
     ORDER BY grantee;
  rrec    udr%ROWTYPE
BEGIN
OPEN udr;
LOOP
  FETCH udr
  INTO rrec;
  IF rrec.grantee != lastusr  -- Has username changed?
     OR udr%NOTFOUND
  THEN      -- process last record
     IF cmd IS NOT NULL
     THEN
        cmd  := 'Alter user '||lastusr||' default role '||cmd||';';
        DBMS_OUTPUT.PUT_LINE(cmd);
```

```
         cmd  := null;            -- Clear the command string
      END IF;
      lastusr := rrec.grantee;  -- Save the current username
   END IF;
   -- Assemble the default roles into a comma separated string
   IF cmd IS NOT NULL
   THEN
      cmd := cmd||', ';
   END IF;
   cmd := cmd||rrec.granted_role;
   IF udr%NOTFOUND
   THEN         -- Loop exit test
     EXIT;
   END IF;
END LOOP;
END;
/
SPOOL OFF
SET TERMOUT ON ECHO ON FEEDBACK ON PAGESIZE 24 VERIFY ON
```

The first part of the script is the conventional SQL section. It selects the string that consists of the command to GRANT the role to a user. The DECODE section is used to add the "WITH GRANT OPTION" clause, but only if the value in the admin_option column is "YES." The UPPER function is used, so only a test for uppercase is needed; otherwise, tests for all eight possible combinations would be required.

Default role assignment is determined and output by the PL/SQL section. This section starts with the keyword "declare" and ends with the "/" that executes the block.

We use PL/SQL because the roles are stored in individual records or rows. If SQL were used to retrieve the default roles, then there would be multiple ALTER USER statements. However, as we've discussed previously, only the last default role assignment is registered. We must have only one statement, and that statement must include all of the default roles. Since SQL does not loop and PL/SQL does, we'll use PL/SQL. To illustrate, when the ALTER USER statement is executed:

```
ALTER USER mary DEFAULT ROLE dba;
```

then that is the only default role the user will have. But most users will have more than one default role. If a subsequent command is given:

```
ALTER USER mary DEFAULT ROLE connect;
```

then the first assignment is discarded and replaced by the second. All default roles must be specified in one command:

```
ALTER USER mary DEFAULT ROLE connect, dba;
```

and the PL/SQL block accomplishes that. On execution, the program output for the *CRUSRGRT.SQL* script is:

```
GRANT dba TO ralph;
GRANT connect TO mary;
GRANT dba TO mary;
GRANT admin_usr_role TO ed;
ALTER USER ralph DEFAULT ROLE dba;
ALTER USER mary DEFAULT ROLE connect, dba;
ALTER USER ed DEFAULT ROLE admin_usr_role;
```

Note that user *mary* has been given both roles as defaults in a single statement.

A Disclaimer

While the *CRUSRGRT.SQL* script we've described in this chapter works, it would not be suitable for large systems because there is a limit to the number of records PL/SQL can buffer when the DBMS_OUTPUT.PUT_LINE command is used. There are two options you can use in place of this function:

- The records could be written into a table, and, after the PL/SQL block completes, another SQL statement would select the values as part of the current spool file.
- You could use the file input and output functions found in the Oracle-provided UTL_FILE package to open an operating system file and write directly to it. For large systems, two files may be preferred simply to keep down the file size and keep each file performing only one function.

The UTL_FILE functions and some documentation may be found in the file *UTLFILE.SQL* in the *RDBMS/ADMIN* directory. The exact location of these directories will vary by operating system.

III

Enhanced Oracle Security

This part of the book describes some security features that might be appropriate in certain types of environments. It discusses the use of the Oracle Security Server (supplied with the basic Oracle RDBMS), which uses encryption and certificates of authority to protect your data. It suggests a number of strategies for protecting your site from the risks posed by Internet and World Wide Web connections. And it looks briefly at several extra-cost Oracle products you may wish to purchase for enhanced security.

In this chapter:
- *About Cryptography*
- *Ways to Authenticate Users*
- *What's in the OSS?*
- *Configuring and Using the OSS*

15

Using the Oracle Security Server

The Oracle Security Server (OSS) product was introduced with the basic Oracle8 software delivery. Although OSS is new with Oracle8, you can use it with Oracle7 as well. You do not need to purchase anything else from Oracle Corporation to be able to install, configure, and use this product. Why would you want to install and use the OSS? To see more clearly why you would want OSS and what you'd do with it, let's look first at some things you might do to prove your identity.

When you travel from one country to another, you may be required to carry a passport or some other form of identification to prove who you are and where you came from. To obtain the passport, you generally need to go to a government agency carrying a picture of yourself and a birth certificate to prove your identity. You fill out a form and provide your picture and identification, and the agency will issue a passport to you. You then carry the passport with you as you travel and show your passport to any agents who request it. In this way, you will be able to successfully prove who you are and will be permitted to travel anywhere within the area without having to display your passport again.

Basically, the concepts of *single sign-on* and *certificates of authority*, which we'll explore in this chapter, are very similar to using a passport to travel from one country to another. Once a user has logged on to a "trusted" system and been authenticated using the OSS, that user can carry the electronic certificate granted by the Oracle Security System and "travel" from one area of computing or database to another without having to explicitly produce a username and password again to access each separate system or area.

This chapter describes the basic use of the Oracle Security Server. We'll first look at the fundamentals of the cryptography concepts that underlie the OSS technology. Then we'll explore the OSS architecture, installation, and configuration.

Finally, we'll look at the concepts and use of OSS identities, servers, and server authorization, as well as enterprise authorizations.

About Cryptography

Years ago, there was a television show that offered a special decoder ring you could send away for. Each week, there would be another secret message you could decode using your ring. You had to know where the starting point for decoding was but, once you knew where to start, you could decode any message that was sent. You could even send coded messages to your friends and receive messages from them. That decoder ring used a simple form of cryptography. Today's highly secure systems obviously use more complex forms of cryptography to protect their messages and file, but the basic principles are the same.

A Simple Code

The code used by the decoder ring was a very simple letter substitution cipher. Even if you did not have the ring, you could decipher the code by listing the alphabet and building your own decoder ring key. For example, if the television host said to "start with M" for the first letter of the message, you would list out your alphabet starting with the letter "M" like this:

```
M N O P Q R S T U V W X Y Z A B C D E F G H I J K L
```

Below the letters listed, you would write another alphabet starting with "A" like this:

```
M N O P Q R S T U V W X Y Z A B C D E F G H I J K L
A B C D E F G H I J K L M N O P Q R S T U V W X Y Z
```

The message which was presented could now be deciphered. Presented with the message:

```
NDUZS TQXB. UY MF FTQ AW OADDM.
```

and looking at the key, you could determine that the hero was at the OK Corral and needed help. Obviously, a code as simple as this is easily broken, but it illustrates the basics of how encryption and decryption work.

Algorithms, Plaintext, and Ciphertext

More complicated forms of cryptography use an algorithm—a method or procedure for completing a specific task—and one or more keys for the encryption and decryption of data stored on and transmitted via secure systems in the computer world. When you want to transcribe data into a coded form (encode), a computer program (which can be an implementation of an *algorithm)* is called and one or more parameters are passed to the program as *keys*. The algorithm, along with the key or keys, is applied to a readable text message, sometimes referred to as *plaintext*. This procedure, which is referred to as *encryption*, produces a coded or *ciphertext* output. Likewise, if a ciphertext message is presented to the algorithm, along with the appropriate key or keys, the message can be translated into plaintext. This procedure is referred to as *decryption*.

Thus, each encryption and decryption requires:

- An algorithm used to convert messages to and from ciphertext
- A ciphertext or plaintext message
- One or more keys to be passed as parameters to the algorithm

If one or more of these elements is missing, a message cannot easily be encrypted or decrypted. For example, if a person has the ciphertext file and the algorithm but no keys, the ciphertext cannot easily be decrypted into a plaintext message.

Figure 15-1 shows an example of simple encryption and decryption.

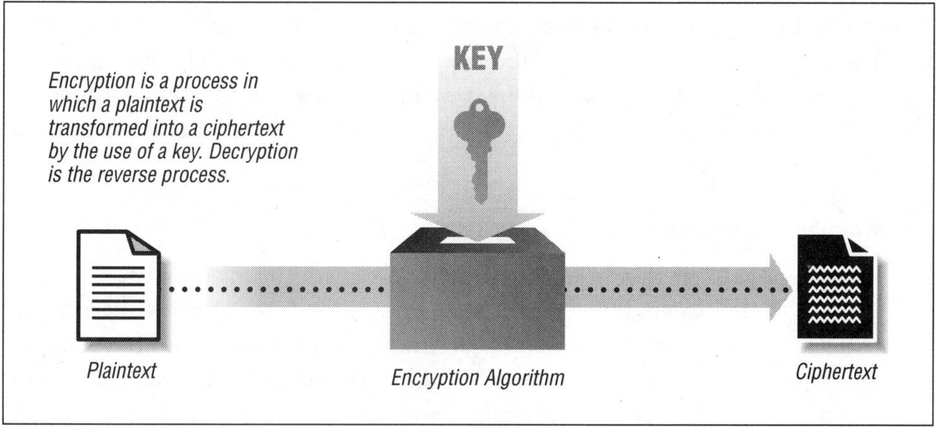

Figure 15-1. Simple encryption and decryption

Ways to Authenticate Users

As we said in the previous section, keys are actually parameters you reference when you run your program (algorithm) to either encrypt or decrypt a message or a piece of data. Keys were first used with algorithms to enable people to communicate electronically in a more private manner. Originally, the same algorithm was used to both encrypt and decrypt a message. But that approach often proved vulnerable to the sophisticated computer programs hackers wrote to break the encrypted messages. By necessity, keys have had to become more complex, and their use and protection more secure. Different approaches have been used to try to ensure that encrypted material cannot be decrypted by anyone other than the intended receiver. This section describes some of these approaches.

Private Keys

One way for two people who want to communicate privately with each other to do so is for them to ensure that they each have a copy of the same key, referred to as a *private key*, which they use for both encryption and decryption of their message. But to use this approach, they need to find a way to exchange the key information so no one else can get the key.

If Mary and Ralph want to communicate, they will each need a copy of a key to encrypt and decrypt their messages. Let's say that Ralph and Ed also want to communicate privately. They will need a different key so that Mary cannot read their messages. Now Ralph needs to maintain, protect, and track two different keys—one for communication with Mary and one for communication with Ed. If Ralph wants to communicate with a third or fourth person, his key maintenance will quickly compound.

A number of commonly used cryptography approaches are based on the notion of the sharing of private keys. Two of the best known private key algorithms are the Data Encryption Standard (DES), published in 1975 by the National Institute of Standards and Technology (NIST) and the International Data Encryption Algorithm (IDEA), published in 1990.

The problem with private keys

On a company-wide basis, the need for users to get and maintain multiple private keys becomes a managerial nightmare. As the number of users grows, the number of possible keys required grows proportionally. Some companies have implemented various forms of central key servers to provide users with a place to obtain a key each time they want to communicate with another user in a private manner. The problems with this approach are that the centralized key server:

- Becomes a single point of failure
- May become a bottleneck point on the system

Both of these problems are really time-based. If everyone is relying on obtaining their private keys from a centralized key server and that key server crashes, no one will be able to obtain a key until the server is back online and available. Without a backup server, secure communication might have to be halted until the key server can be repaired or recovered. Likewise, if a substantial number of users are obtaining private keys frequently, the key server could become overwhelmed. Response times for obtaining private keys could impact your system and user performance.

Public Keys

Another approach to encrypting secret communications is to use a public key system. With public key systems, each user has a set of two keys—a public key to which everyone can have access, and a private key which is available to only the owner of that key. The public key is made available to anyone who wants to communicate in a secure manner with you. The public key is truly public—it can be placed anywhere on a system, including a web page.

The public key is used to encrypt the plaintext message, while the private key is used to decrypt the message. Anyone can use the public key to encrypt a message, while only someone who has the corresponding private key can decrypt it. The keys are generally complex enough that the private key cannot be easily derived from the public key. Public key algorithms are usually much larger than private key algorithms and, therefore, are generally much slower to use.

The beauty of the public key/private key approach is that it provides much greater security and privacy. Going back to our example earlier, if Mary wants to communicate with Ralph, she will encrypt her message using Ralph's public key. Since Ralph is the only one who has his private key (we hope) Ralph will use his private key and easily decrypt Mary's message. Likewise, if Ralph wants to communicate with Ed, Ralph will use Ed's public key to encrypt the message.

Private keys, public keys, and authentication

In a reverse manner, with public key systems, private keys can be used to authenticate a user—just as you proved you were who you said you were by showing your birth certificate and driver's license to an official to obtain a passport. Let's say that Mary encrypts a message using her private key. Anyone who has Mary's public key can decrypt her message since the keys can work in either order—public to private or private to public. However, unless someone else has access to Mary's private key, duplicating Mary's encryption would be very difficult.

Advantages of a public key system

Since each person maintains his or her own private key, there is no single point of failure in a public key system. People have the ability to authenticate themselves by using their own private key to encrypt something that can be decrypted with their own public key. Key distribution is simplified since private keys do not need to be shared between two people to be useful.

Figure 15-2 shows an example of public key encryption and decryption.

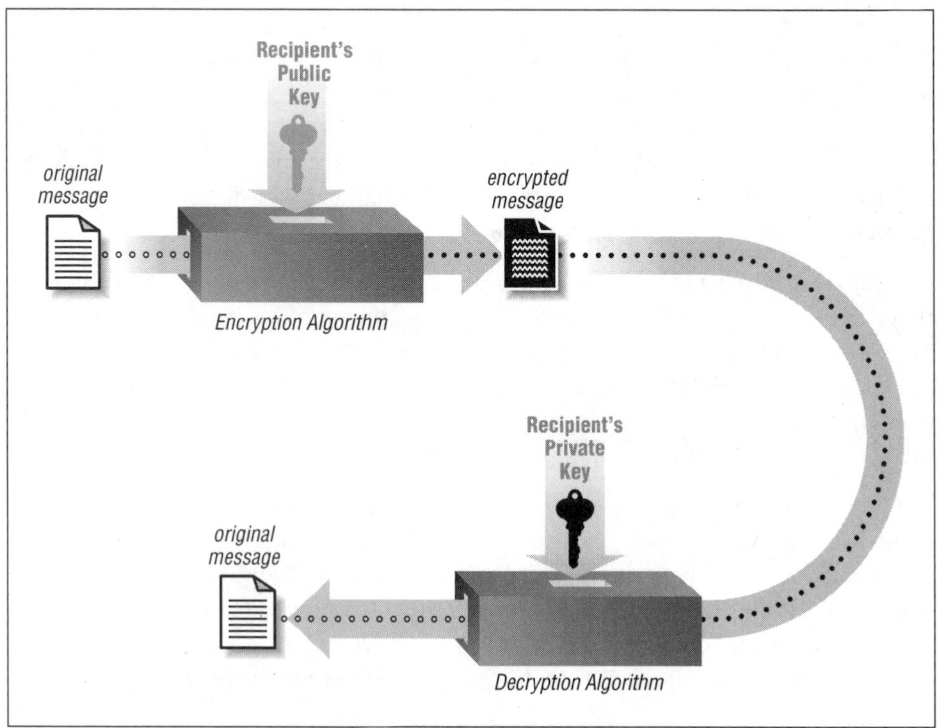

Figure 15-2. Public key encryption and decryption

Digital Signatures

In earlier times, when a military leader wanted to communicate with his troops who were some distance away from him, the leader would write his message, fold the paper, and affix a special wax seal. The seal was recognized to be his alone. The seal was affixed to the open edge of the message, thus both sealing the message closed so that no one could read it without disturbing the seal, and authenticating the message as having been sent by the leader personally. The seal was recognized by the troops, and the directives within the message were followed as if the military leader were present and issuing the orders himself.

In a similar way, *digital signatures* have become a way to authenticate that a message was sent by a specific user. The digital signature is generated using a two-step process. First, the sender uses a *one-way hash function* to generate a specific-length number known as a *message digest*. The hash function can take a message of any length and generate a fixed-length number. Next, the sender uses his or her private key to encrypt the message digest. The digital signature—the encrypted message digest—can be attached to any message.

When someone receives a message with a digital signature, the receiver goes through a two-step process to decrypt the signature and verify that the message was actually sent by the person who claimed to send the message. The receiver would apply the same one-way hash function the sender used to generate the message digest and then apply the sender's public key to decrypt the received message digest. The result should be a match of the sender's transmitted message digest. If it is a match, the receiver can feel pretty comfortable that the message has not been tampered with.

Figure 15-3 shows an example of using a digital signature.

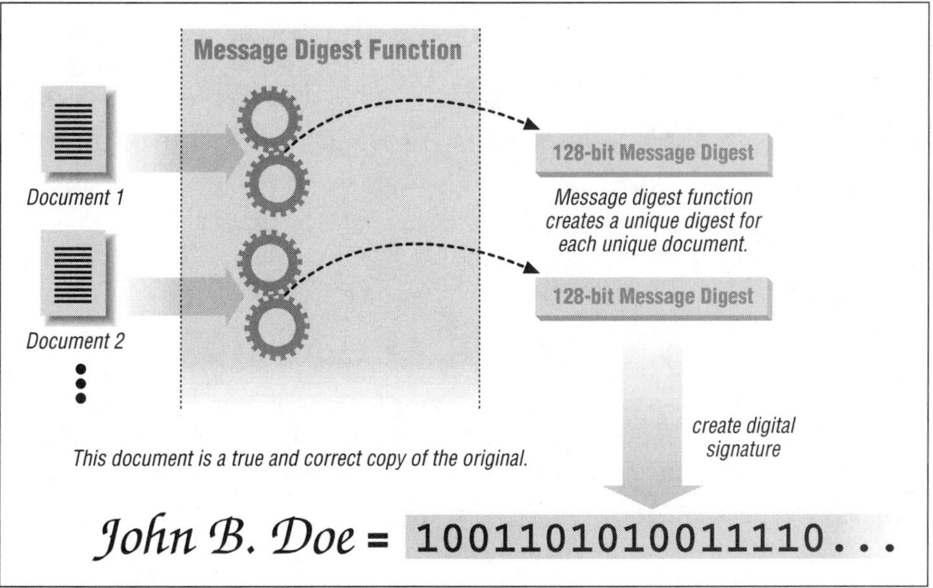

Figure 15-3. Digital signature

Certificates of Authority

With a digital signature, the person who receives a message takes responsibility for authenticating the message. Another approach to security is to have a trusted entity, referred to as a *certificate authority* (CA), validate that someone is who he says he is. At the beginning of the chapter, we talked about a government agency you go to when you need a passport issued. The CA, like the government agency, validates that you are who you claim to be and issues an appropriate credential, the certificate of authority, to you.

A *certificate of authority* is an electronic message digitally signed by the CA. It states that a public key belongs to a specific user or process. The CA signs a certificate by using its private key to encrypt the signature and place it on the certificate. Anyone or anything receiving a certificate can decrypt the signature using the public key and thereby verify the authenticity of the CA. Based on the trust in the CA, the receiver can trust whoever presents a certificate from the CA.

Think back to our initial example of an agency issuing a passport and the traveler then showing his passport to move from place to place in a trusted manner. In similar fashion, the certificate that is electronically signed by a CA can enable a user or process to be trusted and allowed to move from system to system or to transact business in a trusted manner.

The OSS provides the ability for a user or process to obtain a certificate of authority to enable the process or person to perform one or many transactions, with one or several databases, without having to use a username and password for each interaction. The OSS supports a form of certificates known as X.509 version 1 (a standard protocol). The OSS places the certificate of authority, otherwise referred to as an *X.509 certificate*, along with a public and private key pair, into a structure called a *wallet*.

Certificate format

An X.509 certificate has a standard format; here we show the values generally used by the OSS:

Version
: Currently, this value for an OSS is always "0," which refers to the X.509 version 1 certificates. In future releases, the OSS will support X.509 version 3 certificates. These future certificates will use a version value of "1."

Serial number
: A unique identifier for the certificate.

Algorithm identifier
: The algorithm the CA used and any necessary parameters for validation.

Issuer
: The name of the CA.

Period of validity
: The range of dates over which the certificate is valid. Usually, it is the range of dates requested by the certificate requester, which would typically span the period from the date of creation to a specified end time.

Subject
: Identifies to whom the certificate belongs.

Subject's public key
: This area includes the certificate owner's public key, identifies which algorithm the CA used, and includes any necessary parameters.

Signature
The digital signature of the CA.

As you can see, the information contained in a certificate is enough for a receiver to validate the CA and the owner of the certificate.

Period of validity and revocation

The period of validity for a certificate (see the list of certificate elements above) is the amount of time requested by the certificate owner during which the certificate will be able to be accepted. At the end of that period of time, the certificate becomes invalid. A certificate can also be revoked (so it is no longer valid) before its period of validity expires. Even though a certificate may still have a valid time period, something might have happened to cause the CA to revoke the use of a specific certificate.

There are a number of events that might cause the revocation of a certificate. For example, the certificate owner's key or the CA's key might have been compromised, or an event might have occurred that makes the certificate owner no longer worthy of trust. Leaving the company would generally be a reason for the CA to revoke a user's certificate before it had automatically expired.

Periodically, the CA will issue, sign, and timestamp a list of certificates which have been revoked. Referred to as a *certificate revocation list* (CRL), the list can be checked by any receiver to verify the status of a certificate. However, since checking the CRL can be a very slow process, verification against the CRL is generally reserved for really important or critical documents or might be used only infrequently to perform complete verification checks.

Distinguished names

The concept of a *distinguished name* (DN) is used not only by Oracle Corporation for its OSS product, but by other companies and products as well. For example, Verisign Corporation, when issuing a digital identification for a server, requires the server's distinguished name as part of the certification process. In Verisign's case, the requirement is to present the server name as the fully qualified domain name used for standard Internet DNS (Domain Name System) lookups for a server location—like a web server address (e.g., *www.my_web_address.com*).

In Oracle's case, the DN has a very specific structure:

```
DN=([Country,][Organization,][OrganizationUnit,][State,][Locality,] CommonName)
```

The one mandatory value in the distinguished name definition is the common name. The other values are optional, but the order in which the values are entered is very important. The rules associated with a distinguished name are the following:

- A distinguished name must have at least the common name
- All of the other elements, if used, must be in the specific listed order: "C=,O=,OU=,S=,L=,CN="
- All element labels used for a distinguished name must be uppercase, though the elements can be upper/lower
- The actual definition values must match exactly the values used in the OSS identity
- Elements in the distinguished name definition cannot have any spaces between the elements
- The elements in the distinguished name definition can only be separated by a comma (,)

The order in which the values are entered when defining a distinguished name becomes important when a "global user" definition is entered. (The OSS global definitions are discussed in a later section.)

An example of a valid DN structure would be:

```
DN='C=US,O=MyCompany,OU=MyDept,ST=VA,L=Vienna,CN=mary'
```

The only mandatory value in this example is the "CN=mary" at the end of the string; this is the common name. The Country is "US"; the Organization is "MyCompany"; the OrganizationUnit is "MyDept"; the State is "VA"; the Locality is "Vienna"; and the CommonName is "mary."

The OSS toolset is case-sensitive and, if you actually enter the values as shown here (i.e., "C=US, CN=mary"), you will have to ensure that you carry the upper/lowercase entries throughout the steps exactly as you have entered them initially. A much better approach would be to *always* use uppercase.

What's in the OSS?

The OSS is comprised of several components that use underlying protocols to enable its wide assortment of security features. The features the OSS provides are:

- User authentication
- Certificates of authority

- Digital signatures
- Public and private key pairs

We have already discussed, in a general way, the meaning and function of each of these security approaches. This section examines the OSS structure and what protocols are used to support the features.

The OSS Architecture

The OSS is made up of the following components:

- The OSS Repository
- The OSS Manager
- The OSS Authentication Adapter

The person who interacts with and manages the tool is referred to as the security administrator. As we've discussed earlier in the book, the security administrator at a site might be a DBA or someone whose basic job is as a security manager or system administrator. In other words, the security administrator does not have to be a DBA to work with the OSS toolset. Each piece of the OSS—the repository, the Manager, the Authentication Adapter, and the security administrator himself or herself—combines to comprise a certificate authority. The OSS toolset can be used with both Oracle7—from version 7.3.2 forward—and Oracle8.

The OSS Repository

As with some other Oracle products, such as the Oracle Enterprise Manager (OEM) and the Oracle Recovery Manger (RMAN), the Oracle Security Server requires an area of a database in which information can be stored about encrypted private keys as well as certification authorities. The actions supported by the OSS Repository are:

- The generation and storage of certificates requested by the security administrator or manager
- Responses to queries about the status of certificates (whether they have expired or have been revoked)
- The storage of information about Oracle Application Server certificate requests

As with the other Oracle repositories, you must carefully select the database in which the OSS Repository will reside, as well as what procedures will be used to protect and back up the repository. When you install the OSS, the tablespace and associated datafiles to house the repository and the repository itself are created, along with two users: *oracle_security_service* and *oracle_security_service_admin.*

After installation of the OSS product, the OSS code is located in the *$ORACLE_HOME/Oss* directory. You should examine the script *NZDOCRT.SQL*, which is used to create the OSS repository. Since this script creates the tablespace in which the OSS repository will reside, you might want to change the disk location or size used as the creation defaults. At the very least, you want to look at this script just to ensure you know what it is doing. Make sure the version of the RDBMS is 8.0.4 or higher and the version of Net8 (formerly SQL*Net) is 8.0.4 or higher.

When setting up the OSS Repository, take the same steps you'd follow to establish any other OSS user. In other words, to create a usable OSS repository, you must set up a SQL*Net connection listing in the *SQLNET.ORA* file of the database that will house the repository. You'll also use the *osslogin* tool to install a wallet for the repository. By following these steps, you'll enable a secure environment from which the OSS can function.

The OSS Manager

As we will see in the later section, "Installing the OSS," the OSS Manager is composed of software that lets you interact with the OSS through the Oracle Enterprise Manager product set. The OSS Manager is used to perform these tasks:

- Administer the OSS repository
- Define global users and global roles
- Define and maintain information about identities
- Track authorizations granted to identities

The OSS Authentication Adapter

The OSS Authentication Adapter is used by Net8 clients, Oracle7 databases, and/or Oracle8 databases to enable interaction with the OSS Repository. Using OSS Authentication Adapters, processes can deal with certificates of authority in various ways:

- Request certificates
- Obtain certificates
- Use certificates
- Query the status of a certificate to verify if the certificate has expired, has been revoked, or is valid
- Mutually authenticate themselves and retrieve role information to enable the process to perform work

Authentication occurs using OSS Authentication Adapters. All communication between the various components of the OSS and other entities is done using SQL*Net and/or Net8.

Protocols and Algorithms

Oracle Corporation has taken advantage of several industry-standard protocols to provide various forms of security within the OSS:

- For authentication, a version of the Security Exchange Mechanism (SKEME) protocol developed by Hugo Krawczyk is used.
- For certificates of authority, the X.509 version 1 protocol is used.
- For public/private key pairs, RSA Data Security's TIPEM library function (currently a 512-bit version) is used.
- For digital signatures, an RSA cryptographic algorithm and RSA's Message Digest 5 (MD5) one-way hash function algorithm (using functions in the RSA TIPEM and BSAFE security tools) is used. The RSA algorithm is the 512-bit US-exportable version; MD5 produces a 128-bit hash value.

The OSS allows you to define several forms of subjects:

- Individual users
- Database servers
- Oracle Application Servers

to enhance single sign-on, distributed authentication of entities to each other, and central authorization of users performing global tasks. Let's take a moment to look at what single sign-on can provide for you.

As a DBA, you might have several accounts on different machines from which you administer several different databases per machine. You currently have to remember a separate username and password for each machine and each database account. With the implementation of a single sign-on mechanism, you will only have to remember and use *one* username and password to access *all* of your machines and databases.

In the next chapter, we'll examine more closely the use of the web and security. For now, just note that the OSS can play a vital part in enhancing web-based security.

Global users and global roles with OSS

Suppose you are an accounting clerk in your company and you need to be able to perform the same list of tasks across a group of databases on different machines.

You can log on to each database, specifying your username and password each time, and perform your tasks, but this can be very cumbersome—especially if your password expires on different machines at different times. You might end up having to keep track of several passwords for several different databases on several different machines. Wouldn't it be useful if you only had to log on once to a central location and obtain the ability to connect to each database on any machine without having to use another username and password? If your DBA creates a *global user* for you and creates a *global role* that will give you the privileges you need to perform your set of tasks, you can do just that.

You obtain a certificate of authority (a single set of credentials) from the OSS and then access each database to perform your work. Your certificate enables you to connect to the databases without having to use a separate username and password for each connection. The OSS keeps track of the privileges you have been granted for each database by tracking the global roles that have been created and granted to you across the entire group of machines. Although the OSS will track the global roles, the DBA still must create the global roles in each of the databases in order to give the global roles meaning to the individual, local database servers.

Creating a global user and global role

To create a global user, the DBA issues a command in the form:

```
CREATE USER username
   IDENTIFIED GLOBALLY AS
'C=country,O=organization,OU=organization_unit,ST=state,L=locality,CN=user';
```

Notice that the definition includes the same values, in the same exact order, as the distinguished name described earlier in this chapter (see the "Distinguished names" section). Therefore, a global user created for the distinguished name we created for *mary* would look like this:

```
CREATE USER mary
   IDENTIFIED GLOBALLY AS
'C=US,O=MyCompany,OU=MyDept,ST=VA,L=Vienna,CN=mary'
```

Now, let's give *mary* some privileges so she can perform her tasks. The global role for the user *mary* will be "marys_role", and the syntax to create the global role would look like this:

```
CREATE ROLE marys_role
 IDENTIFIED GLOBALLY;
```

"Ah," you say, "but you haven't really given *mary* privileges to *do* anything!" and you would be correct. Next, we have to grant the appropriate privileges to the global role so *mary* can perform work. We would certainly need to give *mary* the ability to connect to the databases. So, we might say:

```
GRANT create session
   TO marys_role;
```

We might also want the *mary* account to be able to input data, update information, and delete data from the employees table. We would issue the command:

```
GRANT select, insert, update, delete
   ON employees
   TO marys_role;
```

Note that, prior to this script, when we listed duties we wanted the *mary* account to be able to perform, the ability to "look at" (SELECT) the data was not mentioned. However, in Oracle8, the SELECT privilege must be granted if the user is to be able to perform any of the other duties against a table or view. Correspondingly, we would need to create the role "marys_role" in each database *mary* will be working with, and grant the same privileges in each database in order for *mary* to be able to perform tasks.

Configuring and Using the OSS

This section explains how to configure and use the Oracle Security Server at your site. The details of software installation are operating-system dependent and will not be discussed here. Please refer to your operating system documentation for installation instructions.

From the physical installation perspective, the Oracle Security Server consists of three components:

- A command-line tool, which provides the *osslogin* (connect OSS) utilities
- The Advanced Networking Option Authentication Adapter (see Chapter 17, *Using Extra-Cost Options*, for more information on ANO)
- A repository that stores OSS information

The *osslogin* command-line tool is activated from the DOS prompt on your Windows NT or Windows 95 system. You type in the utility name and respond to the prompts. Notice that the prompts are in the opposite order from the order in which you enter information when creating a global user. The interaction for the user *mary*, who we created earlier, would look like the following:

```
C:\> osslogin
Oracle Security Server for 32-bit Windows : version 2.0.4.0.0 - Production on
21-JUN-98  16:35:13
© Copyright 1997 Oracle Corporation.  All rights reserved.
Oracle Security Server Login Program
Please Enter the following information:
Common Name: mary
Locality: Vienna
State: VA
```

```
Organization Unit: MyDept
Organization: MyCompany
Country: US
```

Once you have entered the last piece of information (Country), the utility will generate a wallet for the user *mary*.

The section "More about osslogin" provides additional details about the *osslogin* syntax.

The OSS repository will use the *system* account and will need the *system* password during installation. However, interaction with the OSS will be performed using an account created during installation. The account you must log in to is *oracle_security_service_admin*. The password for this account will also be created during the OSS installation. If you try to create an account with another name to house the repository, the tool's data will not be available.

Creating and Deleting the OSS Repository

After you have installed the OSS toolset, you will find a new entry in the Start → Programs menu of your Windows NT or Windows 95 system. This entry is titled "Oracle Security Server." There are four options available under this entry:

- Create Oracle Security Server
- Oracle Security Server Manager
- README
- Remove Oracle Security Server

Two of the options enable you to create and delete the OSS repository: the "Create Oracle Security Server" and the "Remove Oracle Security Server." When you select the "Create Oracle Security Server" option from the Start → Program → Oracle Security Server menu, the *create* utility runs *NZDOCRT.SQL* and creates an OSS tablespace (*oss*), datafile (*oss.dbf*), and the two user accounts, which will be used to interact with the utility. The script is very straightforward. First, you'll run the *NXDODROP.SQL* script to attempt to remove any existing OSS objects and users. Then, you'll create the tablespace for the repository with the script:

```
CREATE TABLESPACE oss
          DATAFILE 'oss.dbf'
              SIZE 10M;
```

Finally, you'll run the script *NZDOUSER.SQL* to create the users. The script performs the following commands:

```
CREATE USER oracle_security_service_admin
IDENTIFIED BY oss
DEFAULT TABLESPACE oss
QUOTA UNLIMITED ON oss;

GRANT CREATE SESSION TO oracle_security_service_admin;
GRANT CREATE TABLE TO oracle_security_service_admin;
GRANT CREATE SEQUENCE TO oracle_security_service_admin;
GRANT CREATE PROCEDURE TO oracle_security_service_admin;
GRANT CREATE TRIGGER TO oracle_security_service_admin;
GRANT CREATE VIEW TO oracle_security_service_admin;

CREATE USER oracle_security_service
IDENTIFIED BY oracle_security_service;

GRANT CREATE SESSION TO oracle_security_service;
GRANT CREATE SYNONYM TO oracle_security_service;
GRANT CREATE ANY SYNONYM to oracle_security_service_admin;
GRANT DROP ANY SYNONYM TO oracle_security_service_admin;
```

Make a note of the passwords used for the two accounts, since you will need to know them to interact with the OSS. If you run the "Create Oracle Security Server" option interactively, a DOS window appears and you are prompted with a Username/Password screen—with no guidance or indication of what you are expected to enter. The expected response is *system/<current_system_password>* and the correct network connection, if you are not using a default database on your current system. If a repository already exists, you will be notified of that fact and asked if you want to continue. If you continue, the current repository is dropped and a new one is created.

If you decide that the OSS must be removed, you can invoke the "Remove Oracle Security Server" option to remove the account. You select the Start → Program → Oracle Security Server → Remove Oracle Security Server menu option. However, the *remove* utility script that is run will completely erase all of the contents in the OSS repository and should be used only if you are absolutely sure you want to destroy *all* of the identities and authorizations that exist. Be sure you do not run the *remove* utility script while anyone is logged on to the OSS as the *oracle_security_service_admin* user.

While running either the *create* utility or the *remove* utility, you will be prompted to supply information about the database in which you are creating or destroying the repository. You will be asked for the *system* username, its password, and the Net8 information. Since the utilities are written to assume a local database, if the database with which you are interacting is not a remote one, you will only need to supply the *system* username and password.

A Known Problem

In the Oracle 8.0.4.0.0 version, a known problem exists with the OSS utility. If you have already run either the "Create Oracle Security Server" (*create*) or the "Remove Oracle Security Server" (*remove*) script against a database and you rerun the *create* script, you may receive the following set of errors:

```
XP-07016: A database error has occurred:
create tablespace oss
datafile 'oss.dbf' SIZE 10M
ORA-01119: error in creating database file 'oss.dbf'
ORA-27038: skgfrcre: file exists
XP-07031: An error occurred while processing file C:\ORANT/OSS/nzdocrt.sql
```

The errors occur because the datafile to support the OSS tablespace exists in the *$ORACLE_HOME/Database* or *$ORACLE_HOME/DBS* directory. If you look at the *NZDODROP.SQL* script, which performs the work of dropping the tablespace and users, the internal comments within the script show that the developer realized that the datafile will not be removed. Perhaps the file is left behind because it could easily be relocated to another location on the system.

If the errors are encountered and the *remove* script was previously run, you should first ensure that the OSS tablespace has been logically removed by logging on as a DBA account and issuing the commands:

```
ALTER TABLESPACE oss OFFLINE;
 DROP TABLESPACE oss INCLUDING CONTENTS;
```

Even if the tablespace has already been successfully removed, issuing these commands will not hurt anything. You can then physically delete the *oss.dbf* file from the appropriate directory and rerun the *create* script if you want to be able to continue to use OSS.

Before you alter the OSS tablespace offline and drop it, take the time to identify where the actual physical file is located so that you can remove it. Next, ensure that you *really* want to take this action. If you have accidentally run the "Create Oracle Security Server" script on a database in which the repository currently exists and you take action to drop the tablespace, you will destroy your current OSS repository and its contents.

Securing the OSS Repository

The Oracle documentation indicates that the Oracle Security Server is run from the Oracle Enterprise Manager tool. When the OSS is installed on a Windows NT system, however, the Start → Programs menu currently shows the listing in a separate set of menu options. See the "Creating and Deleting the OSS Repository" section above.

Be aware that the Oracle Enterprise Manager tool offers a "Security Manager" menu option. This option is used to administer roles and users in a database and is *not* the same option as the OSS.

After you have run the script to create the OSS repository, you can activate the OSS tool by selecting the "Oracle Security Server Manager" option from the Start → Programs → Oracle Security Server menu option. You will be prompted for a username and password. Use the *oracle_security_service_admin* account with the *oss* password and the appropriate network connection string to your OSS repository location. Since this is the first connection to the OSS, you are prompted with the information that the proposed action is to create the Oracle Repository Manager. Responding by clicking on the "OK" button enables the tool to run the appropriate *create* scripts to create the repository. A box appears and messages are displayed as the repository is built. Once the script has completed, the actual OSS window is displayed. Figure 15-4 shows the initial login screen with the account *oracle_security_service_admin* and password *oss*.

Figure 15-4. The OSS login screen

Once you are in the OSS application (see Figure 15-5), notice that there are options available from the pull-down menu:

- Identity
- Server
- Authorization
- Enterprise Authorization

In each available menu action, there is a Create, Create like, Drop, and Delete option. There is no Modify option available in this application for any object. If you need to modify an object, you must drop or delete that object and then create it again.

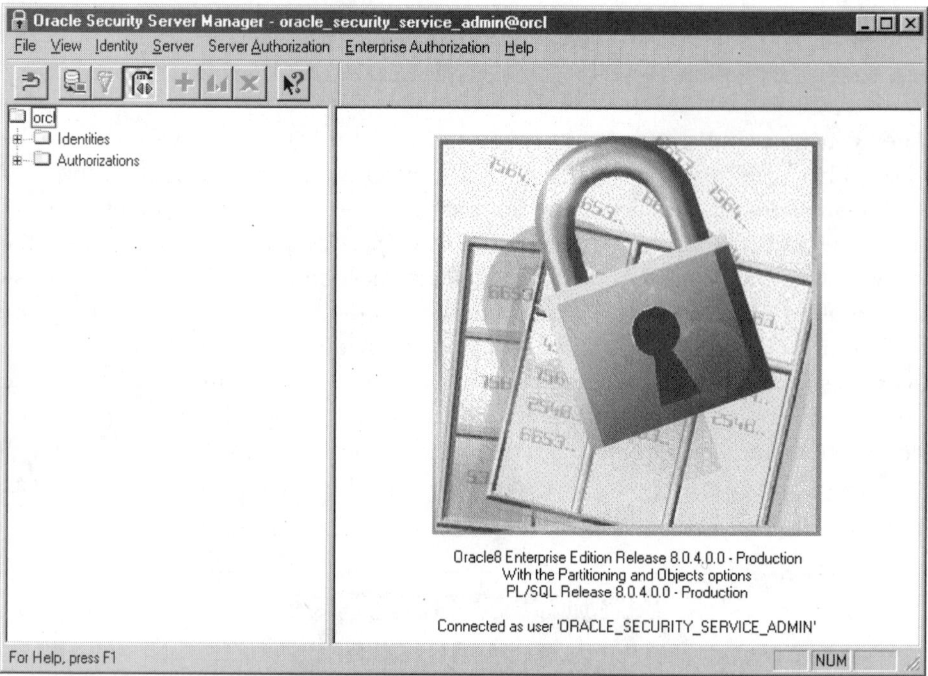

Figure 15-5. Initial OSS window

Creating the OSS certificate authority

Because the appearance and functionality of the OSS application seems to be changing with each new release of the product set, we won't present the step-by-step details on interacting with the toolset. However, we'll include an overview of the actions you must take to configure and use the tools.

Once you are logged on to the OSS window, you must first create the certificate authority (CA). You create the certificate authority by selecting the "create" option from the Identity pull-down menu. Use the Oracle-provided documentation to perform the appropriate steps to configure the CA. In version 8.0.4.0.0, the first action you take must be to configure the CA. The first Identity option which is presented is, by default, the CA configuration. Once you have walked through and established the first identity, by default, the next identity is the "Repository" identity. After you configure the repository identity, all other identities you create will be global users. In other words, in the 8.0.4.0.0 version, you only get one chance to configure a CA and one chance to configure the repository identity.

Figure 15-6 shows the initial screen you fill out to begin to create the CA. Notice that the radio button at the top of the screen indicates you are creating the certificate authority.

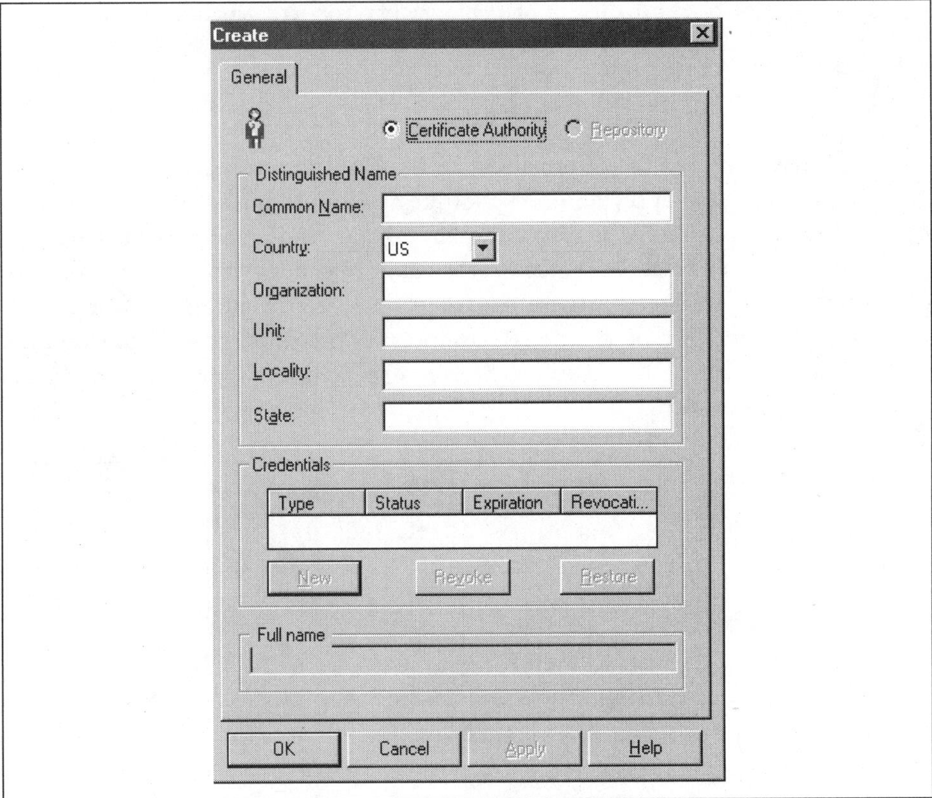

Figure 15-6. The initial CA Create screen

Do not use underscores or other punctuation in the common name in version 8.0.4. The credentials creation will fail.

You do not need to put information into all of the fields. The country and common name are the only Oracle-required fields that must be filled in. However, commercial CAs will insist on the complete list of values being filled in. We therefore encourage you to get into the habit of filling in each of these fields and keeping track of the entries.

Since the product is case-sensitive, decide whether you want to enter all values in uppercase or lowercase and stick with whatever convention you have chosen. When you download a wallet, you will have to exactly mirror the information you are entering during configuration—in the specific case in which it was originally entered here. We recommend entering all values in uppercase.

Once you have entered the information for the CA and pressed the "OK" button, you are prompted to supply an encryption key password in the "Create New Credentials" form, to verify the password, and to enter a random encryption seed. The seed, which will be used as a base for creating the keys, can be any word or phrase which you would like to use. As you can see from Figure 15-7, when creating the CA, you will not be prompted to supply a decryption password. However, for all other identities you create, you will be expected to supply both encryption and decryption passwords.

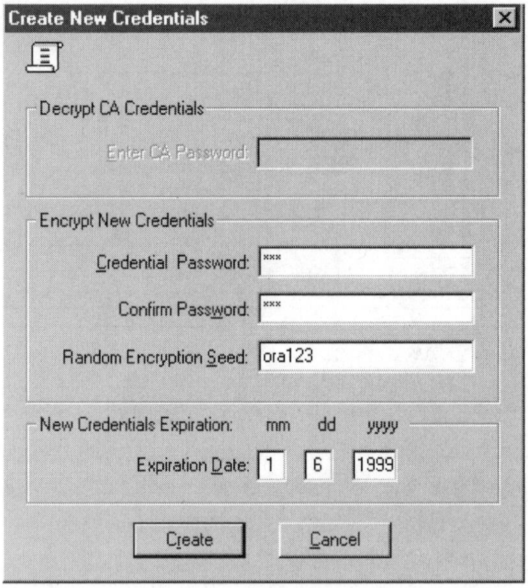

Figure 15-7. The OSS Create New Credentials screen

Be sure to remember the password you enter for the CA identity (or write it down in a truly secret location). You'll need to know the CA's password when you download a wallet later in the configuration process.

The password will be used to decrypt the encrypted private key stored in its wallet. We'll look more closely at wallets later in this chapter.

The tool will present a default expiration date, which is six months from the day on which you create the credential. You can modify this date to whatever value you want. When you complete entering the required information and press the "Create" button, the credential is created and you will see an entry in the credential area of the master OSS screen (see Figure 15-8).

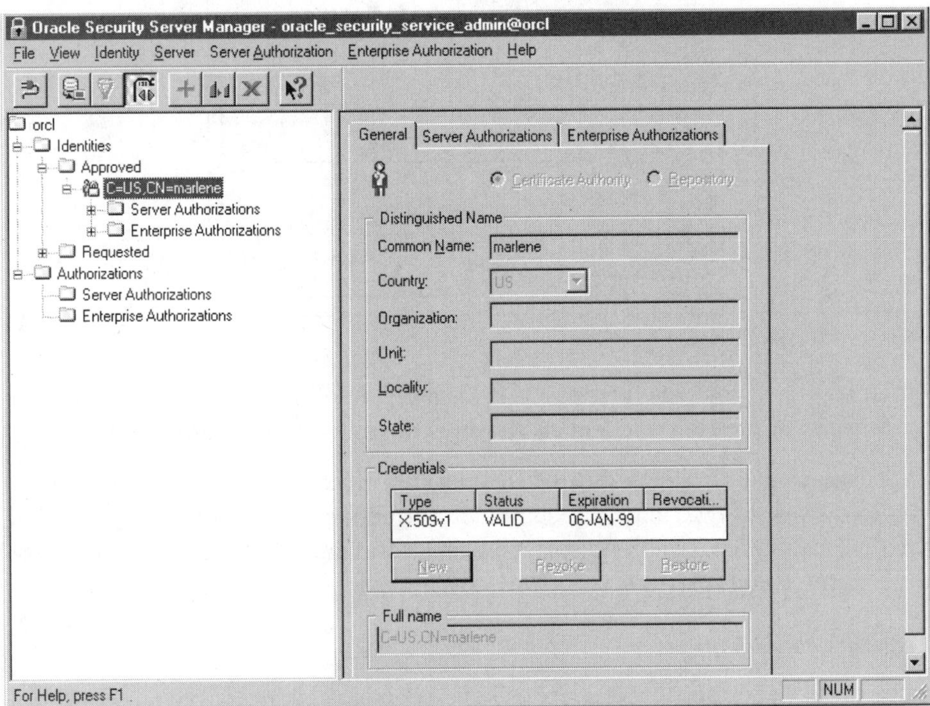

Figure 15-8. The OSS main screen with the CA created and a credential

Creating the repository identity

The next identity you create is the repository. Selecting the Identity pull-down option, choose "Create." Figure 15-9 shows the general Create screen. This time, however, the radio button for repository is marked.

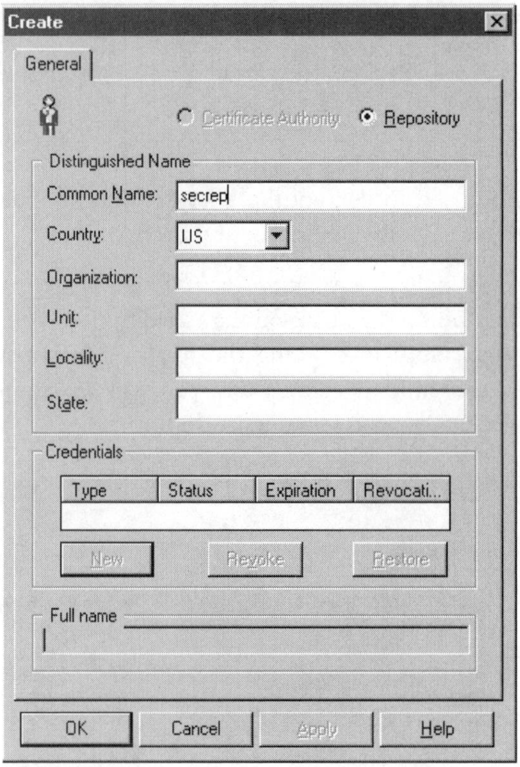

Figure 15-9. Creating the repository

When you have completed filling in the required information, press the "OK" button and the Create New Credentials screen is presented (see Figure 15-10).

This time, you are prompted to fill in both the decrypt and encrypt areas. When you have finished entering the required information, press the "Create" button, and the OSS main screen will be displayed (similar to Figure 15-8 but with the repository information displayed).

Creating other identities

Once the CA and repository identities have been created, every other identity you create will default to being a global user. Figure 15-11 shows the Create screen for a global user. The only difference between this screen and the other Create screens we've displayed is the fact that a radio button is not lit.

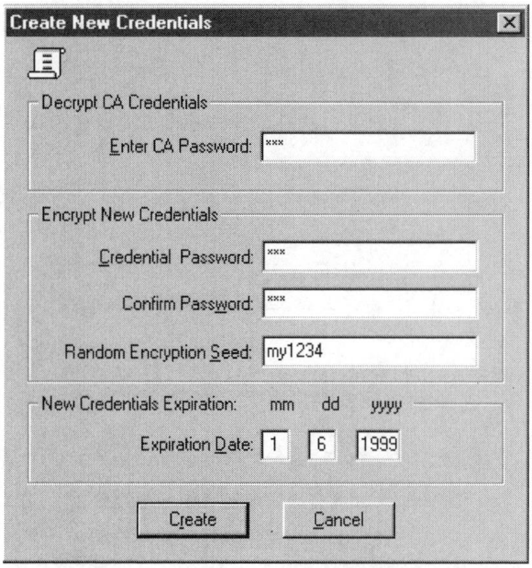

Figure 15-10. Create New Credentials screen for the repository and other identities

Defining a server

Once the CA, repository, and one global user have been created, you can begin to define servers that are to be made available to interact with the OSS. To designate a server value for the repository or, more generally, to define a server to the system, select the "Server → Create" options from the pull-down menu. Enter the name of the server. If you do not have any other servers to define, click "OK." If you have other servers to define, click "Apply" and define the next server. Figure 15-12 shows the server configuration screen.

Defining a Server Authorization

A Server Authorization is a role created in the database on a specific server and identified as a global role. To define a Server Authorization within the OSS application, select the "Server Authorization → Create" options from the pull-down menu. Enter the name for the role you want to designate and select a server from the pull-down list of servers available. Alternatively, you can apply the role to all servers you have identified by selecting the "Create for All servers" option. Again, you can either choose "OK" to exit the option or choose "Apply" to continue to define Server Authorizations. Figure 15-13 shows the "Define a new Server Authorization" screen.

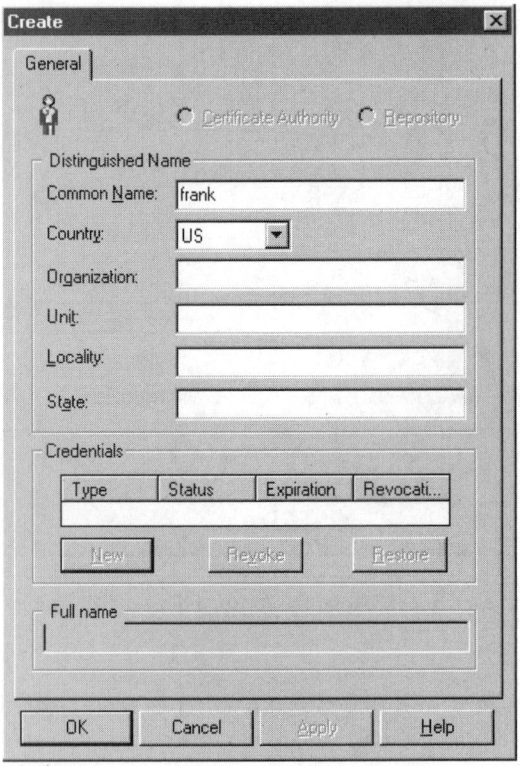

Figure 15-11. The Create screen for a global user

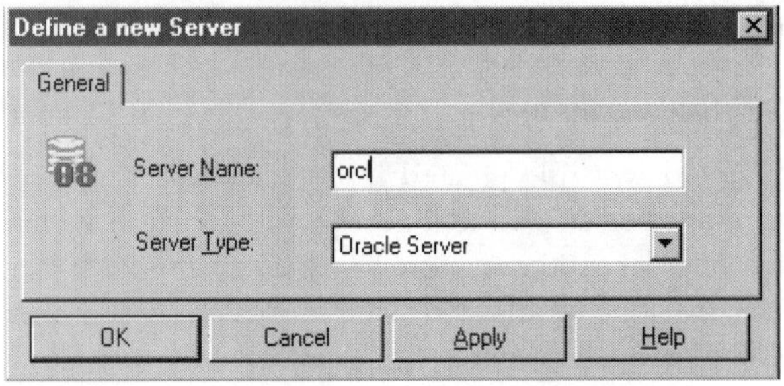

Figure 15-12. The Define a new Server screen

Defining an Enterprise Authorization

An Enterprise Authorization is a role that contains actions a global user can perform across multiple Oracle8 databases. The difference between a Server Authori-

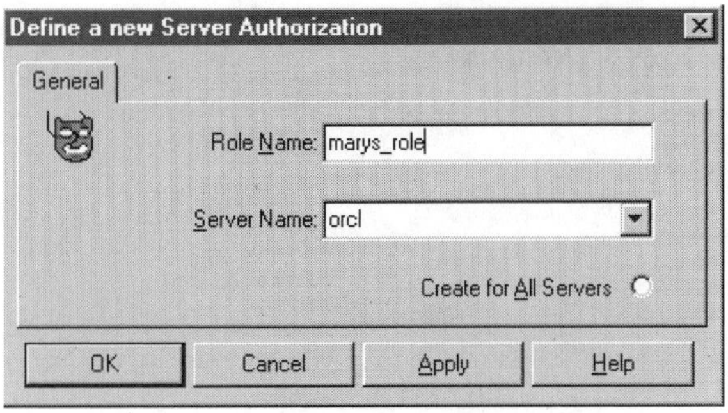

Figure 15-13. The Define a new Server Authorization screen

zation and an Enterprise Authorization seems to be the scope of the role. The Enterprise Authorization can be used to encompass many servers, while a Server Authorization encompasses only one node.

To define an Enterprise Authorization, select the "Enterprise Authorization → Create" options from the pull-down menu. Enter the value for the new Enterprise Authorization and click either "OK" or "Apply."

Creating/downloading a wallet

Once the CA has been defined, a wallet must be created to hold its credentials. A wallet is a file that stores an X.509 certificate and a public/private key pair. The private key stored in the wallet is encrypted. The *SQLNET.ORA* file, which is located on either the Net8 client or Oracle8 server, is used to define where an entity's wallet is stored. A client or server downloads its wallet from the OSS repository. The local client or server has the responsibility of protecting the contents of the wallet. As we saw in the "Create New Credentials" discussion, the password you supply for decryption is used to decrypt the encrypted private key in the wallet. The following template defines a location for a user's wallet:

```
OSS.SOURCE.MY_WALLET=
(SOURCE=
  (METHOD=ORACLE)
     (METHOD=DATA=
        (DIRECTORY= directory path)
     )
  )
```

In this example, directory_path is the *full name* of the appropriate directory being used to store the wallets. If you do not supply a value for the OSS.SOURCE.MY_WALLET location, the default value of *$HOME/oracle/oss* will be used. *$HOME* is

UNIX-specific so, if you are not on a UNIX system, you will want to change this reference.

Once the OSS.SECURITY.MY_WALLET location is defined, the OSS repository location must be defined. The syntax for defining this value is:

```
OSS.SOURCE.LOCATION=
(SOURCE=
  (METHOD=ORACLE)
     (METHOD=DATA=
        (SQLNET_ADDRESS=<service_name>)
     )
 )
```

In this example, service_name is the value defined in the *TNSNAMES.ORA* file for "oracle_repository." If no OSS.SOURCE.LOCATION is supplied, the default is "oss." However, there must be a reference for the OSS repository location either in the *TNSNAMES.ORA* file or in a Names Server definition.

More about osslogin

In the section entitled "Configuring and Using the OSS," we looked briefly at the *osslogin* utility that Oracle supplies to download a wallet or create a clear private key. The *osslogin* utility can take an encrypted private key in a wallet and decrypt it to create the clear private key. The general syntax of the utility is:

```
osslogin [-d] [-f] ['<x.509 name>']
```

The results of the command vary depending on the form of the command you use and the information that exists in various locations on the system. To download a wallet for the global user "mary.us" from the OSS, use the syntax:

```
osslogin -d 'mary.us'
```

The tool will download (–d) a wallet from the OSS repository to the directory location specified for OSS.SOURCE.MY_WALLET in the *SQLNET.ORA* file.

To convert the private key to a decrypted "clear" private key, issue the command (without any options):

```
osslogin 'X.509 name'
```

The utility will first look in the location specified for the OSS.SOURCE.MY_WALLET directory. If the wallet is there, the utility will prompt you for the password to use and the key will be decrypted. If the wallet is not there, the utility will go to the OSS repository and download a wallet using the X.509 name. You will then be prompted for the password and the decryption will occur.

You can force (–f) the tool to go directly to the OSS Repository from the client or server wallet by using the syntax:

```
osslogin -f 'X.509 name'
```

To be prompted for the X.509 name, you can just issue the command without arguments:

```
osslogin
```

The tool will first look for the wallet in the OSS.SOURCE.MY_WALLET directory and, if it doesn't find the wallet, will prompt you for the X.509 name and go to the OSS repository. Once the wallet is downloaded, the tool will prompt you for the password to use to decrypt the encrypted private key.

In all cases, the wallets are protected only by the operating system directory protections available for your system. Therefore, take care to ensure maximum protection for these directories. If users can access the location where clear private keys are stored, there is the potential for a user to masquerade as the client or server on a network and obtain privileged information. Oracle recommends that a wallet and its contents be deleted as soon as a communication session is completed. Either the system administrator or security administrator will potentially need to create an application that could be used to remove wallets when clients complete their communications sessions.

Revoking and restoring credentials

The OSS provides you with the ability to revoke a client's credentials. If an employee leaves the company or goes on an extended leave of absence, you might want to revoke his credentials to ensure that no one can use the account owned by that person.

Revoking a credential is very straightforward. You select the identity within the tree structure displayed in the OSS Manager main screen and click on it. The information for that specific identity will be displayed including the "credentials" area with the options to create new credentials, revoke credentials, or restore credentials. You can then select the credential of interest and click the Revoke option.

To restore a credential, perform the same actions as above, but select Restore instead of Revoke as the option of choice.

The revoke option revokes credentials for a user or process but does not completely remove the identity, making it easy to later restore the credentials if appropriate. To remove completely, see the next section.

Removing an identity

You can completely remove an identity from the system by selecting an identity from the tree structure and then selecting "Drop" from the "Identity" pull-down menu. If you decide to drop the certificate authority's identity, be aware of the fact that you will also remove *all* other established identities in the system.

Removing the Oracle Security Server Repository

As we mentioned earlier, Oracle supplies a utility and menu option for removing the OSS Repository. The option, from the Start → Programs → Oracle Security Server menu, is "Remove Oracle Security Server." Only use this option if you have migrated the Security Server to another location or are really sure that you want to discontinue using certificates of authority on your system through this server.

When you launch the utility to remove the OSS repository, you will be prompted for a username and password. Although there is nothing to advise you, use the system username and password, along with the name of the database in which the repository is resident. You will be prompted to confirm that you want to remove the OSS repository; when you acknowledge that you want to continue, the tool will connect to the database and remove the objects associated with the OSS repository.

In this chapter:

- *Web Basics*
- *Evaluating Web Assets and Risks*
- *Protecting a Web Site*
- *Getting Users Involved*

16

Using the Internet and the Web

Many years ago, in a system administration class one of us attended, the instructor spent an entire afternoon teaching us the step-by-step procedures for breaking into several different models of Digital Equipment Corporation VAX computers. We learned how to "hack" into a computer from an operator's console and how to gain privileged access from a remote terminal. Of course, some ways to break into the computers were easier than others, but all of the models that were current at that time were able to be compromised. The people in the class were amazed that an instructor would so thoroughly teach the art of the break-in. One student expressed this amazement to the teacher. The teacher's reply, which seemed so obvious afterwards, was, "If you don't know all of the ways which someone can use to compromise your system, you won't be able to completely defend that system."

With the explosive way in which the world has embraced the use of the Internet, intranets, and the World Wide Web, we now have more ways in which our systems can be compromised—and there is much more to be learned about defending those systems.

Who's using the Internet today? The large volume of Internet users now includes such diverse populations as private citizens, commercial businesses, universities, hospitals, public institutions, national, state, and local government bodies, and non-profit organizations.

The wealth and volume of information available on the Internet is almost incomprehensible. Information is available on media ranging from newsgroups and electronic mailing lists to product and company information. The United States Government has web sites to supply information about its various organizations and activities. You can "surf" over to the White House home page (*http://www.whitehouse.gov/*) and gather information from "The Virtual Library" to an

"Interactive Citizens' Handbook" to "What's Happening at the White House." Never before in the history of the world have you been able to tap into so much information so easily from the comfort of your own home.

There is an enormous amount to learn about the web and thousands of books written about web use, web page design, and web security. (See Appendix A, *References*, for a few such books we've found helpful.) This book's focus is on Oracle security, so we won't try to teach you about overall web issues. Our goals with this chapter are much more limited:

- Summarize briefly the terminology involved with web technology
- Evaluate your current options for securing your web site
- Examine some steps you can take to help protect your Oracle database while making it available from a web site

We emphasize the approaches you can use to help secure your database, from the Internet or an intranet, without the purchase of additional Oracle-supplied tools. However, you may want to look at the next chapter to see what Oracle products are available, at an additional cost, to help protect your database while still making it available through your web site.

The only real product Oracle supplies with the base RDBMS purchase that might provide some web site security is the Oracle Security Server discussed in Chapter 15, *Using the Oracle Security Server*.

Web Basics

There are many reasons why more and more businesses and government agencies are joining the ranks of those who have (and provide access to information through) web sites. The major reason to host a web site is to improve communication between employees (through an intranet) or between your company and potential, current, or past customers (through the Internet). The ease of reaching a large number of people with minimum expense is very appealing. The Internet enables small businesses with very limited funds to reach larger audiences of potential customers easily. Large companies can also benefit from the high Internet traffic.

Let's look at some services you and your company might provide via the Internet or an intranet:

- Help desks and technical support
- Educational opportunities and computer-based training

- Sales and unique services
- Public announcements and government policies
- Publication of reports and scientific data

Some government agencies are even using the Internet to provide employees with notification of "suspense" dates—dates when specific information is due to be delivered to one or more organizations. The volume of topics on which you can find information on the Internet is almost limitless.

Here's an interesting excerpt from Volume 7—May, 1998 Netscape Netcenter News, "Netscape.htm," an electronic, information document sent out, free of charge, by Netscape Communications Corporation:

"Thanks to everyone who took last month's small-business survey! Here is what you told us:

- 50 percent of you buy products online
- 28 percent of you sell products online
- 44 percent of you have a web page or home page for your company, while 56 percent have yet to make one"

The statistics cited from the Netcenter News indicate that, in just the few years since the World Wide Web originated, at least one-half of the people who use the Internet and web technology have really begun to feel comfortable with the idea of conducting business online—both as buyers and as sellers. This confidence indicates that the public believes the information they supply to vendors, such as credit card numbers and personal data, will be kept safe and secure. Are they right or are they just naïve about the risks involved in placing highly sensitive information on the Internet? We think a lot of the confidence is currently unfounded.

About Networking

Many DBAs have managed to escape the need to learn or understand much about how a network is put together. You receive software from Oracle with documentation that tells you to install the code and configure some files. Once the installation and configuration tasks are completed, you try to start a process called the *SQL*Net Listener* so that you and your users can communicate with the database from a client machine. As you get more skilled with doing the configuration tasks, you are more successful at getting a listener process up and running quickly.

You may be aware that in later versions of Oracle, there is a second listener process called a *bequeath adapter*, which helps you connect to the database directly from an operating system account when you are not using the SQL*Net listener. You might know about the underlying network protocol, usually TCP/IP, that you are running to support your listener processes and your SQL*Net traffic. (Chapter 8, *Installing and Starting Oracle* contains a brief discussion of SQL*Net and security.)

From there, things may get a bit fuzzy. You may hear buzzwords about things like routers, gateways, bridges, and bandwidth, and have a less-than-clear understanding of what they are. To ensure that we are all "singing from the same page," the following sections give an overview of some basic Internet and web concepts. These sections explain (in the simplest terms) how a basic network functions and supply some of the terminology that will help you understand how the Internet and web sites work. Consult some of the references in Appendix A for more technical information.

LANs and WANs

If you connect a group of computers together—both logically (with identifying names) and physically (with cables or fiber optic lines)—in order to exchange information, you have created a *computer network*. If the computers within the network are connected to each other within a short distance (say, a few hundred meters), the network is called a *Local Area Network*, or LAN. On the other hand, if the computers are separated by a substantial distance (several to hundreds of miles), the network is said to be a *Wide Area Network*, or WAN. The Internet is composed of many computer networks. We'll look more closely at the terms Internet and intranet in a moment. For now, let's look at how information is moved over the network from one computer to another.

Moving data around a network

If you were going to design a mechanism to move data from one computer to another, what would your approach be? Realizing that there is a finite amount of information which can flow through a network cable at a time, what would be the best way to enable many people to move data at the same time? You would realize very quickly that if one user were moving a really large file as one complete transaction, no one else would be able to interact with that network line until the file had been completely moved. If the computer receiving the file had a limit on how much data could be received, the file transfer might fail before completion. The approach that makes the most sense would be to break the transmission into many small pieces and send each of the pieces separately. Many people could send information at the same time since there would be room for many pieces to travel across a network at once. If each piece of data contained information about its name and sequence number, the receiving computer could easily reorganize the pieces into their original order.

When you write an electronic mail (email) message and press the "send" button, your email software takes your message and breaks it into many small pieces called *packets*. At the beginning of each packet, there is information, called *header data*, which tells the receiving software how to put the packets back together again in their proper order so that the message you sent will be readable by the person who receives it. The standard used to describe how the messages will be divided up and reassembled is called the Internet Protocol (IP). There are two basic types of protocols which are used to transport information over a network:

- Those that send information in streams—for example, TCP/IP (Transmission Control Protocol/Internet Protocol)
- Those that send information in a series of packets—for example, UDP (User Datagram Protocol)

Internet and intranet terminology

The word *Internet* is derived from the words "interconnect" and "network" and is a worldwide conglomerate of computer networks. No one person or organization owns the Internet; it's a cooperative interconnection of computers around the world with many different types of computers and different technologies. If the Internet is made up of so many diverse computers, how do they all talk to one another? The problem of interconnecting all of the diverse computers to form one network is overcome by using a common communications protocol—TCP/IP. By establishing a standard and ensuring that every organization that wants to participate in the network follows that standard, the dream of being able to communicate with someone you've never met, who lives thousands of miles away from you, has become a reality.

The basic technology of the World Wide Web was developed in 1990 by Tim Berners-Lee while he was at the European Laboratory for Particle Science (CERN) in Switzerland. The web is essentially the combination of an authoring language, a distribution system, and a *web browser*; the first browser, Mosaic, originated at the National Center for Supercomputing Applications (NCSA) at the University of Illinois, Urbana-Champaign.

A *web server* may be a computer that contains web pages. A web server may also be a program that receives and forwards information or fulfills requests for data. A web server may also:

- Run programs to act as an electronic mail server or news server
- Support downloadable files (act as an FTP, or File Transfer Protocol, site)
- Support database query facilities

The term *intranet* is used to describe an internal, corporate network that uses web technologies such as web servers and browsers to provide company employees with easy access to internal data among departments. Web browsers are available for most of the platforms a company might use. Thus, development of web applications can be done on a much more cost-effective basis since the applications do not need to be ported from one platform to another. The information you need can be located in a room down the hall or across the country or halfway around the world—you won't care or need to know the data's physical location. Unlike the Internet, which is not owned by a single person or organization, an intranet is owned by the corporation that creates and supports it. An intranet is not usually available for access by people outside of the business which owns it.

The term *HTTP* is short for HyperText Transport Protocol. HTTP is a set of rules and standards. Client programs use HTTP to read hypertext files on host computers. Along the same lines, the term *HTML* (HyperText Markup Language) is used to describe the authoring language that lets you connect to web sites and communicate with them.

A *cookie* is a block of ASCII text used to keep track of a web user's preferences. A cookie can either be stored in a user's web browser memory or, in the case of persistent cookies, on a user's disk. Although cookies were originally used to help track a user through several HTTP requests, cookies are sometimes used to help validate a user's identity to a web site. We'll discuss cookies further in the "Cookies" section later in this chapter.

The term *firewall* is generally used to describe a hardware and/or software system used to implement and enforce a security policy between two networks. The firewall software selectively forwards information to one or the other of the networks. A firewall may require that users authenticate themselves through the use of a certificate of authority, through an electronically-generated passcode, or possibly through the use of biometrics like fingerprints or retinal scans. We discuss firewalls further in the "Firewalls" section later on.

The World Wide Web is made up of intelligent servers, sometimes called HTTP servers, which perform several different functions:

- Receive, forward, and process information and requests from client machines
- Store vast amounts of information
- Protect information from being accessed by unauthorized users
- Are aware of information stored on other servers
- Log network activity

Several forms of software are used to aid in making information available. HTML, Simple Mail Transfer Protocol (SMTP); web browsers, and other Internet standards are used to enable you to access and transfer data. Because of the potential security advantages offered by the Java language (described in the next section), more and more companies are implementing their applications in Java applets. (Applets are mini-applications, typically designed to be run by a web browser.)

The Java language and security

Java is similar to C++ and is an object-oriented language. One of the major advantages of using Java is that, instead of being compiled for a specific computer operating system, Java is compiled into machine-independent bytecode. After a Java program is compiled, the bytecode is downloaded to an operating system that has a Java Class Loader. The loader is used to upload the bytecode into the computer's memory. A Java Virtual Machine is used to run the bytecode. The bytecode can be run either directly from the operating system using an interpreter or from inside a web browser using a just-in-time compiler to convert the bytecode to the native machine code for that particular computer.

One of the major security advantages of using the Java language is that restraints have been placed on what a downloaded Java program can do. Since Java programs run in a virtual machine, they cannot directly manipulate a computer's hardware. So, if you download a Java script from the Internet, you will not have to worry that the code you download will run a program that will reformat your hard drive or erase files from one of your directories. Java programs are prohibited from making calls to a computer's operating system and are run with limited system privileges. You won't have to worry about a Java script running a program and giving itself enough system privileges to damage your system. Java scripts are not allowed to read the contents of a file or directory on a client machine and cannot make calls to the computer from which the Java applet was downloaded. Since they can't read the contents of files on your system and can't make calls back to their parent machine, you don't have to worry that a Java script is reporting back sensitive information to whoever owns the web site from which you got the Java program you are running.

The way Java script rules are enforced is through the use of an object-oriented class called the Security Manager. The Security Manager class is called before any potentially dangerous operations are executed. The Security Manager class then determines if the operation should or should not be permitted to execute. To ensure that a program is not attempting to tamper with or redefine the Security Manager class, the Class Loader is used to examine each class which is being used.

In early 1998, Larry Ellison, cofounder and Chief Executive Officer of Oracle Corporation, stated that Oracle software is going to become completely Java-based. More and more of the current Oracle code is being delivered as Java applets. In fact, almost the entire Oracle Enterprise Manager toolset (described in Chapter 13, *Using the Oracle Enterprise Manager*) is written using Java applets.

Evaluating Web Assets and Risks

In Chapter 7, *Developing a Database Security Plan*, we looked at the steps you could take to generate and implement an effective and enforceable security approach. Before you establish a web site, you need to consider the potential risks and benefits involved with hosting such a site. You will want to decide how secure your site really needs to be and how much it will cost, both in actual cash outlay for software and in the number of hours it will take to implement and maintain the degree of security you need to keep your site safe.

As with every area of computing, there are specific potential risks involved with hosting a web site. There are several different forms of losses to your computer system and Oracle database that could be suffered if someone manages to break into your system. Some of these risks are:

- Loss of the operating system and its contents from a virus
- Loss of data
- Financial loss (if another company obtains data from your system, giving them a competitive edge)
- Cost in both personnel effort during recovery and delay of access to data if damage occurs
- Loss of personal (or personnel) privacy

An intranet can be either stand-alone or connected to the Internet. If your intranet is a stand-alone system, the risk of the system or database being compromised is potentially reduced. If your intranet is connected to the Internet, the risk is much greater. The larger the Internet to which you are connected, the greater the risk becomes. The Internet is very global and many of the sites offer information, trial copies of their software, and other free materials in the hope of gaining your business. Even Oracle Corporation offers trial software and other "goodies" from their web site.

You need to determine the type of information you plan to offer from your site and how much and what forms of access will be permitted to your database. The degree of sensitivity of the data that will be viewed must also be considered. Some sites offer two versions of their site—one site is more secure than the other and offers much more privileged information. Other companies choose to incorporate different levels of access within one site through the use of password-protected areas.

Let's look at each of the potential losses more closely.

Viruses = disaster!

Ten years ago, the risk of a computer file containing a virus was very low. But over the past decade, more and more incidents of different and more harmful viruses have infected our sites. Like the flu, a virus can be mild and do little or no damage to your files or computer system. But a virus can wreak irreparable damage—destroying the boot sectors of your hard drive or erasing all of the data in your system. One type of virus might replace a word in your document with another word or message just to let you know that your file has been compromised. Other types of viruses might scramble data or make information disappear completely.

There are now thousands of different types and strains of viruses to guard against. Viruses can now be passed from one system to another in Microsoft Word documents, or even through electronic mail, without the sender ever realizing that the file that was forwarded is infected. An article on the front page of *The Washington Post* Business section on Saturday, August 8, 1998, was titled "Flaws Found in 4th E-Mail Program" and subtitled "Hackers Could Hurt Some Eudora Users." The article discussed a security hole which has been identified in Microsoft Corporation's Outlook and Outlook Express, Netscape Communications Corporation's Communicator, and Qualcomm Inc.'s Eudora. The security hole "allows a hacker to create a 'booby trap' with a file that comes attached to a message and looks like a harmless link to an Internet site, but when opened attacks data on the computer." The article stated that both Microsoft and Netscape are providing patches for their flaws on their web sites. Quoting from the article:

> "Computer specialists said the problems highlight the risks involved as e-mail is used to send not just text messages but also rich multimedia documents and computer programs. Such transmissions can contain instructions that venture beyond the confines of the mail software, enabling hackers to spy on or destroy other files..."

You can unwittingly download a virus in a file from the Internet or from a floppy disk.

Viruses do their damage in a variety of ways. Some viruses are designed to enable the attacker to gain entrance to your system. The virus might be designed to help disable some aspect of system security to help the attacker to compromise your system. The virus might establish itself to gather password information and transmit it back to the originator, thereby giving an intruder access to files and data on your system or within your database. Other viruses are like time bombs—set to go off at a later time or date.

You must realize that no matter what type of virus you end up dealing with, viruses can be spread either by accident or intentionally and can potentially do substantial damage. If you or your company have not already done so, you might want to invest in a really good virus detection package and pay to receive the monthly update software to help guard against the worst of these insidious attacks.

It was here just a minute ago...

There are really only two types of computer users in the world: those who have lost data and those who will. And, just as there are two types of computer users, there are two types of data loss: accidental and deliberate.

Loss of data can be the most damaging event with which you might have to cope. If a computer crashes, you may be delayed in performing work, but you can repair the damage fairly easily. You can buy new components to repair an existing system or even buy new equipment, depending on how severe a loss of hardware you face. If vendor software has been damaged, you can always reinstall the code and, if necessary, apply any required patches to bring your software back to where it was before the damage occurred. But replacing data that was stored in a database but has been deleted—either accidentally or maliciously—can be very difficult.

Accidental loss of data can encompass any action you might take to remove information from your system. A friend of ours was sure she was in a directory on her test machine when she began to delete files from the directory. Unfortunately, the directory from which she was deleting files was on her production machine. Accidents resulting in loss of data can be costly.

You can't necessarily prevent against every possible loss of data. But you can plan ahead so the loss of data does not cripple your organization. Frequent backups of your system, coupled with enabling archive logging, can help you recover from loss of data; although the process may not be easy or quick, careful planning can keep the loss from being a catastrophe.

Another way data can be lost is through files being deliberately deleted from your system or through a user intentionally deleting data from your database. As mentioned in Chapter 2, *Oracle System Files*, you should make sure that no one but authorized personnel have access to the system and database files within your operating system.

Loss of competitive edge

Corporate espionage can be ruinous to a business. Let's say that you own a construction company and you have the opportunity to bid on a job that will generate a great deal of income. You have labored night and day to determine exactly how you will implement the specifications and have carefully calculated how much the materials and labor will cost you to accomplish the task. You are almost ready to present your bid when your corporate computer is broken into and your proposal is either copied or removed from your system. Your competition for the job underbids you by just enough to win the contract. Not only have you lost the job, but you've lost the amount of time it took to create the proposal and all the resources you had invested in laying the groundwork to win the job. Unfortunately, this scenario happens far too frequently in the business world. Protecting your computers and databases is vital to ensure that your company is not compromised by either an internal or external corporate spy.

Where did the time go?

As we discussed in Chapter 12, *Backing Up and Recovering the Database*, you must balance the amount of time and effort you spend implementing backup procedures and resources with the amount of time and data your company can afford to lose. If you are supporting a web site on which the data supplied can be easily replaced, you will not have to take as costly measures as would a business offering much less easily replaceable data.

On the other hand, if your data must be available 24 hours a day, 7 days a week, you may need to build redundant systems, including stand-by databases, to support constant data availability.

Breach of privacy

In an ideal world, you should be able to trust everyone. Unfortunately, we do not live in an ideal world, and not everyone is as honest as we would like them to be. Each of us has areas of information we want to keep private from those with whom we do business. The threat to privacy is twofold: from the outside world and internal (as an employee).

If you are conducting commerce from your web site and require your customer to supply a credit card number in order to purchase goods or services, you have an obligation to your customers to treat their credit card information with complete confidentiality. While you, yourself, might be honest and above reproach, your employees might not be as trustworthy. You must be able to assure your customers that none of your employees will tamper with or misuse their information.

You also have an obligation to your employees to ensure that their private information is not compromised in any way. We have mentioned before that salary information is one area that is normally kept very private. How about medical records? You might suffer from a medical condition you might want to keep private from your work associates. You might have gone through a tough time with your spouse or loved one and sought out professional support to help you get through it. You might have participated in a program your company's medical policy paid for. Any of these situations could cause data to be entered into a database. Compromise of your personal medical information is a betrayal of your trust in your company to keep your records private.

Protecting a Web Site

Although Internet technology is fairly old, by computer standards, the options for securing a web site and protecting an Oracle database are relatively young and immature. There are several possible approaches you can implement to help protect your database, including:

- Cookies—with the user's IP address encrypted in a form only your web site can decrypt
- Firewalls—both packet-filtering and application-level proxies
- A security server that issues digitally signed certificates of authority
- Access control at the operating system level
- Blind faith that there are so many packets "floating around" that yours won't be intercepted or targeted

All these methods (except the last one) are valid approaches for implementing web security. Let's examine each one more closely.

Cookies

As mentioned in the terminology section earlier in this chapter, cookies are usually small ASCII text files. Originally, cookies were used by the Netscape browser to help track a user's actions through several HTTP requests. The process of keeping track of a user's movements from one HTTP page to another is known as *instantiation*. The cookie keeps track of the user's movements forward. Then, when a user wants to return to a previous page, the cookie can be used to help guide the browser backwards through previous pages and URLs of interest.

Capturing an IP address

Another potential use for cookies would be to have your web site capture and encrypt the user's Internet Protocol (IP) address the first time that user contacts your site. Each time a user re-enters your site and requests information from your database, the IP address your site's software encrypted would be decrypted and compared to the IP address of the user attempting to gain access to your database. Since your software should be the only code that can decrypt your encryption successfully, if the IP address of the user exactly matches the decrypted IP address in the cookie, you can be pretty confident that the user is who he claims to be and that access can be granted. Since the cookie stores the information, you do not have to code any special application to insert or retrieve information from your site's central database for user authentication.

A dual approach

There is still the slim chance that a sniffer or spoofer could capture your user's IP address and masquerade as your user. Therefore, you might want to implement a dual approach. You could capture the user's IP address to your database the first time the user contacted your site. Each time the user re-entered the site, the visit would be noted in your database by incrementing the site visit column of your tracking table. You might also request and store a password as a column in the tracking table. Suppose that a user suddenly appeared at your site without your site's cookie in the appropriate place (as would be the case with a new user), but with an IP address that matches a known user. You would know—and could code—an action to take to prompt for the password stored in the tracking table. If the IP address matches the one stored in the database and the user can produce the correct password, access is granted and a new cookie with the correct IP address encryption is placed in the appropriate directory for the user's use. The assumption here would be that the user, or the user's system administrator, had removed the cookie your site's software placed in its known directory location.

Obviously, in a corporate intranet, the users and systems administrator would be briefed on the use of the cookie so they would not disturb it. However, systems can be damaged accidentally, so your code would need to be written so that appropriate checks and actions could be taken to not preclude a user from obtaining necessary information from the web site.

Firewalls

A firewall is a hardware and/or software system that enforces security on a network. With a common firewall implementation, software running on a router is used to determine, of the requests presented to the router, whether a request should be:

- Forwarded to a secure computer
- Routed to a less secure machine
- Refused and returned to the requester

Firewalls to protect privacy

A doctor recently discussed her computing concerns with us. She has embraced the latest computer technology by purchasing personal computers for her office and installing software designed to enable her to place all of her patient information online. She is gearing up to make specific parts of her patients' medical records available to some of the hospital staff to improve the turn-around time in getting her patients admitted to the hospital for tests and surgery. But she is concerned with the questions of how to:

- Enable selection from part of a patient's record without compromising the patient's privacy
- Ensure that only the specific people who should access her system actually access it
- Keep track of who has obtained information from her system and when the access occurred

One potential approach the doctor might use to help secure her system would be to have more than one computer. She could compartmentalize her patient information to ensure that only the information she wants accessed will be available to the outside world. Likewise, she could establish a firewall to keep her patients' private information inaccessible to the outside world.

The ease of giving access to the hospital employees via a web site is countered by the possibility that someone might compromise her patient records. Costs and benefits must be carefully weighed when dealing with such delicate situations. A firewall may be a good start towards securing the doctor's system while still accomplishing her goal of helping to ease the delays her patients might face when entering the hospital.

*SQL*Net and firewalls*

We've looked at many ways of keeping people from gaining access to areas of your system and database from a web site. However, there is a situation we haven't yet examined—the ability to allow someone to use SQL*Net (Net8 for Oracle8) to obtain information from your database *through* a firewall. Why would you want to allow this interaction? Let's say you have a group of sales personnel who travel extensively and need to be able to connect to your database from anywhere in the world. The easiest access to a central computer from around the world would be through the Internet and a company-provided web site. Obviously, you would not want any random person to get to your orders database or see the shipping information about your products. You would, however, like to provide your sales force with easy access to this information. By enabling your personnel to get through the firewall, you provide a means for them to do their jobs more effectively and efficiently. They also gain the ability to better support your customers while not compromising your higher security data.

Oracle Corporation has been working with third-party vendors to help them provide ways in which you can enable the access of data from your database through a firewall. As yet, there is little information about the code Oracle has developed to enable users' access through a firewall. The vendor involved must sign an agreement to protect information about the code. You should be seeing this technology from several vendors in the near future. You may want to ask your vendor if this feature can be provided to you and your company.

Oracle Security Server

The Oracle Security Server provides you with a method of authenticating users who access your system to ensure that the data you are releasing is really going to the right person. Chapter 15 contains an extensive explanation and evaluation of this free, Oracle-supplied product.

Controlling Access from the Operating System

This section provides a brief overview of the options you can use to implement operating system access controls. A detailed discussion of operating system security is outside the scope of this book. There are many good books on operating system security; see Appendix A for a list of some suggested ones.

Implementing access controls, either through the creation of directory structures or through the use of group assignments, provides, at best, only limited protection for the files on your system. The determined user who wants to gain access to your files may still be able to do so. As we mentioned, the better approach to securing your system is through the use of file encryption and decryption routines. While not 100% foolproof, encryption and decryption provide a much more imposing barrier to your system files.

There are several options you can use from the operating system level to provide security on your system. You can use Java-based scripts, CGI scripts, or a web security server tool like CERN HTTPD or NCSA to enable or block access to your system by:

- Forcing users to have passwords to access areas of your web site or database
- Limiting access to your web site to known user IP addresses, host IP addresses, or host names
- Placing users in groups and allowing specific privileges to different groups

The methods you might choose to implement any of these approaches can be scripted in HTML. Some very basic examples are presented here.

Using a password file

You can create a password file and store it in a specific directory of your choice. As mentioned in the last section, there are several different web server software packages you can use to create a password file and add users to the file. Be sure the package you choose provides encryption and decryption so your users' password information cannot be easily compromised if someone gains access to the directory in which your file is stored.

Once you have created the password file, you need to add the names and passwords of users you are allowing to access your web site and/or database. Depending on which web server software you are using, you need to modify your security configuration file to add information about the location of your password file. You might want to protect access to a specific directory or set of directories. You would put this information into the configuration file as well.

When a request is presented to your site, the user is prompted to enter a username and password. The server software will verify the information presented by checking for the file in the directory that has been specified in the configuration file. If the information matches, the user is granted access to the directory or database which has been requested.

Again, Java-based scripts, CGI scripts, or a web security server tool like CERN HTTPD or NCSA can be used to implement password-protected web site access.

Access by IP address or host

In a manner similar to that used to implement password protection on your site, you can store a list of accepted IP addresses. When a user presents a request, the server software checks a file of valid user or host IP addresses and determines whether the requester is coming from a known computer. Access can then be granted or denied based on the results of the IP verification process.

A potential problem with using IP address verification is that there are ways to enable a computer to masquerade as another machine and present a seemingly valid IP address.

Access by group

As we saw in Chapter 7, you can set up operating system groups and control access to files by only permitting that access to specific groups. Don't confuse the reference used here to "group" with an operating system group like *osoper* or *osdba*. Just as Oracle roles are used to define privileges for many people both easily and centrally, the web server group access approach is a way to enable many people to access a directory or a database. A group, in this case, is merely an alias for a set of users and is used like an Oracle role. The difference is that the web server group is listed in a file and is identified in the server configuration file rather than in the database.

To define a group, you create a file using your web server software in much the same way you did for usernames and passwords or IP addresses. You will also list the users who are members of the group. When a user attempts to access information on your site or from your database, the user's name will be checked against the list of people in the group who have access to the site area of interest. If the user's name is present in the appropriate group list, the user will be permitted access to the area.

Getting Users Involved

In Chapter 7, we discussed the steps you can take to create and implement a security policy and security plan. When it comes to web site security, one of the steps you can take with the greatest payoff in security is to make your policies clear and available to your users. Here are some ways you can let visitors to your site know what you expect from them and what they can expect from you:

- Create and post a security policy screen that each user must acknowledge each time they access your site
- Force each user to sign an agreement to observe your security policy—before they can get a logon to your site
- Post information about the users' rights when accessing your web site

The policy you post should outline the rules you intend to enforce and the consequences to the user if the rules are broken.

Educating Users

If you post a policy, you will need to ensure that you can enforce that policy. For example, if your intranet policy says that there are sites or newsgroups your employees are not permitted to access, you will have to be able to monitor their activities to ensure that they are not accessing those sites. If you *are* going to audit user actions, you have an obligation to notify your users of that fact.

You should be sure that you are able to enforce any policies you post. In the case of an intranet, you should try to involve your users in helping you enforce policies. Show them what steps they can take to keep the system and their data safe. The more your site visitors know about what you expect:

- The better they can comply with your security requests
- The less likely they are to intentionally violate the rules
- The more they can help you to protect the system

If you can show them the ramifications of having the system compromised—loss of data and time loss from being unable to access the system—you might gain their support to help keep the system safe.

Enforcing Policies

As with any other form of computer security, you need to decide how you are going to enforce the policies you have defined to help ensure that your web site provides a safe place for users to conduct business with your company and a secure environment for your computers and databases.

Although you need to define internally the steps you are prepared to take to enforce your web site policy, you will not want to publicize these steps to the outside community. Publicly mapping out the steps you are taking to close a security hole may actually help outside intruders compromise your system.

Communicating with Other Sites

If you know and trust the people who administer the sites that are either physically or logically near yours, you might want to stay in contact with them to share information. For instance, if you are with the government, you might want to develop contacts with other government web site managers. Likewise, if you are with a university, staying in touch with other university web site managers might be of benefit to you. If another site suffers a break-in and the site administrator lets you know what happened and how, you will be better able to protect your own site from the same situation. However, sharing information can add an extra amount of risk. If your system is compromised, be careful just how much and what kind of information you pass on to other sites with which you are in contact. For example, using email to share information is not a good idea in this situation.

Although operating system intruder detection is beyond the scope of this book, we would like to call your attention to a wonderful intruder detection checklist supplied by CERT-CC (the Computer Engineering Response Team Coordination Center). You can access this list through CERT-CC's web site at *http://www.cert.org* or download it from *ftp://info.cert.org/pub/tech_tips/intruder_detection_checklist*.

17

In this chapter:
- *Trusted Oracle*
- *Advanced Networking Option*
- *Oracle Application Server*

Using Extra-Cost Options

The goal of this book has been to provide you with the background and examples to implement a reasonable degree of security within your Oracle database, based on the software Oracle delivers by default. For example, it describes how you can use roles and views to control user access to different areas of the database, limit access to your operating system files, and implement auditing to further protect your data and database.

The topics discussed in this chapter go beyond the basic security available in the standard Oracle database. Oracle Corporation provides several products that offer additional security at an additional cost. Here we provide a brief discussion of these Oracle products so you will have an idea of other options available to protect your databases:

- Trusted Oracle (TO)
- The Advanced Networking Option (ANO)
- The Oracle Application Server (OAS)

Our hope is that we can supply you with enough information so you'll be able to recognize the terms and concepts pertaining to each of the products described. You can get a great deal more information from Oracle Corporation.

Trusted Oracle

Trusted Oracle is a multi-level security (MLS) product used primarily within government agencies where data access is based on security clearance levels. The government security levels are (in increasing degree of security):

- Unclassified
- Confidential
- Secret
- Top secret

Normally, in highly secure government agencies, information is restricted by a "need to know" basis. Trusted Oracle is intended to allow you to access only the information at the level your security clearance allows. For example, if you have been granted a clearance level of *secret*, you can view information that has been classified at the *confidential* and *secret* levels, but you will not be able to view information at a higher level.

There is one more component to a clearance. You may hold a *secret* clearance but not be permitted to view specific areas of *confidential* or *secret* information because you do not have a need to know that information. In other words, you might be cleared to see information for the ABC program because you are working on that program but not be able to see information for the XYZ program.

There are, therefore, two potential levels of access at play within a single security level:

- The actual security clearance you hold
- The programs you have a need to access

Restriction to data access is enforced by the Trusted Oracle engine and by stored PL/SQL programs.

We stress the use of Trusted Oracle in conjunction with security clearances because that is how the product is most often implemented. However, there are many organizations that could benefit by using this product to ensure the protection of very sensitive data. For example, a company whose profits depend on keeping formulas protected might implement Trusted Oracle using various company-defined levels of privilege. A pharmaceutical company could set up its database with different levels of access to the formulas that it views as *top secret.*

How Trusted Oracle Works

At its simplest level, Trusted Oracle adds a classification column to each table. The information this column contains is called a *label*. Each label is divided into two parts: the *information label* and the *sensitivity label.* Both labels include a classification such as *unclassified, confidential, secret,* and *top secret.* The information label also includes a *marking* section that allows a distinction to be made between different categories of the classification. Each row within the table contains an entry made for the classification level of that particular row.

Each user within the system has a label designation. The user's label identifies exactly what information he or she is permitted to view. A security scheme that implements matching table and column labels to user labels is called *mandatory access control* (MAC). Mandatory access control is implemented above any user-defined data restrictions. Full implementation of Trusted Oracle relies on the use of an approved *trusted operating system* that has been certified at a specific level of trust by the National Computer Security Center (NCSC)—generally B1 or B2.

Accessing a Trusted Oracle Database

Access to a Trusted Oracle database can be enforced in one of two ways:

- From the database level
- From the operating system level

If access is implemented from the database, you have to present a username and password to log on to the operating system and another (or the same) username and password to connect to the database. If access is controlled from the operating system, you just have to enter a username and password to log on to the system. By default, Trusted Oracle will accept the operating system validation as enough proof that you are okay, and you will be granted access to the database. This approach is very similar to the approach taken by the "identified externally" accounts we described in Chapter 8, *Installing and Starting Oracle.*

Certifications

Trusted Oracle (version 7) has been subjected to several U.S. and foreign government certification tests and has been certified as secure according to those tests. Among these are:

1. U.S. National Computer Security Center (NCSC) Trusted Computer System Evaluation Criteria (TCSEC) or "Orange Book," class B1.
2. European Information Technology Security Evaluation Criteria (ITSEC) at assurance E3.

The trusted version of Oracle8 is also being subjected to these tests.

You must remember that the full functionality of Trusted Oracle is only available provided that the computer on which the product is installed is also running a trusted version of the operating system.

Advanced Networking Option

Security—the protection of data—is one of the primary concerns of any business. This book focuses on how the standard features of Oracle can be used to control access within the database and thus improve the security position of your business.

But what happens outside of the database? Is the data safe on a network (LAN), an intranet, a MAN, a WAN, or the World Wide Web? Probably not. In the military security community, a popular and commonly told story concerns the detection of keystrokes from teletypes. Many years ago, an evaluation team went to a popular electronic parts store and, for only a few dollars, bought a handful of electronics components. When properly assembled, these components became a crude but effective receiver that could be tuned to the frequency radiated by the teletype keyboard. This was an excellent example of the interception of data as it was being entered—even before it had a chance to be encrypted. The story ends with the team visiting the "secure" facility with a full copy of the supposedly classified message that had been transmitted only moments earlier.

About Sniffers and Snoopers

A similar situation exists today. Data is not usually encrypted between the workstation and the database. Almost everyone has now heard of the terms *sniffer* and *snooper*. These terms pertain to hardware and software that can be located close to, but not necessarily physically attached to, the network. You could use sniffers or snoopers to intercept network packets. With sniffer or snooper technology, an interloper can: intercept, read, modify, or substitute data as it travels through the network. Most dangerously, the interception of data can include usernames and passwords.

How ANO Works

Oracle provides several products that help you protect the confidentiality and integrity of your data. These products can also help you authenticate users. The base product is called the Advanced Networking Option (ANO); ANO is an option that must be purchased separately from the default RDBMS software bundle.

ANO first appeared with Oracle7 and incorporated features of several previous products, primarily:

- Secure Network Services
- SQL*Net/DECNet

Neither of these products is now available.

ANO is used in conjunction with SQL*Net for Oracle7 or Net8 for Oracle8, and provides all the functionality of those products in addition to data encryption. Several encryption algorithm options are currently supported (some of these are described in greater detail in Chapter 15, *Using the Oracle Security Server*):

RC4 40
: A 40-bit encryption algorithm from RSA Data Security, Inc.

RC4 56
: A 56-bit encryption algorithm from RSA Data Security, Inc.

RC4 128
: A 128-bit encryption algorithm from RSA Data Security, Inc.

DES 40
: A 40-bit encryption algorithm based on the Data Encryption Standard, which uses a security key that is randomly generated for each session

DES 56
: A 56-bit encryption algorithm based on the Data Encryption Standard, which uses a security key that is randomly generated for each session

Over time, these options will probably change. The number that follows the encryption type indicates how many bits the algorithm will support. Smaller numbers—like 40-bit encryption—will pose less of a challenge for an eavesdropper to break to enable him or her to see the information being transported. Although the ANO is available in other countries, slightly different encryption capabilities are delivered outside the United States due to U.S. Government export restrictions on strong cryptography.

For single sign-on support, you can use a third-party single sign-on server such as Kerberos or SESAME, or you can use the Oracle Security Server (described in Chapter 15), which is included with the default Oracle8 bundle. ANO works with both standard Oracle and Trusted Oracle.

When considering the use of any encryption methodology, keep in mind that encryption is another process that has to be completed in the communications process. Each packet you send must be encrypted by your software, and each packet received must be decrypted—both from the client side and the server side. As a result, there will almost always be some performance degradation. You can expect a potential range of performance degradation of between 5 and 20 percent depending on the complexity of the operations you are performing.

Oracle Application Server

Web products are usually implemented with a three-tier configuration if a database is involved. While this usually means three computers—a client PC, a middle-tier computer used to support the application code, and a back-end computer that houses the database, as we discussed in Chapter 8—it does not have to. These are functional concepts, and two computers (or even one) can run with the three-tier model, although that is not common. A two-tier, client server configuration could be used. Most applications dealing with a database must maintain a constant connection. A web application, on the other hand, is stateless and can connect and disconnect from a database as needed to support the web site users' requests. We'll describe what we mean by the terms "constant" and "stateless" in the following section.

Constant-State Versus Stateless Connections

Oracle Corporation provides a product called the Oracle Application Server (OAS), which serves a broad spectrum of applications for web-based interaction. With each new version of the Oracle Application Server, new security features are introduced or current features are enhanced. Therefore, this section provides a very general overview of some basic security features available in the OAS version 3.0 product.

While you are dealing with a database from a web site, the actions of the application are remembered internally by the database. This allows you to either keep what you have done (commit) or undo your work (roll back). The actions you can take rely on the database knowing who you are and what you have done. If you disconnect, the database would have to undo all the work you have not committed before you disconnect. The database must also know that you have modified a record and must prevent other users from modifying the same record. The ability of the database to keep track of your actions—for example:

- Inserting data
- Updating data
- Deleting data
- Committing or rolling back transactions

can only be accomplished if the transactions all occur within one session. The act of remaining connected to the database until a full set of transactions has been completed is referred to as a *constant-state* transaction. If you disconnect, the database should restore the data to the last stable state, that is, to your last commit.

Web applications, on the other hand, are *stateless*. They access the server but do not maintain a constant session connection. When you have downloaded a page from the server, the connection link is idle and the server does not know what you are doing with or to that page.

We will describe the OAS functionality and connection states for two situations, one using a typical Oracle Forms type of application and the other using dynamic HTML.

Running a form using the OAS

The OAS uses a three-tier architecture. Working at tier one, the workstation, you establish a link to tier two, the Oracle Application Server. You initiate an application that uses the database, typically an Oracle form. This application is actually executed on the web server by a modified form engine. The part that handles the display is downloaded to your workstation while the application, running on the web server, establishes a permanent connection with the third tier, the database server.

Tier two, the Oracle Application Server, actually functions as a client with tier three, the database server. The Oracle Application Server maintains the necessary connection to the database while keeping the data link with your workstation free for other users when you are not using it.

From a security standpoint, there is nothing new here. If you consider the web server and the database server to be running in client/server mode, then the usual security problems exist. If the network is external, as with access through the Internet, then anybody can monitor or "sniff" the line. If the access is internal, as with an intranet, sniffing can still occur, but the potential is marginally reduced simply because the population is smaller. Thus, it does not matter if the network is internal or external; the problem of someone else snooping and intercepting your data still exists—whether the data is being transmitted from your client PC to the Oracle Application Server or from the Oracle Application Server to the database. In order to establish a secure environment, the entire session must be encrypted from the point in time when you submit your username and password through your final exit.

As we mentioned before in the "Advanced Networking Option" section, all networks can be sniffed. Data can be intercepted, read, changed, or even completely stopped. The only complete solution to protecting your data and database is to use a secure connection between the workstation and the Oracle Application Server, and between the Oracle Application Server and the database server.

Running a dynamic HTML application

In this scenario, the database PL/SQL packages are used to generate HTML for display on the workstation. The execution of the PL/SQL is handled by a cartridge on the OAS that passes the execution requests with appropriate arguments to the database server. This is a transaction-oriented approach. The user works on the HTML page within the browser until he or she is ready to commit the work. At that time, the data is sent to the OAS where it is packaged with the PL/SQL request and sent to the database. While the cartridge maintains a connection to the database server, it does not maintain a session with the database. Thus, the entire link is stateless except for the brief periods of communication during which data is requested from or passed to the database server. Work is committed whenever the "page" of data is sent. This has a significant impact on the development approach, since a request for "rollback" of the work will now require a DELETE statement and not a ROLLBACK.

The advantage of using dynamic HTML applications is reduced load on the network and generally faster throughput.

How the OAS Works

The Oracle Application Server contains security software from RSA Corporation. There are two types of communications that can be performed with OAS. Each type uses a different form of an Object Request Broker (ORB):

- For distributed communications, an Oracle-provided protocol called Oracle Media Exchange (OMX) is used
- For non-distributed communications, an industry-standard protocol called UDP is used

An Object Request Broker manages objects using an industry standard for cross-platform communications between executable programs called the Common Object Request Broker Architecture (CORBA).

There are several components that make up the OAS. Some of the components are supplied with the Oracle OAS and some are not supplied by Oracle Corporation. The components you need to use the OAS effectively are:

- A browser—usually Netscape Navigator or another form of web-based application (non-Oracle supplied)
- An HTTP listener listening for requests (Oracle provides the Spyglass HTTP listener)
- Cartridges to execute applications and return HTML content back to the browser (six cartridges supplied with OAS 3.0)

- A dispatcher for requests that require cartridges (one dispatcher for each listener) (Oracle-supplied)
- The Web Request Broker (WRB), which creates and destroys cartridges for the network (Oracle-supplied)
- An Oracle database (you build your own using Oracle software)

Cartridges communicate with the database using either Oracle Calls Interface (OCI) calls or PL/SQL.

In OAS 3.0, a version of the Spyglass HTTPS listener is included to support SSL-3 communications (SSL-3 is the Secure Socket Layer protocol). However, you must have a digital certificate issued by Verisign Corporation for the Spyglass HTTPS listener to work. Oracle's OAS also supports Netscape Enterprise and FastTrack HTTPS servers (versions 2.0 and 2.01). Microsoft Internet Information Server (IIS) is supported. The "S" indicates that a Secure Socket Layer (SSL) connection is being requested.

Figure 17-1 shows the OAS architecture.

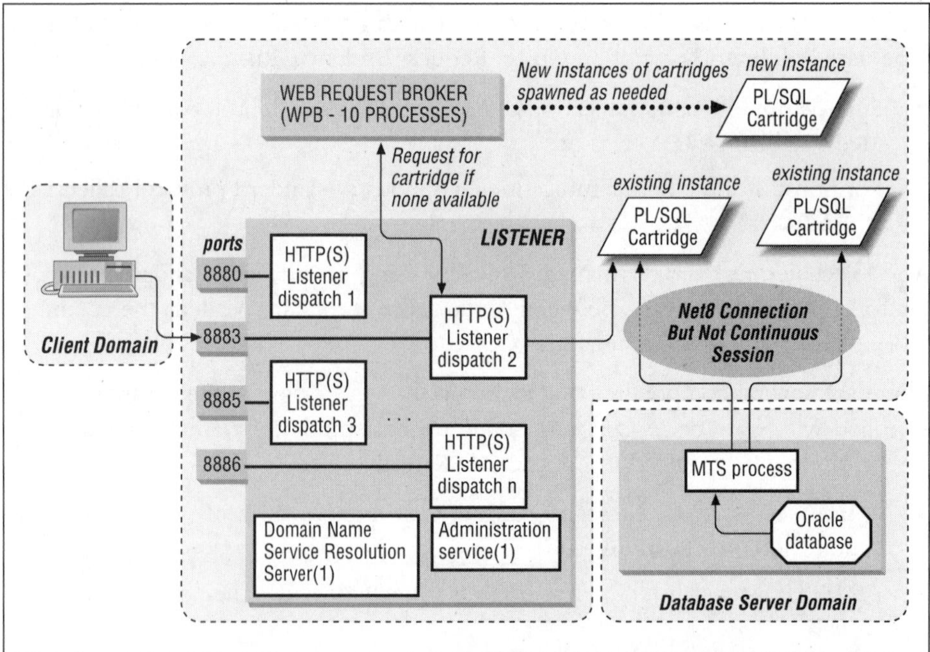

Figure 17-1. The Oracle Application Server architecture

OAS Security

The Oracle Application Server supplies security features for user authorization in several different ways. Based on the way you connect to the web site and which web pages you want to access, the OAS will authorize your access to information using:

- The dispatcher or the cartridge itself for WRB cartridges
- A Secure Socket Layer (SSL) or digest authentication for encryption of passwords over SQL*Net
- The listener for HTTP static pages or CGI scripts
- The database server through username/password (in a file or from the database) and/or roles
- An authentication server with username/password stored in a file or in the database

As we mentioned in Chapter 16, *Using the Internet and the Web*, there are products that can be used to limit access to your web site in several different ways. The Oracle Application Server enables you to restrict access to information by prompting for the username and password, restricting access by IP address and/or domain, or checking for the presence of a digital signature.

References

Because this is the first book devoted exclusively to the topic of Oracle security, we can't direct you to any other books that deal extensively with this topic. However, we've assembled a list of Oracle and security-related books, web sites, newsgroups, and conferences, which we hope will provide you with a starting point for more information on Oracle and security topics.

Technology changes at such a rapid pace that it is hard to keep up. We direct you to Oracle Corporation's web site as a primary starting point for Oracle information. If you have an Oracle support contract, Oracle's Metalink site can provide you with a great deal of in-depth data.

In addition to providing Oracle-specific infomation, we've also included a number of references to some excellent security-related books and web sites. For an extensive bibliography of security references (both online and offline)—particularly those related to UNIX—-we direct you to Appendixes D through F of *Practical UNIX & Internet Security* (cited below). For Windows NT resources, we direct you to Appendix B of *Essential Windows NT System Administration* (also cited below).

Oracle Books

There are many Oracle books available on a variety of topics. If an author has published more than one edition of a book, the following list shows the most current edition (e.g., the Oracle8 edition). If you need earlier (e.g., Oracle7) editions, check with your local book seller or with an online source such as *amazon.com* to see if they are available.

Of General Oracle Interest

Becker, Rachel (Editor). Advanced Information Systems Inc., *Oracle Unleashed.* Sams, 1996.

Bobrowski, Steve. *Oracle8 Architecture.* Osborne McGraw-Hill (Oracle Press), 1997.

Koch, George, Kevin Loney. *Oracle8: The Complete Reference.* Osborne McGraw-Hill (Oracle Press), 1997.

Luers, Tom. *Essential Oracle7.* Sams, 1995.

McCullough, Carol. *Oracle8 for Dummies.* IDG Books Worldwide, 1997.

Database Administration

Abbey, Michael, Michael Corey. *Oracle8: A Beginner's Guide.* Osborne McGraw-Hill (Oracle Press), 1997.

Ault, Michael R. *Oracle8 Administration and Management.* John Wiley & Sons, 1997.

Ault, Michael R. (editor) et al. *Oracle DBA Exam Cram, Tests 1 and 2.* Coriolis Group, 1998.

Ault, Michael R. (editor) et al. *Oracle DBA Exam Cram, Tests 3 and 4.* Coriolis Group, 1998.

Brown, Linwood. *Oracle Database Administation on Unix Systems.* Prentice Hall Computer Books, 1997.

Couchman, Jason. *Oracle Certified Professional/Dba Certification Exam Guide.* Osborne McGraw-Hill (Oracle Press), 1998.

Ensor, Dave, Ian Stevenson. *Oracle Design.* O'Reilly & Associates, 1997.

Ensor, Dave, Ian Stevenson. *Oracle8 Design Tips.* O'Reilly & Associates, 1997

Honour, Edward. *Oracle How-To: The Definitive Problem-Solver for Oracle Developers and Database Administrators.* Waite Group, 1996.

Lomasky, Brian, David C. Kreines. *Oracle Scripts.* O'Reilly and Associates, 1998.

Loney, Kevin. *Oracle8 DBA Handbook.* Osborne McGraw-Hill (Oracle Press), 1997.

Owens, Kevin T. *Building Intelligent Databases With Oracle PL/SQL, Triggers, and Stored Procedures* (2nd Edition). Prentice Hall Computer Books, 1998.

Toledo, Hugo. *Oracle Networking.* Osborne McGraw-Hill (Oracle Press), 1996.

Velpuri, Rama. *Oracle8 Backup & Recovery Handbook.* Osborne McGraw-Hill (Oracle Press), 1997.

Velpuri, Rama, Anand Adkoli. *Oracle Troubleshooting.* Osborne McGraw-Hill (Oracle Press), 1997.

System and Database Tuning

Alomari, Ahmed. *Oracle and Unix Performance Tuning.* Prentice Hall Computer Books, 1997.

Aronoff, Eyal, Kevin Loney, Noorali Sonawalla. *Advanced Oracle Tuning and Administration.* Osborne McGraw-Hill (Oracle Press), 1997.

Corey, Michael J. (Editor), et al. *Oracle8 Tuning.* Osborne McGraw-Hill (Oracle Press), 1997.

Gurry, Mark, Peter Corrigan. *Oracle Performance Tuning* (2nd edition). O'Reilly & Associates, 1997.

Harrison, Guy. *Oracle SQL High-Performance Tuning.* Prentice Hall Computer Books, 1997.

Tools and Languages

Anderson, Carrie, David Wendelken. *The Oracle Designer/2000 Handbook.* Addison Wesley, 1996.

Billings, Chris, et al. *Rapid Application Development With Oracle Designer/2000.* Addison Wesley, 1996.

Dorsey, Paul, Peter Koletzke. *Oracle Designer/2000 Handbook.* Osborne McGraw-Hill (Oracle Press), 1996.

Feuerstein, Steven, and Bill Pribyl. *Oracle PL/SQL: Programming* (2nd edition). O'Reilly & Associates, 1997.

Feuerstein, Steven et al. *Oracle Built-In Packages.* O'Reilly and Associates, 1998.

Feuerstein, Steven. *Advanced Oracle PL/SQL Programming With Packages.* O'Reilly & Associates, 1996.

Hipsley, Paul. *Developing Client/Server Applications With Oracle Developer/2000.* Sams, 1996.

Lockman, David. *Developing Personal Oracle7 for Windows 95 Applications.* Sams, 1997.

Lulushi, Albert. *Developing Oracle Forms Applications.* Prentice Hall Computer Books, 1996.

Lulushi, Albert. *Inside Oracle Designer/2000.* Prentice Hall, 1997.

Muller, Robert J.,Steve Illingworth. *Oracle Developer/2000 Handbook.* Osborne McGraw-Hill (Oracle Press), 1997.

Urman, Scott, Wendy Rinaldi. *Oracle8 Pl/Sql Programming.* Osborne McGraw-Hill (Oracle Press), 1997.

Data Warehousing

Burleson, Donald. *High Performance Oracle Data Warehousing.* The Coriolis Group, 1997.

Corey, Michael J., Michael Abbey. *Oracle Data Warehousing.* Osborne McGraw-Hill (Oracle Press), 1996.

Dodge, Gary, Tim Gorman. *Oracle8 Data Warehousing.* John Wiley and Sons, 1998.

Oracle and the Web

Greenwald, Rick, et al. *Special Edition Using Oracle Web Application Server 3.* Que Education and Training, 1997.

Johnson, Berry. *Oracle Web Application Server Handbook.* Osborne McGraw-Hill (Oracle Press), 1998.

Papaj, Robert, Donald Burleson. *Oracle Database on the Web.* The Coriolis Group, 1997.

Security Books

This section contains references to a variety of security topics; this list represents only a fraction of the many works available; we've tried to mention those likely to be helpful to Oracle sites.

General Computer Security and Risks

Neumann, Peter G. *Computer Related Risks.* Reading, MA: Addison-Wesley, 1995. (Collected from the Internet RISKS mailing list moderated by Neumann.)

National Research Council. *Computers at Risk: Safe Computing in the Information Age.* National Academy Press, 1991.

Pfleeger, Charles P. *Security in Computing* (2nd edition). Prentice Hall, 1996.

Power, Richard. *Current and Future Danger: A CSI Primer on Computer Crime and Information Warfare.* Computer Security Institute, 1995.

Computer Viruses

Denning, Peter J. *Computers Under Attack: Intruders, Worms and Viruses.* ACM Press/Addison-Wesley, 1990.

Ferbrache, David. *The Pathology of Computer Viruses*. Springer-Verlag, 1992.

Hoffman, Lance J. *Rogue Programs: Viruses, Worms and Trojan Horses.* Van Nostrand Reinhold, 1990.

Network Administration and Security

Bellovin, Steve and Bill Cheswick. *Firewalls and Internet Security.* Addison-Wesley, 1994.

Chapman, D. Brent, and Elizabeth D. Zwicky. *Building Internet Firewalls.* O'Reilly & Associates, 1995.

Hunt, Craig. *TCP/IP Network Administration*. O'Reilly & Associates, 1992.

Kaufman, Charles, Radia Perlman, and Mike Speciner. *Network Security: Private Communications in a Public World.* Prentice Hall, 1995.

Schneier, Bruce. *Applied Cryptography: Protocols, Algorithms, and Source Code in C* (2nd edition). John Wiley & Sons, 1996.

Stallings, William. *Network and Internetwork Security: Principles and Practice.* Prentice Hall, 1995.

UNIX Administration and Security

Garfinkel, Simson and Gene Spafford. *Practical UNIX & Internet Security* (2nd edition). O'Reilly & Associates, 1996.

Nemeth, Evi, Garth Snyder, Scott Seebass, and Trent R. Hein. *UNIX System Administration Handbook* (2nd edition). Prentice Hall, 1995.

Windows NT Administration and Security

Frisch, Aeleen. *Essential Windows NT System Administration*. O'Reilly & Associates, 1998.

Sheldon, Tom. *Windows NT Security Handbook*. Osborne McGraw-Hill, 1997.

Sutton, Steve and Trusted Information Systems. *Windows NT Security.* Trusted Systems Training, 1995.

Web and Java Security

Garfinkel, Simson with Gene Spafford. *Web Security & Commerce.* O'Reilly & Associates, 1997.

Oaks, Scott, *Java Security.* O'Reilly & Associates, 1998.

Stein, Lincoln. *Web Security: A Step-by-Step Reference Guide.* Addison-Wesley, 1998.

Oracle Electronic References

This section contains references to helpful Oracle-related web sites, user groups, and newsgroups.

Oracle Web Sites

A major problem encountered as we composed this list of sites was the ever-changing and expanding realm of electronic references on the World Wide Web. As of the day this list was assembled, it was accurate. However, links come and links go. Therefore, if a link we've listed does not work or fails to provide you with the information you are expecting, don't be too hard on us. It was there when we listed it! But do let us know so we can update the book accordingly.

Oracle Corporation

The most obvious Oracle link is, of course, the URL for Oracle Corporation. Oracle's links provide great product information and educational listings.

http://www.oracle.com

OraWorld

The OraWorld site says of itself that it provides "Everything Oracle on the World Wide Web." The site provides many Oracle-related links, scripts, tips, and hints.

http://www.oraworld.com

Oracle User Groups

There are many Oracle user groups throughout the world. The majority of the links to them are provided under the home pages for the various international regions. For the United States, the International Oracle User Group—Americas home page provides links. Likewise, the European Oracle User Group has links for many of the European, Middle East, and African sites. For the Far East, Oracle Corporation provides links to these sites.

International Oracle User Group - Americas

http://www.ioug.org

European Oracle User Group

http://www.eoug.org

Far East Oracle User Groups

http://www.oracle.com/international/html.asia.html

Oracle Usenet Groups

There are several Oracle-related Usenet newsgroups. A warning about all newsgroups: just because you read something in a posting does not make it correct. Please try to take what you read in a newsgroup with a critical eye. It may or may not be true.

comp.databases.oracle
Computer Databases Oracle, a good place to start

comp.databases.oracle.server
Computer Databases Oracle Server

comp.databases.oracle.tools
Computer Databases Oracle Tools

comp.databases.oracle.misc
Computer Databases Oracle Miscellaneous

Security Electronic References

This section contains references to helpful security-related web sites and newsgroups.

Security Web Sites

These web sites are likely to be helpful informational resources. Some will be particularly useful if you have to deal with an attack on your site.

COAST

COAST (Computer Operations, Audit, and Security Technology) is a multi-project, multi-investigator effort in computer security research and education in the Computer Sciences Department at Purdue University. COAST contains information about software, companies, FIRST teams, archives, standards, professional organizations, government agencies, and FAQs*—among other goodies. The WWW hotlist index at COAST is the most comprehensive list of its type available on the Internet at this time. COAST also provides a valuable service to the Internet community by maintaining a current and well-organized repository of the most important security tools and documents on the Internet; you can obtain these via anonymous FTP.

```
http://www.cs.purdue.edu/coast/coast.html
```

FIRST

FIRST (Forum of Incident Response and Security Teams) maintains a large archive of material, including pointers to web pages for other FIRST teams.

```
http://www.first.org
```

CERT-CC

CERT-CC (Computer Emergency Response Team Coordination Center) was founded in response to the Internet worm incident in 1988. CERT-CC acts as a clearinghouse for information, and helps organizations respond to security attacks. You can get on CERT-CC's mailing list for security advisories and fixes, and can obtain archived past advisories via anonymous FTP from:

```
http://www.cert.org
```

World Wide Web Consortium

Here is an explanation of the WWW Consortium (W3C) from their own web site:

> "The W3C was founded in October 1994 to lead the World Wide Web to its full potential by developing common protocols that promote its evolution and ensure its interoperability. We are an international industry consortium, jointly hosted by the Massachusetts Institute of Technology Laboratory of Computer Science (MIT/LCS), the Institut National de Recherche en Informatique et en Automatique (INFRIA) in Europe; and the Keio University Shonan Fujisawa Campus in Japan."

Services provided by the Consortium include: a repository of information about the World Wide Web for developers and users, reference code implementations to embody and promote standards, and various prototype and sample applications to

* Frequently asked questions.

demonstrate use of new technology. We especially like their security Frequently Asked Questions (FAQ) link.

http://www.w3.org

Web security

Lincoln Stein's FAQ about web security contains a lot of good, practical information, and it is updated on a regular basis.

`http://www.genome.wi.mit.edu/WWW/faqs/www-security-faq.html`

Windows NT security

This site contains information and solicits reports of break-ins. You can get on the mailing list for NT security advisories.

`http://www.ntsecurity.net`

Security Usenet Groups

Several Usenet newsgroups are particularly good sources of information on network security and related topics.

comp.security.announce (moderated)
: Computer security announcements, including new CERT-CC advisories

comp.security.misc
: Miscellaneous computer and network security

comp.security.unix
: UNIX security

comp.security.firewalls
: Information about firewalls

comp.virus (moderated)
: Information on computer viruses and related topics

sci.crypt
: Discussions about cryptology research and application

sci.crypt.research (moderated)
: Discussions about cryptology research

comp.risks (moderated)
: Discussions about risks to society from computers and computerization

comp.admin.policy
: Discussions about computer administrative policy issues, including security

Index

A

B

G

H

I

J

K

L

P

T

U

V

W

About the Authors

Marlene Theriault has over 14 years' experience as a database administrator, starting with version 2.0 of the Oracle RDBMS. She has presented papers at numerous conferences throughout the world, including various IOUG-A, DECUS, EOUG, and Oracle OpenWorld conferences. At the 1997 East Coast Oracle conference, Marlene tied for first place with Steven Feuerstein, receiving an "Outstanding Speaker" award. She also received the "Distinguished Speaker" award two years in a row at ECO-'95 and ECO-'96. Marlene's articles have appeared in Pinnacle Press' *Oracle Developer* magazine, IOUG-A's *SELECT* magazine, and many user group publications. Marlene reactivated the Mid-Atlantic Association of Oracle Professionals' Database Administration Special Interest Group and is the current chair of the MAOP DBA SIG. She authors an "Ask The DBA" column for the MAOP newsletter, and her articles and columns are available at *http://www.maop.org/sig-dba/*.

For recreation, Marlene is an avid volksmarcher who has, with her significant other, Nelson Cahill, walked at least 6.2 miles in every one of the United States. She loves to travel and has been on numerous cruises. She can be reached via email at *Marlene.Theriault@jhuapl.edu*.

William Heney started working with version 2.0 of the Oracle database in 1980. After doing application development in FORTRAN and what then passed for "Forms," he began to specialize in DBA work. In the ensuing years he has worked for a wide variety of customers, many of whom wanted some form of access control implemented in the database. Some of the techniques acquired during these experiences are reflected in this book.

Computer programming was not Bill's original occupation. His first Bachelor's degree is in Music Education. It was while serving in the U.S. Navy that he became interested in electronics and, later on, computers.

For relaxation, Bill likes to spend time outdoors with Ellen, his wife, enjoying their mutual interests of camping, biking, and skiing.

Colophon

Our look is the result of reader comments, our own experimentation, and feedback from distribution channels. Distinctive covers complement our distinctive approach to technical topics, breathing personality and life into potentially dry subjects.

The animal on the cover of *Oracle Security* is a tarantula, one of a family (*Theraphosidae*) of hairy spiders, which includes many species—over 30 known species (such as the trap-door spider) are found in the United States alone (mostly in the South and Southwest). Tarantulas are more common in tropical or subtropical areas; they generally live in holes in the ground or under stones, but are occasionally found in human dwellings, under leaves, or in trees. Species vary in size and appearance, with the largest having a leg span of about nine inches. Most species eat large insects such as beetles, but some prey on small reptiles. Some tarantulas live up to 20 years; females live much longer than males. The tarantula can also survive for very long periods without food or water.

The tarantula's vicious, deadly reputation is undeserved; the bite of most species, while about as painful as a bee sting, contains venom that is relatively harmless to humans. Tarantulas are actually shy and nocturnal: they rarely bite people. Another defense is to use one of their four sets of legs to fling hairs from the abdomen at perceived threats. Tarantulas often appear sluggish, but can move quickly when necessary.

Tarantulas molt their skins several times a year until they reach maturity at about three years of age; after this time, they molt about twice a year. The molting process frequently restores lost limbs. The legs of the tarantula each end in two claws, used to climb walls and rocks; the legs rely on blood pressure to function.

Various tarantula species are kept by many people as pets. The name is thought to have come from the Italian town Taranto. Popular wisdom held that the only cure for tarantula bites (tarantism) was a folk dance called the tarantella.

Ellie Fountain Maden was the production editor for *Oracle Security* and performed the copyedit. Seth Maislin wrote the index. Ellie Cutler proofread the book, and Sheryl Avruch, John Files, and Claire Cloutier LeBlanc performed quality checks.

Edie Freedman designed the cover of this book, using a 19th-century engraving from the Dover Pictorial Archive. The cover layout was produced with Quark XPress 3.32 using the ITC Garamond font.

The inside layout was designed by Nancy Priest and implemented in FrameMaker 5.5 by Mike Sierra. The text and heading fonts are ITC Garamond Light and Garamond Book. The illustrations that appear in the book were created in Macromedia FreeHand 8 and Adobe Photoshop 5 by Robert Romano. This colophon was written by Nancy Kotary.

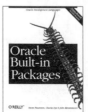

Security

PGP: Pretty Good Privacy

By Simson Garfinkel
1st Edition January 1995
430 pages, ISBN 1-56592-098-8

PGP is a freely available encryption program that protects the privacy of files and electronic mail. It uses powerful public key cryptography and works on virtually every platform. This book is both a readable technical user's guide and a fascinating behind-the-scenes look at cryptography and privacy. It describes how to use PGP and provides background on cryptography, PGP's history, battles over public key cryptography patents and U.S. government export restrictions, and public debates about privacy and free speech.

Computer Crime

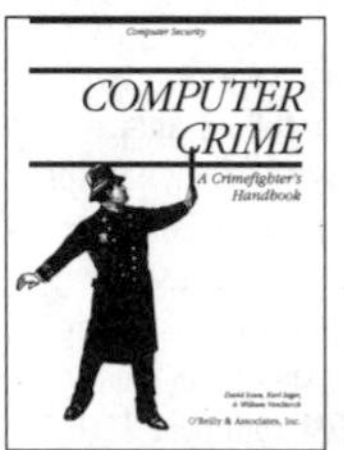

By David Icove, Karl Seger & William VonStorch
(Consulting Editor Eugene H. Spafford)
1st Edition August 1995
462 pages, ISBN 1-56592-086-4

This book is for anyone who needs to know what today's computer crimes look like, how to prevent them, and how to detect, investigate, and prosecute them if they do occur. It contains basic computer security information as well as guidelines for investigators, law enforcement, and system administrators. Also includes computer-related statutes and laws, a resource summary, detailed papers on computer crime, and a sample search warrant.

Computer Security Basics

By Deborah Russell & G.T. Gangemi, Sr.
1st Edition July 1991
464 pages, ISBN 0-937175-71-4

Computer Security Basics provides a broad introduction to the many areas of computer security and a detailed description of current security standards. This handbook describes complicated concepts like trusted systems,encryption, and mandatory access control in simple terms, and contains a thorough, readable introduction to the "Orange Book."

Protecting Networks with SATAN

By Martin Freiss
1st Edition May 1998
128 pages, ISBN 1-56592-425-8

SATAN performs "security audits," scanning host computers for security vulnerabilities. This book describes how to install and use SATAN, and how to adapt it to local requirements and increase its knowledge of specific security vulnerabilities.

Cracking DES

By Electronic Frontier Foundation
1st Edition July 1998
272 pages, ISBN 1-56592-520-3

The Data Encryption Standard withstood the test of time for twenty years. *Cracking DES: Secrets of Encryption Research, Wiretap Politics & Chip Design* shows exactly how it was brought down. Every cryptographer, security designer, and student of cryptography policy should read this book to understand how the world changed as it fell.

Web Programming

Web Client Programming with Perl

By Clinton Wong
1st Edition March 1997
228 pages, ISBN 1-56592-214-X

Web Client Programming with Perl shows you how to extend scripting skills to the Web. This book teaches you the basics of how browsers communicate with servers and how to write your own customized web clients to automate common tasks. It is intended for those who are motivated to develop software that offers a more flexible and dynamic response than a standard web browser.

Web Programming

CGI Programming on the World Wide Web

By Shishir Gundavaram
1st Edition March 1996
450 pages, ISBN 1-56592-168-2

This book offers a comprehensive explanation of CGI and related techniques for people who hold on to the dream of providing their own information servers on the Web. It starts at the beginning, explaining the value of CGI and how it works, then moves swiftly into the subtle details of programming.

Dynamic HTML: The Definitive Reference

By Danny Goodman
1st Edition July 1998
1088 pages, ISBN 1-56592-494-0

Dynamic HTML: The Definitive Reference is an indispensable compendium for Web content developers. It contains complete reference material for all of the HTML tags, CSS style attributes, browser document objects, and JavaScript objects supported by the various standards and the latest versions of Netscape Navigator and Microsoft Internet Explorer.

Frontier: The Definitive Guide

By Matt Neuburg
1st Edition February 1998
618 pages, 1-56592-383-9

This definitive guide is the first book devoted exclusively to teaching and documenting Userland Frontier, a powerful scripting environment for web site management and system level scripting. Packed with examples, advice, tricks, and tips, *Frontier: The Definitive Guide* teaches you Frontier from the ground up. Learn how to automate repetitive processes, control remote computers across a network, beef up your web site by generating hundreds of related web pages automatically, and more. Covers Frontier 4.2.3 for the Macintosh.

JavaScript: The Definitive Guide, 3rd Edition

By David Flanagan & Dan Shafer
3rd Edition June 1998
800 pages, ISBN 1-56592-392-8

This third edition of the definitive reference to JavaScript covers the latest version of the language, JavaScript 1.2, as supported by Netscape Navigator 4.0. JavaScript, which is being standardized under the name ECMAScript, is a scripting language that can be embedded directly in HTML to give web pages programming-language capabilities.

Learning VBScript

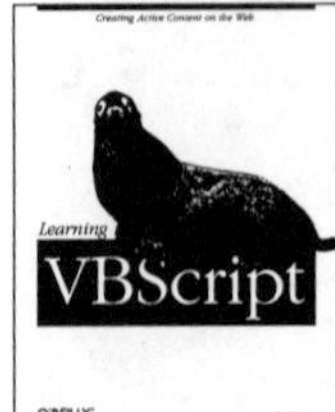

By Paul Lomax
1st Edition July 1997
616 pages, includes CD-ROM
ISBN 1-56592-247-6

This definitive guide shows web developers how to take full advantage of client-side scripting with the VBScript language. In addition to basic language features, it covers the Internet Explorer object model and discusses techniques for client-side scripting, like adding ActiveX controls to a web page or validating data before sending to the server. Includes CD-ROM with over 170 code samples.

Web Authoring and Design

PNG: The Definitive Guide

By Greg Roelofs
1st Edition June 1999 (est.)
500 pages (est.), ISBN 1-56592-542-4

PNG: The Definitive Guide addresses the needs of graphic designers who want to get the most out of this next-generation graphics file format and programmers who want to add full PNG-support to their own applications. It focuses on implementing PNG with the libpng C library and discusses improvements, such as gamma correction and the standard color spaces for precise reproduction of image colors on a wide range of systems.

Web Authoring and Design

Designing with JavaScript

By Nick Heinle
1st Edition September 1997
256 pages, Includes CD-ROM
ISBN 1-56592-300-6

Written by the author of the "JavaScript Tip of the Week" web site, this new Web Review Studio book focuses on the most useful and applicable scripts for making truly interactive, engaging web sites. You'll not only have quick access to the scripts you need, you'll finally understand why the scripts work, how to alter the scripts to get the effects you want, and, ultimately, how to write your own groundbreaking scripts from scratch.

Information Architecture for the World Wide Web

By Louis Rosenfeld & Peter Morville
1st Edition January 1998
226 pages, ISBN 1-56592-282-4

Learn how to merge aesthetics and mechanics to design web sites that "work." This book shows how to apply principles of architecture and library science to design cohesive web sites and intranets that are easy to use, manage, and expand. Covers building complex sites, hierarchy design and organization, and techniques to make your site easier to search. For webmasters, designers, and administrators.

HTML: The Definitive Guide, 3rd Edition

By Chuck Musciano & Bill Kennedy
3rd Edition August 1998
576 pages, ISBN 1-56592-492-4

This complete guide is chock full of examples, sample code, and practical, hands-on advice to help you create truly effective web pages and master advanced features. Learn how to insert images and other multimedia elements, create useful links and searchable documents, use Netscape extensions, design great forms, and lots more. The third edition covers HTML 4.0, Netscape 4.5, and Internet Explorer 4.0, plus all the common extensions.

Photoshop for the Web

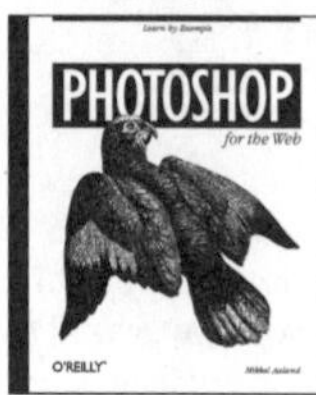

By Mikkel Aaland
1st Edition April 1998
238 pages, ISBN 1-56592-350-2

Photoshop for the Web shows you how to use the world's most popular imaging software to create Web graphics and images that look great and download blazingly fast. The book is crammed full of step-by-step examples and real-world solutions from some of the country's hottest Web producers, including *HotWired*, *c|net*, *Discovery Online*, *Second Story*, *SFGate*, and more than 20 others.

Web Navigation: Designing the User Experience

By Jennifer Fleming
1st Edition September 1998
288 pages, Includes CD-ROM
ISBN 1-56592-351-0

This book takes the first in-depth look at designing Web site navigation through design strategies to help you uncover solutions that work for your site and audience. It focuses on designing by purpose, with chapters on entertainment, shopping, identity, learning, information, and community sites. Comes with a CD-ROM that containing software demos and a "netography" of related Web resources.

Web Server Administration

Building Your Own WebSite™

By Susan B. Peck & Stephen Arrants
1st Edition July 1996
514 pages, Includes CD-ROM
ISBN 1-56592-232-8

This is a hands-on reference for Windows® 95 and Windows NT™ users who want to host a site on the Web or on a corporate intranet. This step-by-step guide will have you creating live web pages in minutes. You'll also learn how to connect your web to information in other Windows applications, such as word processing documents and databases. The book is packed with examples and tutorials on every aspect of web management, and it includes the highly acclaimed WebSite™ 1.1 server software on CD-ROM.

Web Server Administration

Writing Apache Modules with Perl and C

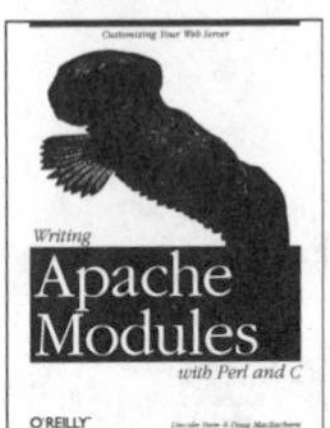

By Lincoln Stein & Doug MacEachern
1st Edition March 1999
746 pages (est.), ISBN 1-56592-567-X

This guide to Web programming teaches you how to extend the capabilities of the Apache Web server. It explains the design of Apache, mod_perl, and the Apache API, then demonstrates how to use them to rewrite CGI scripts, filter HTML documents on the server-side, enhance server log functionality, convert file formats on the fly, and more.

Building Your Own Web Conferences™

By Susan B. Peck & Beverly Murray Scherf
1st Edition March 1997
270 pages, Includes CD-ROM
ISBN 1-56592-279-4

Building Your Own Web Conferences is a complete guide for Windows® 95 and NT™ users on how to set up and manage dynamic virtual communities that improve workgroup collaboration and keep visitors coming back to your site. The second in O'Reilly's "Build Your Own..." series, this book comes with O'Reilly's state-of-the-art WebBoard™ 2.0 software on CD-ROM.

Apache: The Definitive Guide, 2nd Edition

By Ben Laurie & Peter Laurie
2nd Edition February 1999
388 pages, includes CD-ROM
ISBN 1-56592-528-9

Written and reviewed by key members of the Apache group, this book is the only complete guide on the market that describes how to obtain, set up, and secure the Apache software on both UNIX and Windows systems. The second edition fully describes Windows support and all the other Apache 1.3 features. Includes CD-ROM with Apache sources and demo sites discussed in the book.

Web Performance Tuning

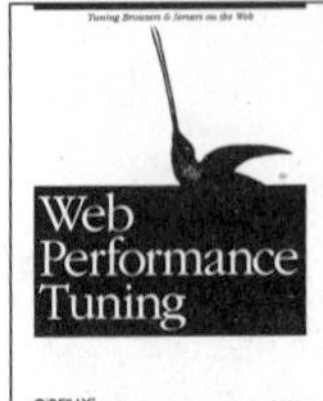

By Patrick Killelea
1st Edition October 1998
374 pages, ISBN 1-56592-379-0

Web Performance Tuning hits the ground running and gives concrete advice for improving crippled Web performance right away. For anyone who has waited too long for a Web page to display or watched servers slow to a crawl, this book includes tips on tuning the server software, operating system, network, and the Web browser itself.

How to stay in touch with O'Reilly

1. Visit Our Award-Winning Web Site

http://www.oreilly.com/

★"Top 100 Sites on the Web" —*PC Magazine*
★"Top 5% Web sites" —*Point Communications*
★"3-Star site" —*The McKinley Group*

Our web site contains a library of comprehensive product information (including book excerpts and tables of contents), downloadable software, background articles, interviews with technology leaders, links to relevant sites, book cover art, and more. File us in your Bookmarks or Hotlist!

2. Join Our Email Mailing Lists

New Product Releases

To receive automatic email with brief descriptions of all new O'Reilly products as they are released, send email to:
listproc@online.oreilly.com
Put the following information in the first line of your message (*not* in the Subject field):
subscribe oreilly-news

O'Reilly Events

If you'd also like us to send information about trade show events, special promotions, and other O'Reilly events, send email to:
listproc@online.oreilly.com
Put the following information in the first line of your message (*not* in the Subject field):
subscribe oreilly-events

3. Get Examples from Our Books via FTP

There are two ways to access an archive of example files from our books:

Regular FTP

- ftp to:
  ftp.oreilly.com
  (login: anonymous
  password: your email address)
- Point your web browser to:
  ftp://ftp.oreilly.com/

FTPMAIL

- Send an email message to:
  ftpmail@online.oreilly.com
  (Write "help" in the message body)

4. Contact Us via Email

order@oreilly.com
To place a book or software order online. Good for North American and international customers.

subscriptions@oreilly.com
To place an order for any of our newsletters or periodicals.

books@oreilly.com
General questions about any of our books.

software@oreilly.com
For general questions and product information about our software. Check out O'Reilly Software Online at **http://software.oreilly.com/** for software and technical support information. Registered O'Reilly software users send your questions to: **website-support@oreilly.com**

cs@oreilly.com
For answers to problems regarding your order or our products.

booktech@oreilly.com
For book content technical questions or corrections.

proposals@oreilly.com
To submit new book or software proposals to our editors and product managers.

international@oreilly.com
For information about our international distributors or translation queries. For a list of our distributors outside of North America check out:
http://www.oreilly.com/www/order/country.html

O'Reilly & Associates, Inc.
101 Morris Street, Sebastopol, CA 95472 USA
TEL 707-829-0515 or 800-998-9938
(6am to 5pm PST)
FAX 707-829-0104

International Distributors

UK, Europe, Middle East and Africa (except France, Germany, Austria, Switzerland, Luxembourg, Liechtenstein, and Eastern Europe)

INQUIRIES
O'Reilly UK Limited
4 Castle Street
Farnham
Surrey, GU9 7HS
United Kingdom
Telephone: 44-1252-711776
Fax: 44-1252-734211
Email: josette@oreilly.com

ORDERS
Wiley Distribution Services Ltd.
1 Oldlands Way
Bognor Regis
West Sussex PO22 9SA
United Kingdom
Telephone: 44-1243-779777
Fax: 44-1243-820250
Email: cs-books@wiley.co.uk

France

Orders
GEODIF
61, Bd Saint-Germain
75240 Paris Cedex 05, France
Tel: 33-1-44-41-46-16 (French books)
Tel: 33-1-44-41-11-87 (English books)
Fax: 33-1-44-41-11-44
Email: distribution@eyrolles.com

Inquiries
Éditions O'Reilly
18 rue Séguier
75006 Paris, France
Tel: 33-1-40-51-52-30
Fax: 33-1-40-51-52-31
Email: france@editions-oreilly.fr

Germany, Switzerland, Austria, Eastern Europe, Luxembourg, and Liechtenstein

INQUIRIES & ORDERS
O'Reilly Verlag
Balthasarstr. 81
D-50670 Köln
Germany
Telephone: 49-221-973160-91
Fax: 49-221-973160-8
Email: anfragen@oreilly.de (inquiries)
Email: order@oreilly.de (orders)

Canada (French language books)

Les Éditions Flammarion ltée
375, Avenue Laurier Ouest
Montréal (Québec) H2V 2K3
Tel: 00-1-514-277-8807
Fax: 00-1-514-278-2085
Email: info@flammarion.qc.ca

Hong Kong

City Discount Subscription Service, Ltd.
Unit D, 3rd Floor, Yan's Tower
27 Wong Chuk Hang Road
Aberdeen, Hong Kong
Tel: 852-2580-3539
Fax: 852-2580-6463
Email: citydis@ppn.com.hk

Korea

Hanbit Media, Inc.
Sonyoung Bldg. 202
Yeksam-dong 736-36
Kangnam-ku
Seoul, Korea
Tel: 822-554-9610
Fax: 822-556-0363
Email: hant93@chollian.dacom.co.kr

Philippines

Mutual Books, Inc.
429-D Shaw Boulevard
Mandaluyong City, Metro
Manila, Philippines
Tel: 632-725-7538
Fax: 632-721-3056
Email: mbikikog@mnl.sequel.net

Taiwan

O'Reilly Taiwan
No. 3, Lane 131
Hang-Chow South Road
Section 1, Taipei, Taiwan
Tel: 886-2-23968990
Fax: 886-2-23968916
Email: benh@oreilly.com

China

O'Reilly Beijing
Room 2410
160, FuXingMenNeiDaJie
XiCheng District
Beijing, China PR 100031
Tel: 86-10-86631006
Fax: 86-10-86631007
Email: frederic@oreilly.com

India

Computer Bookshop (India) Pvt. Ltd.
190 Dr. D.N. Road, Fort
Bombay 400 001 India
Tel: 91-22-207-0989
Fax: 91-22-262-3551
Email: cbsbom@giasbm01.vsnl.net.in

Japan

O'Reilly Japan, Inc.
Kiyoshige Building 2F
12-Bancho, Sanei-cho
Shinjuku-ku
Tokyo 160-0008 Japan
Tel: 81-3-3356-5227
Fax: 81-3-3356-5261
Email: japan@oreilly.com

All Other Asian Countries

O'Reilly & Associates, Inc.
101 Morris Street
Sebastopol, CA 95472 USA
Tel: 707-829-0515
Fax: 707-829-0104
Email: order@oreilly.com

Australia

WoodsLane Pty., Ltd.
7/5 Vuko Place
Warriewood NSW 2102
Australia
Tel: 61-2-9970-5111
Fax: 61-2-9970-5002
Email: info@woodslane.com.au

New Zealand

Woodslane New Zealand, Ltd.
21 Cooks Street (P.O. Box 575)
Waganui, New Zealand
Tel: 64-6-347-6543
Fax: 64-6-345-4840
Email: info@woodslane.com.au

Latin America

McGraw-Hill Interamericana
Editores, S.A. de C.V.
Cedro No. 512
Col. Atlampa
06450, Mexico, D.F.
Tel: 52-5-547-6777
Fax: 52-5-547-3336
Email: mcgraw-hill@infosel.net.mx